SELF-MANAGED TEAMWORKING

SELF-MANAGED
TEAMWORKING

The Flexible Route to
Competitive Advantage

Graham Wilson

FT
PITMAN
PUBLISHING

PITMAN PUBLISHING
128 Long Acre, London WC2E 9AN

A Division of Pearson Professional Limited

First published in Great Britain 1995

British Library Cataloguing in Publication Data
A CIP catalogue record for this book can be obtained
from the British Library.

ISBN 0 273 60714 6

1 3 5 7 9 10 8 6 4 2

Typeset by PanTek Arts, Maidstone, Kent.
Printed and bound in Great Britain by
Biddles Ltd, Guildford and King's Lynn

*The Publishers' policy is to use paper manufactured
from sustainable forests.*

CONTENTS

ACKNOWLEDGEMENTS

This book is the result of a ten-week trip to Japan and the United States. Well over a hundred hours of interviews were carried out, with representatives of commercial and non-commercial organisations, educationalists, legislators, policy makers, and trade unionists. Each gave their time freely, often spending considerable effort to help by providing translators, additional information, making further introductions and responding to subsequent questions by E-mail, telephone and fax.

Three individuals in particular provided exceptional help. Lola Okazaki-Ward of Cranfield School of Management provided introductions to two key organisations in Japan, through which many of my subsequent contacts were made. Hitoshi Suzuki provided a number of useful introductions during my stay in Japan. In the United States, John Robinson at Motorola, on behalf of Bill Wiggenhorn, acted as host and co-ordinated a full programme of visits throughout my stay.

The trip was only possible because of financial support provided by the Winston Churchill Memorial Trust. Established in 1965, the Trust perpetuates Sir Winston's memory by providing Travelling Fellowships. Each year the Council of the UK Trust selects different subjects or categories in which candidates can propose study projects of their own choice. The awards are open to any UK citizen, regardless of race, sexual orientation or age – or, indeed, of academic or professional qualifications. A primary consideration is whether the applicants' contribution to society will be enhanced by personal travel overseas.

Despite the 30 years of change since his death, I feel sure that Sir Winston would have revelled in the sweeping social changes that are reflected in this book. Anyone interested in the Fellowships is welcome to write to the author, care of Pitman Publishing.

A project of this kind, involving three months' absence from home and office, would have been impossible without the support of family, friends and colleagues. My parents, George and Betty Wilson, and Liz Morrison deserve a special mention for responding to often bizarre requests at unusual times. Transcribing and editing interviews, especially in a foreign tongue is an arduous and time-consuming activity and I am grateful to Fiona Taylor, my PA, for her professionalism and perseverance. Finally, a book depends on its index to make it accessible – June Morrison has contributed enormously through her thorough and imaginative indexing efforts.

1

INTRODUCTION –
A REVOLUTION IS BREWING

To most people, in most organisations, there is only one way to organise the group – it is the traditional way – it is the status quo.

- For decades, organisations have formed around functions and perceived specialisations, with their roots firmly in the concepts of Taylorism.

- Functionalisation of this kind stultifies individuals, demotivates the workforce, seriously impedes productivity and waves goodbye to quality improvement.

- Whenever we ask people to work together, we are assuming that the output from the group will be greater than the sum of the individuals – yet we rarely make sure that it is!

- Sadly, for many organisations, business process re-engineering – which offered a real opportunity to break away from the functional mould, has been little more than business process tweaking!

- Self-Managing Work Teams offer a radical alternative – one which allows individuals to grow beyond their wildest expectations, and at the same time allows unprecedented levels of output and quality improvement.

- This is more than just a restructuring, more than simple quality improvement, more than creating a learning organisation – it is a completely different way of life.

TWO APPROACHES TO BUSINESS ORGANISATION

Below are the stories of two very differently run organisations. Which would you prefer to work for?

1 The traditional approach

It's 8.30 in the morning and the traffic on the road to the Research Centre is moving slowly. Terry remembers that, when she left last night, the road-works on the roundabout seemed no closer to finishing. As her car approaches the main gate the security guard recognises her and opens the barrier. Terry's pass is clearly displayed in the upper left-hand side of her windscreen, but speed of entry is based more on personal recognition. It takes only a few moments to slot her car into a vacant space and as she walks to the Admin. Building she notices Jean-Paul's car in the space nearest the door.

There was quite a furore among the managers a couple of years ago when the assigned spaces for senior managers were replaced with a first-come nearest-parked approach. With the exception of shift technicians, the first person to arrive each day was almost invariably Jean-Paul. As Head of the site, the expatriate Frenchman has nearly four hundred people reporting to him. Under the old system he would have had the same space allocated to him anyway!

The staff at the Centre represent a typical R&D operation in their industry. Of the four hundred, roughly half are 'Professionals', mostly graduates in a specialist discipline. The rest are 'Non-Professionals', broken down into Technical and Administrative staff. Not all the Professionals are scientists – about a quarter are general managers pursuing a career that would take them through several distinct functions. It's widely recognised (and a little resented) that these are the people who will be running the company in fifteen years' time.

Terry is Head of Information Technology (IT) and Communications. Although one of the generalist élite, she knows that she has been side-tracked. Nobody quite knows how this happened, or when, but they know that it has. Transfers took place after three years instead of two-and-a-half, they were never quite what she wanted, and others heard of their moves before her. But Terry isn't bitter. She enjoys her job, has a lot of responsibility, and commands a deal of respect from her staff.

As Head of IT and Communications, Terry provides the site with a package of telecommunications, mail and computing services. She has to ensure that services are never interrupted, that expenditure on telecommunications and computing equipment is justifiable and, perhaps most important, that other people don't buy things aren't compatible with the site's systems.

Her staff of forty are divided roughly into three functions: the mailroom team, the technicians' team and the software specialists. None of the mailroom team are Professionals; all were recruited locally, mainly from girls who hadn't yet got the qualifications to become secretaries. Two lads who'd recently joined the team were pleasant enough, but lacking a certain streetwise characteristic that might have led to a job in the test-rigs or laboratories. Terry has had to put up quite a strong case for employing them: there was an unvoiced, but widely held, fear that they wouldn't be satisfied in the mailroom and would become a disruptive influence. The company has an Equal Employment Opportunities policy – indeed in the 1980s it was the subject of at least one sex discrimination case – yet these male/female distinctions continue to apply.

The second group under Terry's care, a small team of technicians, has one Professional nominally in charge. The team is responsible for site systems – the hardware side of the work.

Finally there are the software specialists. Entirely Professionals they provide advice to the other 350 or so personnel on how to use the facilities. She's inherited this functional structure from her predecessor and it was difficult to see how it could be changed. Besides she's always aware that it takes six months to understand a department and six months to change it. By then she's hoping for a change in her own assignment.

There are problems, she knows. People occasionally get hot under the collar when the mail is delayed. Usually this isn't her team's fault – the post might be late in arriving, and they still have to sort it. In the same way, unless letters get to them by mid-afternoon they can't be sure of catching the evening post. But you can't have it both ways: the company bureaucracy certainly couldn't cope if she introduced a shift system for the mail room!

Not that her problems are restricted to the lower grades. The software team are mavericks – the lot of them. Two have already had their cards marked for their arrogance on the telephone, and she still hasn't got to grips with Jim – the longest-serving member of the team. He never seems to be doing anything, never volunteers for anything, and yet his 'charged-out' time-sheet always shows the highest level of utilisation in the Department. He either knows a trick that she doesn't or she isn't aware of what work he's doing (in either case she feels insecure!).

The toughest issue for software is one of control. Firstly, their users demand the latest versions of any product and are always asking for special packages, even though she knows that most never touch half the functions in any product. The company, too, is paranoid about copyright: any illegal copying is a dismissable offence and it is the software specialists' job to prevent this by ensuring that people never need to 'pirate' anything. But a software upgrade to two hundred-plus people is a logistical nightmare, and is considered 'dirty' work by the software team who can't really see why the users don't do it themselves.

The only area that really runs smoothly is the hardware group. Alan, the supervisor, is a dedicated technician who keeps Jim the Professional on a sound path. Though even here Terry can see a problem. At 42, Alan is soon due to complete his Open University degree: as a graduate he would expect to be on the Professional scale – although it didn't apply automatically. Yet, as they both know, the company doesn't have a system for transferring him. She knows too that he will never be promoted at the same pace as one of the 23-year-old graduates. She is bracing herself for a confrontation, the inevitable resignation, a morale slump, and CHAOS! And then it will be her neck that is on the block.

Terry manages her team, as she likes to call them, by means of a series of meetings. Each week she and the nominal leaders of each section get together. The company doesn't recognise 'leaders' as a grade but she has found that larger meetings become unruly – and no-one has complained about her choice of individuals. Much of these meetings is spent on 'firefighting' issues – discussing complaints or substantial problems in each individual section. Inevitably this means that, while one person talks, the others sit – informed but not involved. On the day following such meetings, the three leaders usually hold a meeting with their own teams.

Terry's organisation is typical of many traditionally-based modern businesses. In Figure 1.1, we show the cumulative results of assessments made by the people in her department during the course of a series of seminars. [The activity that produced it is based on one described in the book *Making Change Happen*, also published by Pitman Publishing.]

2 The team-work approach

It's now Saturday, and thirty miles away, Steve's car sweeps through the main entrance of the factory. When he left school at sixteen he worried a great deal about his freedoms. He didn't mind working hard but he hated being constrained. That was probably why he'd rebelled a bit at school – nothing serious, but if there were ever any pranks you could be sure that Steve was somewhere behind them. When his parents had divorced, as he entered his exam years at school, he moved in with his grandparents – they'd been kind and he loved them greatly but they weren't able to understand his friends or him. Little surprise, then, that he'd scraped through two bottom-grade passes and had left school with little hope of a job. For two years he did odds and ends – nothing taxable, of course! At eighteen he had thought of joining the Army, but 'even' they wouldn't employ him.

GROUP PROCESS REVIEW

Participation

1	2	3	4	5	6	7	8	9	10
⑦	⑥	⑦	④		②	①			

Uneven, some dominate, quiet members ignored — Undirected comments, full participation throughout

Influence

1	2	3	4	5	6	7	8	9	10
③	⑦	⑦	⑥	②	②				

Evidence of rivalry, dominance of one person's ideas — Shifting influence, no rivalry, quieter members drawn out

Styles of Influence

1	2	3	4	5	6	7	8	9	10
⑧	⑧	⑨	②						

Tendency to be autocratic with few other styles of influence — Balance of autocrat with democrat, peacemakers etc

Decision Making

1	2	3	4	5	6	7	8	9	10
⑫	⑥	④	③			①	①		

Consequences poorly reviewed, steam-rollering, majorities used — Impacts well considered, group accepts all decisions, no drift

The Job In Hand

1	2	3	4	5	6	7	8	9	10
⑧	⑥	⑧	④	①					

Drift off course, analysis paralysis or over task driven — Stick to goal, base decisions on essential facts, people & task OK

Maintenance of the Group

1	2	3	4	5	6	7	8	9	10
		⑧	⑨	⑦	③				

Little done to support others, some ideas are lost forever — Support given to all; all ideas are discussed

Group Atmosphere

1	2	3	4	5	6	7	8	9	10
	②	⑥	⑦	⑦	④			①	

Excessively congenial or openly sharp — Business-like with all involved and interested

Membership

1	2	3	4	5	6	7	8	9	10	
⑩	⑦	⑤	④							①

Subgroups, cliques "against" outsiders — Subgroups do not interfere; full team membership

Feelings

1	2	3	4	5	6	7	8	9	10	
⑭	⑥	④								③

No expression of feelings; Excessive emotions showed — Balanced emotions shown if appropriate

Group Rules

1	2	3	4	5	6	7	8	9	10	
⑧	⑥	③	③		①			②		④

Excessive politeness or formality, taboos exist — Flexibility, no constraints or constraining rules

Fig 1.1 Group process review (traditional organisation)

Then a friend told him about a job that was going at the factory. It wasn't much but the money sounded fair and Steve had figured that his girlfriend wouldn't put up with him scrounging off her for much longer! He'd rung up. His grandparents had helped him complete the forms; he'd attended an interview with a panel of six people and then he'd been offered the job.

On his first day he was introduced to one of the women in the factory – assuming that they got on alright, she would be his 'buddy' for six months. She was OK – nearly old enough to be his mother, it seemed – but she treated him like an adult. That afternoon they went to a team meeting. He recognised four of the people who had interviewed him. For the first time since he'd gone to secondary school he felt wanted.

Now, twelve years on, Steve still has that sense of belonging. He's done well. Shortly after he'd joined, the team proposed a change to the product that they were working on. It had been simple, but had created a whole new product for a different market. It had been agreed with the Steering Group that they would take it to the market-testing stage.

The team spent several days handing over their existing work to another group, then they closeted themselves alone to draw up a plan of action. One of the company's facilitators had worked with them as they brain-stormed, drew fishbone diagrams, performed SWOT analyses, prepared budgets and forecasts and finally developed a systems design for the new production line. From time to time they had called in members of other teams who had useful experience – but generally all the work was their own.

After nearly three months, the product was ready for testing. Steve hadn't noticed the time pass, so he was a bit surprised when he was called one day and asked by one of the facilitators if he'd like a chat.

Mary, the facilitator, had suggested that they meet for coffee in the canteen a little earlier than the usual break. She explained that, now his probation time was over, it was time to think about his future. The members of his team had all pointed out that he was fun to work with, but they were afraid that he wouldn't get far if his English and maths didn't improve. This wasn't new to him – they'd hinted at it already! Mary explained that for every hour that someone put into formal study, the company matched it in time off. So if he wanted to take a half-day a week in college then they'd give him an extra half-day for private study. He took the chance, and within a year had got top grade passes in Maths, English and Music.

Just as he got these, the company began a programme of college units, with visiting lecturers running courses at the factory. Steve found these fascinating. Within six years he'd done courses in Accountancy, Mechanical Engineering, Adhesives Chemistry, Labour Law and four others. His team had also let him tackle two projects which he had written up for credits. He'd worked with a couple of other team-members on a Market Research analysis, and had redesigned some product quality-testing procedures. His biggest regret was that his grandmother had died shortly before he graduated – the first person in his family to ever get a degree.

The members of his team changed over time. His 'buddy' left for a few months when she had a child and came back into a different team. Two of the older members retired and three new ones joined. Steve in turn 'buddied' one of them.

With each college credit his salary increased, as it did with each new skill that he learned in the team. Their product has done well too – each month's sales figure brought in a healthy bonus. A while ago, one of the team flagged a problem – the packaging was not quite tamper-proof and they were worried about both deliberate and long-term contamination. But the team re-sourced the pack when the original supplier hadn't shown any interest in helping them.

Steve enjoys his work. He can't compare it with other jobs as he's never had another; when his friends moan over a pint he is always sympathetic but he doesn't really understand – most of the time their complaints are to do with pay or internal politics. In his twelve years with the company, Steve can only think of two occasions when his team's ideas haven't been accepted by the Steering Group – in each case they'd had a briefing on providing extra detail. In one case they could see straight away that it was better to take a different view. On the other occasion they still thought that they were right. So the team and the Steering Group held a joint meeting with a facilitator. By the end of the session both groups had changed their views and a better solution emerged. Shortly after that meeting one of their team was invited to join the Steering Group; though, of course, he remained in the team too.

So why is Steve going in to work on a Saturday? One of the production lines is being changed over today and Steve has volunteered to help. 'It must be eighteen months since I did one of these', he muses, but he isn't worried because he knows that the process has been well planned by the team at their meeting on Thursday – any rustiness in his technique was polished off then.

Steve's company is one of a new kind. No longer based on a hierarchy with specialist functions, it uses flexible, multi-skilled teams known as Self-Managing Work Teams. Each team runs a distinct product line. Steve's team also assessed themselves on the same scales as Terry's (Fig 1.2).

To any of us brought up in a traditional structure, this second example may sound far-fetched. This book is about how it works and why some of us believe that it won't be long before Self-Managing Work Teams replace the traditional hierarchy permanently.

GROUP PROCESS REVIEW

Participation

1	2	3	4	5	6		7		8		9		10	Total
						(1)			(6)			(12)		(9)

Uneven, some dominate, quiet members ignored — Undirected comments, full participation throughout

Influence

1	2	3	4	5	6		7		8		9		10	Total
						(2)	(7)		(6)			(6)		(7)

Evidence of rivalry, dominance of one person's ideas — Shifting influence, no rivalry, quieter members drawn out

Styles of Influence

1	2	3	4	5	6	7	8		9		10	Total
							(8)			(8)		(12)

Tendency to be autocratic with few other styles of influence — Balance of autocrat with democrat, peacemakers etc

Decision Making

1	2	3	4	5	6	7	8		9		10	Total
							(6)			(2)		(20)

Consequences poorly reviewed, steam-rollering, majorities used — Impacts well considered, group accepts all decisions, no drift

The Job In Hand

1		2	3	4	5		6	7	8	9		10	Total
	(2)					(2)					(6)		(18)

Drift off course, analysis paralysis or over task driven — Stick to goal, base decisions on essential facts, people & task OK

Maintenance of the Group

1		2		3	4		5		6		7		8		9		10	Total
			(3)			(1)		(3)		(3)	(3)		(5)			(3)		(7)

Little done to support others, some ideas are lost forever — Support given to all; all ideas are discussed

Group Atmosphere

1	2	3	4	5	6	7	8	9		10	Total
									(4)		(24)

Excessively congenial or openly sharp — Business-like with all involved and interested

Membership

1	2	3	4	5	6	7		8		9		10	Total
						(3)		(5)			(8)		(12)

Subgroups, cliques "against" outsiders — Subgroups do not interfere; full team membership

Feelings

1		2	3	4	5	6		7		8		9		10	Total
	(3)						(4)	(8)		(3)			(4)		(6)

No expression of feelings; Excessive emotions showed — Balanced emotions shown if appropriate

Group Rules

1		2		3		4	5		6		7		8		9		10	Total
	(4)		(2)		(1)			(3)		(2)	(2)		(4)			(4)		(6)

Excessive politeness or formality, taboos exist — Flexibility, no constraints or constraining rules

Fig 1.2 Group process review (the high-performance workplace)

SELF-MANAGING WORK TEAMS

Self-Managing Work Teams (or Self-Directed Work Groups, as they are sometimes called) are not a new phenomenon, nor are they as unusual as you might think. Perhaps the earliest example to hit the headlines was the Johnsonville Foods organisation, principally a sausage manufacturer, based in Sheboygan, Wisconsin. They received a great deal of attention in the early 1980s, promoted by management gurus such as Tom Peters. Their Chief Executive, Ralph Stayer, wrote an article in *The Harvard Business Review* which has become a classic of its kind.

In the last ten years, though, Self-Managing Work Teams have become widespread. There are few industries and few non-commercial areas in which they have not been tried. Attendance at the annual conventions for interested organisations has escalated. And yet there is very little information about them, about their common characteristics, their implementation, or the reactions to them of unions, shareholders, management and front-line employees. This book is an attempt to set the record straight, and at the same time to influence a few more people to consider implementing Self-Managing Work Teams in their own organisation.

How do you know they work?

To find out what makes Self-Managing Work Teams different from other team-based activities in organisations, we interviewed and listened to people associated both with Self-Managing Work Teams and with some of the other well-known groups. We also talked to some of the people trying to use Self-Managing Work Teams as part of their armoury to address some of the major issues confronting industry today. The organisations and individuals came from India, Japan and the USA, though their sphere of influence was far wider.

These interviews form the core of this book, together with other information, and an interpretation of some of the events that have led to Self-Managing Work Teams. We have not set out to provide the definitive guide to implementing Self-Managing Work Teams, because we feel that the present priority is to understand what such teams are and why they are so important. Some organisations are much better at recording information than others, but wherever possible we have obtained hard facts rather than hearsay detail.

Why should we be interested?

Before going any further, let's just look back at Terry and Steve's organisations. What is of note in them both?

The traditional organisation

It would be daft to suggest that any organisation is remaining unchanged in this dramatically changing world. Terry is a manager in a changing organisation. As we can see, they have begun to address some of the imbalances that trouble everyone these days. Firstly they have started to look at some of the overt perks that make some individuals feel less significant than others. We heard that the assigned car-parking spaces have been removed. This is just a trivial example, but it's intriguing that such spaces have been known to irritate most employees for a decade at least, and yet we still see them being used. I regularly drive past a factory that has four Senior Managers' spaces clearly marked outside – even though there are always free spaces next to them. Only a little while ago, I visited a company that had differentiated its toilets into 'Gentlemen' and 'Others'. There are signs of this arrogance, this 'I'm better than you' attitude, all around us. Many people are happy to accept certain aspects of privilege due to seniority, expertise, or whatever – while to others these symptoms are purely inflammatory.

At Terry's company they have an Equal Opportunities Policy, even though it is passively flouted where temporary or 'local' employees are concerned. Perhaps much more disturbing is the terminology used to distinguish between graduates and non-graduates, and the inflexibility of the bureaucracy to recognise individuals like Alan who have shown commitment to develop themselves later in life. If barriers of this kind exist, can we expect people to want to develop themselves? And as if this weren't bad enough, it has been compounded by creating an élite stream who will be the captains in years to come. In other words, unless you were selected at the outset of your employment you stand little chance of advancement other than by the 'escalator' system – slow promotion only when a vacancy opens up 'above' you. In Chapter 2 we shall see how seriously this is thought to have hindered Japanese organisations.

Probably the single largest demotivator of employees in traditional organisations is the appraisal system – they have usually had nothing to do with its development and do not know how to improve themselves in order to do well. The rules are often couched in terms that are vague, and are clearly there to protect management decisions rather than to promote excellence. Most assessments are subjective; employees rarely have the opportunity even to understand them without making themselves appear to be trouble-makers.

Terry's role in the company is primarily one of control. This is typical of managers in traditional organisations, who may be responsible for controlling the actions of a group of people or a set of tasks. In Terry's case it is both. She has responsibility for controlling the behaviour of her team (one or two of whom she obviously doesn't feel she controls sufficiently!) and the behaviour of others to do with her IT function. Part of this involves managing (albeit in theory through delegation) the handling of specific tasks such as mail distribution and software upgrades. Again, control is a characteristic role for managers in traditional organisations – although many have been recruited for their specialist knowledge rather than this ability. In Terry's case, the company has decided to separate the roles by recruiting two streams – the specialist and the generalist. This is fine, if the specialists know that this is the case when they are recruited, and understand its inhibiting features.

Terry has organised her people into three groups in a typical functional pattern. In her case it is difficult to see any alternative because the skills involved in each are specialised (or too dirty for some people to handle). Quite how rigid this distinction should be is difficult to say without comparison with other organisations.

The rotation of managerial jobs means that there is potentially a lack of consistency, but at the same time most realise that there isn't time in a position to make radical alterations – so the *status quo* is maintained almost by default. Of course, cynics will also point out that if a change is made and it turns out to be wrong, the miscreant manager will never get caught anyway!

Terry knows that there are problems with her department's output, but she feels powerless to prevent them. The obvious solution, in her eyes, would not be allowed by higher levels of control. We can only hope that she has at least tested this idea out to see if it really is the only solution! Managers in Terry's position often feel unable to discuss problems of this kind with their team, because they 'know' that the solution calls for action beyond their remit. The risks are too high: if the staff agree on a logical solution, they will become demotivated if the idea isn't accepted, and will lose confidence in their manager's leadership if the recommendation falls out at a higher level. So it is often easier to deal with the occasional hassle of a disgruntled user rather than do anything to prevent the problem in the first place.

Terry has already become steeped in the hierarchy of the organisation: she refers to some people as higher grades and some as lower. Although the distinction may fit the corporate personnel system, what exactly are the lower grades lower than, and what are the higher ones higher than? And does the distinction really help anyone?

Terry's control role comes through again when she talks of her problem with Jim. She is afraid that there is something she doesn't know – a lack of knowledge which may end up hurting her. It also illustrates how the company system of measuring people's output doesn't necessarily meet the need of its managers. Jim does well, so Terry doesn't trust him! She'd be much happier if he only did as well as his colleagues!

The company is (quite rightly) concerned about the issue of software piracy. But its solution is to rely upon a prevention mechanism that doesn't have the support of the people it needs to implement it, and a policing function coupled with a stiff sentence. It's been well-known for twenty years that inspection-based quality control doesn't really work – yet here is a case of a company depending upon it to deal with a serious threat.

Poor Alan! He's devoted a personal fortune, together with a massive amount of his spare time (probably to the detriment of his home-life) in trying to better himself. And what is going to happen to him? In a survey of one award-giving body, virtually all recipients said that their current employers didn't credit them for their achievement, and that to make use of their new-found skills and experience they would have to change jobs! What a damning indictment!

Of course, Terry isn't thinking of the issue in this way – but she is aware that if Alan leaves, it will become her problem.

What a different world Steve lives in!

The premise behind this book is simple. Whenever we ask a group of people to work together we are assuming that the group's output will be greater than the sum of the individual contributions. If it is not, there is little point in having a group at all. To most people, in most organisations, there is only one way to organise the group – it is the traditional way – the *status quo*. We may tweak the functions but we still organise people in the same way. With very few exceptions most workplaces are arranged according to the principles described by Taylor a century ago – or at least reflect these through functionalisation and specialisation.

Frederick Winslow Taylor

Frederick Taylor was born in Philadelphia in 1856 and initially worked as an apprentice machinist. At 22 he joined the Midvale Steel Company and became a Superintendent there. His experience was almost entirely with shopfloor employees in heavy industry at a time when most of these people were agricultural immigrants with little or no education and were suffering many economic and social hardships.

Taylor felt that most people wanted to work slowly in order to protect their jobs; that management controls were generally poor enabling these workers to work slowly; and that as working practices weren't controlled in any way workers could choose what they wanted to do with impunity. He believed that output would be increased by reducing any one person's job down to a small number of simple tasks, by supervising them strongly, and paying them a piece rate for their job.

The study that was necessary to break down these jobs into small tasks led to the adoption of the title *scientific management* and could be said to have founded the field known as 'work study'.

Taylor had some strong views about workers. He made a distinction between manual work and mental work – the latter being the job of managers. He believed that by introducing 'scientific' principles managers should no longer need to arbitrarily 'lord' it over workers. But, where necessary, strong discipline should be used.

In 1898, Taylor was hired by the Bethlehem Iron Company to introduce his methods. After a few individual successes, the workers and management became increasingly alarmed at the prospect of widespread redundancy, industrial relations broke down, the local community were up in arms and within less than two years he was told to leave.

In the UK, the techniques were first applied in 1905, though they were subsequently evaluated by trade bodies, strongly criticised and scrapped. When they were introduced to factories in Germany and France there was widespread demotivation and violent industrial action which reached its height in the Renault works at Billancourt in 1912.

At the same time Taylor's approach was being tried at the Watertown Arsenal in the US. Almost immediately the workers went on strike! The US house of Representatives formed a committee to investigate the circumstances around the strike and Taylor's methods. Their initial report was not entirely damning – saying that there were some useful aspects to the methods. However, on the eve of the First World War, an attitude survey was carried out of the Arsenal workforce which revealed a substantial hostility to the approach. As a result, the government banned the use of Taylor's methods throughout the defence industry.

Amazingly, his approach is still applied in workplaces around the world today. A typical application could give a worker one and a half minutes to perform five or six simple fixing activities, such as screwing together components on a car. The line is continuously flowing and if the worker misses their fixings the vehicle will be rejected by quality control inspectors down the line. As you can imagine, if the workers want to go to the toilet they have to ask the supervisor to arrange for cover and then wait for their relief – in more ways than one!

In one large consultancy practice, for example, the consultants are separated into specialisations. The more junior ones are assigned to projects in which they are given small tasks, such as conducting interviews, and then expected to complete many of these, each in like fashion. The consultancy is constantly seeking patterns and routine, and so as they complete one or two similar assignments, a generic methodology emerges. The senior and managing consultants document this, trying to standardise the approach which they perceive gives them a marketing and selling edge. In so doing they further remove the creativity that the juniors can display. As they are not involved in 'client-facing' work, the secretarial staff are usually organised into a distinct hierarchy –

removing the need for the consultants to be involved in their management (and thus reducing their ownership of the work that they are doing on behalf of any client). An us-and-them attitude quickly develops between the two groups – victims of their own organisational structure! There are alternatives (even in this environment), as we shall see later in this book.

Within only a decade of their publication, Taylor's methods had been banned from US government-run organisations by Act of Congress. Such drastic action was necessary because they stultified individuals, demotivated the workforce, and seriously impeded productivity. In the US and Europe (where they were first applied by one major car manufacturer) they led to riots! Despite this we continue to adopt them in organisations around the world.

The reason that we do so is quite simple: it is not through any act of malice but simply that most of us have been brought up in that organisational style and know no other approach. It has become so ingrained that we do not even challenge its effectiveness as a way of delivering productivity from a group of people. This book is about an alternative – one that is increasingly being adopted around the world. It is adopted because it delivers results, such exceptional results that organisations often describe the structure as one of *High Performance Work Teams.* We are not talking about an increase in productivity of a few percentage points, but about changes in orders of magnitude. Not once, not twice but perhaps even three times (i.e. a thousand-fold increase). If productivity itself doesn't increase then quality does to the same extent and these organisations are talking in terms of *Six Sigma* quality – no more than three defects in a million opportunities. How is such an increase possible?

It can only be achieved by dramatically improving the skill-levels of the employees involved. The secret, though, is not to throw training at people. Training on its own achieves relatively little. Real benefits arise when individuals are helped to develop their skills on the job. This calls for a transformation in the approach of managers. However, as the new culture of constant self-development becomes ingrained, so the organisation is known as a 'learning organisation', and becomes not merely an environment of high investment in learning but a place of genuine clamour for enhanced skills among the organisation's members. How is this growth achieved?

The step-change comes slowly, and as it comes the organisation must adapt. Traditional hierarchies must be removed and in their place a new structure evolves. Every one is different, every one is unique, but the structures themselves are increasingly known as *Self-Managing Work Teams*, or *Self-Directing Work Groups*. This book looks at the perceptions of a wide variety of individuals towards such groups. It looks at their success and their failures. It sets out an agenda, not merely for the organisations, their managers and employees, but also for the unions, government and educators. The choice of whether to follow this route is yours. We hope that you will be persuaded by the example of others.

2

THE TURBULENT PAST – THE EVOLUTION OF SELF-MANAGING WORK TEAMS

Even in the mid-1970s over 75% of Japanese manufacturing output came from firms with fewer than ten employees. The practices that were being cited as the panacea for Western industry were actually only being carried out in a handful of Japanese companies!

- Self-Managing Work Teams are a common response to a growing concern – they are neither a Japanese fad nor a Western re-import from Japan!

- SMWTs are an alternative organisation structure – they are not merely the evolution of quality control (QC) circles.

- In Japan, SMWTs are evolving to counteract the rigid, worker-based environment of QC Circles, with their emphasis purely on improvement, and the lacklustre output of the educational system.

- In the US, SMWTs have a longer pedigree – considerably more research has been carried out on the impact of motivation on workers. They may have evolved from 'Quality of Work-Life' initiatives, but have been heavily influenced by other factors too.

- SMWTs take time to implement – unless you are very brave, people need time to learn new skills and new attitudes, and to relearn the 'rules'.

NOT ANOTHER JAPANESE QUALITY IMPROVEMENT IDEA!

I remember running a seminar in the late 1980s in which I mentioned a few facts about Japanese business – I thought that they were pretty innocuous until one senior manager got up and lambasted me for expecting him to believe that what worked in Japan could ever work anywhere else. There is a popular Western perception of Japanese management which is neither accurate nor helpful – and this is as good a place as any to try to lay it to rest!

Give most company managers a list of phrases, and the ones that they use to describe Japanese management will probably include the following (or derivatives of them) (Fig 2.1).

Although there is a degree of truth in some of these, they are by no means universally applicable.

So where has this perception (or mis-perception) come from? In 1958, James Abegglen's book *The Japanese Factory* enumerated several of these practices, which he said were the remnants of the feudalistic Japanese culture which prevailed in the Edo period (1603-1868). He said that these attitudes had allowed modern-day Japanese businesses to adapt rapidly to Western production technology and thus accounted for the Japanese industrial success in the post-war years.

This picture was built on by two widely read, and still widely circulated, articles in *The Economist* in the early 1960s. Then, in 1969, Robert Guillain wrote the book, *Japon Troisieme Grand*. He too related their success to near-feudal behaviour – employees' devotion to the point of self-sacrifice – and employers' protection of the employee at the expense of his own well-being.

- Lifelong employment
- Hierarchy based on seniority
- Employing (even 'owning') the 'whole-person'
- Standardised (and sometimes 'silly') training
- Emphasis on interpersonal harmony rather than fact
- Bottom-up project proposals (Japanese: *Ringi*)
- To the individual the company is more important than him or herself (Japanese: *Omikoshi*)
- Collective responsibility
- Participative management
- Absurd concern for the individual

Fig 2.1 Perceptions of Japanese Management Practice

These sources were all available to, and it is thought were highly influential on, the OECD mission to Japan in 1970. They produced a report which has been referred to by almost every management observer and reporter ever since. In it they attributed the post-war success to the same factors, in particular lifelong employment, seniority-based hierarchy and a different style of union.

Then, Ezra Vogel wrote the best-seller *Japan as Number One* – which hit the bookshops in 1979. His list of the characteristics of Japanese firms that led to their success was even more explicit than the previous authors, but still revolved around the same set of behaviours. In his case the feudal origin was played down, and the emphasis was placed on the sense of belonging and pride in their work. This he said should be transferred to American firms to replace an individualistic attitude.

Throughout this time numerous reporters and journalists were repeating the same information in literature around the world – in Japan as well as in the West. A good example of this was the report which appeared in 1980 in *Newsweek* 'Lessons from Japan, Inc.' – a much referred to and widely repeated analysis. In this case the phenomenon of Quality Control (QC) Circles was put forward as a vestige of an older society and thus entered the picture (to outsiders) of traditional Japanese Management.

Soon, not only were the Westerners treating Japan as a Mecca of good management practice, but the Japanese themselves began to refer to these factors as the basis for their own success – on a number of occasions using them as 'selling characteristics' when taking over European and US companies.

What is intriguing is that in the US, these Japanese practices were being emulated at the same time as the fear of Japanese investment rose, when in reality the level of investment from Britain was far greater.

So what has gone wrong in our analysis of Japanese management, and how significant is it?

A number of the characteristics listed in Fig 2.1 *do* have elements in common with Japan's feudal society that existed between 1603 and 1868. For five hundred years before, though, the country had been locked in combative, highly individualistic conflict and civil war. The Meiji Restoration in 1868, along with the further break-up of close-knit communities in both World Wars, brought a growth of entrepreneurialism in their aftermath. But we have to question just how endemic these 'Japanese' management practices really are.

If they are a throw-back to earlier times, it is much more likely that they originate in the large merchant houses of Osaka, Kyoto and Edo in the late 1700s. Rather like Lloyd's of London, these businesses are still around today and have inevitably had an effect on commercial practice generally.

Japanese productivity has always been more heavily biased to the smaller business sector. Even in the mid-1970s, while the West (particularly Britain) still had many large nationalised industries, over 75% of Japanese manufacturing output came from firms with fewer than ten employees. By the 1980s and the 'Japanese management boom', the practices that were being cited as the panacea for Western industry were actually only being carried out in a handful of Japanese companies!

Remarkably, at the same time as the West was struggling to adopt these approaches, the Japanese were struggling to overcome their negative effects!

Four aspects of the 'traditional' Japanese approach to management were identified as particularly disadvantageous:

1 the encouragement of employee dependency and the conscious suppression of individuality;
2 discriminatory employment was preventing a horizontal labour market;
3 the age-profile of Japan was becoming top-heavy, leading to a promotional bottleneck for middle managers;
4 work in the larger organisations was becoming repetitive and required limited intellectual effort.

1 The encouragement of employee dependency

While employment stability is considered beneficial to most organisations, this depends on the way in which it has been encouraged. The Japanese problem that was that the methods used had actually encouraged employee dependency. Many of the aspects of a Japanese company that caused this were common in the West too, such as strong direction, extensive welfare facilities, tied housing and collectively negotiated wages. Less common elsewhere were the policies to remove interpersonal competition: Japanese firms usually matched workers for skills and age, not making use of their innate talents but instead encouraging a uniformity of skill among all employees in a particular workplace.

This began with the recruitment process – an annual cycle in which employees were selected for their character and likely fit with others, rather than for any particular educational prowess or skills. As we see in Chapter 5, when Brian Morris of Nippon Lever describes their developments in team-working, this practice is a reflection of a nationwide approach to higher (and by definition secondary) education.

In training, too, the Japanese emphasis is on a common set of basic skills rather than on specialist knowledge. In Chapter 7, we see how one company, Juki Sewing Machines, addressed this problem by developing a demanding training programme which also encouraged skills-flexibility.

Any evidence of non-conformity was actively discouraged. In many organisations, individuals who were not prepared to work under the regime were likely to leave and develop their talents elsewhere – usually in their own enterprises.

2 A horizontal labour market

Because Japanese companies recruited most of their employees in an annual cycle, training and other activities (including pay adjustment) were geared to that cycle. Individuals who were not recruited in this way were frequently discriminated against by company practices. Among the groups most affected by this were mid-career changes, temporary employees, female employees, part-timers, and seasonal staff. Although this was a particular problem for Japanese companies (which they began to address), as we shall see it also has many similarities with the systems in contemporary Western traditional organisations.

Such discriminatory practices, then, inhibit the movement of employees between companies (a horizontal labour market).

3 A top-heavy age-profile

In a naturally ageing population, a horizontal labour market creates a predominance of people at the top, and no spaces for rising middle-managers. Couple this with the Japanese practice of separating salary and status from personal achievement and linking them to age and service, and you end up with the potential for a growing number of discontented middle managers. Ironically, avoiding the very thing that demotivates many Western managers – the subjective assessment of their performance by a remote and highly partial senior manager – had led to an even less palatable alternative.

4 Repetitive and routine work

Immediately after the Second World War, the larger Japanese organisations began to move away from the participative practices that have remained in the Western perception of Japanese management. Practices such as *Omikoshi* and bottom-up decision-making were no longer desirable as companies began to implement automation. Had they done so in a small way, perhaps the impact would have been different; but with Japan no longer engaged in military production, and with two new theatres of war on their doorstep (Vietnam and Korea), Japanese companies were in an ideal position to become major suppliers – and they needed to do so with a level of performance that only automation could guarantee. As a result, most employees lost what little creativity and variation there had been in their job.

More than one analyst has correlated this investment in automation, and employees' decreasing identity with their work, as one of the main contributors to the Japanese leisure industry boom of the 1980s and 1990s. Unlike their Western counterparts, the Japanese have reacted fairly passively to job displacement through automation.

Quality Control Circles – cure or placebo?

The growth-spurt of automation in the 1960s, with the consequent reduction in labour requirements, was addressed in many larger organisations by transferring employees to areas of lower automation and generally less interest. (Compare this with the strategy described in Chapter 10 by Russ Robinson of Motorola.) In the 1970s, when the two oil crises and global recession struck, investment in automation continued but with the goal of reducing labour-cost rather than improving production.

The appeal of Quality Control (QC) Circles at the time was twofold: they provided mechanisms:

- for remotivating employees;
- for addressing the problems often experienced in introducing new technology.

In Japan, the number of firms with QC Circles continues to grow, while in the West the concept has largely been abandoned. This is possibly due to a difference in expectations from the Circles.

Are Self-Managing Work Teams just Quality Control Circles under a different guise?

Quality Control Circles (or Quality Circles, as they are usually known in the West) blend beautifully into the largely imaginary Western perception of the Japanese style of management (which so few companies could actually have practised). Indeed, *Newsweek*, in particular, spotlighted QC Circles as contributing much to Japanese corporate performance.

The widespread adoption of QC Circles in Japan has largely been due to the single-minded perseverance of one body, the Union of Japanese Scientists and Engineers (JUSE). Established in May 1946, JUSE received government recognition in 1962 when it was consolidated into the Science and Technology Agency as part of the Japanese national effort to cope with the rapid growth in technology.

JUSE is not a representative union – it is fundamentally an educational and lobbying group. JUSE's main area of involvement since its inception has been the application of mathematics and statistics in management. Their single most significant impact has been in the field of Quality Control which they began promoting in 1949. After some initial lobbying by JUSE, the Japanese Industrial Standardisation Law was passed – and JUSE began its pioneering work in research and education.

In 1950, JUSE invited Dr W. Edwards Deming to conduct some seminars on QC – it was to be the start of a long relationship. He interlaced his material with some elements of modern behavioural philosophy (at that time unproven, but subsequently reasonably well-established) and created a potent mixture. In 1951, Deming offered the royalties from the sales of his books in Japan to the foundation of an annual quality prize. This has continued to this day, evolving to meet the changing needs of industry, and acting as a role model for both European Quality Award (instituted in 1992) and for the Baldrige Award (which was created by Ronald Reagan in 1988).

Throughout the 1950s JUSE maintained its pressure on organisations to adopt the statistical principles of Quality Control. Among the highlights of this period were the initial series of lectures on QC, broadcast by Japan Short-wave Radio, and the inaugural sessions of specific courses for senior and middle management – courses that continue to be run today.

It was in 1962 that JUSE moved from basic education in the principles and methods of QC to begin promoting a structure within which Quality Control could be introduced. Initially this was produced as a book, *Gemba-to-QC*, later renamed *SQC* and eventually *QC Circle*. This was the start of a new era in JUSE. Although the organisation continued to develop its basic principles, it also promoted the development of QC Circles as the medium for their application in organisations. The Japanese have stuck rigorously to the terminology, QC Circle, rather than Quality Circle which is more common in the West.

JUSE recorded the growth of their brainchild by maintaining a register to co-ordinate QC Circles. As a new QC Circle was formed in a company, its existence would be reported to JUSE. By 1967 the number of such groups had risen to 10,000. In 1970 JUSE began to emphasise the importance of these activities in small and medium-sized enterprises. It was in 1971 that they organised the first All-Japan Conference of QC Circles.

Throughout the 1970s JUSE focused on a number of specific industries, such as construction and the service sectors. Despite the worsening economic climate, JUSE's promotional activities continued. Among the gloomier aspects of the decade were the oil crises of 1973 and 1978, the 'Nixon Shock' of 1971 when the yen was devalued overnight from 360 to 308 to the dollar, and, in 1974, Japan's first recorded drop in gross national product (GNP) since the end of the Second World War.

A number of products had demonstrated phenomenal export success – not the least of which were the colour TV sets that every QC student is nowadays taught about! At the same time the 'secrets' of these exceptional performers were being publicised by, among others, Dr J.M.Juran at international conferences and seminars. It was in around 1979 that the 'Japanese Management' boom reached its height in the USA, and *Business Week* published a special issue entitled 'American manufacturers strive for quality – Japanese style'. At this time JUSE were training over 10,000 employees each year on their QC courses. By 1980 the number of foreign visitors to JUSE had grown dramatically, but it was not until 1985 that the organisation began offering literature and some courses in English.

It was also in 1985 that the Japanese Government took steps to denationalise some of their key industries, especially Nippon Telephone & Telegraph (NTT) and Japan Tobacco and Salt. Two other key events of the time, which may help us to put the timing into perspective, were the Chernobyl Reactor accident which happened in 1986 and the 'Black Monday' crash of the New York Stock Exchange in 1987.

JUSE continued to promote basic quality-control education, the QC Circles' route to implementing these tools and sector-specific applications. In the year of the Tiananmen Square riots and the collapse of the Berlin Wall (1989) JUSE took its next step in developing quality improvement activities within Japan – it sent a mission to Europe and the USA to study quality management systems and to discover why Britain, in particular, had adopted them so fervently.

As we reach the middle of the 1990s, JUSE has begun to focus its attention on developments in the technical field of Total Productive Maintenance and the wider adoption of group-based activities (rather than just QC Circles) as a mechanism for implementing quality improvement.

Membership of JUSE remains quite small, despite the very large number of individuals passing through its courses each year. Its membership is limited to corporations – and it currently has just under 2,000 members.

In late 1993 Dr W. Edwards Deming passed away.

THE EVOLUTION OF SELF-MANAGING WORK-TEAMS IN THE US

Links between education and industry go back as far as the Industrial Revolution. Certainly since the 1770s, companies have had to train their employees for specific tools, machines and functions. Extending this learning beyond the workplace began to emerge as a trend in the early 1800s. One of the first 'business schools' was operated in New York by the Grand Masonic Lodge. This was followed by one of the first university-based business schools: in 1830, Columbia University began offering courses to people currently employed in business. Non-managerial training was to follow later and in 1862, the Morrill Act was passed establishing agricultural and mechanical colleges. The need to improve workers' basic skills was widely recognised, but it was Hoe and Co. who introduced the first factory school in 1872. By the mid-1880s adult education had become firmly established as an academic area.

Some of the first union-led training programmes began in the 1920s at the same time as scientific management and a host of other 'academic' concepts began to be applied in the industrial world. Interestingly it was also around this time that many of the modern quality gurus began practising, and the Bell Labs began their work on statistical quality control.

Bell Laboratories

In 1876 Alexander Graham Bell invented the telephone. In 1885, AT&T (American Telephone and Telegraph) was incorporated to distribute the system throughout the USA. The Bell System continued to provide telephone services until AT&T divested its interests into a number of smaller local providers – known popularly as the Baby Bells.

As you would expect for such a fledgling technology, AT&T had to conduct extensive product development and basic research. Established in 1925, the AT&T Bell Laboratories, their R&D division remains the paradigm for industrial research throughout the world. Seven of its scientists have been awarded the Nobel Prize and it continues to earn an average of one patent every day – a consistent pattern since the day it was established!

Among the many spin-offs from their research were the statistical methods of process control devised by W.A. Shewhart. It was these techniques that have formed the backbone of quality improvement throughout the 20th Century.

By the 1930s the importance of employee motivation, development and education had become well established. In 1931, Massachusetts Institute of Technology opened the first executive development course – an away-from-work programme lasting several weeks. Dale Carnegie began promoting his human relations approach to management and sales in 1936, and shortly after the US Government announced its plans for the development of civil servants.

With the Second World War, and the drafting of younger people into the armed forces the workforce rapidly aged. Suddenly, large numbers of people had to be retrained, or trained to work again after having left work for some years. The Training Within Industry Service of the War Manpower Commission established what were to be known as 'J' programmes: these included the first 'train-the-trainers' initiatives and interpersonal skills for workers.

By the 1950s the demotivating aspects of scientific management were beginning to be appreciated, and courses in psychology and human relations were booming. Many supervisors and junior managers were introduced to these concepts, inspired by the lecturers and took up training themselves. The need for senior management involvement too was recognised, and Training Directors were appointed.

Without the barriers of language to contend with, US management academics began to acknowledge the work of people such as Eric Trist[1] who conducted research with groups of miners in the UK – an environment in which multi-skilling, job flexibility and team work were essential. Trist demonstrated two particularly important aspects of the story behind Self-Management:

1 He showed that miners who were given more opportunity to manage their own work produced more and were more motivated.
2 He found that such workers were more aware of, and capable of responding to, changing political and market forces.

In the early 1960s many of the 'modern' management psychology themes emerged, with McGregor's Theory X and Theory Y appearing, Schein's seminal works on organisation development, the Myers-Briggs Type Indicator based on the work of Carl Jung, and Blake and Mouton's Managerial Grid. The 1960s were the decade of organisation development and group behaviour. Leonard Nadler was the first to refer to 'human resource development', and the idea of modular training (known as programmed instruction) took off.

It was in the early 1960s that the Quality of Worklife movement began. Despite some powerful success stories[2] many organisations found that the impact of these involvement initiatives was minimal. This could have been due to the limited amount of top-down commitment: such initiatives were often seen by senior management as peripheral to the main business and, in a *macho* culture, they were rubbished by aspiring managers who could not see a role for themselves.

The training industry has been in the forefront of social trends and so it isn't surprising that by the late 1960s in the US the specific needs of urban regeneration, ethnic groups and women were frequently the subject of employee development initiatives.

Other shop-floor developments included the quality-circle activities of the West. Having a greater emphasis on bottom-line-related results, there was greater management support for these initiatives; and in some organisations many hundreds of teams were introduced. There were many differences between the Quality Circles of the West and the Quality Control Circles of Japan, though these differences tended to revolve around the scope of the projects undertaken rather than any fundamental change in approach.

The importance of managers as modifiers of behaviour rather than controllers of work was first promoted in the early 1970s. In 1971 Henry Mintzberg published an article in which he challenged the 'plan, organise, co-ordinate and control' model of management presented by Henri Fayol in 1916. This picture of the manager as a task-orientated controller of people had become entrenched in the popular mind. Sadly it was so ingrained that knowledge-based training would never shift it and so the mid- to late 1970s saw the introduction of behavioural modelling as an acceptable technique in management development training. New ideas are only ever old ones packaged in a more acceptable framework, and this was certainly the case here as the techniques that were most often used were based very heavily on the role-play and psychodramas of Moreno, first shown in 1910!

Around the same time, the US Congress was enacting legislation to improve widespread worker education, including the Comprehensive Education and Training Act (CETA); exemption from taxes was offered to organisations for their training budget. By the early 1980s, evidence was accumulating of the link between organisational performance and such aspects as quality, management style and employee involvement. In 1982, Tom Peters and Bob Waterman published *In Search of Excellence* – the first management text to make information of this kind accessible to practising managers. At about the same time, the US Congress passed the Job Training Partnership Act, providing assisted employment and training for workers who were in some way disadvantaged.

Remarkable though it may seem now, it was only at this time that Paul Hersey, Ken Blanchard and Robert Guest were developing their concepts of situation-related leadership. The Blake-Mouton Grid had been in use for fifteen years and had been widely interpreted as calling for one style of management – a hands-on but supportive coaching approach. Here the authors were demonstrating that style had to be flexible and appropriate – that leadership of this kind was a complex process, requiring skill and understanding.

Despite a few early attempts, Self-Directed Work Teams did not reach the popular audience in the US until the mid-1980s. This time, they were seen in almost every industry and environment.

In 1987, as the Malcolm Baldrige National Quality Award was introduced by President Reagan, so the Hudson Institute published its report *Workforce 2000,* based on research funded by the US Department of Labor. Its startling statistics on the future of the American workforce (and that of most other industrialised nations) were to provoke a number of employers and unionists rapidly to reassess the needs for worker education to the end of the century.

In late 1990, Texas Instruments and the University of North Texas, convened a conference on Self-Managed Work Teams. They had expected fewer than a hundred participants – they had to close the doors at 350! Of the benefits cited by most organisations of introducing Self-Managing Work-Teams, quality improvement and productivity headed the list. This was the boom of Self-Managed Teams. But today, many of their exponents have begun to move from describing the teams and how they work, to describing the benefits that they produce – the High Performance Workplace.

The concept that an organisation has to take a front-seat role in the development of its employees was encapsulated in Peter Senge's 1991 book, *The Fifth Discipline: the Art and Practice of the Learning Organisation*. At the same time, the American Society for Training and Development (ASTD) published jointly with the US Department of Labor two books by Anthony Carnevale demonstrating the direct link between employee learning and corporate performance. By 1993, Bill Clinton had created the Office of Work-based Learning within the Department of Labor, along with many other significant departures from the traditionally conservative structure.

In the following chapters we look at the different perspectives of people involved in encouraging, implementing, and working within Self-Directing Work Groups. Why have we changed the terminology?

The Japanese, especially at the Japan Productivity Center (JPC) and JUSE were at pains to point out the distinction and it is worth repeating here:

1 Self-management implies that a group is performing the activities of a manager. But these groups go much beyond this: in many cases they are taking significant strategic decisions. For instance, we have helped as teams of front-line employees redesigned their organisational structure, balancing the demands and resourcing of sales, production, maintenance and other support functions in the process. These are decisions that are more commonly associated with directors than managers.
2 The groups are large – often as many as twenty people. Team-working specialists will tell you that twenty is too many for a team. Most of the traditional assumptions about teams are based on groups of fewer than ten. Besides, these groups work alone, in many instances only getting together to review progress.

So the term that is increasingly used is Self-Directing Work Groups rather than Self-Managing Work Teams – nevertheless the two are widely used, SMWTs perhaps more often – hence the title of this book.

References

1 Trist E (1981) *The evolution of sociotechnical systems*. Occ Paper #2, The Quality of Worklife Center, Toronto, Canada.
2 Guest RH, Blanchard KH and Hersey P (1986) *Organizational Change through Effective Leadership*. Prentice-Hall, London.

3

SELF-MANAGING
WORK TEAMS

'How do I see Team Work developing in the future? In the future we shall be looking at the increasing importance of creativity in individuals and teams, and we shall be looking at the value of employee-participation.' (Prof. Kozo Koura, Asahi University)

- Even today, there are consultants who believe that quality can be improved (and equally important, productivity remain unaffected) by writing procedures, explaining how to use them and then sending a team of auditors in to check up on people.

- SMWTs provide the means of improving quality and productivity by several orders of magnitude – even in organisations which already leave the rest standing still!

- SMWTs call for a change in management attitude – relaxing control and devolving authority to an unprecedented degree.

- Implementing SMWTs goes hand-in-hand with evolving a learning culture.

- In the SMWT, group and peer control replaces the power of the paper organogram and management intervention as a means of maintaining standards.

- If you are going to achieve such performance goals as Six Sigma, you have to be prepared to challenge every facet of your organisation – first and foremost, its formal structure needs.

INTRODUCTION

When the phrase, 'Total Quality Management' (TQM) became popular in the 1980s it quickly emerged that it meant very different things to different people. To some, 'doing TQM' meant little more than implementing a basic quality-management system. To others it was a state of relaxation of management control and devolution of authority which could be aspired to, but never reached. Even today, there are consultants who believe that writing procedures, explaining how to use them and then sending a team of auditors in to check up on people will improve quality (and, equally important, not affect productivity).

In a similar way, Self-Managing Work Teams (SMWTs) are prone to a range of interpretations. To some they represent the closest we can get to that state of nirvana that they called TQM, but which was undermined by the systems movement! To others they are little more than an extension of Quality Circles. Whether consciously or subconsciously, some people have focused on the results that these teams produce and have used that to describe the phenomenon – High Performance Workplace or Six Sigma.

Others have concentrated on the culture that evolves with the teams – and especially on its educational aspect. As the teams become established (as we shall see later in the case of the Ford Romeo plant), an organisation evolves in which the *raison d'être* is learning, and the exceptional output appears almost inconsequential. For the last few years the phrase 'learning organisation' has sat on the touchline of the management pitch – SMWTs offer the medium for it to happen in.

In this chapter we look at Self-Managing Work Teams as just one of a range of organisation structures. But first, we examine what an organisation structure is, and how it works.

WHAT IS AN ORGANISATION?

It wouldn't take much to dream up a list of many different types of organisation. But it is much harder to define what we mean by 'organisation'. Three elements common to most definitions are that an organisation:

- is a social arrangement;
- it pursues collective goals;
- it does this through controlled performance.

For anyone interested in understanding SMWTs it is useful to consider what each of these means before looking at how they may differ in the individual SMWT.

1 A social arrangement

An organisation may consist of only one individual – and may provide an excuse for that individual to interact with others: in other words, it has a social function. So, the founder-member of a charity creates an organisation which allows them to interact with other people in a way that wouldn't be open to them if they were operating under their own name. When an organisation has more than one member, those people can get something out of meeting together, without the need for outside interaction. Around the world there are running clubs, called Hash Harriers, which originated in South East Asia. These groups of runners meet, often weekly, for the purpose of running together. Their members do not compete – there is no element of internal competition. Unlike most other sports clubs, though, there is also no element of external competition either. Hash Harriers do not compete as teams against one another.

The two elements of internal and external social interaction are to be found in almost all organisations.

2 Collective goals

Organisations provide a focal point for like-minded individuals – i.e. such individuals have some common or collective goals. For political parties, charities, and caring organisations in particular, this is easy to imagine. It would be wrong to think, though, that the organisation itself has goals – individuals have goals, organisations do not, they simply provide a focal point for people with similar (but often different) goals. Thus a political party can easily be fragmented when two alternative goals, or more often the means of achieving them, compete for resources.

Occasionally the individuals' goals are so clear that they can also be consistent. In this case, there is a good chance of the organisation achieving them and it may well then disappear. A good example of this was the Campaign for Lead-Free Air, an early 1980s pressure group established by Des Wilson, founder of Shelter (a voluntary organisation for the homeless). The members shared such a unified set of goals that they did not compete for resources with each another and presented a consistent argument. Through the organisation, they achieved their goals and it disbanded.

3 Controlled performance

Where the external front of the organisation (its collective purpose) has some community role it is easy to see how the individuals within it might share the same goals. But they may well not, and it is very dangerous to assume that co-members all have the same goals as you. Organisations provide financial support, physical resources, a sense of value, of contribution and meaning, and some order or stability to people who need it. They may also be a source of security and protection, and they often offer support – either directly or through fellow members. They can bolster self-esteem and confidence by building status or prestige through membership of them. And finally, the individuals within them may be able to exert control, power and authority, that would otherwise be impossible. All of these are powerful motivators to become a member without a need to share a common purpose. Some individuals can be so strongly motivated by these personal factors that the collective purpose of the organisation becomes secondary, if not completely irrelevant!

Some organisations are particularly susceptible to this, and carefully screen out potential members whose motives are suspect. This doesn't just mean gun-clubs either! The police and armed forces have their fair share of such problems – and but the church and counselling organisations also have to screen out those whose personal needs may detract from their clients.

The power to define the organisation's collective purpose is not usually distributed evenly across the members. In most organisations, particularly in commercial ones but also in not-for-profit ones, that power is concentrated in a few members. Many are defined in the office of the chief executive. They may take counsel from the directors or from their management team but, more often than not, an individual will have drafted them. As soon as they have passed out of the hands of that individual they have to be 'sold' to other members of the organisation. The commonest 'sales' tactic is to tell people that they are the 'company goals' – implying that they are not negotiable: you accept them or you get out! This ploy usually takes place at the first level beyond the senior management team, and may be used throughout the rest of the organisation. Thus the chief executive announces the goals, and invites discussion in the Senior Management Team. At this stage they may be modified. The senior managers then describe the goals and invite discussion among their staff, but by now there will be no further modifications.

In the 1980s, one management guru advocated cascading this goal-setting process throughout an organisation. Although in theory this might work, in practice it led to widespread demotivation and eventually to outright hostility. Two managers from one of his former clients summed up the predictable range of reactions: 'Don't the directors know what they're doing? Why do they have to come asking us?' and 'They've never consulted us before – they'll never consult us again – it's a whitewash and they'll blame us when it goes wrong!'

So organisations exist to provide social interaction, pursue collective goals and achieve controlled performance. You might like to consider how the growth of self-employment is affecting people. Once their primary source of social intervention has gone, their goals may be misaligned with their needs and controls on performance are changed.

WHAT IS AN ORGANISATION STRUCTURE?

So how is performance controlled within an organisation? Managers control their employees with rewards, motivation and discipline – and perhaps less obviously by grouping functions and establishing hierarchies to affect decision-making. The advantages of an organisation structure are wide-ranging. For example, by introducing a rigid structure, managers can save themselves effort by avoiding adjudicating over conflicts of resources. Structures are not restricted to paper organograms. For instance all the same purposes are achieved in schools through the imposition of a set of common rules. Exactly the same thing happens at work – though here there are also many unwritten rules that have become a part of the culture. When organisations try to improve innovation or quality, they often seek ideas from employees. There is a common cry when someone suggests something novel: 'We can't do that: it's against the rules!'

We often find that the environment in which people work has a bigger impact on their attitudes and behaviour than any basic personality types. Take a sales manager from the regional office to headquarters and his or her behaviour can change almost overnight.

Thus organisations (or more accurately their managers) rely upon structures as a way of controlling people's behaviour at work. Provided that their personal goals and social needs are met, employees will go along with this. But what happens if they are not? Fortunately this doesn't often happen except in disputes over wages.

Nevertheless, in the late 1980s especially, many people at the top of organisations began to question their own right to decide how their employees should behave. Many of the earliest Self-Managing Work Teams were introduced by top managers who had in their own words; 'gone through some kind of personality crisis'. There is, however, a continuum between those people who believe in the importance of social interaction as the means of controlling behaviour and the rule makers. Even in the mid-1960s, when the structural view was already under considerable threat from the human relations school, Alan Fox reported the findings of a Royal Commission on Trades Unions and Employers Associations and bucked the trend by emphasising the structural dimension again. By the 1980s popular empathy was with the employees and their importance, now in the 1990s as Business Process Re-engineering has taken hold, we see a swing back.

If neither is right or wrong, what are the important elements of organisation structure? It is useful to distinguish between the **basic structure** (possibly written down and referred to as the organisation structure) and the **operating structure**. It is the operating structure, if anything, which affects people's behaviour at work. The operating structure is based on acquired wisdom, politics, seniority of service, qualifications, who is married to whom and a host of other factors. It may also be influenced by management decisions and formal procedures, working practices and shared training. In Activity 3.1 (at the end of this chapter) we describe a simple exercise which illustrates many of the different ways in which an organisation is structured.

THE NATURE OF GROUPS

Most of us belong to five groups. Most groups consist of a maximum of five people. Our lives are organised around groups, at school, at work and socially. When two people develop a relationship – at work, in the home or wherever – their behaviour with one another becomes predictable and they adopt quite clear roles.

In groups, there are many one-to-one relationships, but there are two others that are important: a group itself takes on an identity, and a group interacts with other groups.

Most people have heard of the early social science experiments conducted by Elton Mayo at the Hawthorne works of Western Electric between 1927 and 1932. Popular memory distorts the real findings of the experiments, the main conclusions of which were:

- individuals benefit from groups, just as organisations do;
- there are formal and informal functions within groups;
- the informal functions can conflict with and overcome the external ones;
- in this way groups of workers can unite against their managers;
- the individual benefits of group membership can offer greater rewards than management can.

Before these experiments it had been thought that groups were responding to another leader. Even today there is a blind assumption that all groups must have a leader. This is far from the case, and a lot is now known about group behaviour and how it operates.

By groups we mean collections of people who share some psychological links. This excludes people who have gathered together by chance – such as the group of people commuting on the 7.24 train from Leatherhead to London. The psychological links mean that *all* the members of the group interact, are aware of each other and believe that they are a group. There are some common characteristics of psychological groups:

1 a sense of collective identity;
2 shared goals;
3 group structure – with different roles and group rules;
4 a means of communication with one another.

It is quite easy for a collection of people to become a group. This is the stuff of disaster movies, but it can apply whenever the group goes through a shared experience that they perceive is unique to them. It was this simple transition which was abused so much by the outdoor 'education' schools of the 1970s – throw people on to a moor for the night and they become a psychological group!

The role of groups

We keep saying that groups serve both the organisation and the individual. The organisational goals are usually concerned with the output from tasks – whether this is sales made or widgets produced. The individual goals may include friendship, control over others, subservience to others, or achieving a common purpose. Once the main goals have formed, accessory goals develop. This is very common with pressure groups, and may be one explanation why the same people are frequently seen supporting successive causes. Intriguingly, the psychological satisfaction of belonging to a group can dwarf individual identity. Next time you go to a party, ask a few people who they are and you could be surprised by the number that don't give their name but instead say which group they belong to! For each of the needs described by Abraham Maslow there will be members of a group.

To Maslow the most important need was self-actualisation. He didn't actually use that word, but he did define a desire for self-fulfilment, to become everything that a person is capable of becoming.

In Chapter 2 we saw how the Self-Managing Work Team movement has evolved. From its origins in the human relations school and the quality

- To know and understand
- Freedom of inquiry and expression
- Self-actualisation
- Self-esteem and the respect of others
- Love and a feeling of belonging
- Safety and being organised
- Physiological

Fig 3.1 Maslow's hierarchy of needs

arena, it has moved from management-led formal groups to employee-led informal groups (especially western Quality Circles). In some ways, the Self-Managing Work-Teams are the formalisation of these employee-led groups.

To the members such groups are deliberately constructed to satisfy needs for self-actualisation. As Maslow demonstrated in the late 1940s, this need depends upon the needs to learn more and to express oneself freely. SMWTs are the perfect breeding-ground for these abilities.

But why should traditional organisations move towards SMWTs as an organisation structure? The Hawthorne experiments showed that if the groups developed relevant standards of behaviour, they could organise themselves to be more efficient, more effective and produce better-quality results. In the 1950s George Homen described how a group evolves these internal standards or patterns of behaviour – 'emergent' behaviours, as he called them, as distinct from 'required' behaviours.

Think of the cabin-crew on an aircraft: they each have their own tasks and generally don't need to interact with one another very much. They are not working under ideal conditions for their tasks, but they perform adequately. When the chief steward or purser encourages the group to have a friendly banter, performance goes up (and with it morale). Recent statistics from Southwest Airlines suggest that this kind of friendly banter can stimulate performance by several orders of magnitude!

Subsequent work by Tuckman, Hersey, Blanchard and Guest, among others, have shown how the group evolves to this condition of high-performance. The benefits of improved productivity and quality give an enormous incentive to the organisation, along with the advantage of stimulating self-development and so preparing the workforce for more demanding roles in the future.

But what are the risks?

Most managers' greatest fear is of losing control. They argue that without direction and control, the group will spend excessively, allow productivity and quality to drop, antagonise customers, endanger themselves and others, and encourage working practices and procedures to be abandoned. In short, industrial anarchy!

In practice this never happens directly with Self-Managed Work Teams. If it does it is for some other reason. Why?

When we look at the behaviour of people in groups we can separate what they are tackling (Task Content) from the way in which they are tackling it (Process). We can also distinguish the methods that they use to tackle the task (Task Process) from the ways in which they work with one another (People Process). This People Process can be broken down further still:

- **Factors between individuals**: the impact of differences between people – their personality, learning styles, motivation and motives.
- **Group characteristics**: where the focus is on the group – its hierarchy, roles people are given or take, elements of formality and informality.
- **Interactions**: how the communication between individuals affects their behaviour (for instance, if one person uses an arrogant tone, do others take umbrage, recede into a subservient role or ostracise the individual?)

From a study of these factors we begin to see how a group regulates the behaviour of its members. Members of a group gain little if being in the group is itself stressful, produces little, or conflicts with personal needs. The desire to achieve these personal needs creates a cohesiveness which is influenced by similarities between members, the size of the group, communication between them, isolation from outside influences and many others.

To maintain cohesiveness, groups form their own rules of conduct and the means of enforcing them. These 'norms' are often produced as a clear step in the development of a team. Tuckman described four stages in team development: forming, storming, norming, and performing. Enforcement methods can range from practical jokes and temporary or permanent ostracism to outright violence. As a consultant I have twice seen board members of large companies locked by the lapels!

Take a moment to think of some of the things that you wouldn't do if someone else were present. Why wouldn't you? What would happen if you did? In society we use this as a form of punishment. In prisons, individuals are degraded by being forced to do things that they wouldn't do normally – in front of others. There is a strong moral debate about the extent to which this should be done and whether it achieves any long-term benefit. The mere presence or absence of others, and the way it affects our behaviour, is known as 'social influence'.

Social influence can stimulate certain behaviours, just as it can inhibit them. When a group's effect is to increase the productivity or quality of an individual, we talk of 'social facilitation'. There's nothing new about this – we all expect a football team to do better in front of a home-crowd, and most sports competitors say that they achieve personal bests against good competition, and with a supportive crowd.

Besides the impact on individual performance, there are certain tasks that benefit from the combined strengths of the members of a team. This may be simply a matter of more hands to turn a wheel, or more heads to tackle a problem – or it could be that the creativity of one individual is complemented by the practicality of another, or the sheer get-up-and-go mentality of another.

These factors alone would tend to improve people's performance as they become team members. But the scale of the impact can be increased enormously by helping the group to develop a shared frame of reference or common purpose and set of norms. Much of the early training and development of SMWT members revolves around developing that purpose and the group's norms. It can be shown that, once developed, these will last a long time, will be referred to subconsciously and used covertly. Despite the almost constant talk of the importance of a shared vision, organisations frequently fail to give teams a good picture of their objective.

So how does the SMWT prevent the anarchic, demotivated employee from ripping the organisation off? Not only does the group establish norms (which inevitably incorporate moral values), inhibit behaviour that falls outside them and 'facilitate' improved performance, it also affects people's perceptions. An early, and now classic, experiment was carried out by Muzafer Sharif in 1936. He demonstrated that, if a group of people who are getting to know one another is placed in a situation where information or direction isn't given, the individuals' viewpoints will quickly fall in line with one another. What happens is that an individual who flouts the group's accepted behaviour and norms will be 'punished' by the group – often quite openly. Anything that threatens the group cohesion will provoke a response.

Of course, this needs to be managed. If members of the team are trained and informed, little can go wrong; but if alternative solutions and views are discouraged, then the group could press ahead with inadequate solutions, ultimately leading to the phenomenon known as Groupthink.

THE INTERVIEWEES

We interviewed three leading Japanese management observers on issues of team-work and employee development.

Professor Koza Koura is active within JUSE (the Japan Union of Scientists and Engineers). He is widely recognised for his contributions to management science and especially to team-working. Professor Koura summarises the state of teams in Japan generally and highlights their future role.

The Japan Productivity Center is one of the country's leading providers of training to junior management. It runs many basic skills courses, workshops on advanced techniques and conferences and seminars. It is increasingly taking a role in promoting adult-worker training as an essential component in the economic strength of the Pacific Rim. **Yasuhiko Inoue** explains their origin, future direction and current thinking on self-management.

The Keidanren is a powerful lobby representing major industry. Situated close to the Imperial Palace, its impressive offices are constantly hosting meetings between powerful industrialists from the Keiretsus. **Motori Hirose** is the manager of their Industry and Telecommunications Department whose teams are constantly evaluating new developments. He summarises the problems confronting Japanese business leaders in the area of employee development.

INTERVIEW 3.1 TEAMS, PRESENT AND FUTURE

Kozo Koura, Professor of Business Administration,
Asahi University, Tokyo, Japan

Koura made the interesting point that SMWTs are an evolution of Western team working. Although some people might think that they were transferred from Japan they are nevertheless essentially Western. So when we look for the characteristics of SMWTs in Japanese organisations we should look at their 'traditional' structures too and the latest evolutions of them .

Let's begin by clearing up a small confusion – there are three types of teamwork approach common in Japan:

- Committee;
- Team;
- QC Circle.

There are three types of 'team' too:

- Project teams;
- Product teams;
- Strategic Business Unit (SBU) teams.

The different teams may affect one another, but they are different. For example, a project team may make a recommendation that involves attending some workshops and as a result of these the workers may create an action in their QC Circle.

Exactly what is a QC Circle? The QC Circle is a group of workers which, with their Foreman as the Leader, tackles problems of Quality Control. They never include more senior people. They address problems of relevance to their daily work. Some QC Circles have been very rewarding – in a survey we found that the usual benefit from a QC Circle was between 100,000 and 1.5 million Yen ($650 to $10000).

A typical product-line passing through many different functions could be influenced by a lot of QC Circles.

Some groups have a learning function too. We can call these PTAs (Parent-Teacher Associations). There are three main differences between QC Circles and PTAs.

1 In a normal QC Circle the group selects their own problems to tackle; in a 'PTA' they usually respond to a suggestion from their manager.

2 A QC Circle may seek advice about which tools to use or approach to take, but this is not usual; a PTA, on the other hand, will be guided by their manager in the process of interpreting the problem and may be coached in the use of certain techniques.

3 A QC Circle produces its own team-report – if necessary to senior management; the PTA, on the other hand, is usually evaluated for them.

The other arrangement to mention is the Cross-Functional team, composed of managers and not the workers.

How do I see Team Work developing in the future? In the future we shall be looking at the increasing importance of creativity in individuals and teams, and we shall be looking at the value of employee-participation. Professor Kondo of Kyoto University has been reflecting on this for a long time.

You should look at two organisations on this subject: Toyota, which has gone a long way in reducing the number of managers by empowering their employees more; and Juki, which is the best example that I know of collaboration with the Union – an important issue.

INTERVIEW 3.2 SELF-MANAGEMENT IN JAPAN

Yasuhiko Inoue, Deputy Director, Japan Productivity Center

The JPC, while being a key provider of training, is also an economic lobbying organisation. They have been concerned for some years about the disparity between the ability of pupils leaving school and the needs of industry. Inoue pointed out the serious national economic consequences of not taking action about this.

Brief history of the Japan Productivity Centre

The Asian Productivity Organisation (APO) is a regional eighteen-strong organisation founded in 1960 on the recommendation of the Japanese Government. It has recently been announced that Australia will become a member next year. The US, Canada and Mexico will be forming the Asian Pacific Economic Committee. Our Director, Mr Miyai presented a paper in February, in which he explained the macro level of change that we feel is important.

In April, the Japan Productivity Center (JPC) and the Social Economic Congress of Japan (SECOJ) will merge to tackle social productivity. JPC has been concerned with manufacturing productivity, but many things cannot be solved by organisational effort, such as social, national and international factors.

SECOJ has been tackling things like basic education, labour law, economics and transport. Our area is more concerned with implementation but they are highly complementary.

JPC has three basic characteristics: it is non-profit-making, self-sustaining (from training, sales of books and audio-visual aids, and consultancy) and impartial. We currently run 1,500 programmes each year – the longest being a one-year full-time consultancy skills programme, while the shortest lasts just four days.

This building has 350-400 employees; there are seven regional offices and twenty local offices with a total of roughly 500-540 employees. To each seminar, the average response is 40-50 – the consultancy programme has fifty people. The main candidates for the consultancy programme (80-90%) are bankers: younger bankers are sent by their company to learn to assess company performance. It is a unique course though.

The courses are mainly on corporate performance, but some are at a very macro level – such as environment for top-level managers. Our courses range from top management information-sharing seminars (on energy, the environment and so on) to very practical skill-development for newly recruited sales teams – how to bow for example!

We do not touch specific technology – but our courses are for management level – supervisors, foremen etc. We cover problem-solving skills, like JUSE, but our courses have much wider coverage than just the quality area.

We are a non-governmental body – our third characteristic is impartiality: we are supported by management, unions, and academics – we are concerned with what academics have to offer management and unions.

The increasing relevance of Self-Management

Through their own researches JPC feel that they have sufficient real evidence to support a macro-economic argument that empowerment (and reduction of hierarchy) is tied to productivity and quality, and that these two drive consumer spending.

Mr Miyai presented a paper in Manila in October 1991 which reinforced the fact that productivity and quality are not a trade-off. What is a productive workforce and productive management? He discussed Human Resource effectiveness.

Our main activity is Human Resource Development. Of course, we need tools and techniques for certain technologies, but we particularly refer to Self-Management of Workforces. Tasks should be the responsibility of a small group of the workforce – each individual is expected to deal with each problem with a level of care or attention. The person who they deal with is their customer – and people should be very careful in dealing with the products or services that they give to their customers. They themselves need to be a disciplined, well-managed and responsible group.

Self-Management is growing to some extent in all Japanese companies, but in a very dynamic, very flexible way. Some organisations are making more changes than others – steel making, car assembly, manufacturing, finance – in all these industries there is evidence of this.

Self-Management is not carried out in taskforce-types of groups like QC Circles. We are talking about day-to-day work. The Japanese way of working is in small groups – led by a foreman or supervisor – consisting of a maximum of ten people. These are mainly organised according to functions – marketing, accounts, production and so on. But the function of each sub-department is changing – the traditional responsibilities of, say, the Quality Department are in fact better handled by each individual department – design, marketing, customer services and so on. The Departments themselves exist. The recent trend is to 'market-in' not 'product-out'. The information flows that way – and the result is a flatter organisation.

Management reaction to Self-Management

Self-Management isn't that easy for managers to accept – traditionally they needed to control. There must be more trust between managers and sub-ordinates. This exists in a family, and the workplace must be an extension of this – since we are in the workplace for eight hours or more a day. We need to stop people behaving like machines. The new style is almost paternalistic, in a way. Managers need to trust, to have a form of control, but the basic idea is that they assist their subordinates.

Impacts on rewards systems

At the macro level, productivity increases and nominal wages are linked to consumer spending. We have three guiding principles:

- productivity increase should bring an increase in employment;
- labour should be involved in productivity increase;
- gains should be shared fairly (not equally) between management, employees and consumers.

Companies are carefully reviewing the wage system in Japan right now – wages, life-style and seniority are all interrelated. For instance, the needs of a typical 35-year-old change because of his family, while at 49 or 50 his needs are fewer. The recent economic recession is encouraging this review. But the idea of payment for skills is built into our seniority system – the more knowledge, the more they will be paid.

However this payment isn't immediate, and this is particularly unpopular with young people. Job-hopping was never very common but now it is increasing – (though not dramatically) from 20 to 28%: still most people prefer to work for one employer.

INTERVIEW 3.3 EMPLOYEE DEVELOPMENT

Motori Hirose, Manager of the Industry & Telecommunications Department, Keidanren (the Japan Federation of Economic Organisations)

Brief background to the Keidanren

The Keidanren is a think-tank. Essentially we represent large industrial and commercial organisations in Japan. Our structure reflects the very wide range of issues that we feel need to be reviewed and in which industry – especially large-scale industry – needs to have a voice. The policy committees, which draft and respond on each area, are chaired by some of the country's most pre-eminent businessmen, most often the chairmen of our member companies. Areas in which we express a policy include political reform, government reform, international co-ordination of economic policies, competition policy, and quality of life – as well as all the issues that you would automatically expect a movement such as ours to be involved in (energy, environment, safety, taxation and so on).

Japanese management style

Firstly, you must recognise that the nature of Japanese management is changing. The style has been well described and has many historical roots – what is important, though, is the impact of those today, rather than how they evolved.

For instance, the idea that there is a Japanese management style, whether it is true or not, has had an effect on the attitudes of many business people. Books, like *Japan – Number One*, have been remarkably popular – they appeal to people who would not be prepared to read a more academic study. The image that Japan's success is due to our management style is, in a way, history repeating itself – we have an unfortunate trait of being rather arrogant. We were before and during the War – and we have been afterwards.

The social structure of Japanese organisations

i Age of management

Senior management in many large organisations comprises men who were managing at the time of the Japanese Austerity Plan, men who have always had an eye for detail in the use of resources: they have had to because Japan has very few natural resources – only human ones.

ii Class divisions

However, these managers also really pre-date the efforts to remove the class-based society in the aftermath of the Second World War. To pretend that it has been removed would be foolish – many people believe that other countries (such as the UK) have a much more extensive class system – but ours is still there.

iii Ethnic diversity

This also creates a problem for the large companies. Japan has always, and continues to, contribute heavily to the economic growth of our neighbours, especially in Korea and Vietnam. But nowadays, our society includes fourth generation representatives of these communities, and they represent a social time-bomb.

Employment and employee development practices

Many companies have begun to recognise that there is a need for change in their procedures of employment and development: there are concerns about the educational system (which produces people who are good at repetitive learning but not at analysis and interpretation), about the annual recruitment procedure and limited mid-career change, about the college system, and about the way in which employee development produces compliance, and removes or wears down individuals who do not conform.

The limited power of shareholders

The shareholders have relatively little power – apart from annual stockholders' meetings they cannot interfere in the management of a business. A recent case established this very clearly.

I'd add that although we have been successful in many respects, there are also some startling anomalies that people are beginning to challenge: for instance, basic infrastructure – very little stands today that was created a hundred years ago. We do not build for durability – and that applies to things like sewers too. A basic requirement for a civilised society is good sewerage – and we are not that good.

What can be done to address these issues?

So what are we doing to try to address these issues? Well, there are the extensive policy committees – each has its own remit and each has importance. In the same way, though, that the Confederation of British Industry (CBI), for example, has its core issues – I guess that ours are:

* the need for a very clear policy on the 'slump';
* the need to build on and improve Japanese–US relations;
* widespread de-regulation;

- increases in areas of capital expenditure ;
- the encouragement of new management styles.

Beyond that it is perhaps too early to say. In May our new chairman takes up his post – Mr Toyoda has had a long association with the Keidanren but is seen as a very different person from others in the organisation. Not only is he from a consumer-driven business (Toyota), but he is also much younger than many others. He and Mr Morita have both been very well received abroad as spokesmen for Japanese business.

Activity 3.1: Concepts of organisation

We use a straightforward game to help groups think about and discuss concepts of organisation structure. Cut up some sheets of plain paper into pieces about 3" x 5", and write the following roles on them:

- Owner
- First Team Squad
- First Team Captain
- Second Team Squad
- Second Team Captain
- Youth Team Squad
- Youth Team Captain
- Saturday Club Children
- Mums and Dads
- Launderers
- Manager
- First Team Coach
- Ground Staff (Permanent)
- Ground Staff (Temporary)
- Team Doctor
- Team Physiotherapist
- First Aiders
- Cleaners
- Security Officers
- Police Officers
- Chaperones
- Food Franchisees
- Mobile 'Hawkers'
- Programme Sellers
- Souvenir Sellers
- Ticket Sales Clerks
- Restaurant Waiting Staff
- Restaurant Chef
- Restaurant Cooks
- Restaurant Plongeurs

Have a few blank pieces too to add to your list if you spot any obvious gaps.

Now working with a couple of others (your family will be good at this), arrange the people in some form of organisational structure.

You should begin to see functions, teams and groups emerging. You will find examples of positional authority, peer pressure and familiar power determining behaviour. There are positions based on skill, experience, financial commitment, and individual relationships. Some roles have a large span of control and others a small one. A few posts might be very clearly defined while others will be very loosely defined. Some parts of the hierarchy are flat, while others are not. Some people have a line relationship, others are specialists and have a 'staff relationship', while still more have functional relationships. Look for situations where people have responsibility for something, may be held accountable, but lack the authority to *force* it to happen. Some of the jobs are grouped according to their output, others by function, some by customer-type. There will be groups according to geography, time and technology.

4

IMPLICATIONS

'We spend money to give people specific subject-matter training, and we spend money to raise people's capabilities so that they can grow, because we think that is one of our requirements – to enable every person to have success in their life.'

Paul Noakes, Motorola.

- **High-performance companies balance short-term targets and goals with a longer-term vision.**

- **Most strategic initiatives take many years to come to fruition – without a longer-term vision they are doomed from the outset.**

- **The high-performance company depends on the performance of its suppliers – of people, services and materials. It is no longer sufficient to specify and inspect as a means of ensuring quality in these – you have to be actively involved in their development and production.**

- **With a long-term vision, the degree of this involvement is much greater. We can develop partnerships with our raw materials suppliers, spawn new businesses to service our organisation, and, through schools and teachers, educate the workforce of tomorrow.**

INTRODUCTION

The difference between an ordinary driver and an advanced motorist is said to be the distance ahead that they are considering. The regular motorist rarely considers beyond the car in front, while the advanced driver is constantly scanning the horizon. Much the same could be said of high-performance companies, which, just like the motorist, balance short-term targets and goals with a longer-term vision. For many years, a common observation of Japanese companies has been that they tend to spend extended periods of time planning, and a relative short period of time implementing, a policy. Though it may be for different reasons, Western companies which can be seen to be pursuing a high-performance route are also concentrating on short-term targets that lead to a long-term goal. This could be misinterpreted as encouraging a lack of innovation, whereas in fact the contrary is true. Because they have a long-term vision, these organisations are able to invest considerable amounts of energy in speculative areas, provided that they tie in with the longer-term picture.

The Rentokil success story

The recent emergence of Rentokil as one of Britain's most admired companies is a perfect example of this approach. Twelve years ago, they were a £100-million-turnover business, and were a household name in the UK for pest control and in particular for the treatment of woodworm. Twelve years ago, the newly-appointed Chief Executive, Clive Thompson, began a long-term transformation of the organisation. It now has a turnover measured in billions of pounds and employs 30,000 people around the world. In 1982, environmental issues were beginning to attract attention, but to most organisations, they were a 'nice to have', without representing any significant opportunity. Most emphasis in environmental matters was concentrated on the negative impact of organisations on their immediate environment. One classic Environmental Consultant's report tried to evaluate the heat-loss from a UK factory building in terms of trees consumed in South American forests. Such information, while raising eyebrows, did little to promote the recognition that the environment was a significant, market-shaping factor.

At the helm of Rentokil, however, Thompson recognised a longer-term future in the real world of business services. At that time it would have been easy for Rentokil to have fallen foul of environmentalists because of the nature of its products and the type of treatments that it carried out. Today, however, it is a multinational services group offering a broad base of specialist services protecting people's health and property, and improving the environment. As stock exchanges around the world strove to identify such businesses for their environmentally conscious portfolios, Rentokil became the 'Green Stock par Excellence'. By 1992 it was awarded a royal warrant for environmental services.

The range of Rentokil's environmental products today include water and ventilation services, medical services, tropical plant-care, health-care services, security and communications. It has regularly grown by acquisition, incorporating innovative approaches to its already impressive portfolio. The company has identified eight major environmental impacts, and within each they have adopted an innovative growth process:

- **Food**: bacteria, additives and preparation.
- **Air**: quality, airborne germs, viruses, smoke and air conditioning.
- **Water**: contamination and disease carrying.
- **Light**: its adequacy and offensive or oppressive nature.
- **Noise**: excessive, unpleasant, unceasing and damaging.
- **Equipment**: harmful and threatening.
- **Amenity**: unpleasant, unsociable, depressing and oppressive.
- **People**: safety, epidemiology, density and sociability.

It would have been possible for Rentokil to have squandered its efforts and resources in a random trawl through these many emerging fields. However, the second element to Thompson's vision was the single-minded pursuit of a financial performance goal of achieving growth of more than 20% per annum. It has done this in two respects: in the twelve-year period, it has grown by an average of more than 22% per annum in profits, and by more than 24% per annum in earnings per share. From a financial perspective its performance has been incredible. The company is now among the seventy largest in the UK, and the top 200 in Europe. The Daily Telegraph acclaimed it as the best performer of all present members of the FT/SE index in the past five years. No matter which criterion you use, Rentokil is now among the top in the UK.

So the aspirations of the high performance company are high whether in terms of financial performance, or perhaps quality defects – and such companies look into the longer term, whether that means the twelve-year-plus horizon of Rentokil or the fifty-year plan of Motorola. Such an attitude has many implications for the wider community beyond the organisation. In this chapter we want to focus on two implications:

- the preparation of the ground for the future;
- the involvement of organisations outside the high-performance one.

Development of the market for the future

It may seem far-fetched to believe that Motorola has a regular fifty-year planning process. In today's technology-driven world, this means that they are often now considering issues of the market-place that realistically have never been considered before. Take Rentokil's case: if it is to continue to hit its 20% growth factor for capitalisation, then in fifty years' time, on the basis of present-day employment levels, it will need to be employing over 270 million people. Clearly they cannot do so, and so their strategies must evolve to provide the same return for a smaller number.

Take the sales area alone: contracts will be larger and the order-value of an individual sales-person will be considerably greater. To achieve this, they must in turn develop and employ 'the super-sales people' of the day. Such long-term planning also means that certain areas will probably be identified as 'no-hopers' – ones that the company cannot afford to invest in because perceived developments will not meet the targets. Almost certainly the organisation needs to be examining emerging market places and moving into them soon enough to establish a presence. In the case of Motorola, major investments in the former Soviet Union and South America are just beginning to develop and show signs of yielding a return. Plans need to be made and an investment, however small, must be committed early in the process of development.

Involvement

The high-performance organisation is characterised by the alliances that it has with its suppliers, customers and non-competitive organisations. The most obvious area to start is that of customers. The company seamlessly integrates its customers into the production and development of its products and services. One of Motorola's Total Customer Satisfaction (TCS) teams which was concerned with improving broadcast equipment for public-service vehicles, included representatives from the local police force. Juki, the sewing machine company, encourages women from the neighbourhood surrounding its factory to become involved in problem-solving activities. Toyota is reported to involve customers in the evaluation of concept-designs by taking full-scale mock-ups to railway concourses and allowing people to examine and 'play' with them.

Many companies have invested heavily in the development of their distribution channels. Surely none more so than the Ford Motor Company, which provides an incredible portfolio of training, IT, financial and consultancy support to its many dealerships. One well-known watch manufacturer provided extensive sales training for jewellery store staff, despite the fact that they would frequently use their new-found skills to sell lower-valued competitive products.

Similarly, an increasing number of organisations are involving their suppliers in quality improvement and partnership-type arrangements. In the UK in particular, the concept of 'partnership sourcing' became very popular and continues to be talked about, although initially many partnership sourcing initiatives involved one large customer influencing smaller suppliers.

While partnership sourcing has concentrated on the co-development of products and services, many of the collaborative arrangements between supplier and customer revolve around training. We read elsewhere in this book of the major investment made by Motorola in encouraging its suppliers' staff to attend Motorola University courses. Similar activities are carried out by Ford, General Motors and most other high-performance companies.

Alternatively such organisations may recognise that an exchange of labour between their businesses is healthy and that there is a benefit in developing common training. Through their early commitment to a nationwide network of community colleges, Motorola, Kodak, General Motors and Ford, among others, have co-developed training programmes in several basic technical disciplines. They now recognise each other's in-house training based on these units, so employees can move from one to another without retraining.

In some cases, consultancy support is provided. For many years IBM positioned itself as one of the few hardware manufacturers to offer a comprehensive range of IT consultancy services. Although its attempts were curtailed in the early 1990s, other organisations continued to follow suit. For example, one pharmaceutical company recently engaged our consultants to help their suppliers progressively eradicate defects from their products and production processes. In the past, the attitude would have been to change suppliers, thereby throwing away the benefit of a long-term relationship for the sake of a slightly better product. This drug company however, recognised that ultimately it was paying for the production: by screening out defects – through investment in technical support – costs could be brought down and profitability to both parties enhanced.

THE INTERVIEWEES

Paul Noakes is Director of External Quality Programmes for Motorola. While many organisations offer their suppliers the opportunity to participate in External Quality Programmes, they tend to do so by focusing on Quality Assurance, Quality Control and occasionally (though rarely) Management Skills. In his interview, Paul outlines the sheer scale of Motorola's commitment to quality.

Jerry Janka is responsible for Motorola's external education programmes. Many of these are in the mid-ground of Motorola's fifty-year planning process. No longer hypothetical, they demonstrate vividly the scale of commitment and far-sightedness necessary for the high-performance organisation.

INTERVIEW 4.1 FOCUS ON QUALITY
Paul Noakes, Director of External Quality Programmes, Motorola

Sharing the benefits: internally

In today's climate, almost all improvement activities result in fewer jobs. Even in a boom time advancing automation means that there will never be the opportunity for full-scale, full employment. So why should employees collaborate on initiatives that will put them at risk of unemployment?

The usual response is to incentivise them. In Motorola in the 1970s performance-related pay based around teams was introduced.

> Our first work teams were called PMP, Participative Management Process, Teams. These were like Quality Circles or Quality Teams in our factories; they worked on quality, productivity, and safety issues – anything that could improve the business. We shared the gains over a twelve-month period, paying the team a twelfth each month, rather like people who sell insurance for commission.
>
> We did this for about ten years, and then we spread the idea from the factory only into the rest of the organisation. We didn't have the same ability to analyse costs and so forth outside the factory, but we did have a formula to share some gains in the non-manufacturing areas. We did that on a quarterly basis.
>
> Sometimes the goals were competitive rather than being supportive of one another, so in about 1987 or 1988 we moved to the new process that we currently use around the country. Again for a PMP team gains were shared on a twice-a-year basis and the size of the benefit was determined by return on net assets (RONA). The corporation had a target which we had to meet before there were any payouts. Beyond that, each major business-unit had a target, and if they made their RONA goal, that target created a percentage. From the formula we were able to say, 'We are going to pay out 5% of your base earnings for the last six months'. The major business units were allowed to decide whether to distribute the 5% equally to everybody, whether to pass 1% to everybody and put the other 4% in a competition, or whatever. We have been averaging between 4.5% and 5% of base payroll dollars – though some areas don't make their RONA goal and therefore get nothing. Others go way over and therefore they get much more than 5%. In some countries we can't do this: the labour laws make it almost impossible to have any form of incentive.
>
> We found that we get the same rate of improvement, with or without incentives! I think part of the reason for that is the degree of maturity that we have reached in our business process and in our team efforts. Some teams have earned as much as 30% of their base earnings – a pretty big sum of money. It is quite attractive.

Creating competition

But there are alternatives to financial incentives. Competition used carefully can be one. Following the emergence of the team competitions among organisations in S.E. Asia, Motorola instituted its own – highly structured – approach to achieving this. Paul Noakes highlights the problems as well as the successes.

By late 1989, a number of our executives in Asia noticed that local businesses were holding competitions between their Quality Circles, both within companies and even between companies. We thought it was a good idea, and worth trying – so we created a set of guidelines by which we would judge these teams, and announced to the organisation that at the beginning of 1990 we were going to hold a world-wide competition among our improvement teams, which by now had been renamed TCS teams (Total Customer Satisfaction).

We were totally amazed at the competition's success. Initially we said that we would have eighteen finalists; this was based on the population as a percentage of the total population of each of the major business units. You get three, you get two, corporate gets one, etc. We had over 2,000 teams in the first year, over 3,000 in the second year, 3,700 to 3,800 in the third year and about 4,300 last year! After the first year we increased the number of finalists to twenty-four. It was a great success.

The driving factor here is people. People enjoy this. They organise it. These teams are self-organised; they are not yet Self-Directed Work Teams. A lot of Quality Improvement teams are appointed and monitored by a steering committee, which we don't have and we don't believe in. We never know how many teams we have; we only know how many teams enter the competition. This is very important. Our teams are self-organised; they do their own thing. They may or may not elect to enter the competition. We believe that we have several hundred more teams that want to enter the competition.

What do people get out of it? Well, in order to get to the finals you have to get through three eliminating rounds. You travel from place to place for these competitions. There is a lot of sharing. Many people have never been out of their home-town or even been on an airplane. When they get to the finals they perform in front of top management, because our judges consist of the CEO, the President and the top ten or twelve executives, plus a member of the board in some cases. So they get the recognition. We have been holding our finals in January and so they all get a parka, gloves, and a little duffel bag. Nothing of real value. Recognition is the driving force.

When you get to the last twenty-four, they are all winners. We try to choose six gold and eighteen silver, but we inevitably end up with ten or eleven gold and about six silver. My own view is that this will backfire on us. I think we should make every finalist a gold. We hold the competition in the daytime when the judges have reached their decision, we all have dinner. I've sat at a table with one of the silver medallist teams: they've gone flat even though they have made it to the finals. But that is a side point.

So we have had a lot of team experience. We encourage it. We tell our people what our goals are in the areas of quality, cycle-time and so forth, and give them basic training. We believe in empowerment. We empower them to a point where we retain certain guidelines – in other words, you are not just free to go and do whatever you want to do: here are some limits. So they make things happen.

Self-Directed Work Teams

To implement SMWTs you don't have to hand over all control to the workers! There are limitations within Motorola. Most of these concern 'fundamental' values of the company such as lifetime employment.

We got into Self-Directed Work Teams (SDWTs) six or seven years ago. It started slowly and in a couple of the facilities. One facility outside Buffalo, New York, is called Elmer New York: their production operation consists totally of SDWTs. They have no supervision. They have a production manager and the teams are organised there. They will be teams of typically about fifteen or twenty people. These teams set their own objectives.

We have a corporate quality goal, a cycle-time goal and everything else that drives it, and a customer satisfaction criterion which that says that we cannot let anything happen to disturb the customer.

The teams do their own interviewing for their members. They have asked for the right to terminate, which we have not given them, because we have a company policy, whereby if you have ten or more years of service, you can't be terminated for any reason without the Chairman's approval. We also operate in a non-union environment around the world. Those things we are very careful about.

The teams also decide how to divide up their work. They are mostly trained in more than one job. If they want to trade off, that is their business. They elect their own team-leader who in a sense is a supervisor. Their team-leader reports on what they are doing and so forth. There is great satisfaction from this: people really do enjoy their work.

Role of managers

I give lots of quality presentations around the world and my message is that our role as managers today is to get out of people's way. We have got to give them the resources, the tools and to see that they are properly trained. As old-style managers we created many problems. People say: 'How do you get your people motivated?' and I reply: 'We've never had a people problem. What we really had was a management problem.' When I used to run factories, people would say: 'Give me some smart people and I'll show you what I can do. All I have is a bunch of dummies!' Back then, we always spoke about our people being the problem. But really we were the problem!

All our facilities have a number of teams at various stages. We try not to drop into SDWTs too fast because it is a learning situation, and basically management has to learn more than the people. The people pick this up very quickly; they are not really worried about it. We have to decide where to draw the line.

Motorola University has put together some courses, we share experiences and so forth. Our Government Electronics Group in Arizona are well on along on this Self-Directed route. Don King is the supervisor of a project in Phoenix, and they have now produced a video on it, called *The Side Arms Story*. In Arlington Heights, Rick Chandler is General Manager, and he is a great believer in team efforts and so forth: they are well on along the way.

The worst thing, which we had for years but are now getting away from, was a culture of control by budget and head-counting. If you had tough times, you hold head-count or you squeeze the budget, because that was the only sure way we knew of controlling the money. We are making progress there, but we still have some managers who only know those methods.

The other thing is that in some companies now, if you are given a job to do and you don't do it, out you go. But for us, the challenge is to get you to be able to do it, or to get you to be a square peg in a square hole. So we spend a tremendous amount of effort on career planning and employee development, so that we can get the maximum out of our people, and, at the same time, not have people with problems.

I don't think we sell the lack of control, or apparent lack of control, to other people in other organisations. I spent the last 4 years solely dedicated to communicating the quality message and Motorola's message outside Motorola. I am a hell of a salesman, but I'm not very successful. They will listen but they won't accept it. One of the problems is that this quality improvement process is not easy – it takes a lot of effort because you go through a transition – a mindset change – starting from the top. I don't think we ever had a people problem, just a management problem. What I run into with many, many CEOs is that they are always looking for the silver bullet. The latest buzz word, 'Re-engineering the corporation' is a best-seller. We teach process re-engineering as part of our basic quality course to our entry-level people when they come into Motorola. They are not experts, but at least they understand what it's about. What we try to do, is to implement the quality process in each of the business processes. It's done without an overlay team, or it's done without a big task force, and so forth, or any overview. Our role in the quality organisation is to champion them, see that they are going in the right direction.

EXTERNAL QUALITY PROGRAMS

My title is Director of External Quality Programs. It means absolutely nothing! I am a Vice-President, but these external programs are both communicating the quality message, and working with other companies trying to help them. We got so much good and so much help from other companies when we started our quality processes, many of whom we have passed over, but we have had people come in from IBM and Xerox. Hewlett Packard and other executives come and spend a day with us. There has been a willingness on the part of Motorola to fund myself and others. When we won the Baldrige Award we were supposed to share it, but that could basically be done by just a few speeches in one year. Our approach has been to share and share and share. We work with our competitors as well. I have, in some cases, worked with the parent company. I have been in General Electric with the jet engine division and now with medical systems, and I had a phone call yesterday asking me to come back again. This morning I have had a phone call from Scotland, from a company wanting to know if I would come over there again.

It's very easy to read about Six Sigma and think that it's a technique, and that as long as you have learnt the technique, that's OK, it's going to happen. Getting this message across to people, particularly senior executives is an important part of sharing experiences.

My message to them is that Six Sigma is really a statistical term which we use to define a defect rate which is essentially perfection, because people won't respond well to zero-defect objectives. At one time I was reasonably grounded in statistics, and I tell people that this quality improvement process is more psychological than statistical. What we are fundamentally doing is changing basic beliefs or mind-sets. The Six Sigma objective happened to be our second set of quality rules. The first set was to increase ten-fold in five years, (we reached it in two), a hundred-fold in four years and Six Sigma by the end of our fifth year. We have not made that, but we have many processes that are at Six Sigma, and we are coming along.

Quality, to us, is more than just a defect rate: it means satisfying and delighting the customer. In everything we do we have to get to the point where we can give the customer nothing to challenge us on. We are long way from that – but we are making progress.

We are great believers in stretch goals, because stretch goals are not intended just to make it difficult for the organisation. We want to make it to the point where there is absolutely no way of achieving this goal unless you fundamentally change the way that you run the business.

That is the advantage of the Six Sigma objective. Six Sigma is, to me, like sailing: it is like a point on the horizon; when you reach that point, it's gone, it's somewhere off in the future, but you can keep your eye on it. So it is the focal point; it is a rallying point. And it's easy to communicate. People come in and say, 'What kind of a weekend did you have?' 'I had a Two Sigma weekend.' There's no statistical meaning there – it was just a lousy weekend. We can talk about customer satisfaction, and we don't attempt to measure the sigma levels. But we do measure and convert to defect rates or error rates, ppm – parts per million – and put it on a chart for comparison purposes. I would rather not see you focusing on what your sigma level is, but just concentrating on improvements. Our goal is to reduce our defect rate, expressed as defects per unit of work, by ten times every two years, or roughly 68% per year.

When we started that process, some people said, 'Why work so hard? We are already the best.' The message was: 'We are so far off where we ought to be that we want everyone to improve ten times every two years regardless.' We haven't made it every year, but we have made it in a number of years. We are behind our goal but we are moving, we are getting there. Over the last five or six years we have been saving money through this process of defect elimination in our factories. Last year, it allowed us to reduce our manufacturing costs by $1.6 billion versus our 1986 revenue. The cumulative total is $4.6 million in seven years,. In seven years, our sales have risen by 183% and are worth 2.83 times what they were back in 1986. Our employee-counts are only up 25%. Our sales per employee are up to about 127%. We are running at a compounded rate of improvement of 12.4% per year, while the US average is less than 2%, so we are running at more than six times the US average. Part of that is a change in technology, but we create the technology from the savings that we make in cost reduction.

TCS: Total Customer Satisfaction

Just to go back to something I said earlier: I was surprised at how the TCS teams had taken off in terms of their enthusiasm, the way in which the competition works, first of all in Asia and then elsewhere. That is surprising, because all the books say that you should not create competition between teams, because it is more demotivating for the ones that don't win. I've hinted at that at the top level of the competition, the ones who make it through the competition and get silver medals not gold.

I am sure some demotivation occurs down in the ranks when teams don't win. We are a fairly competitive society. We are a very competitive country. It's part of the US culture, whether it be in baseball, football, or whatever. This is all voluntary. We don't tell people to compete, and that is why we have some people who elect to compete and a lot who don't. We also have a lot of self-confidence in our people. We can do anything. That does not get plastered on the wall, but there is no question that there is a high level of confidence.

Rick Chandler's group hasn't been as active in TCS because Rick's boss, their sector director, didn't believe in it. He is very successful, and the corporation has tolerated him; if he had not been as successful he would not be the way he is. They didn't participate in the first year of TCS. They sent just one team, maybe, the second year, and the third year they had just a few. They finally got to the point, though, where George Fisher, our former chairman who is now with Kodak, intervened.

What has happened is that some organisations have four or five hundred teams. They see these, they learn from one another, they make video tapes, they see those, and so when you run into a situation where you don't have the history it is a learning curve. We pass out a lot of video tapes.

We get some fantastic efforts: at one presentation in the Philippines, a group of young ladies fresh out of high school had learned everything that they had to do in English – they'd memorised it. They couldn't speak a word otherwise, and I couldn't speak Spanish – but what an effort they had made. They went through their story – what they did was just amazing. That's the advantage of this thing – it's not just for the people who are involved, it's for the managers too: they will tell you that those who have sat through these presentations – the experience was mostly for them. They learnt the most.

We have around 4,300 teams competing, with an average of ten people in each, so we have over 40,000 people involved. But at any one time we think we have 5,000 teams – roughly half our population. We have somewhere between 118,000 to 120,000 people lined up.

Change from the top down

There is little doubt that SMWTs are a strategic rearrangement of the business. Instituting them calls for demonstrable involvement by senior managers and for this they need to appreciate the extent of the problem that is being dealt with.

One of the big things is the way that the person at the top is involved. The Galvins have been the driving force. A new CEO would have a hard time changing it. One of the other things is that we do very little recruiting from outside – we hire engineers each year, and a few specialists. Once in a while we bring in somebody to middle management – I joined the company in middle management – twenty-six years ago, running a factory. They hired in three or four people at that time because they were trailing behind in manufacturing. But by and large, we hire people fresh out of university, we grow them, and so they have a lifetime of culture within the company.

So the question is, can teams work without this identity? I tell people that they can, but they don't work as well, they don't progress as rapidly. I'm a firm believer that if you want a successful quality process you must have senior management involvement. It is easy to be committed – in the US we talk about 'apple pie', 'American flag' and 'motherhood': we can all be committed to that. But the issue of being involved is something else. That takes time. You have to get to the point where your opening comment is not, 'How much did we ship today?' or 'What are our financial numbers?' – which we are usually driven by. Instead it needs to be, 'How is our quality?'. Quality is the first thing on the agenda of every business review meeting, it has been for a number of years – that was something that Galvin said: 'From this point forward...' He was referring to his review meetings at the operations level, but they found a way of filtering down.

I think that you have to have senior management involvement; you must also tell the organisation WHY you are implementing this. Is it survival? Is it share of market? Is it cost issues? Is it because it is the latest fad? Is it because you want to improve the quality of work-life? It is probably a bit of all of them. But you have to tell people, and you have to tell them what we expect out of this. So many companies start a TQM effort, they hire a young woman or a young man and they are the TQM-make-it-happen person. They don't have a chance in hell! One of the things we did – which was wrong now, with hindsight – when we started our training effort in 1981, we had all these people down here at the bottom of the organisation – problem-solving techniques, SPC, fishbone/Ishikawa diagrams and so on. And what was happening was that we were focusing on changing the behaviour at the bottom of the organisation. We were working at the wrong end of the organisation. I can list in my mind three or four things that a CEO must do first, before starting a training programme. So many people in the US call themselves consultants, but all they're selling is training. They want to move down the ladder as soon as possible – suddenly they've involved everyone in teams, which we are all for. But if your only focus is getting people in teams, then you get into counting how many teams you have! That's why they need a quality administrator – to count the teams and 'approve' their projects. We say you work on anything you want to, as long as it supports one of our five key business initiatives.

There is no question that Art Sundry was the trigger for Motorola; I was at that meeting. We didn't believe that we had a quality problem. We had a reputation for superior reliability, but we were having a lot of early life- failures and so we'd send out someone from the service organisation and they'd fix the problem – but we'd already alienated the customer. We could see Japan coming over the horizon, even targeting specific industries that we were in. Then, in 1974, we sold our consumer electronics business to Matsushita. They took our people, our factories, our processes, our designs – and they performed miracles. For years, we said it was automation, or they did this or that, or they made major investments. But basically they managed better than we did! There was a great sense of embarrassment among senior executives who had been involved in that part of the business, doubtless not excluding Bob. That is not often talked about, but I think it was another factor which said: 'We've got to watch Japan because of this', and 'We have quality problems'. From day one, Bob was a champion.

Understanding self-direction

I think it is probably true that for many managers understanding self-direction is a matter of a life crisis. I mentioned Don King in our government electronics group: he came up here to go to a two-week school which we have called 'Motorola Manufacturing Institute', now called 'Motorola Management Institute' (MMI). He went home, very excited about what he'd heard; it's a very intensive course. They'd just had a project where a contractor built some stuff for the side-arm project. It was twenty-year-old technology, it was a reorder, we were about the only source, the government said, 'We want you to do it'. They tight-scheduled, no chats to anybody, and he said to his people; 'We've got this kind of problem...'

Even in the Self-Directed Work Teams there was a wake-up call. I don't know what the wake-up call was at Elmer in New York – I do know that they were in a business that we kept selling off! They were in a little town that was nearby and we sold that business; some people kept part of it and moved to a new location. I think it was a sort of 'what's our future?' wake-up call. So there's probably one individual, a manager, who was open to this and said, 'Let's try this!'

Barriers to Self-Directed Work Teams

I spent time in Australia and Canada and also covered Central South America for a few years, but the legislative barriers that we have here – I'm not aware of any other countries that have a similar situation to ours. Ours had primarily to do with incentive-type pay-outs, but other legislation or precedents have an effect – for example, I haven't done any recruiting for a while, but today I would have a hard time staying within the rules. We have them because we are overwhelmed with regulations of what you can and cannot ask and so forth. Interesting thing: we are very concerned with safety, very involved in it – but it isn't evident. Each facility has a safety committee of some kind and so on. I used to manage facilities and got a monthly accident report – other than cuts, burns and eye injuries we were pretty safe. All of our manufacturing facilities have gone to mandatory safety glasses. Our accident rate is about half the industry average. We do track this, we have OHSA (Occupational Health and Safety Act), and we track statistics of both frequency and severity, and we analyse them – there's a lot of work, but it's very quietly done. My first reaction is that if it were visible, this might drop to a quarter. There are so many things that we are doing well, but there are many where we haven't even scratched the surface.

What we have learned is that we can drive anything, we can make anything happen if we communicate it, give our people special training if necessary, if we create ground-rules and give them regular visibility. That is why we have moved so far on quality and cycle time. We are now talking of a tenfold increase in five years on cycle-time.

Suggestions

There's a serious point too on suggestions. We used to have a suggestions scheme where we paid out. We don't do that now. We studied so many to death that there was no motivation. Today, when people say, 'How many suggestions do you get from the organisation?', nobody knows. Each business unit knows, but we are fairly autonomous so we don't add them up. It is not a corporate programme, it is a business-unit programme. We have a name which has been used in a number of locations called, 'I recommend'. We have some facilities which get one per employee per year and some which get forty per employee per year. What's the difference? It's the manager. It's down to where they put it on their priority lists and in their conversation. We talk about it, we recognise it, we reward by praise and that's sufficient. The more I see this, the more I believe it; the more we're doing something, the more we're talking about it.

Taking the message outside Motorola

Notwithstanding its commitment to promulgate the quality message having won the Baldrige Award, Motorola had many initiatives underway to both spread the message and prepare its workforce and marketplace of the future.

We are currently engaged in a lot of different initiatives, both to improve our national and local education system, and also in relationships with organisations around the world – you've heard of the ones in Mexico, for example. If we had made a better job of education in this country we wouldn't be spending so much inside Motorola on training. We spend money to give people specific subject-matter training, and we spend money to raise people's capabilities so that they can grow, because we think that is one of our requirements to enable every person to have success in their life. We spend a lot of money just doing remedial training; remedial training can first get people just to fifth grade capability, then to seventh, then to ninth, and so on.

In Mexico, where we now have one facility, it is going to be a booming market when we go forward. If we can influence them early, I think there's justification. The organisation believes that there is a benefit to our customers and suppliers, and beyond that to major government bodies and universities. If we were a less substantial organisation in a market that wasn't booming, we couldn't afford to do this. We're fortunate. There's another thing in my mind – we could take a lot of these things we're doing, and start them, improving our profits in a two- or four-year period, but Galvin and other people in the organisation have got people thinking: 'What do we do fifty years from now?' You may have heard of our fifty- year plan – we don't know the numbers and the technologies, but we typically grow our business by 15% each year. It doubles every five years – we have a history of doing that. It so happens we have done much more than that in the last three years but let's say we are a $17bn company now. Five years from now it would be $34bn, five years later it's $60bn, then $120bn, and so forth. By the year 2020 we're a $500bn corporation. Will this happen? Nobody knows, except that we've been pretty good at doing it in the past. Somewhere out there we're going to be adding a $100bn sales in one year! Wow!

One of the things we found when we started analysing the issues was not the technology – we can understand that and create it as well – it's how we recruit and develop our people to a point where we have an available supply of managers to grow our business by $50bn in five years. We have to find a way of having people become division managers at twenty-eight rather than forty-two. That means that we have to have ways of accelerating the learning process and recruit younger. That led them to say: 'We've got to get to Motorola employees and their families – see them first because that's our first source'. So this past year we have run six-day sessions, the equivalent of a space camp, as a technology camp for 12-14 year-old children of Motorola employees. The object is to interest them in science and engineering, and to interest them in Motorola. The idea is that they would go through this several times, they would work here during high school as soon as they were of an age where they could work. They would work during college, and by the time they leave college they'll be totally committed to Motorola. We have a certain percentage of them taking engineering and science, and they gain a basic understanding of the business by working three or four summers for us. We already do a lot on career planning, and so the objective is to take those high-potential people – the ones we identify – and start special plans for them with the object of having them skilled and polished enough for them to become a division manager at twenty-eight. To me that is a by-product of this fifty-year thought process. Yet there is nothing magic about it – it just says it's a continuing process of challenging everything we do. Of course we have communicated to the organisation that it is our intention to become the world's premier company.

We are in the electronics environment where prices decline every year. This is part of the business. If we were in a flat, no-growth business, we'd have problems. If we had the same culture of process improvement, we'd end up cutting process and growing volume. Assuming there's a market there! But if there's no market – you'd better get out of the business. We have created the paging business, the two-way radio business, the car radio business – though we're no longer in that any more – we were very heavy in the early TV market, we created the cellular market, the next business will be satellite communications systems, we were very early in the semiconductor business, we were the first merchant supplier selling outside IBM who were producing themselves. In fact, Bob Galvin gave a talk once called; 'Eight times in a lifetime'.

We are spending a good chunk of money in schools – we are working in the grade school system, K through 12 (it's really K through 16).

The US education system is based on on grades rather than years. In theory a child that fails to pass examinations at the end of the school year will not move up to the next grade. The starting point is Kindergarten (K). Students that leave school at 16 will have probably reached grade 12. University courses are four years long, so a degree graduate will leave university at grade 16 (often at 21 years old).

We have the quality challenge in universities. We host the annual TQM symposium. And we talk to undergraduate and graduate students. I'll do that any time. If there were a negative reaction to what we are doing, we'd find a way around it – we'd invite them in to be a part of it. What creates jobs? It's industry. We've got to be involved. A few university professors have said to me that this is their domain. The problem is that their domain doesn't cover enough, and the product of their domain is not good in the job! I had a group of vice-chancellors from the State of Illinois here the other day. It comes right down to them having customers – the customers are more than just students – the market-place that takes their graduates is the customer – if they can't sell their graduates in the market-place then at some point they'll have a problem. If they can't sell their education system because their tuition fees are so high that no one can afford them, then they've got problems and they're aware of this. All I'm trying to do is push them over the edge – get them excited about something.

INTERVIEW 4.2 COMMITMENT AND FAR-SIGHTEDNESS
Jerry Janka, Corporate Alliances, Motorola

There are many reasons why Jerry Janka's area is of interest. Two that are worth considering here are:

- How it is possible to introduce systematic quality improvement to such a nebulous subject as personal relationships.
- How quality improvement can become an alternative control mechanism to managerial intervention.

I have been with Motorola University for about twelve years and with Motorola for fourteen. Most of my working life with Motorola has been with the University and it has been a special experience that it's hard to imagine working elsewhere. Within Motorola University I've held a number of positions. Five years were spent working to obtain Federal training grants for Motorola University and for the corporation. That was where I began to get my external focus, because virtually everything I did was externally based. One way or another, I was interfacing with other companies or other organisations, government agencies, 'non-profit-making' organisations and so on. This led to the establishment of our corporate alliances programme a year and a half ago. It is called 'Corporate Alliances', though our scope for the most part has been Motorola University's alliances and interfaces.

We felt that we needed to organise this vast realm of relationships which Motorola University had with external organisations. We realised that we had to manage them properly, because over the years some had worked very well while some had worked very badly. Probably most importantly, we realised that we didn't have any strategy as to why we were working with one partner as opposed to another; why we were doing it, how we evaluated whether it was good or bad, how we determined when to start it, to end it or to expand it. We explored a variety of possible questions that could come into the management of those sort of relationships. So that was really the reason why we decided to formalise the management of this function.

Defining the purpose of relationships

Very importantly, we now have criteria for the selection of organisations for alliance development. This helps our people analyse why are they even doing it. Many got involved because it felt good. Rarely does anyone stop to think: 'Why am I doing this? What should the outcome be?' We know we want to, but it's a kind of fuzzy, feel-good factor. Using specific criteria on how to make these selections and criteria for successful outcomes (in other words, a process and some ground-rules) we can measure whether or not we have met our expectations.

It may look on the surface as though what we have done is to take a whole load of really good relationships and tried to lay organisation on top of them, potentially destroying them. Not all relationships have to be alliances – they do not necessarily have to be formalised. People can say; 'We are comfortable keeping this on an informal basis and we'll let it develop as is'. That's OK – the organisation accepts that. If they want to get funding, though, the organisation will only formally provide it if the criteria of an alliance have been met. That's often pretty critical because a lot of relationships start to require funding.

We have a bold and complicated mission statement in which we try to capture why we form an alliance. In summary, it is to make sure that there is some positive outcome, on our part and on the part of the alliance partner, which has some overall direction: they need us and we need them.

Motorola University 'Corporate Alliances' mission statement

> **An integrative relationship constructed with other business enterprises, academic institutions, and government entities which directly impacts critical business issues of mutual importance, leverages the competencies and resources of all organisations to maximise competitive advantage, gains synergy in critical technologies, and strives toward equal investment and return on investment to maximise participation in the alliance.**

What is important about that mission statement is that it really needs to be two-way. We know that a good alliance is a two-way relationship, so we want to be sure that we have that kind of focus.

Our mission is results-driven – that is critical, because a number of these relationships were such that people would question why they were being made. People were sitting on exam boards, for example, donating time and effort and so forth, and yet couldn't vocalise the specific reason why they were doing it. A lot of companies wouldn't have been prepared to make that investment, because they wouldn't have recognised anything coming back. This all shows that there is a return which justifies doing more.

In the early days we were involved in relationship-building. We didn't have to make decisions on why we were doing this and what the return was.

Management of corporate alliances

At Motorola University we see ourselves as the agents of change for Motorola and I think that is important. Providing good training enables us to do that. So we have a very powerful role in the corporation. We have a strong feeling of pride about what we do and the fact that it is an instrumental part of determining what Motorola will be.

Relationships have a role in that. We have a complex process for alliances, consisting of four different stages:

- process initiation;
- project planning;
- alliance deployment;
- alliance measurement.

This is rather structured and is being adjusted as we work with other organisations, but it tries to establish a framework around how to develop an alliance.

To a great extent we act as process consultants to the rest of the organisation, at least with regard to alliance relationships – though it can get a lot broader than that.

Corporate Alliances: services / products provided

1 Briefing services regarding the role and function of Corporate Alliances in relation to Motorola University's critical business issues and business plans.
2 Guidance on the planning, development and management of Corporate Alliances (i.e. the Guidance System).
3 Facilitation and organisational planning and development services to get alliances started (i.e. the Launch Process).
4 Process consultation during the alliance construction and implementation process.
5 Development and management of metrics for Corporate Alliances.
6 Problem solving and trouble shooting for the disconnects between alliances.
7 Management of white space between alliances and other external ventures.
8 Marketing Corporate Alliances to internal and external audiences.
9 Providing ongoing training and briefing presentations to internal and external audiences.
10 Marketing and sales of Motorola University's externally focused products and services, especially as they relate to potential alliance relationships.

Establishing alliances from the outset

Motorola is about to open another, huge facility in the State of Illinois which will almost double the size of our Illinois operation overnight. We are now working with an external technical-training organisation to prepare the technicians who will be needed at that facility. So Corporate Alliances are setting up the whole relationship between the organisation which is establishing the facility and the external training organisation.

Before we get involved in an alliance we first define the rationale for selecting the alliance partners – a questioning process whereby we ask the Motorola person to examine the 'why'. Why are they doing it; what are they hoping to achieve? It is a very useful stage – but usually happens after they have identified a likely provider.

The next stage is a development and planning strategy – we ask them to go through a whole series of items, like the goals of the alliance. A project plan and a knowledge transfer, or communications, plan are developed. This helps them think through why they are doing it, and what it is that they want to achieve, the time-frames and so forth. The reaction might be that there is too much structure here, but we have relationships that are ragged.

Academic alliances form a large part of Motorola University's relationships. We have them with more than forty academic institutions around the world. Two years ago, we held a conference which brought all of these institutions together, and we are doing it again in July 1995. Many of these relationships have been going on for years and years.

Someone has usually found a potential alliance partner beforehand, so the criteria for selection of organisations are usually applied after the fact. They are a kind of analysis to help the person take a fresh look at the whole relationship. Identifying the business needs as strategic goals for the relationship highlights a great deal of that analysis process. The reasons and outcomes from a relationship are plenty; for example, we might want these relationships to provide access to world-class technology.

We need a way of measuring whether a particular alliance satisfies our requirements. Six Sigma was the driver for this, but the mere process of exploring the way in which something is going to be quantified is very useful.

Major alliances

Clearly Corporate Alliances have an important role to play in ensuring that Motorola's employees get the best out of any external relationship. In this section we see the extent of existing relationships. In a large organisation with a strong technical bias many of these relationships will be academic. However, Motorola is using them not only for this purpose, but as a means of market creation, supplier quality assurance and R & D.

SSRI

Some of our larger and more successful alliances illustrate the diversity of issues covered. The Six Sigma Research Institute (SSRI) for example, was initiated in 1991 as an alliance of six organisations, Digital, Texas, IBM, ABB Brown Boveri, Kodak and Motorola. We sought to develop common resources (which calls for a common framework too) to help each other along the road to Six Sigma.

The Consortium for Supplier Training

Another training-related alliance was the Consortium for Supplier Training. Some members are common to the SSRI, including DEC, Kodak, and Texas, but it also includes Chrysler, Texaco, Xerox and SEMATECH. We would like to provide them with the support that they need to develop their own staff and facilities to help us in our evolving improvement initiatives. But their geographic distribution means that this would be prohibitively expensive and logistically difficult. The alliance developed a network of community college-based Supplier Training Centres, co-sponsored by someone from the college and the local consortium member.

You'll see, from our United States initiatives in the area of education, that we take very seriously our responsibilities as one of the major employer institutions. We have a strong social conscience, and as we begin to think more and more globally, it's inevitable that we feel that we should expand those goals. Our Mexican and Hawaiian alliances are excellent examples of a responsible company contributing to the community – and alliances are a very good mechanism to achieve this.

Hawaii links

We were very interested in the measurement of service quality. We all know how important it is, but it is also very poorly researched, especially in the multicultural environments towards which we are moving. The opportunity to do so came through an alliance in Hawaii. Hawaii depends on servicing visitors as a major industry, and the state government saw the opportunity to transform the local economy by improving the way in which this is done.

At first, we ran a CEO event helping them to focus on service quality as a competitive tool. Then we developed a pool of Hawaii-based certified instructors for Motorola University's quality courseware, and licensed them to use it.

Alliance in Mexico

Perhaps, though, the most significant alliance attempted yet, in terms of the ambition of the alliance members, is in Mexico. Mexico is clearly one of the closest export markets for Motorola products – but the Mexican economy cannot support them at the moment. As our products become more sophisticated there is a danger that they will move even further out of reach of the Mexicans. For the economy to improve, so must education; and when the economy develops we shall need technicians capable of building, installing, maintaining and distributing our products. All of these things are interconnected yet, when you examine the quality of education – especially technical education – it is very poor by our standards.

So we responded to an initiative with the Instituto Tecnologico y de Estudios Superiores de Monterey (ITESM) and the Centro de Productividad de Monterey. ITESM is the main technology university in Mexico with twenty-five sites throughout the country. The quality of its courses and lecturers, in terms of content and delivery, are thus crucial to the future of the Mexican economy. Together with Motorola Mexico, we set out to provide a comprehensive and co-ordinated set of education and training services in Mexico through a joint investment of resources.

The four main goals of the alliance are:

- To identify markets and customers for Motorola University's products and services – actually supplying our training to the Mexican domestic market.

- To develop, and then to deliver, models of the content for courses, together with customised materials and the associated learning-support systems too.

- To design and implement administrative systems that encompass everything from career planning, translation and marketing of courses, course delivery and alternative methods of delivering courses.

- Through applications consulting, technology transfer and executive development, to implement strategies for organisational change, especially towards the learning culture.

In the first thirteen months we have helped nearly one dozen lecturers to develop their teaching methods, as well as their knowledge of the latest technology.

Activity 4.1: Inventory of alliances

Whatever the size of your organisation it, or more accurately its employees, will have contacts with many other organisations. Many of these will be based on very good long-term relationships. The reasons that people have developed these are going to be manifold. Some will be based on ego – after all, it is flattering to be asked to do favours for people; others will have begun because the individual saw an opportunity to develop themself. Some will have been inherited, while a few will be a little more than hypothetical.

This is NOT an exercise in control: you need to make sure that this is clear to everyone. Many of these relationships will have been justified as either marketing-related or aimed at product-improvement.

The organisation is paying for all these alliances – some will be producing benefits, others will need more investment, either in funds or in help to the individuals involved – giving them more resources or helping them to withdraw with dignity.

Start an inventory of your organisation's existing relationships – use regular reporting structures properly briefed to tabulate them, together with estimates of effort expended and any benefits that have been gained.

Activity 4.2: Alliances for employee development

Take a detailed look at your existing training and development activities. How many of the activities are the same as those of your neighbour, regardless of the business that they are in? Look at the training of managers, of technicians, and of front-line employees. Look at 'machine' specific training and at the transferable skills – problem-solving, equal employment opportunities, statistical process control, and so on – skills that can be used in any job. You will be surprised at how few of these call for company-specific content. Despite this, in the past most companies have run internal courses: courses involving very specialised machine knowledge might have been provided by the manufacturers or their agents; the more generic courses could be run by training companies; meanwhile, less demanding site or machine specifics, such as safety training, would often be run by local managers.

The down-side of this approach has been cost, logistics and quality. Every course requires development time, and has other quantity related costs – the more courses that are run, the lower these are. Any training manager will explain the logistical nightmare of running regular courses with sufficient delegates. Too often the result is that courses run only sporadically. This in turn means unskilled, or less-than-adequately-skilled, individuals. To compensate, companies resort to a combination of 'sitting with Nellie' and using their own managers as trainers. But adult learning is a very complex process calling for very significant skills – very different from those of the school teachers, who are the only role-model that these 'practising' trainers have.

Now is the time to address this problem. Pick two or three courses and approach one or two non-competitive neighbours. Put together a case for co-running the courses – avoid financial complications and an imbalance of contribution by each company providing one course.

Agree an assessment process after each course is run, and provide delegates with a statement of attendance and content. As your alliance develops, consider external accreditation for the courses either singly or in groups.

As co-training takes off, you will be amazed at the other opportunities that it opens up.

PROBLEM: All of this is fine, but we are a small firm with only five people . . .

ANSWERS:

Many small firms are scaled down versions of the big one that the founders used to work for. Without wanting them, that can often mean pretension, false expectations and unnecessary boundaries. The modern organisation needs to be more flexible, dynamic, entrepreneurial and a host of other things. In the past these were the qualities of the smaller business – so you should be at an advantage. Is that edge being eroded by the new look big firms?

Why not make a start by taking stock and looking at whether the way you do things is shaped by reason or is an artifact?

1 How do you make decisions?

Are they made as a team or as a dictatorship? Does the 'company' work on projects together, in triads, or as individuals? Do you have/need job titles?

2 What opportunities exist for partnerships, either with suppliers or customers?

Could you share office space? Are you sometimes short of meeting rooms or a pair of hands? Could you share in purchasing deals? What about telephone answering and reception duties?

3 What influence can you have on local education for the workforce?

Could you sponsor a student place/prize at a local college? Can you offer work experience? Are you on the governing body of a school? Could you run a two day summer work camp? If you are in a business park, what about pooled training in common skills, like WP or health and safety? Could you get together with your temp agency and their key customers to define a local certificate of good team skills for temps?

4 Who have you harangued today?

Which politician, union leader, or local government officer do you have as a non-executive on your board of directors or management team? What PR opportunities can you create for yourselves and your local MP? What do you do socially to get to know people of influence? Which radio station do you routinely appear on?

5 What are you doing to set your own standards above the rest?

What does 'high performance' mean in your business? How do you measure it? How do you compare with competitors? What added value do you offer that others don't? Reexamine your u.s.p. – is it still unique?

5

A GENETIC DISORDER? – THE EMPLOYER'S PERSPECTIVE

'There is no single starting point, nor is there any real consistency in the process – and even the business reasons are different – but by and large it tends to be: "My God, we have got to be going down this route."'

(Malcolm Fraser, Motorola Executive Education Design Center)

- **Implementing Self-Direction is a threatening prospect. You have grown up in the traditional system – you have been rewarded for conforming to it by promotion, and your results have been achieved through the traditional system.**

- **The transition to SMWTs is a radical one. Most organisations achieve it from the 'top'.**

- **In most cases the leader goes through a rapid growth in self-awareness or, at least, a process of self-exploration, which provokes a transformation in their attitudes to their work and to other people.**

- **Achieving Self-Direction is about enabling people to grow – people who have not done so in the past. Managers who have made it happen have been committed to their own growth too.**

- **The success of Self-Direction is demonstrating that there are many values which have been accepted traditionally and which are no longer so obviously 'right'.**

INTRODUCTION

With the possible exception of one or two cases, Self-Managing Work-Teams (SMWTs) have originated from the 'top' of the traditional organisation and are implemented 'downwards'. In most cases, the senior managers have become supportive of the new structure. This may not be true all the time: there will certainly be reservations, especially in the early days, before the success of the teams becomes self-evident.

In this chapter we hope to reveal the concerns facing senior managers, to consider at the issues that they confronted and may still confront. Many of these will be personal (including self-doubt and perceived criticism from others – hence the chapter title), but there are also other concerns often associated with the apparent loss of control and a lack of predictability.

Throughout the implementation of the SMWTs there are conflicts of roles as a task previously assigned to someone more 'senior' is taken over by a team comprising people who were more junior. How long does this conflict go on for and how did the Senior Managers deal with it?

Management through SMWTs calls for a development of upward communication: how has this been managed and how effective has it been?

What drives an employer to change the traditional organisational structure to one of SMWTs? It seems that almost every such leader goes through a transformation themselves. Implementing self-direction is a threatening prospect. You have grown up in the traditional system; you have been rewarded for conforming to it by promotion; and your results have been achieved through the traditional system. Little else has changed. There may be ever-increasing pressures on your organisation to perform, but they are not usually step-changes: growth of 20% year-on-year is a gradually evolving target, as are progressive tenfold increases in quality targets. These pressures have not been thrown at you suddenly as you step into the 'hot seat'. So why change?

It seems that the decision to move towards self-direction is either associated with one leader or is a natural evolution from the improvement initiatives of previous years, implemented with the sanction of one leader. Do not equate the leadership role exclusively with the person at the top of the traditional hierarchy. There are examples of such changes being effected by individuals with no positional power, but who nevertheless have a degree of commitment and influence to achieve their goals (a good example of this is shown in Chapter 8, when we hear from Bob Baugh of the AFL-CIO – the body that collectively represents trades unions in the US).

So what is the nature of the transformation that leaders experience? The word makes the process sound extraordinary, yet in most cases such transformations are prompted by fairly rapid growth in self-awareness, or at least self-exploration.

Self-awareness

As you meet and discuss self-direction with senior managers, it becomes progressively easier to distinguish between those who have a well-developed level of self-awareness and those who do not. If they are to address the external criticism, the fear of failure, the lack of clarity, and the loss of the comforting existing structure, the 'employer' has to possess the inner strength to cope. It is not entirely surprising that two cultures above all others seem to demonstrate initiative in the forefront of management practice: in Japan, where considerable emphasis is placed on inner strength, and in the US, where for some decades it has been acceptable to undergo prolonged periods of self-examination.

Understanding our likely reactions to different situations and to different people, and then learning what is triggering our emotional responses in these circumstances, helps us to see what is preventing us from achieving our goals. Achieving self-direction is about enabling people who, for many reasons, have not grown in the past to do so now. Those managers that have 'made it happen' have all been committed to their own growth – physical, emotional, intellectual and spiritual. Later in this chapter we hear how the Japanese *sensai,* or consultants, will not allow their clients to proceed without first making sure that the senior managers are sufficiently strong to carry the process forward.

There are three important aspects of this self-awareness that will be explored:

- emotional responses;
- clarification of values;
- prejudices.

Throughout this book you will read interviews about the importance of interpersonal skills in creating the new high-performance workplace. Interviewees talk of management developing these skills, and of employees. It is no coincidence that at least one of the interviewees, a junior manager, was a volunteer involved in providing therapy for substance abusers.

Emotional responses

If the manager isn't aware of the triggers that cause their own embarrassment, fear or anger, then when an employee does or says something that provokes them, they can't stop themself from reacting – indeed, they may not even recognise their own behaviour as a reaction. For example, if loud voices or displays of temper frighten me, and I've never tried to understand why, then confronted by them I will probably try either to placate or deflect the anger. In this way, I simply encourage the other person to bottle it up until another occasion. In the context of self-directed workgroups, if I (through my own lack of self-awareness) assume that the anger is directed at me, then my reaction is likely to be both emotional ('You have no right to speak to me like that!') and angry ('It's not my job to be insulted like that!'). The result is a row. Whether I've deflected or rowed, the result is counterproductive to the longer-term relationship between myself as a manager and the individual.

Often in work settings this type of response-cycle has become part of the culture. If we are prepared to own our own emotions, and recognise that our reactions are only automatic because we haven't looked deeply enough, then we can begin to choose better options and not be drawn in. Furthermore, we can begin to help others express their own feelings more constructively.

Clarifying values

From an early age we are under pressure to accept and adopt other people's values. All of us are capable of recognising when something is being foisted on us – but we often don't know how to respond and are racked with guilt as a consequence! To others we display a contradiction – paying lip-service to values that our behaviour doesn't match.

Some of the most obvious examples come from well-established areas such as racial and sexual discrimination. What do you say when one of your peers (or worse a boss) says something that is sexist or, racist, or insults some other member of society? Most people would be embarrassed but wouldn't say anything. Even if we feel embarrassed, without understanding the source of our feelings, we can't change our behaviour.

To clear up, in our own minds, our own rules of conduct, rather than just accepting the ones that we have taken on board from childhood or work, gives us a far greater freedom to make decisions.

For the employers who have considered implementing self-direction, an important step is to look at the values which they have taken on board and to decide for themselves whether these are both valid and acceptable. For example, I have a university degree (two, in fact). In recent years, within big business, it has been exceptional for a manager not to have a degree. To me and to many of my generation, it is almost inconceivable that someone could be a manager without having a degree. Yet I see many managers today who are clearly more competent than me, and who don't have degrees. Does a degree provide any significant contribution to becoming a good manager? Does any qualification provide evidence of someone's managerial ability?

Self-direction demonstrates that there are many values which have been accepted traditionally and which are no longer so obviously 'right'. The value of qualifications is one example; the importance of length of experience is another. The role of the unions, the divisory nature of individual rewards, the need for central co-ordination and control, are all values which must be scrutinised carefully if we are going to make the transition effectively.

Prejudices

Although prejudices are closely tied up with values, it is useful to consider them separately. It is possible to be prejudiced both towards or against someone. Although we may have strong values about something, through our own self-awareness we can prevent this from prejudicing a situation. Many caring roles call for this – for example, most of us are appalled by child abuse, yet counsellors working with abusers have to prevent their own revulsion from prejudicing them against the individual. To expand on the example from the previous section: as a graduate dealing with many non-graduates, I have to be sure that I do not favour other graduates over their equally able peers. Similarly I have to be aware if I discriminate in favour of the non-graduate who has struggled to achieve in other ways, because of a positive prejudice for the underdog.

All three aspects can be serious barriers to an individual's personal progress and can't be tackled lightly. Without some awareness of them on the part of the employer, we can't be sure of their motives for wanting to implement SMWTs.

A great deal can be done to help individuals to examine these aspects of themselves, and it need not take a prolonged period of time. There is a danger that some companies fall into an analysis-paralysis trap. This is usually a sign that the analysis is of organisational systems, procedures or processes, rather than about improving the individuals' self-awareness.

Positive and negative motives

Here are just a few of the motives – good, bad and questionable – which have been given by managers claiming to have begun implementing self-direction.

Altruism It was Maslow who commented that many of us repress our feelings of altruism to others. 'I suddenly realised that what we were doing was stifling the development of our people! It became obvious to me that we had to help them grow for their own good, and if the company benefited too then that was the icing on the cake!' The problem comes when what you do is more for your own benefit than that of others.

Do-goodism Easily confused with altruism. The motive is to be seen to be a better person by others, or to feel better because of their actions.

Humanism 'I recognised that unless we did something about this, the US economy would inevitably suffer within the next fifty years, to such an extent that we would become a third-world country!' A strong belief that looking at the bigger picture, with a longer-term and more global perspective, will benefit not only the company but also the community as a whole by allowing the development of rational solutions to problems.

The True-Believer Easily confused with a humanist – the big picture in this case becomes a hidden agenda (often political). The TB can become so embroiled in their view of what is right that they subsequently fail to win others to their cause.

People-type of personality 'It's been thought for a long time that some people have a personality that is more compatible with social or caring roles. I just wasn't comfortable with the way we treated our people.'

Curiosity 'It's all been one big experiment to me. We tried doing it this way, then we did it that way, and now we've done it this way – I think the results speak for themselves.'

Having worked through some emotional pain 'It was after my divorce – it hurt me a lot. I got some help in looking at what had gone wrong, and I realised that I had been very unaware of other people's needs.'

Still needing to work through some pain People who try to do the most to help others are often looking for help themselves. The frustrated manager who has always wanted to achieve more himself may launch a process of self-direction to help others achieve what he hasn't, or was prevented from doing.

Commitment to competence 'I like to think that I'm a progressive manager. People need to have the opportunity to excel, and I have always felt that our workers were capable of being extremely professional. This was the obvious chance to make that change.'

Avoiding pain Imagine the manager we described earlier who finds it difficult to cope with people expressing anger, and seeks to deflect their anger in order to avoid their own discomfort. In a setting where conflict has become prevalent – for example in the period after substantial redundancy – the social levelling and development of others less fortunate than oneself can, within the SMWT approach, be an effective way of circumventing further pain.

Expediency Although it can occur in many guises, expediency may be closely related to the pain-avoidance rationale. For example: 'I've decided to implement self-direction as a way of freeing the organisation from these endless political games among managers trying to get into my chair.' Actually, the person is saying that they are tired of battling and this is an expedient way for them to avoiding conflict in the future.

Decisions

There are several issues that daunt employers who are considering implementing SMWTs.

Boundaries

Most organisations, especially larger ones, have many existing delimited boundaries which are bound to influence the way in which they introduce SMWTs. There is usually a healthy debate as to whether each should go ahead individually or together; whether each should follow the same route or different ones; whether the lessons from one can really be applied to the others, and so on. The issue appears to be one of autonomy.

As Motorola clearly shows, provided that a unit is sufficiently independent, it can evolve independently. It is important that this autonomy is real and not simply perceived. It is not uncommon for the members of the senior management team to have a very different perspective from their employees.

Remuneration

Almost all of the organisations that have successfully implemented self-direction have done so by shifting pay from a seniority scale to one based on skills and competencies. This provides a personal reward for learning and thus encourages individuals to move towards a multi-skilled approach.

Most of the organisations also offered a substantial employee share-ownership option. These were not trivial. Many companies have offered such schemes which, while they motivated people in the short term, are ridiculed when the employees discover how little they get each year from the possession of the shares.

Far more popular are performance-related pay schemes, linked directly to the performance of the team in which the individual works.

Target setting

Managers in traditional organisations frequently complain that they cannot get their employees to focus on productivity-related measures of performance. When you look at their approach it isn't difficult to see why. If you are one member of a company employing say 500 people, knowing what the share price is, or the monthly sales volume, or the output of the entire factory, is relatively meaningless. In most cases targets which had originally been assigned to individuals are now allocated to teams.

THE INTERVIEWEES

Brian Morris is Technology Director of Nippon Lever, the Japanese outlet of the Unilever organisation. Well established in Japan and a sizeable company, Nippon Lever already practises many of the activities that would fall under the umbrella of Total Quality in Western eyes. The latest developments have been a company-wide implementation of Total Productive Maintenance (TPM) and a best-partner programme which is extending their team-working activities to their suppliers and the wider community. In this interview, Brian explains some of the practical differences between a top-down implementation in a Japanese organisation and a Western one, and discusses some of the problems faced by Japanese organisations when they try to shift the culture of their front-line employees.

Few organisations have the opportunity to systematically introduce a new culture, let alone one like team-based self-management. Fewer still try to implement such a mechanisem, developed in one country, within another. Yet **Mineo Hanai**, General Manager with Nippondenso, had to do just that. He was responsible for introducing a Japanese team-based culture into a highly demotivated American workforce in one of the first developments of a Pacific-rim country within the States.

Many people criticise modern management initiatives because they say that they are manufacturing-driven and apply only to large organisations. International Public Relations (IPR) is a small Japanese service company. In his interview, **Takeo Nishitani**, the Chief Executive, explains how he has taken the organisation through all the classic organisational structures for a business in their field, but has now established SMWTs. He describes the reasons for the transition, and many of the issues that the teams have had to contend with. Anyone in a consultancy firm will recognise their dilemmas, and the potential threats to utilisation and profitability that the solutions represent – but as Nishitani points out, the results have more than compensated.

To the larger organisation, the definition of 'employer' becomes difficult to tie down. Is it the major shareholder, or the most senior executive? Perhaps it is the almost autonomous general manager, or a corporate panel – the board or an executive committee. Often, this individual or group establishes the philosophy or vision, and then delegates the implementation to others. **Malcolm Fraser,** of the Executive Education Center of Motorola University, explains the history of the organisation's empowerment activities, how they have evolved through experiment rather than grand design. He illustrates the key role of the single-person trigger among all the pressures to change, and shows how it is often the unique experiences of these people that catalyse them into action.

Ford's Romeo Engine Plant is another manufacturing operation. Started as a 'brown-field' site, it is a uniquely autonomous facility with just over 1,000 employees. The entire drive towards self-direction has been provided by **George Pfeil**, the Plant Superintendent. A frequent question at the seminars we conduct is: 'What is the attitude of unions to all this?' George's approach was to involve the union, the UAW, throughout the implementation. The site is now effectively co-managed.

A much smaller manufacturing organisation is GTE Directories. **Steven Scarbury** and **Leslie Watkins** describe the activities within their own operations as the transition to SMTW takes place. Steven is a largely autonomous General Manager, reporting to a remote Divisional Director. His HR Manager, Leslie Watkins, co-steers their process of change. Again we see the role of the key individual and the evolutionary approach. Again we see the importance of education and training in many of the dilemmas facing the policy-setting team.

INTERVIEW 5.1 TOP-DOWN IMPLEMENTATION IN A JAPANESE CONTEXT

Brian Morris, Technology Director, Nippon Lever BV

Background

Nippon Lever have been in Japan for thirty years, operating with our present organisational structure. We came in with foods, and more recently we've acquired, through our relationships with Cheeseborough-Ponds in America, the personal products side of the business. We've now moved into the detergents market through our own internally driven conditions.

We are a growing company beset by the normal problems of a foreign company in Japan, but we have grown from strength to strength in those thirty years with very few set-backs. We currently employ between 1,100 and 1,500 people. Managerial distinctions are different from those in the West. We were originally a joint venture, but we are now wholly owned by our European parent Unilever. We follow all the guidelines and best practices of Unilever.

The history of team working in Nippon Lever

Despite its ancestry Nippon Lever is very much a Japanese institution. In recent years, it has done a great deal to develop an internal quality improvement culture. It is now developing this to create partnerships with its suppliers and the wider community while internally pursuing a Total Productive Maintenance programme.

The company in its entirety is a part of Japan, so it has its own unique relationship with the way in which the Japanese operate. So when you talk about team-work, you've got to realise that this is a Japanese company and team-work is the watch-word in the way the Japanese operate. So if you say: 'Are we a team-work organisation?', the answer has got to be 'Yes'.

The current status of teams at Nippon Lever

The fact that I'm wearing a badge which says that we are engaged in a 'Best Partner' activity tells you that we all work as one team – not only an internal team but also as part of an external team with our suppliers. The 'Best Partner' programme is about becoming a team with our suppliers and the community at large. It's an extension of Total Quality. It's not complicated – it's been put together by a team and it is trying to pull together our corporate image and extend the ideas into our relationships with customers and suppliers. Teams are working on specifics – such as the customer contact, supplier quality assurance, and strategic relationships with their suppliers.

Everyone sees themselves as working in the Unilever team. In the operating plants the structure is based on designated (i.e. named) teams. They have a nickname process which sometimes sounds strange to Westerners. As a board we receive a presentation from these teams every six months: we visit the production place and listen to their concerns and what they've done. In the administrative area it's been much slower to take off, but that is where we're focusing with the Best Partner concept.

The impact of team working on working practices

The Japanese culture, at least to a Westerner's eyes, is extremely pragmatic. Whereas a Western team creates a strong bond and will persist with this for a long time afterwards, Japanese teams create team identities but can quickly break them down and reform them. This has a profound effect on team working and bodes well for the future.

Team-work is a Japanese preoccupation. Nevertheless there are, within the Japanese way of working, sub-teams and sub-groups. The Japanese tend to operate in factions – even in the Diet [Parliament]. On the face of it it's all one big team, but within that there are factions. What is interesting is their ability to build these up and break them down quite dynamically. Teams seem to assemble and reassemble: the Japanese are very pragmatic people – they don't hold on to philosophies when they aren't necessary.

Within an operating company you have to encourage team-work and you have to manage it. Japan has always liked management and identified with corporate goals – and it's very much down to the management of the company to set the strategic direction. Once you have the framework of the company and what it wants to achieve, you can form teams very rapidly. The Japanese are very quick to form teams – but there will still be people forming factions, people with their own independent ideas, traditions, backgrounds, technical expertise.

In Nippon Lever we've recently started to work on team-work for production improvements: Total Productive Maintenance (TPM) is an area in which we've been particularly active for the past eighteen months. TPM is one of the most interesting examples of formalising team-work – taking a procedure of how you form teams, how you carry out improvement activities within an accepted framework. The Japanese are much better when an outside consultancy or group offers a preferred practice for forming teams. It has been very easy to introduce the concepts of TPM as laid down by the Japanese Institute of Plant Maintenance – the inventors of TPM – and there has been a very quick uptake. I'm surprised that it follows a Western model, with the sell-in and emotional commitment of the Senior Management Team, followed by lots of training and shop-floor discussions with the union and so on. In Japan when introducing a *sensai* (consultant) there's no doubt about his expertise: he has the track record. There is a natural assumption from Day 1 that this is the correct thing to do. It's merely a question of implementing it correctly. I'm astonished at how quickly the Japanese have (in my company) taken on TPM.

The importance of Senior Management commitment prior to change is stressed in every OD book. In practice it is often not demonstrated even if it exists. Morris explains how Japanese tradition is exploited by consultants to ensure that managers follow through!.

We went through a ceremony – a typical Japanese ceremony – in which the company made its commitment publicly. The *sensai* doesn't want you to get started until you're ready for it. You go through a process of preparation to demonstrate that you can work in teams, that you can do homework, that people identify with the mission, then he says you can start TPM proper, and you then go through the ceremony to state publicly that for the next three years that is what you will be doing. This is quite different from the UK and America where you tend to see commitment from the board, but not right the way through. So you then have a buy-in process with lots of education and awareness raising. Here I'd say it's the reverse process: the workforce identifies with the solution, sees that the management has introduced it, and recognises the concern that we have given to thinking about it – it wasn't self-seeded by the workforce.

Although organisations in all cultures have multiple structures, the Japanese social structure is complex and well developed and can take precedence over any formally imposed one. In this way decisions by authority figures can be accepted quite readily. Although this might sound dangerous it overcomes 'analysis paralysis' when few facts exist or opinions are divided.

There is not only a difference in the process, but also in the attitude. The difference here is that a person in Japan always looks at their peers and their colleagues to see who is the boss. A card may be given to you before your boss, because they work out their own sense of authority. A *sensai* has authority because of their knowledge, and a boss because of years of experience. In Japanese terms, this gives authority to a person – not to be given in to, but to be listened to carefully. These natural chemistries in Japanese society, we find very hard. In Britain, consultants are often young, energetic and enthusiastic; in Japan people don't become consultants until they have experience that they can communicate. They use the word *'sensai'* like we use 'Sir'. This is important because it means that the Japanese don't have the problem of NIH – Not Invented Here; they will be open to the new ideas because of the authority of the person. This even happens in Japanese politics – the Prime Minister is in a strange position of authority whereby the opposition will be very cautious about upstaging him.

This produces a dilemma in team-work: the speed with which team-work is accepted. This was true from the start: Deming lectured, and almost overnight the country had taken up the team-work philosophy. You see this in advertising today – cigarettes and so on are being advertised by foreigners. I've even experienced this when buying something: I saw a side-table which I liked, and while I was trying to find a sales-person, someone else bought it – my interest had been enough to endorse that it was worth having! It's this ability to take a very rapid initiative because they see someone in authority setting the standard. In Britain we have some very old-fashioned ideas about class, procedures, hierarchy, boss relationships and so on, which get in the way of our taking up ideas rapidly.

The way in which teams operate is very simple. We think of it in almost emotional terms. The Japanese are very much simpler about these things. One of my staff explained it to me by saying that Westerners tend to discuss philosophies in meetings: we don't really do anything until we have discussed the philosophy. Each person has a view of the world – a virtual reality; different people have different views, and 95% of what you are saying is the same – but you won't do anything until you have resolved the differences. The Japanese can't cope with the enormity of this. By contrast, they discuss realities and the steps that are necessary to move from one stage to another – they get emotional only when they haven't established the facts of something, but it's frustration at themselves, not at an individual. A meeting will break up and have to be reconvened once they have established the facts. They will make one change, then another if the first was successful – this is the basis of *Kaizen*. The TPM equivalent is the 'one- point lesson': they try to encapsulate a simple reality that everyone can digest; they don't progress until everyone has that one point. Compare that with training courses in a Western company where we overburden ourselves with great objectives, heavy words, and complexity in a very short time.

Team-work is about identifying the knowledge base, and then establishing the speed with which the team can progress. The Japanese then go to the *sensai* for more information – or to other teams, sometimes outside the company. One of the challenges for the West is maintaining the health of teams.

I am responsible for improving technological knowledge in my company – and I'm very mindful of the need to implement what the company wants, but in a

Japanese society. Learning is a national pre-occupation here. Newspaper readership is the highest, after Sweden. The consumers are very technically aware – they do not buy because of razzmatazz. I'm struck by the rigour with which they do things, with attention to very small details – look at the way that they learn calligraphy. Then there are lots of other aspects, gardening, *Ikebana*, and so on: there's always this attention to detail.

Elsewhere we hear of the basic skills shortage and how it affects organisations. The Japanese problem is slightly different. Among the larger corporations it is expected that the company will invest in its employees' development.

People attend university after a long period of intensive examinations. They have worked so hard that university is a tremendous release. University is about learning social aspects, forming networks and relationships – not about technical knowledge. When we interview in the West, new graduates talk about projects that they've done and aspects of their courses. In Japan it's very different. They haven't done the projects and so on. Once they get to university they're almost guaranteed a degree at the end of three years. So when they join the company it is up to us to select people for their attitude, interest and energy, and then to spend time teaching them the technology that they need. It's very different at postgraduate level – the Masters and Doctorates.

Companies have a tremendous responsibility to train and develop people. People talk of fifteen-year apprenticeships – because you shouldn't be judged until you have the knowledge. This is very different from the Western idea of people coming from a well-respected college and doing a three-year induction training.

As a company we spend a lot of money helping people to attend night school and so on – for non-graduates too. Many companies have extensive technical centres which their new recruits will attend for quite some time – most of them also use some kind of on-the-job element.

Motivating team members

One problem faced by self-managed work teams is the need to prevent the group from adopting a lowest common denominator approach to goal setting. Organisations that have applied them successfully set stretching goals. Motorola's Six Sigma approach is a good example. Morris uses individual targets to achieve the same purpose.

There's a dilemma between motivating people to be in a team and setting individual targets. I used to think that it was a problem – but I don't think so now. Individual target-setting is one of the best ways of avoiding team-stagnation. People seem to get upset because they go to extremes, but it isn't necessary. The aim is to give people something to stretch them beyond the team

– teams themselves avoid stretching. The beauty of setting demanding individual targets is that you can institutionalise disruption – it can put challenge into the team – which won't happen if the team sets its own targets. Target-setting is a very good way of getting management to focus in a strategic direction throughout the organisation – it's much better than team-briefings and so on.

Future trends and issues

The Japanese economy has grown particularly strongly through 'reverse engineering' and the practical application of Western technologies. The opportunity facing them is to innovate in the first place. But innovation is not a strength – several interviewees commented on the impact of the Japanese education system in discouraging problem-solving and creativity. As Morris points out, attention is shifting to this vital dimension.

i TPM and price competitiveness

I see TPM as being a growing philosophy. TQC was excellent on the soft side – getting people to focus on areas that are difficult to quantify. TPM is important because of the threat to the Japanese economy. It is growing in importance – over seventy companies got awards at the ceremony two months ago. Japanese companies are recognising that price competitiveness is critical.

The next area we have tackle is the innovation process. The Japanese are very conscious of the need to look for the winner which will make them the leader again. They know that Britain, the US and Germany have learnt how to cut development-time down to Japanese levels. Reliability has got to the point where the consumer can't detect improvements any more. In the new technologies, like liquid crystals, the Japanese know that their lead is quickly lost when it is reverse-engineered and goods can be made in places with lower labour-rates.

ii The process of intervention

Japan is highly inventive – people are exceptionally good at turning ideas into practical reality. People are now starting to focus on the process by which you invent, so that it can be applied to anything. There will be a big change in teamwork when they make the step between supply chain improvement and the invention process, which is about disruption. The Japanese have an phenomenal ability in breaking up and reforming: if they can systematise the process of invention, and can use their flexibility of teams to change roles, then there will be a very dramatic change – whole industries stopping within a year and starting up anew. We in the West are very bad at doing this. How it has happened I don't know: teams don't just have to work within the company – there's also the big team – Japan itself.

iii Crossing cultural boundaries

On the surface, the same process of team-working goes on in Japan as in the West. Underneath, there are differences – but there's a tremendous homogeneity of approach. The language of teams, goals, overlapping work-groups and so on are all the same. I'm very interested in the work at Nippondenso where they are trying to achieve something by mixing elements of American culture with Japanese. The American system encourages a certain altruism which is lacking in Japan, because people are used to the State or whatever dealing with things. What they are doing is very interesting: they're trying to take the positive aspects of both cultures and build them together.

This uniformity of approach is probably linked to the way in which the Japanese make decisions. Take fashion, for example. They have not developed such a complex set of internal standards of behaviour, so they look to the labels – Burberry, Gucci, Dunhill – to set the standard. It makes decision-making so much easier. You don't waste time thinking about something that isn't important. There are examples of this all over the place: the Navy is based on the British model; The public schoolboys in their immaculate black tunics are based on German ones. And nobody has challenged the issue – they don't have this emotional baggage. The effect is also felt inside a business – they have different pressures.

iv The changing role of managers

Morris makes a very interesting point about the role of the 'controller–cop' manager. Some of us have used catastrophe theory to describe the cyclical changes in management behaviour. Under normal circumstances a manager cycles through a number of leadership styles according to the individual that is being developed. Organisation-wide, as change is introduced so, layered on top of this cyclicity, is a similar pattern of direction, coaching, support and delegation. What Morris suggests is that managing the step-changes calls for a strong command and control style.

The word 'manager' implies command and control – as contrasted with 'team-work', which implies autonomy and self-motivation. The trouble with command and control is that they can give you tremendous movement – but then people are not doing, they are waiting for instruction. I think that you have to move between them – and management's role is to see that process through its oscillations. Organisations are dynamic, not fixed; they change, and a command and control structure moves you through the next discontinuity. An autonomous working group helps you solidify that gain and helps you move forward in a quality way. The role of managers is constantly changing; at one time you're a counsellor – then you are a controller. I think that cynicism grows because people don't recognise that oscillation: they associate the change in stance with a loss of commitment. The Americans do it in a different way – they are very quick at changing the boss. It's a roller-coaster with the focus on the bottom line and they move very quickly. In Japan it's more evolutionary – when the change happens it does so very quickly, but for different reasons.

vi Crossing competitive boundaries

The Japanese are much more closely tied to export markets. As such their ventures take them into the realm of cross-cultural borders frequently. They are now demonstrating that the reserve displayed by Western companies is far weaker in Japan. One boundary is that between competitors. Japanese teams increasingly collaborate with competitors on problem-solving processes.

> The only other area that is perhaps important is working across competitive boundaries. Teams, by their nature, compete. I've started to see that the Japanese are different in the way that teams can work across previously competitive boundaries. For instance, in the automotive industry, teams can agree between two competitors that there's no point in constantly struggling to outdo one another: if you are better than us at making gearboxes, let's accept that and get on with it. We are better at something else. This is an extension of the joint development projects, where the supplier approaches a customer and offers the chance to co-develop something. They've had the idea and now they'll share its development. We are now seeing companies moving beyond this – accepting that a competitor has the edge in specific fields, and not letting that obscure other elements. In America there's a big problem with anti-trust. In Japan they are proving much more flexible, much more sophisticated.
>
> Look at the American restructuring movement, where they are breaking up large companies and creating separate business entities. The interesting thing will be the way in which these re-form for strategic reasons.

INTERVIEW 5.2 WORKING FOR CONTINUOUS IMPROVEMENT

Mineo (Mike) Hanai, Assistant General Manager, Nippondenso Co Ltd

Company background

Our company works with the latest technologies to allow us to deliver a very wide variety of products to our customers – e.g., in the area of micro-machining. We are also very overseas orientated – Europe, Asia, Oceania – we have a total of thirty-eight overseas plants. We have IC (integrated Circuit) plants – from IC making through systems – we have a big test course [for automotive components]. Altogether we have a total of 100,000 staff producing a very wide range of products, about 10% of which are non-automotive. We have many

CIM (Computer-Integrated Manufacture) plants – our original name was UTOPIA. Our machine is home-made and we have a total CIM facility especially for small components. We build almost everything – 90% of our design is in-house, and about 50% of our production.

The Nishio plant is the largest – with nearly 11,000 employees – making mainly air-conditioners. We have a basic research laboratory nearby, while R & D for products is based here at Headquarters. Here we employ about 1,500 engineers. So we have a fairly traditional structure, with product areas and separate administrative functions, including R & D.

We have a wide range of customers – except for Nissan – for historical reasons. [Nippondenso is part of the Toyota Keiretsu.] We are probably the Number 1 or 2 autoparts manufacturer in the world – we have grown considerably.

Development of team working

Hanai had an unusual experience implementing Japanese practices in American plants. He spent a considerable time analysing the potential problems that this would present and was able to draw some interesting comparisons between the two countries.

My own experience of the team working process stems from my role at Nippondenso Manufacturing, USA. At that plant only about 3-4% of the 1,200 employees were Japanese. [Mr Hanai was Vice-President there and grew the business three-fold in number of employees.] The main difference between Western and Japanese teams is that they are more hierarchical in the West. Japanese team-building is softer, more democratic.

We entered the US in 1973 as a sales operation, and began to develop a manufacturing facility in 1984, commencing in 1986. At that time we had 1,240 employees on a site of a hundred acres. We have always tried to manufacture close to our customers. As you see, we tried to introduce manufacturing as soon as the sales figures justified the investment – the capital involved was $125 million.

Our problem here was how to integrate the Nippondenso Japanese culture with the American. We felt that there were three important aspects to our culture with which American culture contrasted: history, geography and religion.

In Japan, our history is a mono-racial culture from Asia. Geographically, Japan is a small island – actually four small islands. We don't have any natural resources – although our population is so large that we do have a vast human resource. Religiously, we are not monotheistic – most Japanese have Buddhist as well as Shinto beliefs. From this we have come to see firstly that long-term relationships are very important. Secondly, we believe teamwork is very important. Thirdly the use of human resources is very important to us – efficiency in terms of the best output from small actions. Finally, we have a Buddhist belief in doing good things. As a result, from our Japanese perspective, five key issues had to be incorporated in the US plant:

- long-term relationships;
- consensus;
- team-work;
- eliminating waste;
- continuous improvement.

The American culture is basically multi-racial; their history has been adventurous – hunting and cowboy-style – and democratic. They are very friendly to newcomers, quick to act, believe in fair play and respect strong leadership. They have a huge natural resource. They have a very diversified, but Christian religion. They seek comfortable lifestyles, free competition. They respect individuals, and look for spirit, but they like to help each other. To the Japanese their lifestyle is different, very comfortable.

The driving force for this development was the need to have a design facility closer to our customers, here the Big Three. In this way we have been able to deliver responses to our customers much more quickly than they expected. We are a preferred supplier to many now.

[Given that the needs are established,] this is effectively all about lead-time reduction – we had one exceptional example – for Chrysler – reducing design change-time from about two months to two weeks (over Christmas too!). To achieve our objectives we had, of course, to establish the best possible practices for in a design and production facility.

The organisation was driven by very clear goals and well documented critical success factors. Before the plant could begin to compete it had to become an exceptional performer. To achieve this Hanai introduced a succession of major change initiatives – most company-wide and most involving substantial training and development.

We did this by combining a number of initiatives under one Steering Group, given the overall title of *Kaizen* [continuous improvement] Steering Group. These were:

- Quality Control Circles (QCC);
- Suggestion Scheme;
- Total Productive Maintenance (TPM);
- Total Industrial Engineering (TIE) – a kind of small-scale Kaizen;
- Total Organisation Production System (TOPS);
- *Manzoku* – this is Japanese for 'satisfaction';
- Model Line Accountability.

In 1989, we implemented TIE, TPM and QCCs. The QCCs met once a week, for an hour or so at a time, with a twice-annual conference. The plant was mass-production, so TPM was very important and was emphasised strongly. All plant employees were involved in QCCs. There were over 120 QC Circles, usually with leaders who were not members of the management. The managers had their own QCC, structured in the same way but dealing with more strategic problems. At the time we did use the QCCs as an Associate-level activity. I can see that the techniques got used at other management levels – but on different problems. Perhaps it would change more readily in smaller organisations.

In 1990, we introduced Model Line Accountability. This is about helping people take responsibility for a model line and identify problems before they arise.

In 1991, we concentrated on *Manzoku*. The idea is for all employees to be satisfied in the path to customer satisfaction. This identified many important issues, many of which were hygiene factors.

Then in 1992, we implemented TOPS company-wide.

Next we considered how to reward people. We consulted experienced people: 'Do you think that your capability is the same as a beginner?' They said no; they had many years' experience. So we began to ask how to distinguish ability-levels – and identified four different levels and established pay-scales for each. Seniority was part of it, but we also had practical tests. Even people at the top took the test – then if a person was very good he could go on to the supervisor scale.

We began to expand their skills – a kind of multi-skilling. The skills were from different processes, which gave the employee better job security.

The new hirings were first screened by the Human Resource Department, and then interviewed by the Department Manager.

Employee communication

In chapter 11, we look at the common implementation steps taken as organisations establish self-managing or autonomous teams. One critical step which is often under-resourced is that of communication. It is so important that we describe it as a targeted marketing activity.

We had a number of communication activities, a hot-line to different departments, an open-box to the President, employee TV, newsletters and so on. We also had a VPs' do, and a group meeting two or three times a month where we would sit with employees. And of course we had an open-door policy. So there was a network of communication approaches.

Training & development

The second under-resourced area is training. As Hanai explains everyone received around 80 hours *non*-job-specific training. That is the equivalent of between 10 and 15 days per year.

We thought that training and education was particularly important. New associates were given a total of twenty-four hours of basic information; then quality control training added a further fifty-eight hours. Safety, a further one to four hours, depending on their role; management education ranged from 60 to 100 hours. There was, however, as much job-specific training as was necessary. Finally, there was anything from two weeks to two months of Japanese language training available.

The results were all measured in terms of productivity and awards from outside bodies.

Organisational structure

The US plant was organised to use multi-skilled, substantially autonomous teams. Hanai remains unconvinced multi-skilling beyond the production area or the administrative area will work. Within these, existing functions persist, organised either by product line or specialist discipline.

> People are arranged in the same sort of functions as in a traditional hierarchy – I do not see that changing.
>
> In the past we focused on the production schedule. How do we put the human factor in? We must change – otherwise...! Multi-skilling is one solution and that can lead to [Self-Managing Work Teams]. This works well in smaller firms where everyone can feel that they are an owner. But we have to ask whether job rotation and so on is necessary. I am not convinced that productivity is so good when people's jobs are not equal. We are moving towards comprehensive multi-skilling. I still think that management is necessary for direction, and so one person is necessary especially when there are critical problems. That leader needs the skills of how to take risks, how to prevent bugs, and so on.

Development of QC Circles

> I think the development of QC Circles is an interesting issue – I think that some QCCs are too mature. The original theme was to improve. But in Japan they seem sometimes to make better presentations than the results they actually achieved. In the US we started QCCs and they didn't inherit the same background – they were very fresh – I think that it would help for all of us to go back to the original.
>
> We didn't increase the amount of time spent on QC Circles – in the past it was additional to, not part of, the job. So every day would be too much – once a week is a good timing. We surveyed the employees and asked if they would be happy just doing QC Circle activities – they said no! They wanted their own individual jobs. I think that we have to consider the human factor always. This point about satisfying ourselves is important. QCC is a sort of introduction. But it is possible to be modified according to the demand.

INTERVIEW 5.3 ESTABLISHING SELF-MANAGED WORK TEAMS

Takeo Nishitani, CEO, International Public Relations, Tokyo

Nishitani takes us through the fascinating evolution of autonomous teams within one of Tokyo's leading consultancy practices. Driven by a need to match their client's needs, IPR spurned traditional structures broke up into very small teams, discovered that this created inter-team rivalry which harmed the business and so established self-managing work teams.

The changing structure

Let me explain how we are set up in this office. As a consulting company we are sizeable, with about 150 employees. The nature of our business is very similar to law firms and accounting firms – we are consultants in the field of communications. This is quite different from manufacturing. We are concerned very much with individual services rather than organisational ones. Therefore it is extremely difficult to organise a sizeable team. In the past we used to have foreign and domestic divisions – according to where our clients were situated. But with the changing environment of our clients this is no longer possible, and we have to have more capabilities supporting their international needs. Therefore we abolished this distinction.

We tried to develop specialisations: hi-tech, automotives, basic industries (steel, petrochemicals, consumer goods) – but even medium-sized units with that kind of specialisation were less successful, for various reasons. It was good, in a way, that we could improve our skills within a sector, but the people in an individual field become very narrow-minded. Such a narrow scope of understanding is not really needed by the clients – they know their own problems and their own industries; we are asked to provide consultation from a wider perspective. This is a real dilemma. Therefore for the past four or five years we have broken these into very small units, or servicing units, which consist of four or five consultants who are really geared to provide services to meet the individual needs of a client. Each unit does not necessarily have special expertise, but a general consulting background in communication skills. We also gave them quite a lot of autonomy, for the management of the small units – not just the management of the services but also the profit. That worked quite effectively for a certain period – but it still lacked flexibility – such a unit cannot necessarily satisfy the clients' diversified needs.

People were very excited at the degree of autonomy – it was like running a very small company. So they were managed for responsiveness, but they couldn't satisfy client-needs, because each unit began to think only of their own turf. We therefore lost flexibility. Team-work was very much encouraged, but each group was competing against the others. So the larger team-work spirit for the corporation, of give-and-take, a complementary spirit, was lost.

Then, this year, we changed again, by grouping those teams into larger ones in four sections. Each section consists of twenty-five people – to provide more cohesive or flexible services, to meet the clients' needs, especially in the recession when clients have started cutting budgets, rationalising and concentrating on how *they* can satisfy the changing consumer needs. Each unit has rather vague characteristics – one group specialises in analysis because they have more staff capable of providing this; one is geared to the hi-tech areas – which are areas of rapid change, so we have younger people in that; another handles the softer side, the entertainment, leisure and consumer sectors; while the fourth is geared to basic industries (pharmaceuticals, minerals, and so on). So the lack of cross-fertilisation has been overcome.

The other problem is providing the package of benefits which an individual might expect in a larger firm. We used to have internal training sessions, two or three times a year, for the freshmen and junior members of staff – for two days we would go away from Tokyo and work in teams, debating quality control, the improvement of skill-levels, how to make proposals, how to present cases effectively, and so forth. But in our profession on-the-job training is the most important. There are not many common theories on PR and so on, and our clients' needs are highly diversified.

The employment demographics of Japan are changing to the same extent as those all around the world. But in Japan especially, the small and medium-sized firms are rapidly attracting younger employees and especially young career women. Motivating these people is a very different proposition to managing a traditional plant.

It is also important to keep the team intact. Until about ten years ago such brotherhood was very popular with Japanese people, but nowadays young people are becoming much more individualistic – so it has become very difficult to keep the brotherhood relationship in a team. At the same time, senior people have been losing their confidence in educating younger people with different ideas. We have to have the training, but it is very difficult to achieve. Through on-the-job training we are still trying to educate and control the work of junior people when they join us. We are very fortunate that people stay relatively longer than in other countries, such as America or Europe, where people join and change companies quite frequently. We are the largest PR company in Tokyo, so we have a reputation and people tend to stay longer with us and can learn more; but the other side of the coin is that if they stay longer they are only introduced to one way of working.

A natural quality-control mechanism is in place: this is a client servicing industry – so the client controls the level and the quality of the services. As their demands increase, so the consultancy responds. This kind of automatic mechanism is different from in the manufacturing sector. In our case, through daily interfacing the feedback is much quicker. It has become more demanding –

tighter QC is required. The difficulty of systematic quality control is addressed by an Account Executive, and their supervisor has less control. Through an internal weekly meeting we try to control and maintain the standard as much as we can.

We have fully responsible support staff, who are handling the clients. We have a supervisor who gives instructions if needed. The Account Executives have the ultimate responsibility for delivery and execution – they are accountable but not responsible for the work. They report to a Director for each unit.

Thus IPR's approach is to organise multi-skilled autonomous teams of 25 each with their own Director. The teams include both consultants and support staff. Each client has an account executive who is a member of the team, but is not in the role of leader.

The impact of culture on structure

These autonomous units have been allocated their own area of the company offices thereby reinforcing the team. By increasing the size of the groups to 25 communication has improved to a satisfactory level while maintaining the team identity – a similar trade-off is reported in most organisations.

There is a logistical movement, but the communications flow is more interesting. We have one big office space, which has been open-plan in the past; now we have screens so that each unit communicates better – but there is less communication between the groups.

We have had problems recently with internal communications resulting from the deployment of computers – people are kept busy with the computers and so human communication suffers. In Japan communication through computers is not good – in the old days we did not have typewriters and so we don't have keyboarding skills. So people weren't trained to communicate through their fingers, but with the pen, the mouth and more importantly through 'temperature'. Japan was an agricultural society, where you saved and reaped and the family stayed together all their life; whereas among the hunting races of North America and Europe the family had to move from one place to another chasing animals: this has produced different attitudes to communications and team spirit. Here, although improvement could be made through computers, we have the word 'nomination' – '*nom*' means to drink. 'Nomination' after work creates a team identity. By enlarging the smaller units we have helped to overcome the problem of poor communications. When we had small units, it was difficult to set up a task-force team to tackle specialist problems.

When a client makes contact for some prospective work, we build up a team of people to make the proposal and present this to the client. So the team is involved throughout.

Why did we change?

I feel that team-work was very good here. In the past decade it has been deterio-rating, and I was concerned that we needed to regain the team-work spirit. I think that Japanese organisations are now beginning to see that they need to change their structure to cope with the changing demands.

I think that as a country we are losing team spirit. In the past we had one goal – which we had to achieve. Now Japan has succeeded in achieving the very high level of output, it is no longer obvious how we get different things from different people. There is confusion, management is losing control – I think that that is bad. In Japan, management was not really competent at controlling – because of the difference in our approach – the famous bottom-up decision-making process. If the team spirit is lost, then you lose the decision-making process. You can sit and watch, but do nothing because of the team. Now the changing environment means that management must have a firmer grip in controlling the company. The Japanese need to learn the top-down decision-making process, especially in such a deep recession.

The results

It is often tempting to measure success of an OD initiative in terms of the bottom-line. Certainly IPR could and does do so. But 'softer' measures are also significant including the perceptions of young entrants to the industry.

When people finish school they want to join a big company. It is better to hide yourself behind a big tree to avoid typhoons and rain: this criterion is foremost in the Japanese mind. People join us for our name in the field. People think it's more prestigious – they will go to any big company rather than a small company.

PR is not a 'real' industry yet – manufacturing companies are considered to be 'real' industries. The service sector is not really needed! When we started thirty-five years ago people said; 'We can do that ourselves!' There was a real difficulty selling ourselves. But the situation has changed. It was once difficult to attract new graduates – now we can attract people from good universities. When they join they are given more responsibility than in big firms – and people find this satisfying.

This was originally a Japanese firm, but six years ago we were taken over by Shandwick. They don't manage the business, just the bottom line. Their philos-ophy is that indigenous businesses should be managed by local people – we have just one non-executive board member.

We have measured the success of these teams through satisfied clients, the number of clients, and objective criteria such as the development of new busi-ness and innovation in new services. Then again, there are compensations, not so much through regular salary but through the bonuses that we have been paying twice a year.

Future challenges

As we discover throughout the world, the education system is not delivering workers with the necessary skills. Whereas in the US most people commented on basic skills, in Japan the issue is one of team working.

> We need to look at the educational system in Japan – this has not yet been changed. To increase our competitiveness in international team-work we must to be re-educated: individualism must be encouraged, and, contradictory though it sounds, the need for team-work must be developed. We not have not had much individualism in the past – in a way, such individualism was wiped out through the educational process. Therefore we had only one goal, and in preparing the curriculum we provided only for that goal. That has changed but unless you can improve your pupil, you cannot really be international. You have to achieve team spirit by encouraging people to accept their differences. But you can't change the education system in ten years – it takes half-a-century or even a century – that is a big challenge.
>
> Outside school, opportunities are limited. For example, we encourage our consultants to be involved in professional bodies, but in PR there isn't really one – it is more relevant in the high-tech areas, though the PR Society of Japan does now have a sort of forum, where people can continue to develop and learn.

INTERVIEW 5.4 SMWTS AND EMPOWERMENT
Malcolm Fraser, Executive Education Design Center, Motorola University

> The first question is how did we get started? What was the background? Where did we come from? What were the tie-ins to what was going on before? Then there is the issue of how did we sell the idea internally? Then there's the question of barriers, personal, organisational, cultural and even legal. And then finally, look at the changes in people's roles.

How did they start?

There are three qualities that have probably enabled Motorola to transform its organisation more than most. As Fraser explains there has always been a tremendous respect for the person who can get to grips with new technologies. Then the enormous growth of the business in both peacetime and during wars has created an an incredibly diverse organisation with opportunities to experiment as much in 'management' issues as in technical ones. Thirdly, Motorola was one of the first organisations to actively pursue participative management.

What's intriguing, and what makes Motorola such a great place, is that there is no single Motorola. There are differences here, there and everywhere. Even within some of the larger sectors, you get very significant differences, which are more evident than you would expect. I think the basic reason for this is that we have pretty much always been a company which has given a certain element of power to the different parts of the organisation. Fairly early in the history of the company, in the post-Second World War era, which was when it started becoming a major corporation, we became a place which had different technologies: we have always had a supreme respect for the technologist. Some of the heroes of the company were extremely brilliant people who were given latitude and told, for instance, to go down to Phoenix and set up a semiconductor operation – or at least a transistor one, as it would have been then! Those folk are different from the people who do FM radio or paging and so on. So there's always been more of a decentralised approach to the granting to people of power than in many more centralised companies.

More particularly, we simultaneously had the old, traditional approach to running a business – more true than in some other companies. But somewhere in the history of the company, probably in the 1950s and 1960s, what had been a fairly paternalistic method of operating was transformed into something that was more participative, so that you heard people, quite early on, using the language of participative management.

The Participative Management Programme

In many companies SMWTs are seen as a natural evolution of team working, at Motorola, too, several people felt that they evolved from a conscious reassessment of the management style and a need to create a culture of participation.

At some point a programme was launched in Franklin Park, which later became known as the Participative Management Programme (PMP). It coalesced in 1990. So it wasn't a corporate-wide programme. This was an approach to involving people's talents in problem-solving. It had a couple of components:

1 The expectation that people would actually start using different tools and different skills to solve operational problems, particularly quality problems, but also any that had become a demanding focus of attention for folk of the day. It was, in a lot of ways, similar to the efforts that were going on around Quality Circles – involving employees in some fashion with their work.

2 We realised that there needed to be a major shift in the way that people managed, so at the same time a lot of training was being put together around teams and their problem-solving approaches. There was also a major focus on the management aspect that was required for that. So there was a great deal going on – this was the start.

A big part of the idea behind Bob Galvin's centralised training function was that we would be able to shift the thinking, the culture and the behaviour of managers so that they involved people in a participative way – so that they worked much more closely with people around the fairly clearly delineated area of operational problem-solving. My sense is that the PMP programme was a little ahead of its time – there was an awful lot of good that came of it, particularly in some of the manufacturing areas, but I think it shared the strengths and also some of the problems of the whole Quality Circle movement in this country. It took things to a certain level and it left them there. The big plus of the PMP effort was that it put the word 'participative' into the thinking of a lot of people in management. I would also say that it became something that the company was committed to. I don't think that there was any question that there was real sincerity behind what was going on. People around the organisation were very committed to this – in fact, some of the senior management were very clear that they were going to lose their jobs if they didn't get on board with this programme. So there was a top-level commitment which was taken to be very serious.

On a personal note, it was in 1986 when I was with my previous employer that I visited here – and one of the key things in my mind was: 'Is this real? Motorola's training and the participative approach is very impressive – but is this for real?' And the sense that I got from the people here was that this really was in the process of being implemented.

There was no real question in the minds of folks running it, either at TAC or the corporation – they were pretty serious about this. They were trying to involve people in what was going on, to shift away from a traditional control function – and I've not changed my mind about it since then. Eight years on I don't think anything else – it is pretty serious.

So there was the plus of making it in participative management. The drawback – and most of us realised this I think – was twofold. One was that it worked pretty well in factory operations but it didn't seem to have the same power in the indirect areas. Within MTAC we had various people working in teams, and I think we did some good and addressed some issues – but you got to the point of wondering; 'Is the deep-level change going to happen here?' And I think for a lot of us it was the same old thing: you address some issues, sort out different things, but it doesn't seem as if you are having the impact that you could be having. So there was a certain sense that we had gone about as far as we could go with this PMP approach. Like so many developments which took place in this country, there was a sense that we were operating with a framework which was clearly going along with the hierarchy and which was only giving a certain element of power to individuals who were on the front lines.

Quality

The second consistent thread in the evolution of SMWTs is the need for quality improvement. Motorola, again, is no exception. It is very unlikely that the goals they strive towards could have been conceived without the movement towards participative management.

The other strand underlying how Motorola got started was that, in many of our factories, we began at about the same time to get very, very serious about quality. We realised just how much of an incredible competitive threat we were under – some of our early executive programmes were basically designed to discriminate and get them realising that this was not just something in newspapers and magazines – we personally were under major threat. So there was a lot of growing attention to quality. One of our cultural stories which has become enshrined was from one of our officers' meetings. Art Sundry was National Sales Manager for land-mobile products, which at the time was the biggest total business unit. In the middle of the meeting he raised his hand and said: 'Bob, I have a question. All this talk about quality. We're not doing it – our quality stinks!' Bob said: 'Excuse me?' He said: 'It stinks – I can't with confidence be with a customer, have him open a new box, and be sure whether the product is going to work or not.' Bob Galvin said: 'Tell us more'. So Art began to review what was going on. That was really when the Office of the CEO, President and Chairman began to focus on the problem. It took several years though. Art's willingness to say: 'The stuff stinks!' is one of those things that everybody knows but nobody ever says. We began to get very serious about it. The quality folks' role went through some very powerful changes with the massive education of people in things like Six Sigma and Quality Control.

So we had what had always been a relatively employee-centred culture, and grafted on to that PMP programme was a very serious business-oriented commitment to quality. What happened in the workplace was that people began to see that a lot of our quality training was also devoted to manufacturing (advanced manufacturing, work cells and so on), approaching the organisation like that differently. We did not even use the concept of teaming very consciously – and yet we started doing it. We started putting into place a whole lot of training, including cross-training, so that employees became able to take on each other's jobs, to do some very straightforward, technical-increasing efficiency – balancing the line, taking redundant steps out of the work. A lot of it, incidentally, using a great deal of internal training.

SMWTs – the inception

The Personnel Manager in one factory was Dick Passmore. This was one of those areas where was a window of opportunity. It was in the small town of Elmer, outside Buffalo – the sort of place that you would not visit unless you had a reason! There is a school of thought that says that this is one reason we used them as a sort of experimental case, as it wouldn't attract a great deal of attention! Elmer's example is so typical of implementation, and how this process often starts. There's been a Quality Circle drive, there's the attention to quality, there is suddenly a lot of focus on the employee and work profitability – and it all comes together.

The other side to it is that, in the last three or four years, the people in corporate, and also the people in the separate business units, realised that there was a whole new dimension to participative management. So a couple of publications had come out, and a certain amount of pull was created by people in the business units who said: 'We can take this a lot further. We can have (and the names for it vary) Self-Managed Work Teams. We are going to flatten the hierarchy in any event, because it improves our efficiency – so we can do that. We can pull some things together. We can involve people much more in what is going on. So a natural evolution in the workplace resulted in a number of places, usually without a lot of prompting, starting up some very interesting experiments in making use of (what our term for it is) 'empowered teams'.

How did we sell the idea internally?

It is often difficult for people to accept a consultant when they say that there is no definitive approach to a particular problem. Often, less competent consultants try to sell themselves on their own distinctive and universal approach to resolving a particular need. Some management teams never get beyond the starting blocks because they feel that they can't start until they have identified the 'correct' approach. As Fraser points out, the success at Motorola was fuelled by this inconsistency.

> We had a number of teams already, but in 1992 the folks in corporate said: 'Empowerment – we believe in that. It is good, we will adopt it and we will build it into our Total Customer Satisfaction (TCS) schema and goals – as being an initiative. We will take out the wording of participative management and replace it with the wording of empowerment for all in a participative corporate and creative workplace.' So the organisation has approached empowerment through top-level support – and yet the top-level, in the form of Gary Tooker, made it very clear that he is not going to mandate that people do certain things.
>
> Therefore, we find this remarkable variation – maybe more than there ought to be, frankly – in how people approach it. And that's really happened because there were so many experiments going on in different places which haven't been pulled together. There has, in fact, been resistance to any overt corporate involvement – I've had direct experience of that myself with people asking: 'Why are you here?' So there's no single starting point, nor is there any real consistency in the process – and even the business reasons are different – but by and large it tends to be: 'My God, we have got to be going down this route.' None of this is surprising for a diverse organisation with many largely autonomous units.
>
> I think the sense has been: with empowerment, what is the role of the centre – in an environment, the essence of which is one of devolution of power? I asked this of Ed Musselwhite who was presenting to a conference: 'What are the challenges to getting empowerment happening in a large multi-faceted company?' His point was that it was a tremendous advantage because you have so many different experiments. I would follow that up by saying that the challenge for the people in the centre is to become catalysts, spreading the information and increasing the learn-

ing of the organisation about what each group is doing. To some extent, that is the role that we have adopted here.

While the environment was right, someone still had to bite the bullet. Every situation needs a champion with the strength of vision to make the changes happen.

It is purely at the site level, not at my level, that real action occurs. I would say that in almost every case there has been an individual who has had some sort of vision. This is as well as all the other stuff that I was talking about, in terms of the business and what have you. Almost always the real starting-point is somebody at site level saying: 'Hey, there's got to be a new way of doing this!'

In a lot of cases there is a philosophical element in this individual: they simply believe that there is real value in this approach – not only commercially, but also philosophically, treating people well, involving them in their work and helping them to grow.

In most cases the individual is the plant manager – in one very different case, in a new factory-within-a-factory in the paging area down in Florida, in essence they brought this individual in on overseas rotation and said: 'Mark, we need you to set up this plant to produce this brand-new kind of pager. Here are the goals – do whatever you want to.' It was almost in that way – which is pretty empowering! He said: 'Well alright, but I saw some incredible things on my trips over in Asia, and I want to do this thing that a lot of people call High Performance Teams.' They said: 'You see these numbers that you're supposed to make? Well, that's what we care about, OK?' He wasn't even a Vice-President! And he put together a remarkable team of teams, and had such phenomenal success that that he converted the Manufacturing VP for whom he worked, whose tough, hard line was always: 'Make the numbers; that's all I really care about.' And the whole group of plants now has some good stuff going on.

So the VP took this guy, Mark, out and said: 'You're too valuable – we don't want you in manufacturing – we want you to be in charge of replicating this process throughout this entire group.'

So it can start like that. It can be an individual who has simply proved themself in some other places, through going about some remarkable turn-arounds. In some cases, the champion of the process – a term we use a lot – can be someone in the human resources area. In our Government Systems area the woman who was involved in the Enfield plant up in Connecticut, which builds rockets, had nothing to do with SMWTs – but she was brought in and basically through force of character said: 'Look, there's got to be a better way of doing this.' And she got the attention of the Senior VP of their entire business-unit there.

So a lot of times there's a commitment and vision, and some kind of internal selling. Most of the time (and I think this is the commonest in Motorola, as you'd expect for a fairly scientific place), some experiment is tried at the plant, which usually works pretty well and which is then migrated in a fairly cautious way throughout the factory – or, in the case of Automotive, is migrating from one factory to another. In a lot of cases, what's involved is taking an individual and turning the person into a kind of ambassador or missionary, to tell the people in the next factory what they've been doing.

How did we overcome the barriers?

In such a diverse organisation as Motorola there are bound to be some areas that succeed less well. As Fraser points out there are some places that teams obviously fit, there is also a base number of people (as Nishitani in IPR also discovered). Perhaps a non-intervention approach doesn't address all the organisation's needs. Other barriers exist too. Business people (though rarely the leaders) often demonstrate an antagonistic attitude towards behavioural issues – one I met recently insisted on calling them 'synchronised hand-waving'. The problem of cross-cultural teams is another well known obstacle.

I think that an organisation which couldn't accommodate a pilot might have difficulty taking off. The fewer the people – we have not quite grasped why, where, when – the less likely it is that you are going to use teams. My sense is that something like 85% of the activities are in factories where the nature of the work makes it just obvious that teams ought to work. They already are teams in a sense – maybe not very functional ones, but teams in the absolute sense of the word. We have not really grasped what it means to be empowered but not in a team. We have not really grasped what an empowered individual would look like, or what empowerment would be like, in the case of a job that involves teaming but is maybe more like case-work – for example, where I have a line manager, but no employees working for me.

I think we as a company need to do more work on smaller areas where people are not, and maybe should not be, in a team. We are doing a couple of things – we see the next big area of opportunity as directories, particularly in the public phones, because we have a potential for a huge reduction in cycle-time which, more than anywhere, is going to pay off quickly. We are getting better at it, but I think we all know that it is a cumbersome, territorial, aggravating one. It's got more to do with sociology than engineering!

We still recognise traditional functions. Very much so. In terms of breaking down functional silos, that really has not really happened here. There have been instances where it has or where we have brought, usually on a temporary basis, a particular order-cycle or issue of inventory and broken them down, but in terms of making a permanent change in the architecture, that hasn't happened. We haven't done much in that area at all – the functional silos are still there – that's probably an area where you'd have to address a lot of internal resistance. Though there is an area – one of the engineering ones – where they have made some big in-roads. It raises lots of questions, because people have chosen professions and feel their identity is being confronted – so there's some resistance there.

The other area in which there is resistance is in managerial devolution – and I'm not sure yet that all the work which has been done in management training (for example, focusing on the necessary leadership traits) has had the impact that it was expected to. In the mixture of individuals at Motorola, there are some in particular who might be much more prepared to devolve management tasks than others. There are many, though, who are still orientated towards personal control and making sure that they are part of the daily checking of every process. The tricky thing is that some of the bastions of that approach happen to be particularly successful! I think there is still more that could be done there – the training is good, and is substantial, but in some places its effects are pretty sketchy.

Management training is linked into Motorola University to a smaller degree than you might think. We have been very effective in executive education over the ten to twelve years that we've been around. We have been involved a lot in the education of corporate executives. Of the other management populations, we have a couple of powerful courses for the middle managers to top up their management skills, and we also have a number of operational management units. Beyond that, most of the management training takes place around the group in which the managers work. The reasons for this are rather vague and lost, but what has happened is that the training has been combined with that for SMWTs – it's important for everyone to have experienced the core curriculum – but it's very much up to the local manager to resource. We'd really like it if we were more involved, but there's an awful lot of investment already going on, and there's a danger that we would appear to be controlling. There's still a lot that we are involved in – for example I've been heavily involved in executive education in Europe and Asia where there's less being done by the local organisation.

There is also another internal barrier which is important. As a company we are very comfortable with things which we can get our hands around – which can be measured; we are not comfortable (we don't have the vocabulary) to deal with the 'soft' side so well. The success of quality is a good example. It was only when it became something concrete and measurable, that people began thinking: 'This means something scientific'. To some extent our empowerment initiatives suffer from the same problem. There are some people who are out to show that it doesn't make a measurable difference – I think that this is unfortunate, and it is one of my priorities to make it a little more tangible. Where it has succeeded, it's because folks have very skilfully and carefully targeted it in to the business results.

The single, most potent signal which can be sent is in terms of who is selected for each leadership position. The choices of the individuals who made up the Senior Executive were very good examples of individuals who were successful business people, but who also had an orientation to people. They were absolute leaders. I think that the selection of people is critical. The movement of folks around the world is the way that individuals can impart a flavour of empowerment to most of the organisation: how they are treated, how they are protected from people to whom they report and who are not in favour of empowerment – all of this is visible and sends incredibly powerful signals.

The intriguing thing about culture is that we know that the barriers between countries are there. It's a bigger thing than people realise. People use the right words, but I'm not sure that they really act upon them. They like to take what comes out of this building and apply it to their environment. Nobody expects it to apply everywhere – in fact Gary Tooker has said quite explicitly that we don't expect it to. The people here would like to be able to go and help people develop our material to suit their culture. A good example of that was in one of our French operations. They took a great deal of time and effort in translating not just the words but the structure to suit their particular culture, both national and organisational – the company was very structured and linear. They found a way of making it sensible for them – and it's that kind of thing which is going to have to happen. By the way, they eliminated several layers of management which was a major achievement in terms of a cultural step. That wasn't expected of them – Gary Tooker made it clear that it might be something that they would do, but it was entirely up to them.

There's one Malaysian factory which has taken a fundamentally different approach – more along the lines of a radical approach to problem solving and Associates' suggestions – in fact, they have taken things about as far as they can. They have not used the same words at all. The General Manager is a woman – which is very unusual for that culture. She has said that the word 'empowerment' is one that won't work in their culture, although she is prepared to accept the idea of teams. She is clearly conversant with what is involved and what it means, but she is sure that talking of empowerment and teams won't work. So she's doing it her way, and she's getting results. So the cultural thing is there – it's not so much a barrier, perhaps, as an issue that has to be managed. You don't get the opportunity to say that you won't get on board with empowerment. It is an initiative, along with quality and cycle-time, but there is a real understanding that it is not going to look the same in every situation.

Supporting the process of change

Confronted with a large organisation comprising many disparate and largely autonomous units, what can the corporate body do to stimulate change?

There is a recognition that there is a lot of training involved – for us at least – and I think people are taking up that challenge. There's also good use of communication channels by the office of the CEO. There are a couple of networks that pull this together, exchange ideas and so forth. There's a new approach, which I'm involved with, called the Empowerment Resource Centre, which grew out of those networking groups saying that there ought to be some single point of contact for the experiences that people are building, copies of world-wide training courses, publications and so on. People will thus be able to find out if someone has done something particular in one area or another. It is a source, but it isn't an influencer itself – it's centralised, but it needs to be decentralised as much as possible. One of the things that Motorola has done fairly well in a couple of areas (some key functions in software, advanced manufacturing and to some extent engineering) is to set up a designated council – individuals with an interest, often high-level managers – who have come together and who are THE corporate manufacturing council, or whatever. Those task forces have often become a kind of nerve-centre for their specialisation. Often they come to Motorola University and say: 'Can you do a programme on ...?' Cycle-time reduction is one such programme that has been tremendously successful.

INTERVIEW 5.5 SMWTS – A JOINT MANAGEMENT UNION INITIATIVE

George Pfeil and Laurie Price, Ford Romeo Engine Plant, Detroit

The early days

A constant source of debate is whether it is possible to create self-managing work teams in an environment that is anything other than a green-field site. Very few cases are green-fields. A large number though might be called 'brown-fields' as was Ford's Romeo plant.

Originally this was the Romeo Tractor Plant. It assembled tractor components until about 1985, when the decision was made to close it down. We had a workforce of UAW employees who were going to be to be without jobs eventually. At about the same time, the company was looking at engines for the future. One of the alternatives was a Nissan engine – it was the first time in the company's history that they had really seriously considered putting a competitor's engine in a Ford vehicle. The engine guys said, 'Wait a minute. We would like an opportunity to be considered for this, too.' So Ford said, 'Fine, but you have to meet all the quality, performance, cost, etc., indicators, that Nissan is able to deliver'. So the engine team convinced Ford to put the business with their division, and Romeo was the successful site identified. Part of the going-in condition was that we would have a modern operating agreement, and that we would have a team concept. Whatever they meant eight years ago, nobody really knew!

That was, I believe, Donald Peterson's stipulation. He was Chairman of the Board at the time. 'Team concept' was a big phrase about eight or ten years ago, and this was the experiment.

They went out and got our Plant Manager, George Pfeil. George grew up in a very successful traditional system, never liked it and had a real vision of what it would mean to empower people: he knew it was the right way of doing business. He had the opportunity to do something different, and the UAW leadership also shared that vision.

Our current Chairman, Dave Weston, would say that his vision is that all our employees will run this plant one day. It is not going to happen in our lifetime, but his vision is that if you empower people enough, they will rise to the occasion.

When the union and management got together at the first meeting, the UAW expected management to hand them the three-ring binder and say, 'OK, this is what you have agreed to'; but when they got into the room it quickly became apparent that they did not know what 'team concept' was. No-one knew how they were going to run or what they were going to do, and that was a good place to start.

They ended up working for months and months piecing together a vision statement. The mission and operating philosophy is :

'The purpose of the Romeo Engine Plant is to produce the highest quality production engines in the world that meet all of our customers' requirements at a cost lower than the competition and to develop teams of employees who are the best engine builders in the world.'

If you are going to develop teams of individuals who are the best engine builders in the world, then you have got to train people. We had a workforce of tractor employees. Tractors were built in eighteen-minute cycles then. Nowadays the jobs are on eighteen-second cycles; so it is drastically different work.

The UAW and management team worked very closely to develop this structure. I believe the first agreement was two pages long. There was a lot of trust built in, and there was a lot of time spent building the mission and operating philosophy. It is shared with every hourly, salaried employee whom we transfer in or whom we hire, and we go back to it whenever things get out of synch.

Elements of success

The close relationship between management and union, and the openness that experimenting provoked meant that both groups were prepared to admit their faults. Together with the time spent codeveloping designs, the employees were therefore able to develop a lot of ownership for the new practices and products.

There are three areas we can talk about:

- the products;
- the process;
- the people.

Our product is a 4.6 litre modular engine and we are now building both the two-valve and the four-valve. We had a really good working relationship with the engineers who were out here daily, and teams of salaried and hourly employees. The blueprints were out and they were discussing and making changes. So this engine was planned with lots of manufacturing input, and our success is because of that really strong relationship with the planning engineers.

The organisational structure

Our structure is very different from a traditional plant. In a traditional plant you have a centralised engineering organisation. At Romeo, our engineers are on the team, so we have teams of salaried and hourly employees around the five major components: machine heads and blocks, cylinder heads and blocks, crank shafts, cam shafts and piston rods. On those teams are engineers who do all the future and current programme work. We have skilled trades, electricians, whatever you might need on that team, and in the numbers that you need.

In traditional plants, skilled trades are also centralised into a maintenance group. We have a very small central maintenance group which takes care of the building, but the machines themselves belong to the teams and are maintained by the same people. So the team should have all the resources it needs to make productivity improvements, and we have absolutely no supervisors on the plant floor. That is the major difference between Romeo and other traditional structures.

People are not rewarded in the same way. Our salaried employees are paid on salaried guidelines, and the hourly employees are UAW represented, so they are paid per contract. We have co-ordinators who are the team facilitators, the hourly leaders of the group. Those folks are selected through an assessment process, and we have co-ordinators for production. So you might have three or four co-ordinators on one team: one will be the production co-ordinator, then you will have an electrical co-ordinator, and you might have some other skilled trades co-ordinators too.

The team co-ordinators are paid 50 cents more than the skilled trades or production. Co-ordinators are selected by assessment. The typical Romeo team composition has a team manager. The team manager is what, in traditional plants, is a superintendent responsible for production. At Romeo, most of our team managers are engineering graduates – or else they have got tremendous experience in a plant, and they might as well be graduates on the basis of their experience. The team managers wear many hats: they handle engineering, maintenance, quality and production. They have many of the functions which in other plants are centralised. In future programmes, on the salaried side they will have a team leader, who is a lead engineer, several engineers and then some type of administrative assistant who keeps track of the money they spend as a separate cost-centre. This administrative assistant will do a lot with the data which is available, to help them analyse and see where they are going.

Teams range in size depending on the area. Some of the smaller areas may have sixteen to twenty hourly people per shift on the team. The salaried structure is much smaller: maybe you will have five salaried employees on that team. Headcount-wise we are very lean; we have under 200 salaried employees at this location, and about 810 hourly-paid.

Our assembly area is organised differently. In the assembly area, teams of up to fifty people are organised around different parts of the line. So it is a lot bigger, and things are a lot more difficult because of that. The assembly area is labour-intensive, while in the machine area you might have one operator for three or four operations. These teams need to have a weekly team-meeting where they do brainstorming. We also have, about 120 small problem-solving groups. These are groups of employees who have volunteered to get together to solve specific problems. Mostly they are management-directed problems. Those teams might include people other than in their specific area if they need people from other areas, using their expertise to resolve the issues. Small problem-solving groups are the most effective. The teams in themselves are sometimes too big, and not everybody is going to be effective.

One of the other requirements of the team-members is that they rotate their jobs. Everyone on the team needs to know all the jobs on it: in the short-term maybe you lose some quality, but in the long-term people can brainstorm better if they know the whole area.

So there are three styles of team operating simultaneously: 1. The product line teams – working as a self-managed unit in machining with all skills represented. 2. The assembly line teams each taking a part of the line for one component, and also self-managing. 3. Problem-solving teams akin to quality circles.

Training

Again, training features highly in the process of change at Ford, initially through awareness raising and then a wide range of business skills – generally taught by line managers. A frequent concern expressed by senior managers is the time off-line spent in training. The investment is not just in trainers and facilities, but if your commitment stops when it gets to this point you have to ask just how serious you are!

Before we launched this plant, we did an enormous amount of training. The training was basically three types:

- a lot of hand-holding;
- team-building type activities;
- courses to get people to 'buy in'!

One of the classes, called 'Vision in team concept', that shows our workforce what the Japanese are doing and how they are doing; helping people to understand that if we are going to compete in a global market, then we have got to get competitive. We share stories about some of the companies that have launched teams successfully, for instance Harley Davidson. So, the class is focused on giving people a reason for wanting to change the way they are doing things, and making sure that people understand that the UAW, Ford and the US Government need to work together to be productive, in the way that the Japanese work together, rather than working against each other. The enemy is not the company, the enemy is not the UAW, not Chrysler, and not GL: we are our own enemies, and we have got to work together. That is one of the classes that builds a foundation by giving people information which makes them want to change their behaviour.

There are about 160 hours of mandatory training – business-related classes with a team of hourly and salaried employees which is going to run a business.

They need a lot of training and information. 'Productivity 101' is a ten-hour class which our Plant Manager teaches. 'Finance 101' is a ten-hour class which our Finance Manager teaches. 'Quality 101' is taught by the Romeo Tractor Quality Manager. Then there are a lot of business-related classes on interpersonal skills. It is one thing to empower people, but you have also got to bring their skills up to level so that they can work effectively.

Those were the first four classes. Before we started building our plant, we were trained for four hours a day, and then we would have on-the-job training for four hours a day. The teams would go through training together, and then they would go out on the floor and do other things together. Our first job was in June 1990, and since that time we have run production all day, so what we do now is train from 2.30 to 4.30. So, for instance, the finance class will take five days. Training is important at Romeo, and everybody is expected to attend a training class. The only way you can be excused from it is with the Plant Manager's permission. We have done over 220,000 hours of training since we started, and we do about 20,000 to 22,000 hours of training every year.

We will have three or five different training classes a week. Those classes are filled with people between 2.30 to 4.30. Not every employee in the plant is in class – we have to run the plant production. We did forty-five technical training classes last year, and they were predominantly classes to meet the needs of hourly employees, as identified by the teams throughout the year. Plant production is not round-the-clock, we have two shifts normally, and three shifts on a couple of operations. What we do is, if a day-shift employee is scheduled for training, we bring in the afternoon shift early to cover, and if the afternoon shift is training, you have the other folks stay. We do coverage for each other.

The salaried jobs do not rotate. The hourly jobs, where you are working on different machines, those are the sort of jobs that rotate.

We do have an 'us and them' attitude between 'hourly' and 'salaried', but the way we look at it is that we all work for the operator. The skilled trades-people work for their operator. The team leader, the engineers, we work for that production operator. The reason why we work for the operator is that he or she is the person who is putting the product out, and so all our jobs are to support him or her in that. So that is the customer. Our maintenance guys, they work for the operator too. That is kind of turning things around. In traditional plants, skilled trades tend to rule.

The role of managers in developing individuals

The training philosophy at Romeo is that our managers and UAW take an active role as instructors. Instead of going out and getting consultants and vendors to teach our training, we decided that our Romeo management team would teach the training. It turned out very well, and it keeps management in contact with the workforce on a name-basis. People will say what is on their mind. It is a great information source. It helps us to live with this concept on a daily basis. You really have to watch what you say and how you say it, and check yourself: 'Is that in support of our mission team concept? Are these actions and behaviours? How are they going to be interpreted?', and so on. It is a tremendous learning process for both the instructors and the employees.

Other classes included 'Engine Functions'. Where everybody tears down and builds up an engine. You need to know not only the function of each component part which you are working on, but also what comes before and after it. Then there are courses on UAW history, safety classes, team-oriented problem-solving, and so on. All salaried and all hourly employees do this. With the training schedule being two hours a day, it can take six months to get through all the training.

We had a number of employees whose benefits were unfortunately running out, and who had to go to other plants. They had to leave because the decision for this to be an engine plant hadn't yet been made, so they had no idea. They elected to go to other plants to protect themselves. In a couple of months, the decision to make this an engine plant came forward, and those folks were not really happy about having moved their families to other parts of the country. Those folks – we term them 'return-homers' – have had the right to come back to Romeo, and we have worked through 200 people who have come back, and only have thirty-five or so more to go. They left a traditional tractor plant; they are coming back to the Romeo engine plant. They are somewhat bitter about what happened, about the fact that the decision was not made in time for them to avoid uprooting their families. They are coming back to a brand-new environment, and they are not prepared for it, they do not understand it and, unfortunately, the day they come back they are either being trained or learning on the floor. They are not getting 160 hours of training up-front, so they get it as time goes on. Sometimes it takes a while, and that can be disruptive because you have got an influx of new people who do not buy-in yet and have not had the chance to get there in their own minds.

But it is really interesting – whenever we have a down-week, or maybe our customers do not need our engines and they are going down, we try to have intensive training during that week. We can knock out an enormous amount of training by running classes all day long. Our managers will be involved in that. And that is nice, because we get a lot of people who just speak right out about what is bothering them, and many issues boil up. By answering the questions effectively, and by dealing with the issues head-on, the 80% or 90% who are hard workers hear what they need to hear to make them get on the right side of the fence. With people who are not going to get on the fence, there is nothing you can say anyway. We have been lucky enough to have a couple of those weeks where we can do a lot of intensive training and get a lot of good discussions going.

Training is one of those things that a lot of people think is easy, but when they stand up and try to do it, they realise that it is a skill in its own right. It is also something that a lot of managers do not see as their responsibility and they are uncomfortable doing. So the transition can be a tough one to make.

I have only been here for two years, so I am telling you what I have been told about what happened. Some managers, if not all of them, who designed and taught classes went on a three-day training-the-trainer course, which focused on how to teach adults, and how to design and deliver information in a way that adults will accept. Every manager had an opportunity to go on that training course. You have got lots of people who maybe never went to college, or who have never sat in a training class – and a lot of our UAW people, probably previous to this training, were not involved in a lot of training. You have to overcome their fears.

Many of the classes were developed by the managers. Our Plant Manager has just developed 'Productivity 201', which he has been piloting with the Steering Committee.

The Steering Committee is a UAW and management team which meets every week. It is very open and honest, and its role is to help the plant to move forward and progress in this team concept: to help plant and teams to be more productive. Any new training, not technical necessarily, but team-concept, vision, that type of training, gets piloted with that group.

One of the new training classes they are working on, where the UAW is taking the lead, is called 'The Need for Change'. It is an updating of the vision and team-concept, of the philosophies, the reasons why we did what we did five or seven years ago, and continuing that education process. UAW knows what it takes to be competitive, just as much as the company knows it. It wants its membership to do what is needed to be successful.

We make engines, and sometimes that becomes the sole focus. We have had a lot of problems, but it was always a rule from Day 1 that there is no excuse for missing a training class. No manager can be excused, no salaried employee, no hourly employee. It is the team manager's and team co-ordinator's job to make arrangements for coverage so that a person can go to the training class. We have a State of the Plant meeting every quarter, and our Plant Manager, the UAW chairperson, and each of the managers, talk about plant performance and up-coming events, our schedules, new programmes, etc. One of the topics recently was 'What was our last year's training?' It is one of the performance indicators, on which we regularly inform the whole workforce. He also said, 'Hey, if you guys need some training, if there is something you need, then please let us know so that we can get you the resources you need'. This is just a restatement of the policy, but sometimes people need to be reminded.

There are all kinds of training classes you can take other than the core ones, and we are developing the second set of core training.

So we are progressively building up. A lot of the training classes have changed, because there are different people in the room with different sets of information. When you get a room of brand-new people to the plant, you have to approach it a little bit differently. When you have a bunch of 'veterans' who accept team-concepts and know where you are going, then the class can take on a different focus.

At the end of every class there is a survey called 'Is this information useful?' That can give feedback to the instructor. Some of the classes are probably not as effective as we would like them to be, and maybe it is because some of the instructors are talking over the heads of the employees, because their team is not doing all the things which they are supposed to be doing. If you talk about all these wonderful things like quality, measurement, or whatever and then you don't go back to your team, or you don't have a team that is really doing that, then it is almost worse to talk about it. So it depends on the team. I know that the Steering Committee has sat in on some training, and I do not know if that was effective or not. It probably was more effective when everyone was going through it at the same time – when you are in a peer-launch – because you have more control. People are all in the same boat. The training now is all good information, but you have gathered together salaried and hourly employees from every different function, so it is bound to be more effective for some than others.

We also have surveys which ask the teams in general whether the training is effective. We do not measure each of the classes. The way it is measured is if we continue to be productive or if our quality results are really good. We do not have a direct measurement.

Other consequences

Even today there are countless hidden perks that create a divide or maintain a status gap between groups of employees. Despite countless books and case studies firms are generally very reluctant to do away with these symbols. Although 'mingling' isn't perfect afterwards, there's no justification for retaining many of these. Retaining these symbols indicates that other attitudes haven't changed.

> Romeo did away with a lot of the traditional perks and distinctions between salaried and hourly employees. We do not have assigned parking. That is a big deal in a lot of places: the parking spots are up-front. First-come first-served, hourly or salaried. We do not have a management dining room – we all eat the same food in the same cafeteria. Our salaried and hourly employees share the same team facilities. About 95% of the workforce wears our plant work-attire, our uniform. I have mine on today. About 95% of the workforce wears some, and we allot sets of pants and shirts and a couple of jackets so you cannot tell an hourly from a salaried employee. Nobody here wears neck-ties.
>
> It makes for some interesting meetings, when your vendors do not know whether they are talking to the plant manager or to the operator! There was a top Ford official out here early in the launch, and one of the teams did a presentation to him. He said, 'Well, that's all well and good', and he had about twenty questions, like Vice-Presidents do, and the team answered his questions satisfactorily. He then said: 'Well, that was a good presentation and I'm pretty impressed, but I would like to talk to some of the hourly employees'. They looked straight at him and said, 'Sir, we *are* the hourly employees'.
>
> Groups who come for tours here are usually hosted by both UAW and our Chairman. A team will do a presentation about the plant. We host about 150

tours a year. Lots of groups are coming in specifically for 'team concepts'. We almost always make it a team presentation. This is not a management programme, this is a total buy-in. The managers have not done it all, or seen it all in this environment. This environment is so challenging – the way you behave, what is acceptable, is totally different from what these guys are used to.

Changes for managers

It is a learning period, and our managers are growing all the time. They are changing the way they talk with, and give assignments to, their salaried employees. They really listen to the hourly workforce. If an hourly employee comes up – and they encourage people to come up with solutions – with a good idea then they will say, 'Let's try it'. The engineers might say, 'We can't. It won't work', and they will say, 'Try it'. Sometimes we do things that maybe are not the best and do not make the most sense, but if the hourly workers bubble up with the idea, you have got to give it a try. You have got to encourage them to keep coming up with ideas. That is part of the small problem-solving teams, and that is something that George has worked very hard on, to get his managers to give their support. Managers have got to learn how to become facilitators, instead of the 'I'm the boss, do as I say' attitude. It is a great learning process.

While they are training, there is a leadership behaviour survey going on. This has been developed outside Romeo. It puts down sixteen expectations: these are things like 'I encourage people to come up with new ideas'; 'I create an environment which empowers people'. Sixteen questions which employees fill out on their managers to give them feedback on whether or not they are empowering their workforce. This survey has been tied to performance reviews, and managers are expected to review the results with their teams, brainstorm, and come up with an action plan on how they are going to address some of the important issues. They review it with their boss, and talk about the process. So it is an open process where managers examine their leadership behaviours and where the top of the house is saying, 'These are the leadership behaviours we need to display in order to empower our employees, so that we can continue to grow and continue to hold our place in global competition, or move up a place.' Those performance reviews are linked to a manager's pay. We have a merit plan which is based on performance. There are also performance-based bonuses.

Skills enrichment

While time off-the-job for training is expensive to the company, so course fees, travel and expenses can prohibit people from seeking new training for themselves. To help address this the plant provides resources and space so that the individuals have only to provide themselves and their time.

In the middle of the plant there is a Skills Enrichment Centre, where people can get their high-school grades. Because we have assessments for people to become co-ordinators and machine operators, and to do those jobs they have to have a certain level of maths skills, etc. So people have to take it out of their own time to get their skills up to the level to compete with those higher-paid jobs. We have got some incredibly intelligent, capable and motivated employees in our hourly workforce who have come up with all kinds of great solutions.

A lot of these folks have businesses they run successfully on the outside. They run farms, orchards, construction companies, they have leadership positions in their communities, churches and schools. They did all this for years outside of Ford, and then they would come inside these four walls and someone would say, 'OK, leave your brain at the door and don't ask any questions; just do this and that'. Now we have an environment which encourages these people to take these skills which they use outside work and employ them inside. Many people are fired up, but you are still going to have some people who just want to do their work and go home. A lot of hourly employees now take home a lot of stress: they do not walk out until things are covered and done. When you do not have supervisors on the floor, then these guys run their own areas.

For the hiring of hourly employees, we have been bringing back return-homers. Anyone who was a former tractor employee has the right to come back here. When we exhaust that, we shall be doing some type of best-in-class hiring. It is something that our UAW here and our management team will agree on. There will be corporate requirements, too. We will try to bring in people who want to work in this type of environment and who have some basic skill-levels. They will incorporate the UAW guidelines who will be giving us a lot of help.

Control and discipline

So does this team-control really work? The biggest fear of newcomers to SMWTs is that what will ensue is chaos.

Personally, I do not think we have a lot of problems. In every workforce, salaried and hourly, you have your 5% element, and we tend to focus on the 5%. We are probably not as rigid as other plants for the following reasons:

1 We do not need to be.
2 We try to bend over backwards to get people to change, to give them the opportunity to, before we slap them down.

Now that we are five or six years into it, we know who is our deviant element and we deal with them accordingly. By the way, their co-workers want us to deal with them more severely than we actually do. When you have got hard-working, good employees out there, they cannot stand it and do not. They have a hard time with the people who are not contributing.

The management team and the UAW hoped that the work teams would exert more peer-pressure on each other. I think we overestimated. We do not have policemen. We are not staffed, and our salaried head-count is too lean. We do not have people out there acting like foremen and supervisors – we are not staffed that way. When they do act in that way, the work teams do not like it. The hope was that the teams would police themselves. That might happen to some extent, but it might have been a tall expectation. Salaried employees, salaried workforces, do not police themselves, so can you expect an hourly workforce to do so? If you focus on the 5%, and on what you have to do to keep them in line, you end up damaging the environment for the other 95%, so we try to focus on the needs of the 95% in the environment, and work out the bad eggs as we go.

I do not think it is a big problem, I just think that for some people discipline is the only thing they will react to. It is a very small population which does not buy into the team concept, and you are always going to have that element in every workforce.

The team manager administers the discipline. This was one of the early things we struggled with when everybody was sitting in rooms, holding hands, talking about team concept, but it is a different thing when you get out there and you start producing products and you have to count on people to show up. Team concept is a little more difficult. I think many of our managers struggled with it because we had a lot of really young, inexperienced managers who did not come from a manufacturing environment, perhaps they had a college degree, and had then grown up in the Romeo system – it is really hard for these people to make the transition between: 'OK, I'm a teamee, I'm supposed to act a certain way   for 95% of the people who are going to respond to the team'; and: 'How can I discipline someone?' My philosophy is that if someone does not buy into the team concept, and is not supporting it, then they are destroying it. They need to be disciplined.

Team concept does not mean anarchy. It is a hard transition to make between acting as a teamee and doing things that are counterproductive to the team. We have found that if you do not address the performance issues, the bad people are sometimes more vocal. It is interesting that sometimes, in a training class, the yahoos will be the vocal ones and you will think the whole room is that way. You then go out and have coffee in the break- sessions, and you work your way into a couple of groups and ask questions. You then discover that there are a lot of people who disagree with that person, but they will not speak up. You say, 'What do you think about what Jack is saying?' and they say, 'I disagree with him. He's an idiot', and I say, 'You really have an interesting perspective on this. Would you speak up when we get back in there?' Sometimes they will. I think our workforce expects management to take on the bad eggs and, if we do not, then those who are on the fence can jump up on the wrong side.

We are learning every day. It is a struggle. There is no cook-book. In terms of the management culture, we hired an awful lot of people, started to train them in this new culture, and a lot of them had never been managers in traditional environments, so it has been easier than trying to change a lot of war-horses. You find that the old war-horses, when the pressure is on, revert back to things they did before. You fight that all the time. With the hourly workforce, it is all a bit different. Here we have got an average of twenty-five years' service in the traditional culture. So this is a real cultural change for them, particularly among the tradesmen. We continually work at that on a daily basis. Most of our employees like the concept and would not want to change. Everybody is one of the team. There is a small percentage out there who do not like it or feel comfortable with it, for whatever reason. It is a constant thing that we have to deal with.

Responsibility and accountability

The other thing is that empowerment is a new concept to them, they really do not understand yet how much power they do have, if they choose to use it. We are further ahead today than we were a couple of years ago, but there is still a lot more that could happen.

The issue of accountability is important, and I assume that this is true of most companies. If an hourly person in a traditional organisation does something on his own and makes a mistake, he is usually disciplined for it. Here, we are telling them, 'Go ahead. You are empowered to make decisions. You will not be right 100% of the time and, if you are not, that's OK. We will accept that.' That is a very hard thing for them to accept, because they believe that if they do make a wrong decision, we are going to come back on them. We have not done that here. I do not know of any case since I have been here where we have disciplined an employee for honestly trying to do something to improve the operation and failing. Again, changing that culture is a laborious process and something you continually have to reinforce, but you cannot be punitive when people do take responsibility. You just cannot, because then they will just sit back and freeze: they will not do it any more.

It's frustrating that you cannot describe this process effectively. You have almost got to be in it permanently, and there is not a good cook-book to handle all the issues which come up! It is something you have got to work at every day. This is a much more difficult thing to manage than it is in a traditional plant.

Relationship with the union

In the union environment it is crucial to get the union committed by the entrance process. You have to establish a level of trust between the unions and management which is above the level normally found. There has got to be integrity between the two. There has got to be an open dialogue constantly. That is not to say that management is shirking any of its responsibilities nor have we shirked any of ours. We have the same objectives in this plant as in all the other plants. We have the same past. We have the same standards as the others. We are not treated any differently outside these four walls.

Corporate influences

An important aspect of implementing change of this kind is one of interference from the corporate centre. It is very easy for company-wide changes to be introduced that undermine the empowerment initiative.

The company has made no changes in its procedures, policies or practices, because these problems that we face are not special to us. There are two contracts: the national contract, which is negotiated at Headquarters and which controls wages and all that; and the local agreement, which focuses on things within the plant, for example, moving people from one department to another. I have no say in any reward system for my staff.

There is a case in point. We have two teams out there. We have a team called the Manufacturers of Connecting Rods, who are extremely efficient – in fact, we do not have any sour reports on them. They run at an efficiency level anywhere from 80 to 95%. They are always on, or ahead of, schedule in terms of parts produced. The system is that if they get ahead of schedule, then you save money, so what do you do with them? You lay these people off for a week, or whatever. Obviously, that penalises them financially.

That is what the company would tell us to do. Now, compare that to another department at the plant where, for a whole lot of reasons, we are only able to get 50% efficiency, and which runs ten hours a day, six days a week. You have got one set of machinists who are efficient and another, inefficient operation.

As far as being able to improve attendance, it is almost impossible. For people who are perfect attendees, we give them a T-shirt or something. That compares with the Toyota system, though they have much better direct incentives, behavioural incentives, where six or seven names of good attendees are pulled out of a hat and they drive away in a new Toyota. That is a pretty good incentive, to come to work every day!

The company and the UAW have pretty good incentives for continuing education. Since we started, we have probably spent $250,000 in terms of providing things. In addition to that, there are some financial incentives to continue education through the UAW and via the corporate route. We have probably got the largest apprenticeship programme going. So, from an educational point of view, the company is progressive. The plant here, in particular, is.

For the most part, for this plant we do a pretty good job. The other thing we have going is that we have classes in, reading, writing, arithmetic, for those who may not have completed school, taken by high-school teachers from the local school systems. We have a full-time maths teacher, a full-time English teacher, and a computer person. If you are going to college, for example, as some of these guys are, you need some private tuition. These people will do that as well, at no charge, so there is a lot of encouragement to people, if they choose, to learn.

After some time, there is still a feeling in many organisations that people are not really making as much use as they could of the power that they have got. This is not a problem felt by the Steering Group at Romeo too.

One of the things we continually tell them is that we have got problems for whatever reasons. Supplier problems – there are materials coming in that are not needed yet, for instance. Our feeling is that an operator has every right to call the supplier, bring him in and talk to him about the issue. Traditionally, the operator would go to the foreman, or the team manager and say, 'I had a problem with such and such', and in a traditional organisation that management person would pick up the phone and handle it from there.

In this organisation, we tell the operator, 'We have got one team manager and he cannot handle every problem that everybody has got out there, so you have to take some of the responsibility for that yourself. You have got to get hold of the supplier and bring him in here. Here is his number – go call him.'

Barriers to management commitment

In a lot of organisations which are trying to implement SMWTs one of the barriers that managers feel is that their career structures are being threatened because they are no longer going to be comparable with a manager of another plant. That then leads to their being less committed, and creates barriers.

> Let me say this: in my opinion, the reason that you do not get management committed to team structures is that they are a big risk. George took a hell of a risk here. The measurables are all the same, and so you are going to go to virgin territory and still be held accountable for all the things that you would do in a traditional organisation. You can't be assured that you are going to get the results you need to be successful. I do not think that most companies have managers who are really willing to take the career risk to do this.
>
> I look at it from my point of view, quite honestly. I think this is the right way to do things. I have worked thirty-three years. They are not going to be promoting me to Vice-President any day soon, so I do not have that concern. At Laurie's age it is a different ball game. George is a unique person in that he has decided that he wants to give this a shot. I would, however, venture a guess that most managers coming into the system, who still have a way to go, are reluctant to put their careers on the line to try this.
>
> I am not saying this is wrong, but management focuses on the objectives. In the case of engine science, there are so many engines, quality level, cost considerations, and all the same things. Quite honestly, they will support the culture that's going to get the best results. I think that Ford's movement towards teams was due to the fact that the management used it as a way of reducing the wage-bill! You don't need foremen, you don't need as many people. The fact is that the right culture is the culture we want to support. That, to me, was a secondary consideration. I think the focus primarily is on what is going to give you results. I am not saying that is bad, but if Romeo were so successful that we could blow all the other plants away in terms of all the measurables, then everybody would probably say, 'Hey, that's probably the environment we need, but we are one of six plants'.

A better test than any straight performance record is a comparison, against similar plants in the same organisation. With five other facilities in the same group as Romeo comparison should be easy.

> At the end of the year we had the best quality engine in the Ford Motor Co. There is only one competitor who is close to us, and we debate back and forth whether we are better than them. Other than that, there is no other engine in this class that comes close to us quality-wise. We ended last year on budget, in fact we were about $20,000 better than budget. We have the lowest inventory. We have the lowest salary head-count. I would say that this plant stands, hourly-wise, best in class levels. We have approximately 800 hourly folks and

some 100 salaried folks. In a traditional engine plant, the salaried head-count would be more, in terms of 100 additional people, than an hourly head-count, and they would probably have 200 or 300 more hourly workers. For example, we do not have any inspectors at our plant, nor many material handling-type assignments, because of the way that it was laid out originally.

I think, by most standards, that we are better than the others. There are two other new programmes coming on-stream, not necessarily new plants. As far as Romeo is concerned, we will have a better competitor once Cleveland is up and running, and we will be able to compare Cleveland/Romeo and Canada/Romeo. I would say right now that we are equal to or better than most plants.

One thing that I can state with certainty: every employee at this plant, however salaried, is absolutely dedicated. Every station we have out there has a whole lot of equipment on the line, and if, for any reason, they feel that the machine is not effective, they can stop it to adjust it. We have never, since we opened this plant, been punitive about anybody doing that.

The assembly line snakes through the plant, so our teams are geographic. Section A is the area, for example, where the block and the crank come together. Section B is where the piston and rods are built in. The people within Section A who assemble the blocks or the frame will rotate within that team. Job to job. That is where the rotation starts. In Section B they rotate, etc. So they do not move with the product, because of the proliferation of our engines, again based on how successfully we work.

There is no new plan in this plant, just the original plan of 535,000 engines with eight engine codes. In 1996 we are going to handle three or four basic engines. For us to handle that level of complexity on a small volume, for example the Mustang engine that we are going to produce here in 1996, we are going to be building what we call an inter-assembly line, which is an assembly line where we will assemble the block and the crank and then we will pull it off and put it on the next line, where they will build upon that. That line will probably be manned by two employees, and as it moves they will move with the engine; so that they build the complete thing – a bit like the Harley Davidson engine-line.

Social Issues

The demographics of the workplace are changing. With diversity comes a benefit of different cultural approaches. The down-side is the varied educational attainment and attitudinal problems. Most companies implementing SMWTs have at the same time provided a host of awareness raising activities to deal with these issues.

We have done a lot of training in the awareness of sexual harassment, for salaried and hourly workers. Our Chairman visited the plant and commented on how employees need to treat each other with respect, and how we need to be more aware of people's sensitivities. We have done a lot of work to communicate this to the workforce, both hourly and salaried. I do not think we really have any more problems than other plants, perhaps even less. We talked before about the uniforms: it breaks down a lot of walls, when everybody is dressed the same.

What also works is your approach to the situation. When you get what could be a sexual harassment claim, a complaint, if you act quickly and investigate it, I would say that more than half – maybe 75% of the time – it is due to misunderstanding, it is an awareness issue and, if you bring the person in, and you talk about it, and you enlighten them, then they will never have the problem again. They can walk out of the room without it damaging their life.

In some plants, maybe in the interim, we may jump the gun and everything turns into a major issue because people are so afraid that it's going on their reference. But if you can get the parties in the room together, find out what is going on, resolve it and get feedback, they can go back and work together, and it does not become job-threatening. In order to do that, however, we have to have people who will come forward early in the process and not wait until it gets way out of hand. And when they do come forward, we have to deal with them in a way that is confidential so that they feel they have been treated fairly and that we can resolve the issue quickly.

As it relates to teams, I do not see an impact at all. If anything, we have team managers, white males or females, black males or females. I do not see it as an issue here. I do not think the teams make a difference one way or another. I do think that in the tone of the plant we have a very firm policy when these issues come up. We have not had that many really job- threatening situations.

INTERVIEW 5.6 INTRODUCING SMWTs
Steven W Scarbury and Leslie Watkins, GTE Directories, Des Plaines, Illinois

As with most of our interviews, the decision to implement SMWTs at GTE was not an overnight change but the result of slow steady evolution. As elsewhere, some parts of their operation are further ahead than others.

You do not have to wait until you are team-based to institute good ideas. By going to teams, you are letting everybody know that their ideas count, that we value them, that we want to use all their knowledge and abilities. As you came in you heard me explaining to one of our people: 'You don't have to be declared a "team". Let us know now and we can start making changes.'

Our involvement with SMWTs goes back to June or July 1993. Our Vice-President of Printing, David Rawles, had just come over from the human resources side, where he was dealing with Motorola, Texas Instruments, and a university down in North Texas which had a Self-Managed Working Congress, where a whole group of people had got together. So he was very keen on the idea of SMWTs. He came over to Printing and said, 'Well, let's try it in Printing.' We had never used the term 'self-direction' but I can now see that a lot of the introductory management courses we have been giving our people over the last ten years or so were a natural progression towards self-direction, self-management, and empowerment.

Here in this facility we have a team that started off around 1 December. In each of the other areas which report to this particular Vice-President, we agreed to have at least one team up and running by last December, and an additional one to two teams starting some time in 1994. We are not going across the board throughout the entire plant saying, 'Now we are all going self-direction.' We realise that some training has to go on, and rather than hit an obstacle here and there, we want to start small with a few successes and build on that.

Last January, before the decision was taken for Printing, I decided to put my group on self-management – I called them into a meeting one day and said that we were going to change the management of the group a little bit. 'Instead of me being the boss on a day-to-day basis, taking care of things, you all handle it in this office. Person A will be the lead person; if you have a problem, see them first, but basically you all will handle everything. If you have a major problem, or something that is beyond the scope of what you'd normally handle here, then come and get me.' So I started them by setting down that guideline, not knowing that this was what was going to be happening.

There are two of us at this facility on what we call the Co-ordinating Council for Self-Managed Teams, at which a representative or two from every area reports to our Vice-President. We try to glean as much information as possible about Self-Managed Team Work through seminars, through readings, so that we can help disperse this out to each of the areas – 'Here is what we have tried. This worked. We tried this, and it didn't' – and try to share the information across the board, to make it successful for everybody.

We are very much in our infancy. We contacted Motorola after we came back from our Dallas trip and they graciously gave us tours; they put on a whole-day programme for us about the evolution which they have undergone over there. We are anxious to be able to share information back and forth as we go. We are also building an infrastructure in GTE to try to establish at the same time: 'Don't do this' or 'This really works'.

In this facility we have 130 people. In all GTE Directories we are talking about 5,000. Basically, it is the printing and distribution areas that we are talking about to start with. In the other areas of the Directory company the intent is to move to self-management, but we are holding that off because of other technology advances that we are installing right now; we felt it was just too much to try to make all these changes at once.

Although the two are seen as distinct initiatives the GTE teams recognise the links between them. They make the point, which is true of so many, that quality was seen as a management issue. SMTW helps involve employees and so addresses quality issues. Before implementing substantial change self-assessment in the form of an employee opinion survey was carried out.

I joined in 1987 when the quality process was really just beginning. We like to think that it is totally separate, but there are integral facets, because a quality process has no end. It starts and we follow it, regardless of any other programmes or processes that we follow. Everything we do is based upon the quality product going out of the door. Everything we do is done with quality in mind.

Every October is Quality Month, and that is when we really get the employees focusing in on what you are doing, the different aspects of the job, how your performance affects the overall quality of the product, and what you can do – what we as the company can do – further to enhance the quality of the job or of the product. So it's not two separate functions, it is all wrapped up in one neat little package with Quality as the foundation.

With that in mind, here especially, when we first started stressing quality, it was, from the management stand-point, 'How can we improve quality?'. We would sit in our offices. We would see if this would help, and if that would help, and we would go out there and say, 'Do this, do that'. It is not necessarily what is going to get us there. Somewhere along the line, the self-managing concept came along. People said, 'Let's empower, let's utilise'. We had an employee opinion survey in which people were saying, 'We don't get the chance to help in the decision-making'. It was a natural progression. As managers, we have done everything as far as we think we can, but there is still something lacking. We are now empowering the employees to make the decisions, to effect change. We feel it has pushed us that much further down the long road.

We are trying it out in small chunks first. I am not sure we can say what sort of things have helped those areas to make it happen yet.

The first step is the training, both our internal classes and the ones taught by instructors from Dallas. Group seminars further enhance their knowledge of the process: how it works in other places, in other types of businesses; how we can take the bits and pieces that have worked for everyone else, adapt them to what we do here, and take the best from all the programmes and hopefully come up with something that is going to work for us. In a sense, we are unique here in that we do things which are not necessarily commonplace in other industries.

The key is empowerment. There is no-one who knows better how to do a job than the person who does it on a daily basis. So we would often ask them for input, they would make the input. It is like dropping a suggestion in the suggestion box. You put it in and you wait, and you wait, and you wait, and you wait. Something may come of it, and something may not, but if you give the employee the power to effect the change himself, without having to run it up the flagpole, it happens quicker and you have a resultingly bigger buy-in from the employee. It is therefore really in our best interests to make sure that it succeeds, because if it does not, what is to say that they are going to pay any attention to any suggestions down the road, or give us the ability to effect any changes down the road on their own?

Elsewhere in this book we stress the extent of the self-awareness that people need to develop if SMTW is to succeed. The first step towards this among team members is inter-personal skills development. This is frequently a surprise to managers.

> Being a manufacturing environment, we are used to training people in how to operate equipment, how to follow our procedures. One of the training aspects that really jumped out at us when we went to Self-Managed Team Working is the managerial training, the interpersonal skills training, which you do not have to have if you stand in one position on a machine and turn widgets every half-hour. We are finding out that we have to develop people's other skills so that this will succeed.
>
> Two years ago, we did some management restructuring. We removed one layer of management. We feel we are now at a good-sized workforce and, in a couple of areas, we have deemed it unwise to attempt to start a team right now, because there may be staff reductions. We do *not* want to go into an area and say, 'Now you are going to be a self-managed team', and then start laying people off. We work as a group, and if somebody leaves whom they do not feel they need to replace, then that is fine, but we do not want to say, 'This is a great idea. It's going to work real fine for everybody. Let's lay off ten people.'
>
> Some of it involves training people in skills that we have not required of them in the past, and a lot of it involves training the management to let loose, to say, 'We are talking empowerment; let's walk empowerment. Let's follow-through with that. Give the employees their right.' That's a little tough to do!

The middle managers and supervisors are the ones that usually find themselves under threat. They have to see that new skills mean better jobs. As teams develop so new roles emerge. It's important not to allow the *status quo* to be restored by traditional roles simply being relabelled.

> A lot of people see this as a way of working themselves out of a job, especially our current supervisors, because we are not going to have supervision. One of the things that we are trying to stress is, 'Yes, you are working your way out of a supervisory job, but we will have jobs as – we started calling them Facilitators, now we are calling them Coaches – somebody to help nurture the team. We are also hoping that as more and more teams develop, instead of having the silo of this manufacturing area and that manufacturing area, we will start getting some better cross-functional processes working. Today's supervisors, may be tomorrow's co-ordinators, or analysts doing research and helping improve the overall process. It's about getting away from the mind-set: 'I'm working myself out of a job', to 'You are working yourself out of this current job; your structure will change.' That was the initial concern. I have not heard much of that lately.
>
> They begin to realise that just because your job disappears it does not necessarily mean that you will disappear. What you will do is gain experience in other areas, become more proficient in those areas, and you will then have a better job. They were the only rumblings I heard initially. Of course, we are still in the early stages and we do not know what is down the road as far as employee

expectations are concerned, or what reservations they might have, but at this point it has been relatively smooth.

We have convened with a team right now, and this morning it was a little bit bumpy because we were trying to define the roles and responsibilities of each of the members of the team. One of the job titles, that they came up with was 'Leader'. Somebody is going to be a leader. It is going to rotate. But the stigma associated with the word 'leader' is that it means 'a person responsible'. We have had to say, 'No, you are not responsible. This is just a role. You have to determine what the leader will do. The role is just a focal point for outside customers, or for the team, to go to and say 'Hey, we are having a problem with this. Can you help us get a meeting set up?' So there are a lot of implications with some of the words which we have used in the past. I do not see a major problem, but I know that it took us about half-an-hour to get through that this morning. Maybe 'leader' is a difficult word – perhaps it should be 'group coordinators', I don't know. It is an excellent learning process and my team is very, very happy to be a part of this. They have already had about a year's experience, not knowing that the company was getting into SMTW! That team comprises five people.

At GTE the teams are smaller than most – size being decided by the number of people carrying out a particular stage in the production process. They already realise that this isn't right and are working on ways of introducing cross-functional teams to break it down.

I think five is the smallest of the teams. One area has a team of about eighteen people. Right now we are structuring the teams around a specific work area. We are toying with our second group here being a cross-functional team, taking groups from what are now two separate areas. This group feeds that group. Even though they are part of this manufacturing area (just because of the nature of their work) here is where they should be classified, but their work only affects this one area. In this larger group of people, they have two distinct functions. They do not inter-react this way, so we are looking to split into something a little bit different with the next one. Even in the press room, there are only four job descriptions, so you will have four different levels of people working, but in the press room there are sixty or so people. That is an area where we are going to have a sixty-person team – or perhaps split it up into press crews. We have not made that decision yet.

We run two shifts fully staffed, with a skeleton crew on the third (midnight). That is another thing that comes up. How are you going to handle team meetings when you have cross-shift functions? That is something we will have to address when we get there. Right now, we are not addressing it because we do not have that problem. Some of the other areas are addressing cross-shift areas right now, trying to make something that will work initially and get one or two successes and then start branching out.

How much training have people had? This group, which has just started out, has already attended courses which we teach internally at GTE on how to set objectives, how to run a meeting, team problem-solving, and process management. They have been to one seminar, and they have been to Motorola for a site visit. This is just since 1 December, so we have had three months now. Twice a month they have something going on.

Some of the next steps are going to be in interpersonal skills. This is the customer service group and it was the first team. They have already got some skills in interpersonal communications, because they are dealing with the customers on a daily basis. I see the training for them probably going quicker than if we were in a manufacturing area with people who have never had to have communication skills. We have a rough layout which was given to us at our first meeting when we were told that these were 'some of the trainings that we think should occur in the first three months', 'some of the trainings for the next three months', or, 'all this should be accomplished some time in the first twelve to eighteen months'. We realised that it had to be paced to suit our abilities.

People at GTE were generally quite favourable to the idea. In many organisations they turn round and say, 'The guy has lost his marbles' in a natural reaction of disbelief. So what makes some organisations so well disposed towards it?

I truly think it is because this location has a unique familiarity about it. I was at our St Petersburg facility for thirteen years. I have only been here for three years; but when you walk in the door here on Day 1, you feel like a part of the family. There is something intangible about this. I do not know what it is, but there is something about the way this group has worked together over the years which makes for a lot of trust and confidence in the management here. People have been given freedoms in years past to operate as they needed to. A few people are hesitant at first: they ask questions, we explain things to them, and they say: 'I can understand that. I believe that.' There is a strong level of trust here.

They can also see from the commitment from management that this is not a programme, this is not something that is going to start here, we are going to see if it works and, if it does not work, we will shelve it and try something else. This is a path which we have chosen to follow and, good or bad, we are going to follow it to the bitter end from now on. These people have the understanding and the belief that we can make this work. If we can make it work, who is to say what else is down that road for us? It may be beneficial not only for us, but for the company as well. These are people who want to show what they can do on their own. They want to show that we can make this work. We do not need someone staring over our shoulder telling us how to do the job which we have always done.

I also believe that some of it is a little bit of misunderstanding. They think self-management means that there are not going to be any managers around here. One of the concepts they will have to learn is that self-management does not mean a lack of management, just a different kind of management. Once some of the administrative duties come their way, some of them may balk a little bit, but by the time we get there, we hope that we will have given them enough training, background and information so that it will be more readily accepted.

Because at this point, you have individuals floating in uncharted waters. You are going to have peers rating, appraising and reviewing peers. You are going to have involvement in the salary tree, in the salary processes. These are areas where they have been on the receiving end for years and years, but which they have never actually had to do. When they come to the realisation that everything which was done for them in the past is now going to be on their plate for them to do, then at that point, when the reality strikes, it might be overwhelming. Are they up to the challenge? I think so. I believe that we will have prepared them enough so that when the challenge arises they will be prepared not only mentally, but also with all the tools necessary for them to succeed and accept the challenge. I do not think they are going to back down. I do not think they will say, 'Well, this is a little too much for us', and try to shirk the responsibility.

I am very impressed. They are very progressive people at this location. I cannot tell you what it is, but it is special, and it is progressive. I think it comes from the guidance of upper management. Part of management has always given help to the leader to go out and take that initiative, take the risk here and there. This builds on itself. The organisation will care for and nurture you, but the emphasis is that if you want to get on in this world, you have got to think about yourself. I think that part and parcel of that is the fact that our work group is stable. There is not a lot of staff turnover, there is not a lot of in and out. You have people who have been in one department for ten or twelve years. So these are people who have been doing this work for an on-going period of time, and they know their jobs very well. What they are saying is, 'We could have done this a long time ago. We could have pushed the management out a long time ago and run the whole show ourselves, but we were not empowered to do so and, if we had mentioned it, management would probably have laughed us right out of the building. But now management has become a little more enlightened and what they are saying is that we could have done it all along, so just step aside and just let us see if we can do it.' I think that is the attitude here:

'Give us the tools and let us see if we can do it'.

A lot of companies have provided employee share ownership programmes in the belief that they would improve motivation. In practice few have, and there is a growing feeling that they can demotivate as employees realise the very limited value of their holding.

The business is a publicly-held corporation, and most of the employees are stockholders. We have an employee stock purchase plan. We hold it once a year and it effectively allows employees to purchase shares at a significant discount. We make it very attractive for them to reinvest in the company and, by being a stockholder and owner, so to speak, they have a greater care over what happens to the company, because the fate of the company is also part of their fate. So I want to make sure that the company does well, not only because I am an employee, but also I am a stockholder. If the company does not do well, and if by not doing well the end-result may be the company disbanding, disjoining, disappearing, where is that going to leave me? As a stockholder, therefore, I am going to have a little ownership in this programme and be a little more thoughtful as far as my own job and the things that happen around me.

I would say that almost 75% of employees hold stock. It would vary as to the amount. Of course, the longer-term employees are going to have more, but I would say that everybody buys two shares, some as many as 200-300 shares, a year, dependent upon their salary. The way the formula is based, you can purchase a maximum of one share for each $100 of your salary. You can use it for different purposes: as a nest-egg for retirement, to provide college education for the kids, or just to have something down the road, a hedge against inflation, or whatever. But the bottom line is, they can go out and buy shares in anybody's stock. Granted, we give them the extra incentive by giving them the 15% discount, but the fact remains that some people own no other stock.

The GTE employee survey also provides a valuable benchmark for managers and can be used to routinely monitor the impact of changes.

Every other year, we have an employee survey. We started that back in 1982. I think I have participated in eight surveys since the early 1980s and every two years they have this survey at some point. It is about ten page long, and it addresses a number of issues within the company. Trust in management, compensation, benefits, faith in the direction of the company. Just a pot-pourri of different areas of concern. We poll each and every employee. We get an overall result and we poll employees by employee-group. We do not know what each person said, but we have a pretty good idea of the feelings of each group. Once we get that down, we go back to the group and say, 'Your response to this question was this. Given that you made the statement, what did you really mean? What areas of concern do you really have, and what would you, as an employee, do to fix it?' We act as nothing but notetakers. It is up to the individuals to sit down, thrash it all out and come up with a proposal. Once they have a proposal of what they would do, or what they would like to see done, we then transmit that information to the functional Vice-President. It is up to him to respond to the employees on what we can address and on what we cannot address.

What would you like to do that you are not doing now? What would you like to have? How would you make this input? How would you like to see this inputted by management? Those are the things to which the employee has to respond. They know that they are not going to be able just to say this is what we want. They are going to have to hold some legitimate plan which we can take to management and say, 'This is what they said, this is what they meant, this is what they would like to see done', and the management responds accordingly.

One example of that is that typically in the past, if the company were going to spend $1.5 million on a piece of equipment, management would look all round and say, 'That's the best piece. Let's buy it.' They then put it on the floor and say, 'Now, you guys have to work with it'. One of the complaints was, 'Decision-making. We ought to have some say in what equipment we are going to work with.'

We have not purchased anything major here since then, but a couple of years ago, in St Petersburg, one of our folding machines was very, very old and in need of serious repairs; so rather than invest the money repairing and have an old, repaired folder, we decided to buy a new one. We took two or three main operators and sent them to various trade shows and, various manufacturers to look, and let them make the decision. They are going to be running it day in, day out. We gave them the budgetary guidelines with which we had to live, along with the company's expectations of what that machine would be capable of in the production centre, and we let them make the decisions.

This was a couple of years ago, before anybody came along and said, 'Let's go and be a Self-Managed Work Team'. It is a natural progression. We have done things over the years that unknowingly have led us to this next natural step. So let us go ahead, let us jump in the boat and go full tilt and empower them.

One of the areas that GTE is exploring carefully is the idea of performance appraisals and salary setting. Their experiences are a useful account of the teething troubles experienced as SMWTs are introduced.

At this location we have done nothing on peer appraisal and salary setting. We have two teams in Directories which have been in place for a little over a year now. One of them was started up brand-new as a SMWT; they had never been in our business operation. So they went in knowing they would be a SMWT. They had problems at their first review period. They did not like some of the ways the system was set up. They had inadequate measures available. They wanted to change the whole review process. They were told they were not just going to overhaul the review process. Certain guidelines had to be followed, and we had to stay within the guidelines for the time being. Right now, they will be going through their second review process, so I do not know what the feedback is. I hope that it is positive this time. The second group had the training on interpersonal communications and conflict management; they know how to deal with an issue as opposed to dealing with a personality problem. They felt very good about being able to sit down and review each other.

One of the things they said when they handled their group of eight or nine people: 'We are going to review Bob, all the rest of the eight of us go out of the review'. Their coach compiled everything on to one form, reviewed it with the group first to make sure everything was there, and then reviewed it with the individual. If there was a statement on that review which the individual wanted to contest, the person who made that statement had to back it up; if they were not able to do so, the statement was struck out. They had a very, very good success with their personal consultant. We have seen two ends of the spectrum so far. I think that as long as we continue to make sure that these people are given the proper training on how to do the appraisals, and what they should be looking at, I do not think we will have the problems. One group may get to that point in a year's time, another group may take two or three years to get to the point where that comfort-level says it can effectively be done that way.

There has not been an overall decision made as to how salary setting is going to be approached. Currently, each job and each position within the company has a salary range. Even though people are in teams, they still have those job-titles, and the salary ranges that are attached to those titles. We have not got to the point yet where the decision has been made to scrap that and go with something else, or to modify it and go with that. At this point, I do not know if anyone knows how that is going to be addressed. That is one of those pot-holes that we are going to find. We know it is down there, and we know that we are going to hit it, but we will try to make some inroads as to what we are going to do when we get to that point, but at this point we do not know.

The people at Motorola have said that they are going through the same thing. They are rewriting job descriptions. They had forty-eight different jobs and they pinned this down to five or six at two different levels. We know at some point that we will have to rewrite the job descriptions. That may also tie in with the salary structure. Right now, co-ordinating time-frames is the only aspect of salary administration that they would be able to get in to, when it is felt that they are ready for that or they feel that they are ready to accept it. Again, we have ranges, we have a matrix depending upon how you are rated during your appraisal, where you fall in your range. It is pretty much cut-and-dried. You run your fingers down the charts and say, 'You qualify for $x\%$ at this point of time'. That would be their only input, initially.

If there is going to be an annual 4% increase across-the-board for budgetary purposes, we have talked about the idea of possibly taking that 4% for each work group, pooling that money and letting them decide how it is split – whether they split it evenly across the board, or whether Person A has more skills, has done extra this year – we do not know. Again, that is down the road. That is one of the pot-holes that we know is out there. When the snow melts...!

The hiring of new employees hasn't yet happened. Another aspect though which is common in the early stages is the selection of teams from existing employees. Some organisations base the decision on individual past performance, others on team-based activities (including adventure weekends). Some invite applications by individuals and others by teams.

To date, except the 'Spec Art' Team, teams don't get involved in hiring and firing. This was the team that, from its inception, was designed to be self-managed. As a matter of fact, I went down to help to staff up for that team: it was interviewed as a team, the selection was a team, and the concept was for the bulk of the decisions to be made at team level. I can only assume, because I have not been down there since two years ago in September, that they were responsible for the hiring, and they would also give some input as to those individuals that didn't cut the mustard and they let go.

We have a training class available on selective interviewing. It is to teach an individual how to interview, so that you can make the right selection from the beginning and, hopefully, eradicate the need to let somebody go down the road. We know that training will have to be offered to people for that. One of the questions in the initial overview which I presented to the plant at one of our monthly plant meetings – I call everybody in and the two of us explain what we do with teams today. One of the guys said: 'We are all a team, that means if Leslie isn't cutting mustard we can fire him, right?' I said, 'Teams will have a lot of power, but you have to stay within the company guidelines, so it could be a personality issue that now that we are a team we are going to run Leslie down on a rail. We have corrective counselling procedures. We have things that have got to be accomplished before you can take the step of sacking someone'. All those steps are actually meant to improve the employee and not force him out of the door.

Everyone is controlled by the overlying company policy. Even if you were in a team and even if you wanted to put someone out of the door, there is a reason for the performance, and what we would like to do initially is to try to alter the performance. Get that member or employee up to the standard that the overall team would like to see the individual reach. It is up to us administrators, and his team members, to do whatever is in their power to turn his performance around. There are going to be some instances and some circumstances where we are not going to be able to do that. In that situation, it is probably best to have a parting of the ways, but I would think that in most cases it is a personality conflict, or the fact that the individual either has no clear understanding of the expectations, or has not been properly trained.

To date, compensation doesn't depend on daily activity. It has been individual pay per performance at this location. We do have a trial 'team incentive' programme here now, for instance in the press room. It is just a pilot to see where the bugs are and to make sure it is fair and equitable to everybody. At some point, I would think that is one of the issues that we are going to have to address. It is going to be a team issue as well as an individual issue to help attain whatever levels are out there.

Those organisations that have successfully implemented SMWTs usually report the importance of a clear vision and relevant critical success factors. At this stage GTE are tending to experiment and are not modifying their existing measures. That won't continue for much longer.

The measurement of success is in its infancy. We do not have a lot of expectations at this point. They are basically finding their way along. We are trying to make sure that they have all the basics as far as what we are doing right now. Once we figure out what ground we have covered now, we want them to take the next step and start it as soon as possible.

At that point, we know whether measurement will be through customer complaints or through some of the measuring and reporting systems that we have in place now. We should be able to measure whether it is a success or whether there are some shortcomings. Some of the other areas have definite measures. They have productivity goals. In our customer service department, we have not got set productivity goals, we just work! It is not as though you are trying to turn out a thousand-a-day which may not be there. Some of our reporting and responses from the customers I think we could measure and in manufacturing we have many productivity and quality ratios as well as statistical process-control.

One of the things that we do have in our Dallas office is a directory rating system which is published on a monthly basis. Our books are rated, as well as St Petersburg's and Los Angeles's books, and as well as those of some outside vendors whose books we use during peak-time when we do not have the capacity. That quality rating is probably across seven or eight plants, and there is something there that, yes, they could know how well we are doing. Up until 1993 we had a President's printing trophy which measured eight or nine areas. That was strictly a comparison of the three GTE print plants, and so we knew how we stood against our other internal operations. We eliminated that trophy in 1993 – there were some major changes in the way we were doing business, and we didn't feel that some of the old measurements were fair to all three print works. They are in the process of re-evaluating what we should be measuring. Maybe we should reinstate the trophy competition.

Communication, or targeted marketing is vital. Gone are the days of annual visits from a senior manager when the path was swept and the woodwork painted! Every form of media can be used to good effect.

We have a monthly department meeting throughout all the groups. On occasion, if there is something we want to share immediately, we have a spontaneous meeting. We get together for an hour here, an hour there. We had a half-day session recently where two of the Executive Vice-Presidents came through and shared some information with us. We have employee bulletins that come out forty-eight times a day, it seems like! Probably two or three times a week, we get employee bulletins. Company newsletters. I think that is about it. We have quarterly meetings, and letters which go out to the employees' homes. That really keeps them abreast of what is going on company-wise; it's not specific to this location but that is specific to Directories. We also get the quarterly GTE Newsletter which tells us what is going on GTE-wide.

We have some posters which are legally mandatory: these concern the Equal Employment Opportunity process, the non-discriminatory process, the rights of an employee, or the rights of an applicant. Then, of course, there are safety posters exhorting people towards safety, and to exhibit caution in the workplace. Then there are some that are there for the sake of being there, or to exhibit some company motto like, this one here that says, '100% customer satisfaction through quality'.

Rewards can often be supplemented very effectively by recognition. GTE have developed many of these pats on the back. At the moment though most are geared towards individual good performance.

We have a discretionary award programme. If somebody does something exceptional, or something that really impresses the supervisor, they have the right to authorise $250 and nobody asks any questions. We can offer them either a monetary gift or a gift certificate to their favourite store, dinner for two at a restaurant, sporting event tickets, whatever we want. We have the right to say, 'Thanks, that was special. We appreciate that.'

And there is no limit to the number of discretionary awards that an employee can receive. It gives the employee some encouragement because he knows that we are not constantly monitoring him. 'We do see what you are doing and we do appreciate it', and not by just saying 'You have done a good job and here's your normal pay cheque, but if you care enough to go out of your way, to go out of your normal job-span to do a job, we feel that you should be rewarded for it.' A pat on the back is one thing. That is all well and good; but sometimes we should go that extra step. It is not necessarily the amount, it is the fact that we recognise what you are doing and we are willing for that recognition to be known.

Some people do not want their peer group to know. Some are embarrassed and some are afraid of negative feedback. Some feel that, 'This is my job and you do not need to do this because I am just doing my job.' So we have the entire spectrum here, and we try to make compensation or adjustments, wherever possible, to fit within the needs or the desires of the employee.

After an extremely busy period when something exceptional happens we will bring in catering lunch for the entire plant.

There are some other corporate mandates: every five years of service you qualify for a lunch, and you take off with the afternoon off. We have a perfect attendance-incentive programme: if you are here for six months, you get a gift and a certificate; if you are here for a year, you get the same gift and certificate, luncheon, half-a-day off. Every six months you continue to get a gift. Every two years, for every multiple year after the first, you get $150 as well. 1993 was our sixth year of the attendance programme and we had six or seven people receive six years. Some of them have longer than six years, but we have only had the programme that long.

Safety is another issue. We have a safety programme that keeps everybody aware of being safe. Everybody is divided into work-rooms, and if somebody in the work-room gets hurt, your team does not have a chance of winning, so it is a way of getting the employees to watch out for each other. We also have scholarship programmes for the children of employees. We have support for junior high school and college students. They go into competition with the other children, other employees, and the winners get a maximum of $5,000, based on their needs. So if you do not need it, or you do not need it as much, then we try to give it to the most needy.

We give an Award of Excellence twice a year and you can be nominated by your peers. We have categories for quality and customer service, innovation and technology. We have quality improvement teams, which we invite people to be on, to share information and get them to help change the process or part of the operation. The quality improvement teams have an award, and there is an annual presidential award for the idea of the year from each region.

Activity 5.1: Envisaging the future

This is an exercise in envisaging the future. It is not intended that, in doing this, you will produce a definitive plan for the changes which have got to happen in your organisation. The object is to provoke some thinking about alternatives to the way things are done now. We are going to flag a number of areas which we believe are important, as being likely places for change to happen in the course of transition from traditional structures to SMWTs. Depending on your preference, either create a mind-map for the topics, or head a separate page of paper with each, and list bullet points underneath them.

1 Extent

The first area to think about is the extent to which you see SMWTs becoming established in your organisation. Are there any areas that you feel would not be suitable? Will the development occur equally on all sites? Are certain functions sufficiently remote that they are unlikely to become involved? Do you foresee that parts of the organisation will change in size? If you currently employ 250, do you think this is likely to go up, down, or stay the same?

2 Structure

Next, look at the type of organisation that you think SMWTs will be best aligned with. Do your product lines appear to be autonomous? Do certain customer-groups demand sufficiently different services that the SMWT could operate autonomously? Are some functional areas likely to remain, but as a SMWT, and do certain process steps represent a discreet and substantial chunk that can be regarded as an autonomous group?

3 Activities

You can probably identify a number of activities which at present are carried out by a supervisor, foreman, or manager of some other kind, and which you would like to see carried out by front-line staff. Similarly there may be some items which you consider are too sensitive, in your particular organisation, for you to allow front-line staff to tackle. This doesn't mean to say, of course, that this couldn't change – but, for example, there may be commercial constraints with existing customers which require certain activities to be carried out by certain individuals.

4 Measures

Try listing some of the success factors which you will use to measure progress. How will you know that the SMWTs are succeeding? Think, too, of the measures which you will need to give employees in the form of regular information to allow them to monitor their performance.

5 Reward and recognition

Try identifying some of the changes which you think will need to be made to the reward and recognition systems that you have in place. Think of the appraisal system, and methods of negotiation. Think also about your system of representation. Are there unions involved? Is there a staff association? Think of corporate pay and reward systems which may apply throughout the organisation at the moment, but which will not do so in the future. For example, you may wish to give a greater incentive to the people involved in SMWTs in the form of short-term rewards which you have not needed in the past.

6 Product development
Think about the product development process. What currently happens, and how do you think it will be affected by SMWTs? The evidence is that, once these teams become established, they have a great deal to contribute in the area of new product development.

7 Training and development
Look critically at the training service which you have provided to date. Think carefully of the skills you will need for SMWTs to be effective. Planning for this training is a very serious and pressing need. You may feel that you have to launch a training process before SMWTs can be introduced. What will be involved? How many hours per employee? What will the impact be on budgeting? Now look at who will provide this training. Do you see it coming from the Training Department or Personnel, or is it to be a role for managers? If so, will the managers need preparatory training and development, or are they already fulfiling a training role? How will you measure the success of training, beyond the smile factor of course? Try to document as many as possible of the detailed aspects of each of these areas, while you think of them.

8 Social arrangements
Some people think of SMWTs as organisational structures for front-line employees, forgetting that it has as big an impact on the management team as it does on the front-line. In many organisations, particularly large ones, most of the social arrangements have been made by employees from the front-line and although on occasions, the company may have supported them, the initiatives usually lay with the staff association or other group. You are about to change the relationship between managers and other employees. One of the more tangible examples of an 'us and them' culture is where front-line employees do not share social facilities with managers. Take an objective look at your own organisation. What sort of facilities do staff have? Who owns them? Who participates in them? Will any of these arrangements need changing or opening up?

It is worth carrying a note-book with you, or your mind-map, so that you can annotate it in spare moments. The reasons for doing this are manifold. The managers who have done so, find it particularly useful to remind themselves later that, though they may have thought through the approach which is to be followed, they may not have involved others doing so.

Activity 5.2: Self Awareness

Use a video recorder to tape a group discussion from television. There are many suitable programmes shown these days. Try to pick one with a group of four or five people, probably discussing current affairs or the background to news events.

Play back the tape. Ignore the content of the discussion – we're not interested in your views about the death penalty, hostages or civil war! Concentrate on who is saying what, and how they are saying it. Listen for words that suggest opinions rather than facts ('I think'; 'I believe'; and so on). Listen for words that express feelings ('It really upsets me'; 'I felt so annoyed!') Spot anecdotes where people are sharing experiences without so much interpretation. Finally, look for bits of the dialogue where someone else interprets another person's comments ('So what you're saying is ...'; 'That seems very significant to you...'). In each case make a note of who said what. Look through your notes. For each of the people try to spot something that falls into each of the 'panes' of the Johari Window (Fig. 5.1).

	Known to self	Unknown to self
Known to others	**Free and open** You know and others know.	**Blind self:** You don't know but others do.
Unknown to others	**Hidden self:** You know but others do not.	**Unknown self:** You don't know and others don't know.

Fig 5.1 The Johari Window

Source: Munro EA, Manthei RJ and Small JJ (1979) *Counselling – A Skills Approach*, Methuen, Wellington, NZ. Reproduced with permission of Methuen and Co.

The Johari Window is used as a model to understand our openness to others. It takes its name from the two authors who originally described it: Joe Luft and Harry Ingham. At any time, there are some things we allow other people to know about us and there are some we keep hidden to ourselves. Similarly, there are some things we know about ourselves, and some even we are not aware of. This 'unknown self' may have been subconsciously locked away in our minds, or it may be that we've simply never thought about it.

The purpose of this exercise is to begin to improve your powers of observation, and to introduce the idea of aspects of ourselves being open to others or unknown.

Repeat the exercise, but this time tape-record a conversation over dinner with a similar number of friends. It's up to you to decide if you want to explain why – they'll probably be interested. Why not seed it a little?

- "Have you thought of companies getting involved in schools? What do you think of the idea?"
- "We're thinking of changing some of the pay systems at work – what sort of arrangements do you think are best?"
- "When you did the ISO 9000 thing the other year – what sort of problems did you have?"

Activity 5.3: Opening Up

To risk doing something new or difficult, you need to increase your own self-awareness. Doing so involves expanding the 'Free and open' part of the Johari Window and correspondingly reducing the others. This involves two important behaviours: you need to take risks by revealing parts of yourself to others; and you must be willing to ask for, and receive, feedback from others, especially about how you affect them and how well your behaviour matches what you say you will do.

This is not an overnight skill. You won't read this book and suddenly 'do' it. Typically, the process of acquiring, balancing and using this skill takes four years.

Give yourself a taste of what is involved.

Pick a member of your family who knows you well. Explain to them that you are trying to understand yourself a bit better (in preparation for some changes at work) and ask if they will help you. Let them know that it will take a bit of time and that you'll understand if they don't want to. Above all, make it clear that you won't hold anything against them if they'll be honest with you.

There's no reason for picking your spouse. Some people find one of their adolescent children is much better than other family members. A 'hidden' benefit from this is also that your relationship can be strengthened as a result.

Now select an activity which is physical, but not too demanding, and which will last a day. Decorating a room, building some shelves, climbing a mountain, cycling a forty-mile route – all are good. The idea is to share an activity equally, and for the task not to prevent conversation but at the same time to allow you both to have periods of silence. If there is a tangible output then you will probably look back on it years later as a significant aspect of your growth.

Put aside the time, gather your resources and start the activity. Explain to your partner that you need to begin to see yourself as others see you. Get them to give you their thoughts. NEVER argue, and NEVER interrupt. Some of the aspects you might try are:

- What do you think people notice about me?
- If I'm nervous, how do you think I come across?
- When I come in – what tells you whether I've had a good or bad day?
- What hobby-horses have I got?
- What differences do you see in me from before?
- Are there any other people that I remind you of? – What is it about them?
- If there was anything about me that you could change, what would it be?

As you get responses, remember them and refer back to them:

- You said earlier that I get bolshy when I've driven a long way: what other times do you see me as being bolshy?
- Try paraphasing things to get more detail: So what you seem to be saying is that I let other parents over-bear on me?
- Don't forget to thank your partner for their help and for being honest with you. (You might find it helps to give them a hug too!)

Now using the information and self-knowledge which you've gained, write a summary for yourself. Aim for at least a page. Don't share this with anyone unless you want to. As you summarise, keep asking yourself: 'Why am I like this?', 'What has led to me being this way?', 'When have I seen this behaviour in others?'

6

THE LEGISLATORS

'How do you achieve cultural change? ... You have got to hit it from every available institution, over and over and over, doing it so that you can do so over time, and have the peers in the communities drive themselves. It can't be driven by government.'

(Bob Baugh, AFL–CIO)

- **Even when there are substantial internal benefits, companies prove remarkably reluctant to change.**

- **While government can raise awareness through the media, tangible actions are much more likely to result from financial incentives.**

- **Support for small and medium enterprises has to encourage risk-taking – encourage the entrepreneur at their heart – not stifle creativity through fear of failure.**

- **Government example is a powerful motivation to the private sector.**

- **An aggressive stance has to be taken to remove antiquated legislation and replace it with better protection. Legislators and the judiciary need to be kept in touch with modern practices.**

- **We need to publicise our successes to encourage others to try.**

GOVERNMENT INTERVENTION – ENCOURAGING INDUSTRY TO ADOPT SELF-MANAGEMENT

It seems highly unlikely that employers will take the initiative of implementing high-performance work-places, empowering their employees through Self-Directed Work Groups, and collaborating extensively with educators unless they are encouraged by government. Even when there has been a substantial internal financial benefit, as was the case for quality improvement, companies have proved remarkably reluctant to change. Surprisingly, quite small sums provided externally have a far more persuasive power.

Previous initiatives have demonstrated the importance of government involvement in ensuring their success. For instance, the awareness-raising programmes for Quality in Britain in the late 1970s and in the 1980s were extremely successful. Tangible actions, as opposed to awareness-raising, have been strongly influenced through budgetary control – either through tax incentives or disincentives, or through financial investment.

More recently, governments have demonstrated that leading by example can be an effective way of achieving change. In the US, the government restructuring programmes have begun to legitimise similar initiatives in smaller industries. (The lead seems to have been taken by larger institutions such as Kodak and IBM.)

Raising the awareness of industry and the community

Three ways in which the government could stimulate interest in high-performance, self-direction and educational involvement, would be through publicity campaigns, award schemes and their own example. We shall briefly consider the first two of these.

Publicity campaigns

Publicity campaigns have the advantage of being relatively inexpensive, of having established precedents, and of requiring little internal change. Good examples from the past include the 'Keep Britain Tidy' campaign and the 'National Quality Campaign'. However, in recent years there have been some startlingly ineffective examples: in the UK and the USA considerable effort has been spent in AIDS awareness programmes which many people feel have been poorly researched, poorly targeted, and which, according to statistics, have produced little or no effect. If such a campaign is initiated for self-management it needs to be very carefully designed and its effectiveness needs to be closely monitored.

Award schemes

Japan, the USA, Europe, and most recently the UK have all launched Quality Awards. Only the Japanese award, the Deming Prize, has a substantial track record (it was instituted in 1954) and continues to prove effective without attracting criticism. The Baldrige Award (USA) proved popular in the first few years, 1988–1990; since then it has attracted progressively fewer applications and has come in for substantial media criticism. In Europe, perhaps for cross-cultural reasons, the EQA has been popular with its winners, but shows little signs of being an effective tool in the wider forum.

Now Britain has launched its own quality award. Few of the people who were interviewed could see any benefit in this. They felt that it was over a decade too late, couldn't possibly gain the respect of the Deming and the Baldrige awards for its breadth of assessment and impartiality, and was more likely to be counterproductive by attracting negative publicity. It seems that awards are only appropriate when they are the first, and then only really to raise awareness.

Financial Aid

For obvious reasons, direct financial incentives are not the most popular choice for government, involving, as they must, either increased 'taxation' in some form or re-allocation of resources from an equally justifiable programme. However, the UK's experience with the Enterprise Initiative has shown how popular they can be to recipients.

This approach has not been repeated elsewhere. In Japan, few people expected the government to intervene in this way as there is no precedent. In the US, the budgetary process would make it slow to achieve, especially at a federal level. There was a little more optimism that it could be achieved at a state level – a good example of such an approach having been set in Oregon. In Oregon, too, the use of lottery proceeds was also earmarked for individual training grants.

Tax incentives

Tax incentives were seen by many people as the only likely way in which government might become involved in stimulating this process. Credits for investment in non-manufacturing activities, such as employee education, local community education, and schools and colleges were obvious. A scale of employer social-security contributions, depending on the skill-level of employees, was one of the more controversial suggestions – concerns especially focusing on the danger of encouraging recruitment of more highly qualified personnel, rather than contributing to the skills of people in-house.

Tax disincentives

Tax disincentives are another possibility mooted. Most of the people spoken to felt that this was the wrong approach. In both Japan and the USA, where the political balance of power has shifted suddenly, there was concern that another shift would simply negate this approach. However, on a local level again, this was more achievable, particularly as it could involve a local policing effort. Generally, though, both employers and government were wary of its effectiveness.

Direct taxation

Least popular, though still a clear possibility, is direct taxation – in the form of a per-employee fee collected for direct allocation to employee training. Surprisingly, although this was not favoured by many people, it is the method with the longest track record. The UAW contract, established some time ago, specifies a 'dime' (five cents) levy payable to a fund for direct allocation to employee training. In 1994, each Ford worker at the Romeo plant near Detroit was able to spend up to $3,100 towards approved courses.

The range of courses offered is worth mentioning, as people often expect them to be directly related to the employee's work. In 1994, courses ranged from workshop-based programmes on domestic computers, air conditioning, refrigeration and video-recorder maintenance, to classroom-based programmes on setting up a small business and financial planning. There are also courses associated with managing a domestic property, and college credit classes.

THE INTERVIEWEES

The problem of influencing government internationally, nationally and locally is not unique to organisations trying to encourage or promote the high-performance workplace. Our interviewees come from very different types of organisation, and they examine the lessons that can be learnt from others' experiences in similar or related initiatives. **Bob Baugh**, Special Assistant to the Executive Director of the American Federation of Labor and Congress of Industrial Organisations, offers an unusual combination of experience. The AFL–CIO is the co-ordinating body of American Unions, comparable in the UK to the TUC. Bob Baugh's role involves a considerable amount of strategic planning, policy development and lobbying of national government. He has a special interest in the development of the high-performance workplace and the implementation of SMWTs. We include more of his interview in Chapter 8 on trade unions. Before joining the AFL–CIO, Baugh was responsible for steering a radical transformation in the culture and viability of an entire state: as Workforce Development Manager of the Oregon Economic Development Department, in the late 1980s and early 1990s, Baugh facilitated the process of strategic planning for the whole of Oregon. Among the initiatives undertaken were the development of values and beliefs representing the views of the community as a whole, together with detailed plans for the development of education and training, employee involvement and links between business and public institutions. The process included the adoption of a state-wide total quality curriculum and quality plan, the development of funding, in-depth benchmarking, communication processes to the community, and the involvement of many local, town and state-wide organisations. It was Baugh's experience in Oregon that led to his appointment with the AFL–CIO. In this section of his interview, he describes some of the ways in which his organisation progressively influenced government at all levels.

Yasuhiko Inoue is Deputy Director of the Japan Productivity Center (JPC). Throughout the Second World War and early post-war years, Japan had largely focused on military expenditure and, coupled with its isolation from Western technology, her industrial development had lagged behind. In the early 1950s it became clear that some kind of systematic attack had to be made on the problems of low productivity and high costs which were endemic throughout Japanese industry. Under the guidance of the US Government, in December 1953, a US technical aid programme was extended to Japan, mirroring the earlier programmes which had operated throughout Europe. In 1955, the JPC was established as a non-profit-organisation co-operating between management, labour and academia. Later that year, the technical co-operation programme was more closely defined by Japan and the United States. In the early days, most of the Japanese labour unions were suspicious of US involvement, and so later in 1955, the JPC published three guiding principles of the productivity movement in an attempt to address the labour unions' suspicions. Since that time, all influential private-sector unions in Japan have joined the JPC movement.

US aid was eventually withdrawn at the end of 1961, and the JPC's programmes continued largely on a self-funding basis. In the early days of the JPC movement, the emphasis was on educating the general public on the theories and practice of productivity. This was achieved through all of the usual communications media: newspapers, magazines, publications, films, radio and TV. The emphasis was largely on management development, and drew heavily on American experts. By 1960, a full network of regional productivity centres had been established throughout Japan. Just as the European nations had formed a joint European productivity agency, so in April 1961, representatives of eight Asian countries met in Manila and signed an agreement to establish the Asian Productivity Organisation (APO). The eight countries were: South Korea, the Republic of China, the Philippines, Thailand, India, Pakistan, Nepal, and Japan. Today the number of member nations has risen to eighteen and the APO and JPC have co-operated in raising productivity and living standards throughout the Asian region. Most recently, as the CIS strives to introduce a free market to the Russian economy, the All Union Productivity Centre, established by the Russian government in February 1991, has been involved in a number of consultation activities, counselling and sharing of materials and information with the JPC.

Today the JPC's activities within Japan focus on management training, strengthening labour–management relations and creating people-centred workplaces. Much of their work has become definitive. For example, the Academy of Management Development, established by the JPC in 1965, was the country's first true business school, and since it was established, more than 9,000 graduates have passed through its gates. Reacting to growing concerns about changes in the workplace, the JPC established a standing committee on Labour Management joint consultation. They have produced a number of definitive reports and their annual white paper on Labour Management Relations has become a bible for business both in Japan, and throughout the West. The range of initiatives pioneered by the JPC, and in which its expertise has been established, is remarkable, ranging from studies on the mental health of industrial workers, through to the transformation of the gross national product towards smaller businesses. In this interview, Yasuhiko Inoue outlines a few of the JPC's concerns for the future, and the emphasis that they are placing on their lobbying activities.

We have already seen how Motorola invests in the social development of the communities in which it operates. This interview illustrates, too, the role that large organisations, as well as small ones, can take in steering national policy. **Jim Burge** is the Vice-President of Motorola, tasked with managing their Washington-based government relations office. In this interview, he discusses an enormous range of issues relating to the implementation of SMWTs, the impact of demographic change on society, and the process by which an organisation such as Motorola can influence national and state government.

The American Society for Training and Development (ASTD) is a professional society representing individuals working in the fields of training and development. Like most professional organisations, it has a role of promoting the profession to a wider audience. With 55,000 members it has a key role in influencing national and local government in issues affecting worker training. Within the ASTD, **Dr Mary McCain** is responsible for the drafting of policy and for its promotion nationally. The ASTD is meticulous in the depth of its research on many issues related to the high-performance work-place. In this interview, she outlines some of these key issues, and the policy-lines that the ASTD is taking.

The Office of the American Workplace (OAW), is a new agency in the US Department of Labor, created by Secretary Robert Reich, to promote better jobs for American workers. The OAW's role is to work in partnership with business, labour and government to encourage organisations both in the private and public sectors to adopt high-performance work-practices. They do this through a combination of research activities (correlating work practices with corporate results), the development of partnerships with business to identify best practices, the channelling of this information through a workplace clearing house to encourage benchmarking between organisations, the development and distribution of federal and state support through organisations particularly in the small and medium-sized enterprises (SME) sector, the promotion of employee ownership and, unusually, a government-provided Union Leadership Institute. This last organisation is training union leaders in the design and management of workplace programmes as a worker-driven alternative to the top-down implementation process commonly found in the private sector.

The OAW is trying to encourage its own organisation to adopt a team-working approach. Rob Portman, the Assistant Secretary responsible for the OAW, very kindly invited the author to take part in a group discussion with various members of his organisation at their head office in Washington. Although they had only been operating a few months, the discussion illustrates many of the initiatives that had been undertaken and suggests a number of ways in which other countries could follow similar routes.

INTERVIEW 6.1 INFLUENCING GOVERNMENT AND THE PUBLIC SECTOR

Bob Baugh, Special Assistant to the Executive Director, American Federation of Labor and Congress of Industrial Organisations

Most of the initiatives which we've undertaken in the UK in the past have been directed towards old-style, big businesses, manufacturing-biased and, to a lesser extent, union organised. There has been a shift towards smaller, service-orientated, entrepreneurial ones. What do we do to try to capture the attention of the new style?

Bob Baugh begins by explaining how he approached this in Oregon, using business to drive change in the public sector through the government's own advisory boards, while at the same time using public sector change to provide similar responses in the private sector.

Government's role as a catalyst towards change is exactly what I spent the last six years dealing with and particularly with the issue of getting to the medium and smaller firms, In the State of Oregon, we adopted the 'America's Choice' study; it's a high-wage, high-skill game we're in here. We formed a state workforce council, which tried to pull together training and education. But we began from the economic development side: how do you effect transformation in business?

When we formed the council, I got them to adopt operating principles, two of which were:

- It's fundamental that business has got to invest more in the education and training of its workers.
- Government should play the role as a catalyst to get business and itself to move to being high-performance organisations.

What's different about this is that this isn't a normal advisory council. Traditionally you operate an advisory board or committee, to 'advise' government – to tell it how it should engage in best practice to achieve whatever the government wants. Part of what I was trying to get to with this council was reform, and Oregon is now considered the model state for doing this. We said: 'How do you get from here to there? If you want to reform your schools, to try and connect school and work, it's great – but what does that mean? It means that by the year 2000 you have 35,000 juniors and seniors in school work-experience.' They cried: 'We only have 40,000 businesses, how are we going to do that?'

It's all about following through on these things. We had to start asking ourselves a different set of questions. These are the principles of what we're supposed to do but once you get buried in an advisory council, you tell the public what to do without ever thinking about what *we* need to do ourselves.

Advisory committees have got to start operating differently. There should be a set of obligations on how they're organised, how they contact and communicate with their peers, and on the expectations of private-sector members going the other way. You have to be strategic about who you want to get on these committees – and very clear about their expectations.

When I did this, even the political parties asked: 'What do you mean?' So we did benchmarks, and I found that business was saying: 'Damn right, we should invest 1.5% of the payroll on training, and we should do 2% by 1995.' The public-sector people thought we were out of our minds; they told me: 'No, you can't do that'. I said: 'Ask the business people'. And the business people said: 'This is so; we're serious – we need to do these things'.

So the activities within the economic development agency became a private-sector strategy in the long run.

Having stimulated education and training reform within government and the private sector, Baugh went on to involve the unions, as representatives of the workforce.

I went to the AFL–CIO and said: 'We've got all this education and training and reform agenda coming up – what do you people think about it? Think about it strategically, form a permanent committee, pass resolutions, institutionalise this, and come to some decisions about what you want to see as a vision related to the strategy.' It took a year to do – but they did institutionalise it and now they've got a group of people working around it.

With the unions involved in the debate he then turned the argument around to look at reform within the union itself.

Then we turned round and asked the unions the question: 'What do you need to do to transform yourselves, you people out there who are being affected by workplace change? I invested a bunch of money in a labour education centre, and the state AFL–CIO, to go out and start.

Reform overall depends on identifying committed individuals.

If you can begin addressing technology and education in the workplace, you find the people who really get into it, and they become viable members of local education boards and commissions at the same time. They connect work to school in another way, and so we gave them money to self-organise five or six major pilots, and a manual on how to do this.

Different groups have different motives for joining in.

On the business side of the ledger, we went to the business community and said: 'OK, we need a quality initiative. We used various mechanisms to identify a set of firms that seemed to be engaging in this already. There were a lot from manufacturing, but also service-sector firms. We identified who we wanted from the firms, and then we wrote a letter to the CEOs too. We were trying to get them into a culture of working with each other. So we invited 100 CEOs to a meeting on two subjects:

- 'Do you want to do a mini-Baldrige?' This was a source of publicity and a template that people could use to effect change.
- 'Do you want to help design a curriculum so that we could pull all these community college partners together across the state, so we can meet the needs of small firms at a reasonable cost?' They can't afford these consultants – all of whom are pitching their own products – and we would also then have some sort of industry standard that says this is good, this is the right way to go.

Seventy of them showed up, and sat there for five hours straight, non-stop, and said damn straight: 'We're not so sure about the awards; we don't want to have one winner. But we want to do the curriculum, and we want to build the mentoring network, etc., etc., etc.. We want to do all this.'

We just took off and ran with it through our sub-committees. It's been astonishingly successful. It became a network. It's peer-to-peer selling, and the theory behind it was: 'You find the ones who are doing it, get them in there, get them investing; you then reach out to find the wanna-bes and help them become.'

So we launched the quality initiative and invested money to seed it as it got going. We staffed it up, organised the sub-committees and then put money into it for two years to make it go.

But reform doesn't just involve customers and the source of funds, it has to involve the suppliers too! So Baugh's team in Oregon directed some of their efforts to the educators.

> On a parallel track, we organised the twelve or thirteen community college partners to reform too. We helped seed the road map of how you develop a quality curriculum. They used curricula obtained from those businesses who were already engaged in this process and were serving as advisors to us. So they're off and running with this.

Such wholesale reform has already directly affected many of the local inhabitants; however a state like Oregon has a vast silent majority who need to be involved too. Any local economy depends to a greater or lesser degree on the balance of trade into and out of it. For exports to boom quality and price must be better than elsewhere. For quality and price to be good the local demand must be high and this depends on educated and involved consumers. So the Economic Development Unit turned its attention to the state's inhabitants.

> We went back to the Work Force Council and said: 'You've got to have a private-sector driven initiative within the communities of our state.' So we had got one going on quality, so that you have high-performance work organisations. The Labor side was addressing transformation of work and how to do these things. The third piece was school reform, because you want kids who are going to be high-performance workers when you've got workplaces that are high performance!
>
> To organise the business community to participate, we got a foundation to put money in, and that funded a multi-year project of community-based organising.

We often talk of transformation involving two sides: the hearts and the minds. Often reform depends upon convincing intellectual evidence so Baugh's team set about collecting this material.

> We engaged in a study of all the workplaces in the state. It is the largest per capita database in the nation, with responses from 1,700 workplaces in the state, public and private, about training and education for the current workforce, their connections to the education system in the state, what would they like them to be, and examining the characteristics of how the system performs and what kind of businesses they were.
>
> The state had the strategic plan, which said: 'We want the best workforce'. There was a very high-powered council set up, called the Progress Board, and we then benchmarked the whole state.[1] We benchmarked the entire state around environment, jobs and training and laid out a series of twenty-year markers. Figuring out how you measure yourself as a state, as an institution, helps drive the agenda.

All of this was designed, by the people who did it, to achieve cultural transformation. You have got to hit it from every available institution, over and over and over, doing it so that you can do so over time, and have the peers in the communities drive themselves. It can't be driven by government. You've got to be smart about how you organise behind it to be dynamic. You've got to change their mind-set.

When we came in as Economic Development, the businesses said: 'We've never worked with a governmental institution,' (meaning 'we hate government'), 'but you guys are OK. Would you join our board?' Every one of these things we started, they always wanted us on the board – not just because we were a source of funds, but because we weren't what they thought we were going to be. We did come with a bit of a vision, but also a fairly solid sense of organising to meet their own interests. In a way, we talked and acted more like business than most government did. We negotiated hard at times. I told my government partners to go screw themselves because they wanted us just to provide everything for business. I said: 'If they don't want to play, then let them leave – they're not partners and we don't want them because when we're gone, then they'll be gone too. That's not the name of the game here.' When that happened, they were stunned to find out I was a labour leader; they thought I was a businessman that had gone into government!

We're three to five years down the path on these things – and it's worked. I think it's the right way to do it because I know other ways don't work. We really won't know more for another five years. That's one of the very tough things in this business. I gave a speech yesterday, and I was talking about the two great American imperatives: one is patience, and the other is entropy. You find it's a fine line between the bureaucracies and impatience for quarterly results from Wall Street. You've got to find a way continually to support a movement towards the change over time. That's why I like what we did with benchmarks; that really cast it in another light, and setting up an institution to help, which was designed exclusively to keep you on target.

Baugh's approach with the Oregon state and its Economic Development Unit dramatically iillustrates the importance of a multifaceted approach.

INTERVIEW 6.2 LOOKING TO THE FUTURE
Yasuhiko Inoue, Deputy Director, Japan Productivity Center

The Japanese economy presents a special set of problems when establishing the high-performance workplace. As Yasuhiko Inoue explains, the predominance of smaller businesses makes change very difficult.

The small and medium enterprise sector

We have always had a very high proportion of smaller businesses in Japan. This has an economic impact, because it leads to double or even triple wage-structures through the use of subcontractors and sub-subcontractors. This approach needs to be re-examined.

We are very lucky in that the union structure, the social system, the economic climate – including international and government – all the infrastructure is well-established for productivity, but not for control, as the co-ordination is down to luck rather than deliberate choice. In most cases, our success has been in taking a new technology and expanding its application – as with carbon-fibre or transistor radios, and so on. We are not that technologically advanced – in some areas maybe – but that's not what we are good at. For productivity we are far behind the USA, UK and OECD members. A superficial part of the economy is attractive – but the reality is very much slower.

Funding of small businesses stimulates this activity in applied technology, by encouraging entrepreneurs repeatedly to attempt to establish a going business. Whereas in Britain, small business funding is largely from the banks and depends upon security offered by borrowers, the system is very different in Japan.

Each month more than 1,000 companies go into bankruptcy – each year 15,000 – that's been happening for twenty years or more. There's a very high turnover of companies – you've heard of the 'peculiar' Japanese management style, but when you compare it in those terms you've got to ask whether the claims made for it are real. The funding for businesses is different from that in other countries – it is quite normal for people to set up 'venture' businesses. Large businesses are used to support them – but the government scheme is quite dynamic: since 99% of the workforce is in this area, both national and regional government help such businesses, either directly or by providing very cheap consultancy. Take a five- or six-person family business: suppose that they want to buy a robot costing £200,000 – provided that they have been performing just averagely, then a Japanese company or bank would easily give them the money they need. The money would be offered on security if banks were involved, but for government support, previous performance is more closely studied than security. Between 1988 and 1991, when land prices were tripling and it was easy to make money in land, people were over-investing and collapsing, but the scheme of support for small businesses is well-established, and has not been affected by this.

What can be done to stimulate Self-Management?

Inoue has also developed a three-pronged approach to achieving high performance. In Japan, basic education produces a literate and numerate workforce, although earlier on we have seen that problem-solving ability is underdeveloped. The starting point then is developing these skills and a management approach that encourages them.

Let's look at what we are doing to encourage Self-Management. JUSE's QCCs are a type of Self-Management, but from our productivity viewpoint, we call it small group activities – this is a formal structure. From one worker to a

group of people (usually five to ten), sometimes even more. Our training programmes have been developed to stimulate interest in this area. For instance, at
the lowest levels they now reflect on the benefits to be gained from, and the
skills to help, a group of others to contribute to their work. We believe that generally a group of workers produces better results than a single worker. We have
to encourage these people – and from the HRM perspective, we encourage managers to stimulate their employees.

As with Oregon, Inoue feels that the lead needs to come from government. Much of the effectiveness of Japanese infrastructure comes from
strong government control, but control through bureaucracy. Most people
interviewed felt that this bureaucracy was a barrier to high performance.

Now what about the macro-level? According to the report of the Social Economic Congress of Japan (SECOJ), the first priority is government
administrative reform. To stimulate company activities overall, there are so
many constraints – governmental, bureaucratic control; so this is the first priority. The second is education. The third is transportation, energy and
international relations.

Whereas the Oregon study set about benchmarking state performance in
such areas as transport and energy, before it began to accept them as part of
the problem, Inoue is saying that we know they are not good enough, so let's
do something now. His call is for organisations to take a wider perspective,
looking at their own needs as only one part of a larger picture. High performance in individual organisations calls for a high-performance infrastructure.

Transportation has to be considered from a productivity-related system.
For instance, traditionally we have focused on immediate performance – I can
send a two-wheel courier with a single package and it will be there within the
hour, or I can send it overnight. The first one causes a traffic jam, the other
doesn't, and is more productive. But nowhere is there any encouragement to
think in these terms. We must have a more effective way of looking at this.
The standard of the public transport system is alright – but sometimes it is too
much – you need a balance. Of course, you don't want to encourage people to
take to the roads, but you also have to ensure that these facilities are near
capacity. It is time for us to review balanced productivity increases. This is
true in everything – environment, transport and safety.

INTERVIEW 6.3 SMWTs AND GOVERNMENT POLICIES
Jim Burge, Vice-President, Motorola

As Burge explains, the very legislation intended to provide workers with
protection is now in danger of denying them opportunities.

Government relations are an important aspect of Motorola's operations, not only internationally but nationally, regionally and locally.

> We have state government representatives in each of the four states where we have large numbers of employees, including Texas and Arizona. So I have a responsibility of co-ordinating what we do at the federal level, and to ensure that we are consistent in our positions at the state level as well. An example of that is the current debate in health-care, because there are a number of state initiatives going on at the same time.
>
> I work extensively with associations – such as SHRM – I'm on their advisory board. I deal extensively with the Business Round Table and the National Association of Manufacturers (NAM) (that is, nationalised business) and a lesser-known group, but a very effective one in the area of company welfare, known as the ERISA Industry Committee (ERIC), to shape large business policy on health-care, pension and welfare – public policy decisions. [ERISA stands for the Employee Retirement Income Security Act of 1974.]

Burge worked on an early project with the NAM to spread best practice.

> We created incentives for member-companies to move into the workplace of the future, by putting together success stories and creating executive-to-executive forums where those who had been successful in making this transition could share their successes with others.[2]

Anyone looking at the portfolio of legislation currently passing through the national assemblies can't fail to be impressed with the way politicians have grasped the nettle of high performance. Examples include: The Teamwork and Employees Management Act, Goals 2000 Educate America Act, School to Work Opportunities Act, The National School to Work Transition and Youth Apprenticeship Act, Career Pathways Act and so on. Many of these have been tabled but are not likely to move. But some do have the support of the business world. One of these involves defining the skills that are needed to work in a high-performance organisation.

> There is, along with Education 2000, a Title four provision that deals with national skills-standards. A number of us have been working with the Administration to draft it, as we feel it is important to the nation. It would create a skills-standards forum – the intention is to set up a national board which would put the government in the role of a convenor pulling together knowledgeable people to look at the competencies which exist in a high- performance workplace.
>
> As you walk through our manufacturing facilities you meet factory assemblers who, twenty years ago, were performing work in the classic Tayloristic segmented pattern – check your brains at the door, do rote assembly, if you have a problem hold up your hand and someone comes over and solves the problem. Today they schedule their own work, they deal with vendors, they deal with customers, and they form teams to solve problems. They need new kinds of skills.

Establishing a national board to identify these competencies will help us better to communicate to educational institutions that, coming out of schools today, we need students who are equipped for an environment that involves teaming, so there is a need for good communication skills, and the ability to give and receive constructive criticism. We need problem-solving skills – not just rote memory – and this has to do as much with how you teach as what you teach. We think that the time has long passed for memorising and regurgitating material in multiple-choice questions which are easy for teachers to grade. We need to put together teams of students to solve problems, and who have learning experiences which are relevant to today's workplace.

This legislation would allow a lot of people to get involved in identifying those competencies, identifying to the schools what those competencies are, and asking them to think about changing the way they teach. They could still have their core curriculum, but would teach it in such a way that allows teaming and involves problem-solving.

It will also help those businesses which haven't yet made the transition to become high performance workplaces to understand what they are and why those competencies are needed. And finally it would serve as a road map for both applicants and current workers to get their skills upgraded to work in this high performance workplace.

We work hard to make sure that the legislation is flexible, is voluntary and that we don't create another government bureaucracy that's going to be overbearing on how businesses run their business.

New situations require new approaches

Burge also encourages the active participation of government in reform and is not afraid to use what negotiating tools he has available. There is a constant fear, with new legislation, that it will create another bureaucratic burden.

> The Re-employment Act of 1994 is an attempt to take about half-a-dozen federally supported worker-training programmes and re-evaluate them, to converge them into a single programme, realising efficiencies in doing that, and at the same time reassessing the training to ensure that it is relevant to current jobs.
>
> Clinton wanted people like me standing up with him when he introduced the programme. We have said: 'Thanks, but no thanks'. There's additional savings that they're not pursuing. Businesses go through restructuring and generate savings to fund new programmes without creating incremental cost – we think the government should do the same thing. We're encouraging them to move ahead on the consolidation, but insisting that it be done out of general revenues.

The role that Burge plays involves dealing directly with the legislature, Secretary Reich in Labor, Riley in Education and their staffs, as they draw up respective legislation. He then works with associations to help shape their opinion and form coalitions of other like-thinking companies, either to support or raise concerns about legislation.

The legislative process is often a laborious one, yet if we are going to have an impact we need to understand it and how we can influence it.

> When Clinton introduces legislation it will be the Administration's proposal. Now it must move through the legislative process where he will find members of both the House and Senate who will sign on to his bill. There will be others who have a different point of view, and they will either draft their own bill or attach amendments. The Bill will be assigned to various committees in the House and Senate, and they will hold hearings. Associations like the National Association of Manufacturers will come and testify. Individual companies like Motorola might testify and offer opinions. Ultimately they will get to the point where they mark up the bill, and it leaves committees and eventually moves to the House and Senate floor. If they pass something it will be a year, or a year-and-a-half, or even two years down the road. Then the Senate and the House versions must be brought together through a conference committee, and coming out of that will be a final bill which they vote on again, and then that goes to the President. So all through that process there is an opportunity to influence and shape that legislation. I assess whether a given piece of legislation is likely to move and, if it is, how important is it to Motorola? You can't be all things to all people; we have to prioritise.

Typical of the problems of government intervention is the creation of a burdensome set of reporting requirements. If an organisation like Motorola is to divert resources to preparing for the high performance workplace it needs to minimise other overheads and the government relations role can be an important one.

> A comprehensive reform of occupational safety and health is being introduced; it is a very onerous bill which would place a tremendous burden with respect of training, and notice, and reporting to the government. So we have quantified that. We have taken the bill and said, what if this were enacted in its present form today; we have analysed what kind of incremental cost it would place on us to do business with this new legislation. If they're going to create an additional burden of several tens of millions of dollars to the cost of doing business with the United States, and if we have alternative ways, which we think are less burdensome and more effective, then that's a strong argument on US competitiveness.
>
> Now we have also formed coalitions of companies who have contributed to funding third-party research on a nationwide basis and we estimate the cost of a piece of legislation, should it be enacted, on US business in total. That's a very effective message to government.

Shifting GNP to smaller and medium-sized enterprises has a significant effect on the legislative process. Smaller firms can afford less time and effort in lobbying against counterproductive legislation and are less likely to be effectively organised to lobby as anything other than a lone voice.

In the 1992 Workplace Readiness survey there was a lot of emphasis on the small and medium-sized organisation. What the CEOs tell us is that they know they need to change in order to remain competitive. But they don't know quite what to do, and they are looking for guidance. We see associations like the Chambers or NAM being a national resource to these small companies, allowing them to identify common needs in a region, perhaps coming together to go to the community colleges to develop training programmes for a number of small companies, training programmes for supervisors and managers, encouraging the transition, and always remembering this role-model concept – creating a resource of these small to medium-sized companies who have made the transition and are willing to share their experience with others.

Larger organisations, though, can play their part too, and need to do so as many of the SMEs are their critical suppliers or distributors. As Burge explains, this may involve cost, but some at least can be self-financing.

The Galvin Center, or Motorola University, is now selling as much as $10m per year of training, at cost, to our vendors, to customers and to government agencies. We think that this is another way – if we can encourage more and more companies to complete this chain, this link with the vendors who are frequently the smaller and medium-sized companies, then you are also going to create a domino-effect of success which will spill on. We now have a well-trained team of people who have their bags packed, with training ready to deliver on-site to our customers at very reasonable cost, and we think that will have a contagious effect.

Another aspect of the demographics of the next few years is that workers are becoming far more mobile. They are not only having to relocate in order to find work, but the skills that they have are in demand in a more diverse set of workplaces. Furthermore, the leisure boom of the 1970s and 1980s means that long-distance travel is less daunting than ever before. To organisations investing in training this poses a serious threat. Training carries a substantial up-front cost, so it's important either to retain your trained employees or accept that you will recruit equally trained and experienced personnel. But how do you know that one company's in-house training is the same as another's? In the UK, a system of vocational qualifications has begun to evolve, but we are a long way from establishing equivalents of in-house training on a formal basis. In the US the larger companies are beginning to do so.

We are working with other companies to recognise each other's training programmes. Based upon our agreement to have a standard curriculum, let's say on SPC, we have formed a coalition of companies, IBM, Xerox, Kodak, Motorola and several others. We have now got core courses, and if SPC is taught at Motorola and somebody comes to us from, say, Kodak, who has been through the same course, then we recognise that course because we have developed it together. I think that this can spill over to smaller companies too, and help them in the efficiency of their training.

The SMEs are most often in the service sector while larger organisations are split between manufacturing, service, or both. There is often a perception that larger manufacturing organisations have the strongest (or at least more acceptable) voice in political sectors. We hear of the drinks industry, the motor manufacturers, and the tobacco lobby, but we rarely come across the courier lobby, the voice of interior decorators and so on. Will this distort the legislative process?

There's a sensitivity to the concern that the small business is largely service – one of the strongest lobbying organisations in Washington is the NFIB (National Federation of Independent Businesses) they have a huge grass-roots mechanism available that's all the little Mom-and-Pop shops that can range from one to ten people; a lot of them are in retail, small manufacturing, courier, whatever it might be. At the opposite end of the spectrum is the Business Round Table, which is made up of the 200 largest companies, which can be a combination of manufacturing and service.

The legislative process, with all of its public airing, hears from all of these bodies. NFIB represents the real small businesses – the Chambers & Commerce fit into a lot of retail elements, and small to medium-sized companies. You get a vertical slice through them like the National Association of Manufacturers. Then you get industry associations like the American Electronics Association, in which Motorola has a leadership role. We approach legislation from an electronics industry point of view. Again, we have some common values – the electronics industry is largely non-union, high technology and uses state-of-the-art manufacturing techniques. We have a different agenda from the old smoke-stack industries, such as steel and autos.

You get all of these different groups coming at members of Congress as they debate the legislation. So the interest of the service sector is heard very well in this forum, and there is a strong sensitivity to the fact that this is where job-growth will occur.

The impacts of job mobility, and skills increases are widespread. The social security systems that have evolved in most developed countries, for example, are based around a concept of lifetime employment and single skills.

The right-sizing that large business has gone through has created a whole new mind-set. We are no longer going through the old traditional lay-offs where you assume that you are going to go back to your old job. What has happened now is that companies have developed new efficiencies to reduce the number of people they have on a permanent basis. The jobs have changed dramatically – if you do go back, you will go back to a new job, and you will need new skills for that. In most cases, you won't go back ever – so those people have to be retrained. That's the theme behind the Re-employment Act. Our old unemployment system was to tide you over for six months until you went back to your old job. The new legislation widens that with investment and gives dislocated workers up to seventy-eight weeks of income support while they are trained with new skills to re-enter employment.

Justifying the investment

These investments in partnering, education, training and lobbying are difficult to justify to shareholders at the best of times, but how do we do so in leaner periods? Even for organisations with a strong financial base, it is one thing for the senior managers to state their commitment and another for the employees to go along with it.

> Maybe ten years ago I was sitting with Bob Galvin talking about how, as businesses prospered, they would invest heavily in training and education – and as things got tough, so it was one of the first budget items to go. I said that the only way that we are going to maintain a sustained long-term return on our education and training investment is to make sure that it continues, through both good times and bad. Despite all the encouragement from corporate offices, the businesses still behaved as you would expect them to. We finally mandated through our corporate office that every one of our businesses must spend 1.5% of payroll on training and education each year, and if they didn't show justification that they had spent that amount, then they would be assessed on that by corporate office and it would be part of their P&L performance. Our general managers went to their HR person and said: 'Make sure we take advantage of this because we are going to be charged anyway'. Over a period of time they started seeing the long-term results of this continuing commitment to education, and we're now running in the vicinity of 3% of payroll. We now have changed that 1.5% directive to one which states that every employee should have forty hours of training per year. The reason is that we saw that it wasn't being fairly allocated in some of the businesses. There was a heavy emphasis on engineering and management training, rather than training for the front-line worker.
>
> As we went through this transition, we assessed our current workers and found that long-term, loyal Motorolans who were tasked to do the old-style segmented work were severely lacking in the skills we needed. Half of our factory workforce could not read at seventh-grade level, or complete math appropriately. We needed what we called 'Manufacturing Letters' in order for them to understand the more sophisticated training programmes which we would deliver to them in the company. They needed to learn how to do a Pareto analysis, SPC, teaming, and communications skills. So we engaged in a heavy investment in 'English as a Second Language', math, reading and communication skills, spending over $30m over a five-year period. Then we started assessing our job-applicants, and started finding the same thing. We started running an employment screen – half the applicants coming to us couldn't achieve this seventh-grade reading and fifth-grade math test.
>
> We said that we really needed to develop our partnership with the local schools who are providing the workforce of the future. So Ed Bales was asked

to take a full-time assignment, reporting to the CEO, developing a corporate initiative to create a partnership with the school systems in every location where we have a large population. The objective is that by the year 2000, the students coming out of that school system will have the competencies that we need in the high performance work place. That met with a lot of resistance at first. Schools said: 'You're meddling – we don't want you'. We kept coming back and coming back, and they realised that we were not there to bash them, but to co-operate.

Now why should we make that kind of investment? It is a heavy investment that was largely based around Galvin saying: 'We've got to have a faith that there is going to be a return'. In dealing with education systems it's a kind of trust – the faith that if we invest in them then it will come back many times over. Our corporation really doesn't ask us to quantify this. There's a high level of trust that our investment really will come back, and won't just help us but will help this nation, and if the nation prospers then Motorola will too. There are many cases where I have taken to the CEO issues which are important, but not critical, to the company – but where it is the right thing to do for the nation – and the latter weighs as heavily as the former. If you feel that this is right for the nation, then it has got to be right for Motorola.

We have tried to quantify results sometimes – there have been some cases where there has been little change in the process or the product, but the only thing that has changed has been the significant commitment to the education of the workforce. We have got some documentation to show a 30:1 return. In terms of quality, productivity, lower turnover, cycle-time reduction. In other cases it is much more difficult because there are many things going on at the same time – there might be investment in new capital equipment, technology might change, the process might change, as you are also investing in education. As you'll see from our assessment techniques – we are really trying to get away from the 'halo effect', smiles on the faces. We go back after a period of time and test whether what you've learned in a classroom is really being applied on a job, and then measure the results of that application in a way that particularly suits.

Influencing other organisations

In a firm that is little removed from a family concern such arguments can still hold sway, but surely the rest of us will need a lot more convincing? Organisations are notoriously bad at correlating investments and returns on anything, let alone training, so how can we convince them that this investment is worthwhile?

More and more companies are getting smart about benchmarking. In the last five years, Motorola has doubled its revenues, increased productivity by 78% measured on sales per employee, and created 17,000 new jobs when many other companies have been through just the opposite in down-sizing.

The cynics would say that that's because we're in an emerging technology and has nothing to do with High Performance, but so was IBM! We think that our competitors can make the same kind of capital investment as we can make. We think that technology is only a momentary advantage – it doesn't take long for a competitor to reverse-engineer the latest cellular telephone and come out with one that weighs half-an-ounce less. The long-term, sustainable, competitive advantage is only achieved by investing in and using your human resources. If you think of your human resources as an asset not as a cost – we think that is a culture that someone can't easily replicate or take away from you.

What we're seeing are empowered teams of associates on a world-wide basis doing remarkably creative things which are continuously helping us to reduce cost, to reduce cycle-time, and to improve our service to the customer. Just from the ones that we have been able to quantify, we know as a result since we started our march on Six Sigma that we have quantifiable savings of over $4 billion. We don't think that we would have realised these unless we had invested in the education and empowerment of our workers. Those are powerful arguments that drop right to the bottom line.

Cultural diversity and self-direction

Another dimension to the demographic shift that we are witnessing is the globalisation of races. In the past, discrimination has been met with legislation. Racism remains an important aspect of any political agenda. If we are moving towards Self-Managing Work Teams and issues of discrimination are not addressed, what are the likely consequences and how will they be dealt with? In some organisations, moving towards high performance workplaces, considerable EEO training has been delivered. In others, despite the shift in working arrangements, established discrimination persists and teams show a continuing pattern of disproportionate representation.

Jim Burge highlighted another dimension to this issue.

A lot of our managers are coming to the conclusion that solving problems with teams of people from a diverse cultural background adds value – we don't talk about EEO (equal employment opportunities) and similar issues. We have facilities around the world and through our continuous improvement teams we are able to see the performance of these groups from a rich variety of backgrounds. The line managers are telling me that a diverse background gives improved quality to the problem-solving process. They haven't tied down what it is, but it could be an important future development.

Unions, management unions and labour representation

Labour laws differ widely from country to country. Many were designed to protect workers in an environment that was quite the opposite to that of the high performance workplace. This doesn't mean that the laws that exist favour such a culture though. Both unions and management would like to see these changed, but to what extent and how do their approaches differ?

In recent years the power of the unions has been changed in many ways. There are some exceptional examples of collaborative management, such as the GM/NUMMI plant.

The nature of unions too differ enormously around the world. Could the high performance workplace provide an opportunity for old antagonisms to be put aside as the goals of management and labour coincide?

In Washington, the AFL–CIO claims to represent the American worker: yet only 11% of the private-sector workforce is unionised. There are a lot of well-meaning companies which continue to earn the trust of their employees who otherwise could join a union but who choose to deal directly with their management. There is a whole host of pending labour law reforms, which are being promoted by AFL–CIO, that will make it easier to unionise. I argue that their declining membership is because enlightened management has a higher degree of respect for human resources, rather than any problem with the law, so we are in totally opposite positions.

There are areas where we do find some partnerships with the unions – this whole area of the education field, for example. But the concept of empowerment is a threat to them. If you let empowerment go to its ultimate conclusion, you have to ask the question: why would an employee want to pay union dues if indeed they have control over their own work environment?

At the Department of Labor they are having a hard time wrestling with this, because it is not the Department of the Employer – it is the Department of Labor – and they have traditionally looked upon themselves as the one cabinet post that represents the American worker. They deal with the portion of labour laws which have in the past typically dealt with union relationships. Most of our laws were created in the 1930s when they only anticipated adversarial relationships – our national Labor Relations Act is designed to give employees the right to choose to form a union for protection to deal collectively with management. So now you get today's environment, with laws that were created in the 1930s, and the Department of Labor's trying to decide what role they play.

The Office of the American Workforce was created this year to deal with the workplace of the future. They started focusing on co-operative relationships between management and unions as showcase examples. They finally came to the realisation that there is the 89% out there who are not unionised, so they have got to rethink their role and encourage these co-operative relationships in non-union facilities. They are wrestling with how to do that, because the Department of Labor has traditionally had close relationships with organised labour rather than with management.

Under the National Labor Relations Act, created in the 1930s, there is a provision that prohibits the creation of sham unions. Many companies created in-house unions, dominated by the company, to keep legitimate international unions from organising, and that was prohibited by law.

If you look at the letter of the law, teams are groups of employees dealing with the management on terms and conditions of employment. While their primary charter is to deal with issues of cost, quality and the customers, they also get involved in rearranging work-schedules, terms and conditions, and so on. Some teams are now deciding how they allocate their merit increases based upon team performance, so under the letter of the law they are violating the law and there's a lot of debate going on now – whether we should modify it to accommodate teams.

We get in to the problem of political debate – if they open up the Act and give this concession to companies like Motorola, then the labour movement is going to want some concessions to help them organise, and so you get into reform that you may just as well not have. So that issue is sitting there simmering. There have been some recent decisions made by the National Labor Relations commission (one case called Electromation, and another one with Du Pont) that have recently ordered the disbanding of teams.

At Motorola our teams concept has nothing to do with unions and is a way of doing business. While we recognise that we are at risk, we feel that the risk is very low because it is such a certain way of preserving jobs and involving our associates in running the company on a global basis.

There is now the Team Act, which has been introduced by Secretary Nancy Casbaum. A group of us wrote the paper and got her involvement. What that does is to correct this deficiency in the National Labor Relations Act, exempting the kind of teams that you see at Motorola from the terms of the Act. Some day we might find the opportunity to attach it to another piece of legislation and it might go through without opening up the Act to all the other reform issues.

INTERVIEW 6.4 TRAINING AND DEVELOPMENT – THE ISSUES
Dr Mary McCain, The American Society for Training and Development

As we've seen, achieving a high performance workplace calls for a substantial investment in training and development. Existing workers may well be in need of this as much as new recruits. Traditional reluctance on the part of government to fund such training may need to be challenged, as Mary McCain explains.

From the point of view of adult-worker training, there are really two areas of policy in which we are involved. The obvious one is adult-worker or currently-employed worker training, which we are now calling incumbent-worker training. This does not have much going on in terms of federal policy because there is a bias against the government's funding activities which the private sector should perhaps be paying for itself. We are seeing, for the first time this year, some interest in this activity. A senator from New Mexico has considered introducing a bill to provide an incremental tax credit for incumbent-worker training in order to encourage more of that particularly in manufacturing companies.

The source of new jobs

Although the trend is for GNP to shift towards smaller service providers, many people believe that manufacturing deserves preferential treatment. Is this analysis solid or is it simply based on outmoded thinking?

> The emphasis on manufacturing arises partly from the nature of the senator's district, but I have recently been to several conferences and seminars dealing with this issue, and it is supported by all sectors. There is a received wisdom in this country that the best jobs, and most new jobs, are created in the manufacturing sector. Even if you admit that service jobs are not all so-called 'hamburger-flipping' jobs, the line goes that the best jobs are still in manufacturing, and we need to get manufacturing competing in this country. Those are the jobs that we need – the genuine high-skill, high-wage jobs.
>
> Many analysts argue that it is small manufacturing companies which are really creating new jobs. So we need to act as a catalyst for those companies. They have the least resources to become competitive, yet they are the ones which most need them.

Of course the problem becomes cloudier still when we look at the nature of people's tasks at work – even if they are employed in a manufacturing organisation.

> Looking at manufacturing as a monolithic activity is a mistake: there are a lot of service jobs within manufacturing. The service sector itself is more complex and includes things like health and transportation, which are not included in manufacturing. There is clearly some discussion about whether or not the best jobs are really in manufacturing, but that continues to be the given. As a result, most of the legislative activity to do with the private sector is focused on manufacturing.
>
> Motorola had a plant manager doing a presentation recently, and he was saying that eight or nine years ago they did a task analysis of some of their technical people. They found that over 70% of their time was spent on non-technically related activity. At any rate, most of the federal policy, either the discussion of it or the actual policy itself, is focused towards manufacturing.

Promoting training and development

The ASTD, then, is concentrating its policy efforts on the manufacturing sector. As we saw with Jim Burge at Motorola, the first priority is to provide support for smaller organisations to invest in their employees. The second is to provide inspiration. While Motorola are mainly doing this by opening up their doors and by pooling experience, the ASTD is endeavouring to do so through government intervention.

> The other policy area in which we have been very involved is manufacturing and industrial extension activity, which the Clinton administration strongly supports. The idea is that various state, local, regional or federal centres provide information and technical assistance to small or medium-sized manufacturers about what they need to become competitive. The early centres focused on technology, but they learned that a lot of small companies did not necessarily need sophisticated technology. They needed training, business-planning skills, or organisation of the workplace. Policy tends to be controlled by engineering technologists who accept the importance of training but don't really understand how that fits in.

So the drivers within industry are often the technologists, yet they frequently lack sufficient understanding of human issues. These differences are reflected again at a government level.

There are often conflicting interests even within the same government and adult worker training is not exempt from this.

> In this country, workforce, employee, and labour issues are controlled, both in terms of money and federal regulation, by the Department of Labor and the Committees and the Congress who are responsible for employee concerns. The manufacturing interests, business interests, technology development, R & D issues, technology transfer issues, are all in the Department of Commerce and the commerce-orientated committees. So you have completely different constituencies, officials and elected representatives. The technology people tend to be the ones who have driven the manufacturing technology-transfer activity, and most of those folks are engineers. It has been an interesting experience to represent the human side, in the technology community.

Legislative barriers to teams

At government level the human dimension though can become confused with barriers such as the National Labor Relations Board which Jim Burge referred to, and its recent rulings on management unions. As McCain points out, these disparities are now being investigated.

> There is a commission looking into this called the Commission on Labor – Management Relations or the Dunlop Commission, after the labour economist who heads it. It has been holding hearings on this issue for several months and the testimony has been about the use of teams.

The changing roles of training and development

The ASTD is not a corporate lobby. It represents individual members, many of whom have functional responsibilities for training and development. Despite the increasing need for training at work it is not necessarily being provided by these members. Similarly corporate performance is not often linked to the activities of the 'Training' function.

> Our 55,000 members are professionals in their organisations. In some instances, line managers are replacing the training professionals, and so they are under threat. In fact, the more sophisticated training is not coming from the training and development people. The responsibility is being given to line people, quality specialists and so on, or else the teams are being trained to carry all of this forward themselves.
>
> The demographics of the members in our organisation are changing. That is something we are wrestling with and trying to figure out. The profession is changing. One of our responsibilities is clear to us, at any rate, and that is to tell them this! To make them aware that they may need to rethink how they are developing their careers. Most of our members are still people who have training and development titles. One of the effects of the changing field is that it is harder to identify those people who might actually be doing training, because they no longer have 'training' in their job-title. Increasingly, when companies begin to deal with becoming more competitive, they are doing it as a whole. Therefore, you would not drive it from your training department. It would not make sense to do that. When they begin to address the training need, they will just call 'Training' in.

One implication of this is that minor legislation, or changes in the field that might previously have been communicated through training functions, can't be relied upon to reach the right audience. In the UK, recent activities like the Management Charter Initiative, Investors In People and the Diploma in Company Direction have tried to target these mixed audiences, but with only partial success. Achieving change towards high performance needs strong support to promote to both.

Influencing change

Conflicting agendas can hamper this movement too. As McCain points out national interests can easily conflict with local and company ones.

> There are examples here of local consortia which have developed among themselves, working with a community college, or a lot of small companies in the area making the same machine tool, or whatever. There have been a lot of successes with these. In some cases, they have developed a 'teaching factory' which allows them to go and use the latest technology and that kind of thing. So that is really a private version of a 'manufacturing extension centre'.

These rarely originate from a federal level, because the federal government would just make it easier to develop private ones. So really it is almost impossible for somebody, regardless of the topic, to create any kind of national momentum.

Very few places are really nationally connected, and those companies that are, are already doing it and don't really want federal government to do anything. Motorola would prefer the federal government to do nothing; they don't need it, or it gets in their way – although they will say it would be useful for their suppliers.

The concept of manufacturing extension centres remains an important one. There are examples around the world.

I was lucky enough to represent ASTD on a team that went to Germany and Denmark, to look at youth apprenticeship programmes. One of the things that I was struck by in Germany was their so-called Training Centres which, in many ways, were like the best of our 'Manufacturing Extension Centres.' They were created by the Chambers of Commerce. There is mandatory membership of the Chambers there, and they are not only able to control and generate an enormous amount of forward movement, but there is something for the government to work with. Even if they do not do what the government says, they are another partner. We do not have that in this country. I was so struck by how handy it was to have these institutions.

We spend so much time talking about how organised labour is weak here compared to European countries but organised management is really something. We do not have effective employer organisations, or effective small business organisations. We have groups that ostensibly represent them, but they do not have power. They cannot represent them in any decision-making capacity. This is a terrible handicap. It seems clear to me how much of a handicap it is now having seen how they operate elsewhere.

The dissemination of better practice through technical assistance is largely coming out of the manufacturing extension activities. The Clinton administration proposes to have about a hundred established by 1996, small local ones, federal ones, and larger ones. Many exist already, but they are going to fold them in, not start from scratch. They are supposed to be active in seeking out small and medium-sized companies, and offering advice and assistance. Most of them just work on one thing at a time, though. They don't go in and say, 'You need this technology and these kinds of training, and this marketing, and this is a quality problem – you should do all of these things'.

Similar problems have been encountered by UK Training and Enterprise Councils (TECs).

Many companies today are spurred to action by witnessing exceptional feats in other organisations. This is one reason why benchmarking is so popular as a trigger for change. Is there a need for legislation to encourage this? As McCain points out, one significant incentive for lobbying is not just to achieve legislation but also financial backing.

There is a bill being debated in the Senate which would encourage the development of a national computer or electronic network to carry best practice for different vertical and horizontal cuts for industry, technology and company size. Companies could tap into this to find out what a similar small company which made wood products, using XYZ type technology, in the North-west, did to solve a problem.

Some of this is happening on a smaller level – they do have some of these networks – but this initiative is designed to make them uniform and provide access for people who cannot afford them, because right now they are driven by companies and 'for profit' agencies which can afford it, while most companies that need it can't.

An initiative like this needs authorising by legislation. Money must be appropriated for it. This bill is an authorising bill: it could pass and, if no-one appropriates the money, it will just sit there. Occasionally they appropriate money before they have got authorising legislation, which always confuses people enormously. It is part of the tension between the legislative branch and the administrative branch, and part of a general concern about so-called 'industrial policy' and whether the federal government should be mucking around in the private sector. Training, teams, electronic networks, manufacturing extension, are considered by many people to be industrial policies. They are described as a sort of creeping socialism that shouldn't be done at all by the federal government.

The impact of technology

We have heard that the high performance workplace is being driven by increasing sophistication at work. But there are other technology impacts on training and development too.

The use of technology to deliver training is a major issue. Is it efficient and effective, and how much sense does it make to promote training through something that is not accessible for most of the world because of its expense? Computer-based training is also said to become out-moded rather quickly, and it lends itself to some kinds of training more than others.

Another aspect is the use of performance-based technology which supports what you are supposed to do, so you don't have to remember. You have the computer with you and, when you have got to fix a jet engine, you plug it in and it says, 'Turn this screw'. It's a bit more sophisticated than that, but that is very much in vogue. The training implications are considerable. For example, do you train people to follow the technology without the basic knowledge, or do you insist on their pre-qualification? The impact is greatest where you begin to cross-train.

It is so ridiculous. Everyone knows this. It's not as if we don't know it. You can't learn without those fundamental skills. The key to competitiveness is being able to learn new things increasingly rapidly. Once we have all said that, and everyone nods, nodding is about the furthest that we go. That's a little unfair. There are a lot of communities and school systems and companies in the US which are working mightily to change this, but it is slow going!

This might sound semantic, yet it is a crucial point especially when the need for training is being driven by the technologists. Frequently, we train employees to handle a specific instrument or task without helping them to understand why it works. If we then measure the volume of training received, it appears as though we are achieving great things – yet in practice the people have gained little.

Incumbent-worker training

The importance of incumbent-worker training highlights another significant role that lobbyists have. It is easy to assume that the legislators understand a topic well. Many lobbyists fail by assuming just this. Instead their role is really one of educator.

> We have focused so much energy and attention on school-leavers and drop-outs and people who have lost their jobs. There is beginning to be a recognition that a substantial majority of the workforce will continue to be people who are already working. Some attention must be given to them, because most of them are not going to be able to do the jobs that they currently hold if they don't receive any additional training. It is a sort of preventative measure against unemployment. The small-business sector does a proportionally much smaller amount of training, which is why so much of the attention at the federal level is focused on them.
>
> Because these issues are fairly new in terms of policy, we spend a lot of our time, not so much lobbying but educating members of Congress and members of the administration as to what it is about. National government policy about training tends to be for people who have lost their jobs and don't have jobs, so when you talk about training, everyone assumes immediately that is what you mean, and we are constantly saying, 'No, there is this other training. There are other people who need training, people who are already working.'

6.5 GROUP DISCUSSION: BETTER JOBS THROUGH PARTNERSHIP
The Office of the American Workplace, US Department of Labor

The Office of the American Workplace (OAW) was created in 1993 by Secretary Robert Reich to home-in on new workplace practices and new ways of doing work. The OAW mission is to promote those kind of innovative workplace practices, as well as more effective and productive labour-management relations. They are trying to demonstrate how you get to the high performance workplace through partnerships between management and labour.

The need was perceived for an agency to encourage what is already a growing trend in the United States. Recent studies have shown that there are more companies using new workplace initiatives than we thought a year ago. We don't have a mandate or a regulatory basis: we are purely here to provide services, encouragement and inspiration to both businesses and labour unions. We do that by providing information, technical assistance, and partnerships.

We're also trying to do some research that ties in. We did a summary in mid-1993 on the link between innovative workplace practices and long-term performance. There is a growing volume of evidence which shows that what's good for the worker and the workplace is also good for the bottom line. Most people in business agree with that, but it's really difficult to make the change. We thought that, especially for small and medium-sized businesses, it would be useful to have someone from the federal government, with a labour perspective, promoting and advocating these concepts.

Mary McCain mentioned the Department of Commerce Manufacturing Extension Centres. Based on the earlier Agricultural Extension Centres they are developing technology awareness among smaller businesses.

We're trying to work closely with them to bring the human resources element into that equation; to have people who not only talk about new technologies and new production methods, but who also know how to integrate those with your workforce; how to use your people; and how to give them the skills they need.

The skills issue

Before action can be taken, key questions have to be asked and solutions found. The OAW is leading the way through its research-based approach.

In the US there is a growing consensus that there is a wide disparity created by income, based on education. Seventy per cent of the people in the US will never get a college degree. There's a direct correlation in the gap between the upper and lower income groups, based on education, where the top 75% of income is earned by the 25% best-educated. Businesses are crying out to increase their pool of skilled labour, and there are cries for educational reform because workers don't have the basic skills in many cases. Yet, people are also asking, 'What are we going to train them for? What are the jobs? What good jobs are out there?'

In 1993, more than half of the new jobs created in the US were managerial or professional. There are a lot of good jobs out there, with the emergence of new information technologies and changes in the service sector. There's more and more emphasis on higher skills, more flexibility and adaptability. So what we've been trying to do in the Labor Department, and with the Department of Education, is to reform the educational system; to create more partnerships between education and business; to stress innovative models and to create national standards.

We often hear that school students are not emotionally prepared for work as well as educationally. The OAW are addressing this too.

> We're working with the Department of Education on a new 'school-to- work' transition system, creating partnerships and providing opportunities for high school students to go into the workplace while they're still at school.
>
> This will help them structure the high school curriculum so it's more relevant to the students' needs when they leave, and could mean that they have jobs waiting for them because they've already worked with companies, the companies know them, and they know what they need to do to be a good worker.

Common standards are being developed around the world – the vocational qualifications in Britain being a good example. Again the development of these is a responsibility shared by the OAW.

> The same education reform is creating a national system of skill standards, similar to that in Germany, where you can take a course and a test, and then get a certificate for certain kinds of occupational skills, using that as a credential to take to an employer. Like someone in a law firm who knows that you're going to a procedures law school, and when you've passed the bar, they know that you can do certain types of tasks or have certain skills.

The political significance of unemployment is enormous, and no government can afford not to have a variable policy to deal with it. The OAW are part of this policy by working on transitional unemployment.

> Most people who lose their jobs now don't get them back with the same company, or even in the same industry, so we're making a major effort to reinvent the re-employment system, to consolidate retraining programmes and to create better reemployment services. We're using new information technologies and creating a national labour-market system and a customer-orientated service in our job centres.

Addressing the needs of SMEs

The OAW is particularly concerned with achieving change among the smaller employers.

> One proposal that's come to us has been to create regional skills consortia linked to the Manufacturing Technology Centres, where small companies could come together, pool their resources and create learning centres for their workers.
>
> There is not a co-ordinated system in the US. Once people leave high-school, it is really up to them to get ongoing skills training. We have a community college system and a university system. Community colleges try and provide those services, but they have to do that in an entrepreneurial way, working with individual businesses. At certain times they make partnerships with state governments – but there is no network or national framework for that.

Of course providing such facilities is a first step, but sadly the evidence is that even then SMEs won't take up the opportunity unless they are paid to do so.

> It would never be a complete gratuity. At some point there would have to be some cost sharing. I would see though, at least initially, some seed money and perhaps ongoing subsidies. At the moment, though, there's really no money left for large-scale initiatives like that, and so probably it would be in the form of tax credits or a small subsidy that would be contributed partly by federal and partly by state governments.

Stimulating interest

Government endorsement often adds weight. Such endorsement needs to be properly researched, hence the OAW's research activities. It also has to be delivered in a manner that creates ownership and is not patronising. The use of best practice works well in this context. Organisations with a story to tell are identified and then others interested in a similar phenomenon are put in touch. In this way the government doesn't jeopardise the transfer of information and motivation.

> We are creating a national clearing house of best practices, covering about 400 or 500 companies which we consider to be engaging in innovative workplace practices. We are also keeping track of the best articles and information on particular issues. We'll become a resource for people who want to know about events that are going on, a national calendar and route to organisations which are involved in this. Another key initiative is to create better measures for workplace practices, and to collect better evidence of the linkage between practices and performance. We're calling that our Performance Measurement Project. Our third initiative is to form partnerships with trade associations and businesses; and the fourth initiative is to look at ways in which companies down-size and, whether or not there are alternatives to down-sizing.
>
> There are currently more initiatives in the service sector outside the government than inside it. A lot of our partnerships with trade associations involve service-orientated industries. Retail, hotel, hospital and restaurant industries are just some. If you look at our roster of companies, at least 25–30% are service-orientated.

Linking practices to performance

> The Department of Labor looked at past evidence on workplace practices and performance productivity and saw that it lacked rigour. We now have an ongoing effort to collect evidence and work with people doing that research. The Department will also fund some of the initial research.

Shareholders play a crucial role. If the perceived value of an organisation drops, the bolder initiatives will be sacrificed. So it is important for shareholders to have good indices of future value. Unfortunately few of these exist and so a key role to be played by the OAW is to identify and define them. Once defined they can be communicated to the investors.

> We're working with large investors who understand there's a problem which they're not seeing. Some of the leading indicators which they're looking at record what happened last year, instead of saying what's going to happen next year. They understand there is a problem, and they want the Boards of Directors, and business organisations, to figure out how they can better monitor leading indicators like workplace practices. Our role involves trying to convince managers and boards that these workplace practices matter, and then helping the investors convince boards that they'd better be well-informed.
>
> From our perspective, it's just another strategy for influencing change; trying to use the investors and the boards as a lever to get managers to pay more attention to this. We'd just as soon not have to do it, but it's good to substantiate what we're doing, and we're committed to the idea that workplace practices matter. Not everybody feels that way, so a lot of people need to have more meat, more specific information. Some people are driven by information like that and some are not. Some are going to be more influenced if they're rewarded by the finance and capital markets for making larger investments.
>
> Right now if you say: 'I'm going to take lower earnings for two years while I train everybody and reorganise the work', you're getting at best a neutral reaction from investors.

In the UK the Total Quality (TQ) movement was blighted by disinformation. Stories circulated about how it had adversely affected the performance of businesses. If you've got the research there you can prevent that from happening.

> That is what the research tends to show. If you do things piecemeal, they're not likely to work very well, but if you do them systematically they work better. As part of this project, we put out a request for proposals to get more research done on these issues. We've also created a new National Centre on the Workplace. It is statutorily mandated, and we've funded it this year to do more research on high performance workplace practices. The National Science Foundation is also doing a $9 million project on the workplace, not just workplace practices, but what they're calling total quality management, though we are assured that it's broader than just TQM.
>
> By sharing information, encouraging businesses, by our business outreach effort; and by working with the associations, with the Performance Measurements Project adding credibility, we hope to establish that this isn't a gut-reaction. We're not suggesting that people consider these practices because it's the 'right thing to do', or because it treats workers well. Being the Department of Labor, we are the advocacy agency for the American worker, so it helps

to be able to demonstrate that this benefits the bottom line, besides the fact that we're advocating better treatment of workers. All of these pieces fit together. The whole cycle is a dramatic change from where this country has been. This whole agenda is very exciting, because it's a way to tie together all the changes from TQM, and everything we're learning about high performance workplaces, and not only justify it but allow it to move us forward.

Providing recognition

One approach that governments tend to favour to stimulate interest is the use of award schemes to provide recognition for best practice. The OAW is looking at these and considering examples from abroad.

We have thought about two things:

- having a recognition programme for individuals and teams within companies which have done great things in the workplace;
- a certification programme, like Investors in People, IIP.

Australia also has a 'best practices' programme where they award a seal of approval. The thinking behind this is that a small group of companies will vie for the certificate, though whether or not it would have a broad effect is actually quite doubtful. From an agency perspective, it would show that we were trying to be proactive, but it's hard to tell how effective it would be.

We have had a proposal from the National Association of Manufacturers to create a supplier network. This would involve a number of larger companies with whom we would work to develop supplier networks. It's not clear what the standards would be, but ISO 9000 would be one possibility.

A new approach to government

The Employment Training Administration has some separate initiatives, one of which is the school-to-work transition. They're involved with a voluntary pairing of the Departments of Education and Labor in being able to run parallel projects, take new approaches, and form coalitions at a local level.

It's very difficult to look at any one of our initiatives without seeing how it links to the other pieces: this is a total systems change. We're also looking for a new approach to government, in that we don't have funding. We are trying an entrepreneurial approach in all of these efforts by forming coalitions with the Commerce Department, and with Education. Pairings of government agencies are occurring at this level which have never occurred before. Our office has to pull that together; it's an advocacy group that's trying to encourage things like the measurements project.

For other parts of the Department of Labor, like the 'schools-to-work' initiative and the 'skill standards', the approach that's been taken is that, rather than completely fund projects (which has been the traditional approach), existing funds which would have been spent on those are now being divided up. It's being viewed with an entrepreneurial eye – it's being seeded with initial investment funding. There are many others where the understanding is that it's going to be matched by the private sector, by pairing with business at the local level. So we're not completely funding this. On some of the other projects, we are very much hoping that the private sector will join with federal government.

The school-to-work legislation is providing grants for innovative projects, for pairing between business and education at the local level, and for running pilots. Among the possible kinds of project might be:

- How do we change the curriculum?
- How do we get partners together?
- Can we develop businesses to partner specific schools, so that students can spend part of their day in the classroom and part of the day at a real work-site?
- Could they all come out with a certificate, when they graduated from school, to show what they have done in this area?
- If they choose not to follow the college track, can they come out with skill standards that actually mean something?
- How will the employer know what skill this person comes in with?

Much of the emphasis throughout this book has been on organisations or institutions. But there's another aspect – the individual worker. What can government do to improve their understanding and acceptance that jobs are no longer for life, that training goes on throughout our working lives, and that we each need to be driving our own development?

The other element of this which is addressed in the Re-employment Act is the system of job centres and labour-market information. There will be a series of 'one-stop centres', so that every community has a listing of data that's available to employers, not only for vacancies but for what training is available, what workers are available, who is trained, what training programmes are available for consumers to look at, what has been their success rate, how many graduates get work as a result, and what is the quality of their training. We shall provide information for consumers to make informed choices through a central system. In this one-stop centre, school students will be able to learn about different career-opportunities, the kinds of skills which are involved, the kinds of things they need to know if they had a job in this, what their day would look like, what kinds of skills they would have, and what they would do? 'If I do this, what kind of training would I need? Would it be advanced training? Would it be university?' We could be looking at students using this, and teachers using it as a learning tool in their classrooms. Students would also have apprenticeship opportunities while they're in school.

People who are changing careers would be able to come to this same place. They could do work on résumés. They could get additional training throughout the year. They might be laid off and come in. In their lifetime, we would see the same system being used from school-age through to retirement, and probably folks would use it a number of times throughout their life. It would be linked, so that if you went from one state to another the skill standards would be the same.

This office is particularly focused on the other side. Now that we've put all these workforce issues together, what do we do for the workplace and what will it look like, as we prepare these workers? Then, of course, we are also working with the Department of Commerce in trying to ensure that, as we prepare all of these workers, the jobs will exist for them to enter. I think this is probably the first time we've begun to view the whole cycle in a systematic way; they are interdependent, but we have previously done everything very individually; it's the first time we've looked at this as a concerted whole.

The organised labour-management relationship

Change in the unions varies. In some cases they are adapting better than others, but certainly unions are also recognising a need to reinvent, and to view their role more as advocates for the worker, rather than the traditional adversarial role. In high performance workplaces, where unions have existed, and have partnered with management, they have been successful. That's been quite dramatic, and everyone sees that as an example of how we move down the road. They are ensuring that workers are educated to be able to use the broader information which companies share with them. That adversarial role has to change to become a partnership, but developing their trust is a real challenge. We have examples of where it's occurred, but it's not as mainstreamed as we would like. We also have another division within OAW that's called Labor Management Programmes. This works more directly with some of the larger unions, developing training programmes for the unions themselves in a 'train-the-trainer' fashion, so that they will then be able to turn around their training and disseminate it.

Activity 6.1 Lobbying for change

We hope that you have begun to recognise, as you read this book, that organisations large and small not only have the opportunity to influence matters locally, regionally and nationally, but also have increasingly recognised that they have a responsibility to do so. We hope that you will feel a need to do the same. While creating a lobbying activity is not a trivial undertaking, your ambitions should only be limited by the resources available; and it is quite possible that despite this limitation, by acting within another initiative, you can achieve a great deal.

There are often existing initiatives which have realistic financial or support resources but which lack a motivated pilot. Alternatively, there are motivated pilots who lack an aircraft to fly – and perhaps your role could be to supply that aircraft, or to find someone who can.

Stage 1: Identify your cause
In the course of reading this book, you may well have discovered professional, personal or corporate issues which have been bugging you and preventing

you from moving towards self-direction within your own organisation. The first step, then, is to identify concrete issues to be addressed if self-direction is to be achieved. What single or small group of related issues needs to be addressed? We recommend one or two simple tools which could be used as a way of highlighting the focus of your attention. We also suggest that you use these firstly on your own and then as one member of a slightly larger group. On the first pass you should improve your own understanding of the issues and on the second you will benefit from the insights of the other people. The two techniques that we have found most effective in helping groups of people to identify schemes at the centre of a lobbying activity are force-field analysis, and SWOT analysis.

SWOT analysis

A SWOT analysis (strengths, weaknesses, opportunities and threats) is a tool which has been popular in marketing organisations for some years, but has only recently begun to be used in problem-solving as a way of structuring data. Many sources of information can be used, ranging from the output from brainstorming to the results of surveys and questionnaires, and the analysis of comparisons such as competitors and benchmarking. The SWOT analysis can be written on flip charts or an entire report can be structured to reflect the four categories represented by a combination of positive and negative influences operating within and outside an organisation (see Fig 6.1). The approach can be adapted to a wide range of situations and is very popular with senior management teams because of its ability to consider both internal and external factors.

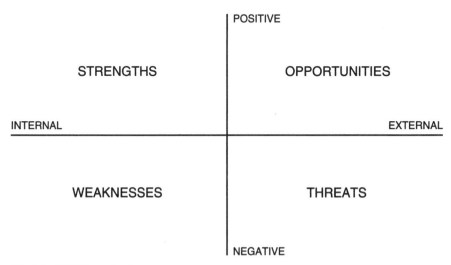

Fig 6.1 SWOT analysis

Using a SWOT analysis to identify the issues calls for an initial statement of subject. In this case such statements might be 'Self-Direction in the South-East of England', 'Self-Direction in the Offshore Oil Industry', 'Employee Empowerment in the Armed Services', 'High-Performance in the Hotel Industry', 'Six Sigma and Retail Banking', 'High-Performance in the Civil Service', 'Self-Managing Work Teams in a Local Tax Inspectorate'.

You will quickly see that what we are trying to do is to define the 'envelope', the framework in which you wish to operate. The next step is to begin to list, over a period of time, the factors which impede and accelerate the approach you wish to adopt.

Under 'Strengths', what encourages you in your particular situation to adopt this approach? Under 'Opportunities', list factors which encourage you from outside your organisation, such as the availability of grants, or local promotion of Investors in People. Under 'Weaknesses' list the factors within your organisation which discourage you from pursuing your direction (such as autocratic leadership or previous lack of investment). Finally, under 'Threats', list those factors outside your organisation which you believe will impede your progress. You may want to build up your list of factors by working with representatives of professional organisations or with your colleagues. We shall talk about this in more detail later. For a SWOT analysis, it is likely that the focus of your attention for a lobbying activity will be on those areas which are external to the organisation i.e. the opportunities and threats.

Force-field analysis

At any given moment, there are forces acting on almost everything; most situations to do with work can be envisaged as having two sets of forces, those which encourage the situation and those which prevent or discourage it. Problem-solving is often concerned with shifting the balance, e.g., in the case of lobbying, we are concerned with moving the balance by reducing the barriers and increasing the positive forces. In many situations, people try to encourage the promoting forces without paying sufficient attention to the restraining barriers, or forces. Although force-field analysis can be applied in a quantitative way, your first attempt will probably just consider positive and negative factors. When you come to prioritise your lobbying activities, you may well want to rank these in a scale according to the severity of their effect. There is a great deal of sophistication available to improve the effectiveness of a force-field analysis. In particular, when considering the relative importance of different elements, four common scales are used:

- their importance;
- their influence;
- their urgency;
- the cost.

For more information about using force-field and SWOT analyses you may like to refer to *Problem Solving and Decision Making*[3].

Stage 2: Identifying the key influencers
Now that you have begun to look at some of the factors which are influencing your progress towards self-direction, you will begin to be in a position to decide who the key influencers are. By key influencer, we mean in lobbying terms, prospects or targets. Who do you believe is in the best position to change the factors which you have identified and prioritised? Depending on your focus, this may be central government, local government or some other organisation.

To consider the local situation first: it is important to break down local government into the real area which needs to be influenced. Local government is a meaningless term, as it represents many diverse, unco-ordinated organisations. For example, are the key influencers a local council, social services, education authority, school, or perhaps a strong trade body such as the Chamber of Commerce? Similarly, within central government, many departments, though seemingly separate entities, have overlapping areas of responsibility and it is likely that you will be trying to influence more than one such area. It is not uncommon for one organisation within central government to be promoting an activity, while another discourages it, either deliberately or unintentionally.

Begin to develop a list of those organisations, and the contacts within them, which you can establish. In most cases, there will be three or four distinct groups of people. At the local level there are paid employees – some of whom are responsible for developing policy, while others are responsible for implementing it. It often comes as a surprise to UK citizens that many local authorities have a chief executive, who will also be clerk to the elected representatives. The chief executive has a substantial role in developing policy and making representations to the elected representatives. Although your lobbying activity needs to deal with this group, it equally needs to focus on the policy makers within the local authority.

Most lobbying activities are multi-pronged. Try to recognise why people are in their current position, and why they fall into that particular category, without letting it become a barrier to you. For example, the elected representatives are elected to represent you. Almost certainly they have strong personal opinions and beliefs, and if they are going to support you and represent you, you need to make sure that, if they don't already, by the time you have finished lobbying, their beliefs are the same as yours. But you need to win them over; you can't expect them to adopt your beliefs without critical thought. However, once you have won them over, they are your ally.

The employed representatives, particularly those responsible for implementation, may not feel that they have the power to influence policy but they can certainly give you insights into the ways in which to influence the policy-makers. In Britain at least, local government officers generally recognise the importance of the local citizens as their customers, though they still to some extent treat the elected representatives as a more significant source of ideas. Particularly at the local level, identifying the right individuals, meeting and discussing the situation and offering to provide the necessary evidence for them to make a decision is often far less painful than many expect. In central government, a similar breakdown exists, though here the elected representatives often have a responsibility to their party which can prevent them from endorsing a policy of which they might otherwise approve. In just the same way, you need to develop a list of the key influencers, and the people within those parts of the organisation to whom you can gain access.

No matter what the issue, writing a letter to the Prime Minister is unlikely to be successful – whereas meeting, talking to, and providing the necessary evidence to a key civil servant or individual representative could be far more effective. Despite the image presented by television, political parties are not always at loggerheads, and a considerable amount of informal contact is made between members of parliament (MPs) with an interest in a particular topic, regardless of their political affiliation. Issues such as 'high-performance' and 'self-direction' need not have a political agenda, and if the aspect you have identified is relatively straightforward, an approach to the appropriate civil servant, to the Secretary of State and their shadow counterpart, may be all that is necessary to raise the profile of a particular topic sufficiently.

Stage 3: The state of change

For most issues, and for most individuals or groups, it is possible to identify a sequence of reactions to a new idea. Their stage in this sequence determines the type of activity which you need to consider in order to win them over. The stages are found universally in situations where an individual or group is confronted by a new setting, or by change of any kind. It was first described as the sequence of reactions that an individual goes through when they are grieving for the loss of a close friend. The four stages in what is therefore called the grieving process are disbelief, emotion, low-energy acceptance and high-energy adaptation.

In the first stage, individuals do not really believe the situation by which they are confronted. For some time, often for years, the circumstances have been of a particular kind. Suddenly, or seemingly suddenly, the situation has changed and understandably they do not believe it.

The second stage in this process, as the evidence comes flooding in that the situation has changed, is usually one of emotion. This can reveal itself in distress, anger or even delight. Don't fool yourself, though – despite all the noise, even if it is positive, the individuals have not yet accepted that the change has happened.

The third stage is one of low-energy acceptance. Once the evidence has built up, the individual is literally overwhelmed. They lose energy, feel lost, lack direction and don't know what they do. They have, though, accepted the change and if you bombard them with more evidence, they are as likely to rebel against it and go back to the emotional stage as they are to adopt and adapt.

The fourth stage is one of high-energy adaptation. It is at this point that individuals will become the zealous convert whom you need if you are going to achieve a wider change.

In a lobbying setting, you need to consider what stage has been reached in the process by each key individual and organisation that you are trying to influence. If you would like some examples to work with, three well-documented situations have occurred in the UK in recent years. There is a wealth of information about the campaign to revoke the poll tax. Similarly the four stages of the grieving process are very clear in Des Wilson's account of the successful campaign for lead free air that was mounted in the early 1980s. The activities that you will need to engage in for the four stages are essentially: awareness-raising, overcoming resistance, providing help with implementation, and supporting through positive recognition. Your campaign needs to have the appropriate resources and materials for each of these elements.

Stage 4: Allies

Many of the larger professional organisations, such as the Institute of Directors, the Institute of Biology or the various Engineering Institutes, have a lobbying role. In most countries there are other organisations, either representing individuals or collective groups of companies, which are engaged in lobbying activities – not all of these are politically motivated nor are they are all charities. There are research and policy units, some of which may have been established by the government, but nevertheless they have a lobbying role.

As soon as you have identified the issues you wish to pursue, you will begin to come across other organisations which are trying to achieve the same end. Having established the key influencers, it is time to identify those organisations which can be useful allies in your own campaign. Some will be organisations which clearly have links to your targets. They may or may not be pursuing your particular issue, but you can save yourself considerable effort by piggy-backing on their initiatives. Alternatively, you may identify organisations which are concerned with the same issue as you, and who are trying to make contacts.

Before taking the process any further, it is worth collecting information from these bodies and trying to discuss the issues informally with people within them. It always pays to set your sights high. If they have a national and local structure, approach them at a national level first, to gain an organisational perspective, before contacting local representatives – but don't make the mistake of assuming that, at the local level, they must share the same views! Don't ignore the role of the media in these activities. Journalists make their living out of communication. Your problem will call for a journalist's skills. We have already mentioned Des Wilson as an excellent example of a committed journalist achieving tremendous results through a highly-targeted lobbying activity, not just once but several times.

Stage 5: The campaign

It is very unlikely that you will have identified an issue which can be addressed in one step. All the rules of marketing apply to a lobbying campaign. It is worthwhile at the outset planning at least twelve months of activities, whether you are doing this alone or with a group of others. Think about the materials that you will need – information packs, leaflets and so on. Consider the PR elements that will be involved. You are unlikely to be successful if you appear to present a disjointed approach, so the first few months of your campaign may be devoted to drawing together a common statement. Whatever happens, it is important that communications with other people are crisp and to the point. The following are a few guidelines for dealing with MPs:

1 All MPs have a better position of influence than you. They may 'only' be a back-bencher, but they could serve on an influential Standing Committee or Select Committee. Whatever their position, MPs have a chance to raise questions, and put points direct to ministers.

2 The better briefed your MP is, the more effective their efforts will be. Remember that, whether writing as a member of a company or of another organisation, as a source of employment, your organisation is of importance to the MP. So it is important to establish your credibility when you write.

3 Most lobbyists believe that the best first step is to make contact by letter. It is against the rules to send more than one letter in an envelope, so if you want to contact several MPs, you must do so under separate cover.

4 It is always better, whenever a formal document has been issued, such as an Consultation Paper or Green Paper, that you have a ready channel for the communication of your views. Now is the time to give your MP the detail that they need.

5 There is no shortage of views and opinions in parliament. What is desperately needed is facts. Make sure that your approach arms the MP with real examples. The more practical and tangible the information, the better the case will be. It is often better to mention the detail, and ask for it to be referred to anonymously, rather than rendering your argument weak because it appears to be too general.

6 When writing, identify the subject clearly, outline your credentials – why is your organisation important and why should your opinion be taken above others. Give tangible examples of the effect of *not* taking action on the issue concerned. Keep the document as short as possible. Don't burden the initial contact with too much detail. Close the correspondence by asking the MP to state their position on the matter. Always remember to keep the tone positive and helpful. There is no point antagonising your key link with parliament.

7 Offer to visit the House to explain your point further or invite the MP to visit your company, but don't make it an either/or offer.

8 In theory, you should be able to visit your MP without an appointment, but in just the same way as your own employees would probably have difficulty in walking into your office on occasions, MPs work anti-social hours and are frequently engaged in committees and fixed appointments. Without an appointment, you will have to queue several times and rely upon other people to get in. It is much better to try telephoning to arrange a time convenient to the MP.

9 Once you have made an appointment, make sure that you take along a well-written brief of the issue that concerns you. Not only will the MP appreciate this, as it saves them effort during the meeting, but it will also act as a powerful prop when the issue is taken elsewhere.

10 Finally, it does no harm to offer to take the MP for lunch, though some will insist on paying for their own. This can be a useful time to fix an appointment in an otherwise crowded diary, but you should be sensitive to the MP's need to get on to their next appointment.

References

1 Roberts. Gov. Birabur (1992) *Oregon Benchmarks – Standards for measuring statewide progress and government performance.* Oregon Progress Board, Salem.
2 Reymond Renee & Jeanne Sano (1991). *The High Performance Work Force.* N.A.M, Washington DC.
3 Wilson GB (1993) *Problem Solving and Decision Making*, Kogan Page.

7

THE EMPLOYEE'S PERSPECTIVE

'Somebody has got to manage the business. Somebody has got to plan, control and direct... the question is: "Who?' ... We are working on getting people to manage the business ... and getting the management to provide the leadership to enable them to do that.'

(Motorola employees, Cellular Infrastructure)

- This is not a process change – it is not re-engineering or re-mapping – it is a cultural change. It is about allowing people to behave differently.

- Being allowed to manage means that you have to know what the business is about. You need to be educated.

- If there are problems, you don't go to your supervisor. Instead you go to a team member and work it out together.

- Flexibility is key. If you feel that you've done enough in one place, then you arrange to learn new skills in a new area. That way, when there's a demand, you can step in and keep things moving.

- If the organisational bureaucracy gets in the way, it's probably because it hasn't adapted to the new environment – when you go ahead there can be some trouble but it's never that bad!

- You have the opportunity to succeed or fail. You make the most of it. If you can prove that you can handle different situations, you are going to excel.

INTRODUCTION

'When Ralph told us what he was planning... we thought he'd lost his marbles!' – one employee's comment on Ralph Stayer at Johnsonville Foods, an early exponent of Self-Managing Work Teams (SMWTs).

To the middle manager, already climbing the ladder, the SMWT can represent a considerable threat. The power and influence of position are lost, and the only way to greater influence is through performance in areas that are perhaps alien to you. You have probably been brought up to believe in the traditional hierarchy and it will take a lot of persuading to believe that SMWTs can work.

To a junior manager, the SMWT can represent a step back down the ladder. Hard-earned status as a foreman or supervisor could be lost when the SMWTs select their own team leader or decide not to have leaders at all. Alternatively, the new structure could be a heaven-sent opportunity with the chance for an aspiring leader to move forward faster than ever before. In this chapter, we talk to managers who have experienced these problems first-hand, who review their feelings both before and after SMWTs were introduced.

As a member of a team, what were your thoughts when the new structure was first voiced? Were you impressed or distressed? How much information should you have had before agreeing to the change? Were the incentives sufficient? And how well did things settle down in the new structure? Given the chance again, what would you do differently?

INTERVIEW 7.1 QUALITY CIRCLES AND TEAM-WORK
Yoshio Hata, Manager of TQC Promotion, Juki Sewing Machines

The Juki hierarchy has been reduced to three or four layers, with a formal quality system within which employees are free to act. The hierarchy persists more strongly at the top of the organisation. There are still a number of specialist functions where teams cannot be introduced because of the limited number of people.

The present extent of team-work

When something happens that calls for a change in company policy, the President of the Company or the Vice-President and the Directors would be involved. The departments represented on the Organisation Chart each have a manager, with people reporting in, and there is one director for each department. And the people in the department who are reporting in to the director – each reports to the manager, and if they are given some work they do it, according to company policy – and within that they can use their own judgement. Take the TQC Promotion Department, which has a staff of four people. Each person has their own activities – it depends on the assignment: sometimes there will be two people involved, but usually there's only one.

Quality control circles as a pre-cursor to other teams

Juki has 222 Quality Control Circles (QCCs) with about 1,080 employees in them (out of 3,033) – i.e., most of the 'workers'. Each employee spends about an hour each week in formal QCC activities – they may also develop questionnaires or whatever, which they have to do outside this time.

Juki has a QC Convention twice a year and the President and Vice- President make a point of praising their employees, as they were encouraged to do by Dr Ishikawa the quality authority and inventor of Ishikawa or Fishbone Diagrams. There is a leaders' meeting once a year, and a month before that, each leader has an individual meeting with the President. He won't let anything take over from this – it demonstrates his commitment.

Our President has also been Regional President of Tokyo Area – these posts are honorary and are held by leading industrialists – usually the President of one of the leading companies. He took the post because he wanted to advocate the TQC approach for the last year.

Each QCC involves seven or eight people who do the same type of work. QCCs have five possible themes: quality, cost, speed of delivery, safety and morale. They can pursue any one of these.

They have meetings where the circles can exchange information. These usually involve the leaders. Two different kinds of meetings – some for circles from within Juki, and others where other companies may meet together. Last year there was a meeting where the team met with another from a beer factory!

Juki has fewer women: one circle is made up only of women – they made a point of meeting many of the different men's circles. They were trying to get the teams to agree to use a standardised system of writing because the engineers' writing wasn't easily legible! This system has been introduced not only to Juki but also to five other companies who have attended our conferences.

The nature of the QCCs has changed over the years. Earlier they used to rely on books to help them solve problems; now supervisors go to lectures (like the ones run by JUSE) and then they can use more sophisticated approaches, so they train their people. There are no other people involved in the QCCs – only the leaders and the members, though we also have part-time members (because they work part-time) and sometimes other people are brought in as experts.

If a circle has a problem, and cannot find the reason behind it, then they have meetings with members of other circles for advice.

The QCCs report to the senior managers through the supervisors – there is a standard letter-format in which they have to write. Each section has a QC Convention – there are two big conventions each year, but there are four or five others each year. Each QCC reports there what they have done.

There are examples where the factory's physical layout has had to be changed because of a team's activity. They are constantly analysing ways of taking up space more efficiently, and at the same time improving speed of delivery. We have a space problem anyway. This often means reallocating space in the factory areas. But the biggest change was in the early days. The main room downstairs consisted of lots of small rooms – the QCCs recommended removing the walls and making it one big area. They then had a small area enclosed for meetings – so that they could have quiet and in turn didn't disturb other people.

The ability test

Some time ago, Juki recognised the importance of basic skills in the workforce of the future. Rather than replicate external exams they incorporated these skills in an assessment of employees' understanding of their main production processes.

As an example of the state-of-the-art 'traditional' Japanese Quality Control Circles (QCCs), you cannot do much better than look to Juki. One of Japan's leading small-arms manufacturers, since the Second World War their efforts have switched to the production of sewing machines and related technology.

Their industry is an interesting one economically. While the cost of labour in neighbouring Korea, in other parts of Asia, South America and parts of Europe remains low, the demand for technological development will remain low too. The domestic user demands quality, but not necessarily high technology. But labour cost is an unstable factor. Politics can change overnight, as can the demand for high volumes of low-cost but well-fitted uniforms! In the longer term those regions where labour has been cheap are turning their economies around too. Eventually, and probably within the lifetime of the current workforce, Juki expects a radical change in the world market for their products.

The company knows that it must prepare itself for change. Three dimensions to their strategy have emerged: developing their people's skills, engaging their front-line staff in Research and Development, and transforming the nature of their managers.

> The Ability Test involves all the stages in the production of the machines – from the design and drawings to the production process. Not every employee had to pass the test – only the employees who were able enough – and for that also there was an ability test, a pre-assessment. There are two kinds of test – one is a theory and the other a practical. It takes them about to two to three months to prepare for the ability test, and it is held every six months. About forty people took it in the first year.

The role of the supervisor

Juki has made a substantial investment in QCCs and sees them as the main structure of the future. Their QCCs are led by supervisors and are run with the dual agendas of continuous improvement and employee development. Nevertheless individual accountability remains with the supervisors.

> Do teams have responsibility for parts of the process or for products? Supervisors have responsibility – but not the workers. The supervisors are usually the leaders of QCCs – they hope to develop others so that they can take over eventually, but for three to four years they will lead. They will then select another.
>
> The role of the managers here has not changed. The managers are not involved in the QCCs, apart from the supervisors. If you separate the task from the process – they each have tasks assigned to them individually, and they analyse them.

Future developments

> We are going to have to improve the methods we use to solve problems and also enhance the ways in which we promote TQC. There is a tendency to tackle the symptoms rather than the causes of problems. We are trying to improve the creativity of our members. We are now sending our supervisors on a fourteen-hour Creativity Course, to make them more effective at problem-solving. Teams are not turning to outsiders as often as they used to: they are finding that they have the necessary experience to tackle problems.

People are constantly learning, with product and process skills being used as an environment to develop basic and transferable skills. The ability test is used to create an above-average workforce, despite the relatively low technology of their industrial market. Employees are provided with the opportunity to apply their skills, not only on what remain as QCCs, but also in teams that have evolved an R & D focus. The excitement that this produces is difficult to convey, but it is typical of the culture that the management is promoting. Experimental work in their R & D teams is mind-boggling! While some organisations choose to emphasise the aspect of learning, Juki constantly reinforces the importance of creativity.

INTERVIEW 7.2 TEAM-WORK IN TOYOTA
Zenzaburo Katayama, General Manager, Toyota Motor Corporation

Superficially Toyota is another example of a Japanese organisation that adapted QCCs 'by the book'. In practice they have evolved a structure that migrates between classical quality circles and SMWTs. Firstly the amount of time allocated to QCCs was increased. Then the decision to switch from normal operations to QCC activities was delegated to the foreman.

Team-work in Toyota is distinctly different and has its own motivations towards reward and quality control to improve work. In 1965 many companies started to organise their factory using the team-work system (basically QCC) and this contributed to the motivation of employees.

QC teams are composed of engineers and technicians. They are supposed to contribute to Quality Control and, depending on the teams recruiting the appropriate personnel, the company also proposed many problems for them to solve. QCCs and their representatives are educated in QC.

These QCCs started group-working. This has had an impact on the routine jobs – while at the same time employees have learned how to improve in terms of QC. At their place of work the employees are given a job description – this is how they have to work. The company's management thinks that this is not enough. It's difficult to say how much time is spent on QCCs by employees. During working hours they discuss the problems, but in-house activities are not all that they do. With their leaders, they study outside, elsewhere, in their homes and other places, so the company cannot survey exactly the hours spent on QCCs. The Toyota Company proposes that employees spend at least two hours per month during working hours devoted to QCCs. QCC members usually gather twice a month for one hour, and the time needed to solve a problem is typically three to six months – though it is up to the team leaders to fix the time-period for solutions to the problems.

Two hours a month was a minimum – if they wished to spend more time they could do so. At the workplace the employees had to do their own task according to their job description, and they joined a QCC on top of doing their job. The foreman acted as a co-ordinator – if he felt that time was spare, he called out people to the QCC. Depending on the factory, the factory manager also decided on certain days of the month being for QCC activities.

QCCs in Toyota are better seen as an individual development environment. As team members develop they take over more responsibility including a leadership role. This is resulting in the dropping of formal status.

In Japanese companies we have foremen and sub-foremen. The team leaders are separate from these positions. There has been an evolution from one to the other. These foremen and sub-foremen, depending on the ability of their employees, could pick on one of them as a team leader. In the QCCs it is not allowed to call people by their titles. Now the foreman is called an 'adviser' by the team; the sub-foremen is called a sub-adviser or something like that! In the early stages the team leader was often a foreman, but nowadays it can be someone below them. QCC personnel have increased, and therefore the teams can now pick up individuals with skills. Suppose that there were several themes or agendas for the QCC – the team leader could change – for one it could be one person and for another it could be a different person.

When QCCs were introduced in Japan (Toyota actually started this) it was to activate the workplace – as the routine work was not enough. People chose themes close to their workplace, which contributed a great deal to the level of 'activation' of the employees.

JUSE continues to recommend that QCCs do not have managers involved. But as long ago as 1976 Toyota felt that this was a mistake. They deliberately opened up the teams to involve shop-floor, foremen and more experienced managers.

> In former days, the amount of management involvement in QCC was limited – management had to change its policy. This came about eighteen years ago – around 1976 – people didn't know what to do, and it took eight years to work out the principles. Toyota Company is proud of their involvement in developing the concepts of QCCs in Japan. The company aims to take the leadership in this field. Some companies prohibited managers from joining – while, for about nine years, we have encouraged them to be involved. By joining the teams, managers also have a lot to learn and this improves team spirit.

By extending the duration of QCCs, bringing them into the working day, integrating them vertically and removing status, Toyota have substantially different structures to JUSE's original, so it seems confusing when they continue to refer to QCCs. They still distinguish between regular jobs and continuous improvement activitites but, as Katayama explains, this distinction may well disappear in the near future.

> The company thinks that if regular job descriptions and QCC are the same, then the QCC is dead. The managers spend a greater amount of their time supporting these QCCs. In QCC, the directors above the managers are called 'caretakers'. If both join, then we have 'caretakers' and 'sub-caretakers'.
> At first, employees had a negative reaction, but eventually they learned that QCCs had a positive effect on their workplace. Managers and directors, when they were asked to join, also had a negative reaction! At present, other companies have kept QCC principles as an absolute – this is why they don't like to change. Still, QCC activities are continuing and in due course the principles could be changed – Toyota Company wants to change the QCC principles for Japan. In the promotion of QCCs very able persons have been dormant: the Toyota Company wants to activate these people. In Toyota Companies there are 2,000 managers, all of whom take part in QCCs.

Toyota have begun to transfer their strucure to one based on teams. A division would typically comprise a major product segment, such as the power train of a car. Within these a separate steering group manages the transformation, coordinated centrally. Managers' effort is not strongly focused on the QCCs.

The QCCs are now dealing with major projects such as production set-up and factory design and layout.

> Our Organisation Chart shows different divisions – each division has a committee to promote QCCs. There is also a whole company committee. My department works as a secretariat to these committees.

Thirty per cent of a manager's time is spent in support of the QCCs. Manager's performance of their jobs, the themes of the QCCs is a variation of the manager's responsibility, and they have the opportunity to state opinions and the reward of the QCCs. These are all roles of managers. The QCC is a part of the company and so it is part of the manager's job. Engineers and office workers are also given the chance to organise QCCs but it doesn't take off very well. The company is convinced that the same kind of QCC could be done in the office environment. QCCs work on the design of new models or factory improvement, and so on. Given a project it becomes an aim of the QCC. To the company it is important that when they have an aim they must go actively for that aim.

The role of QCCs in developing skill-sets

The job evaluation system, the education system and the training system to teach skills to the workers are company systems and are not neglected at all, but the company also recognises that to solve a new problem – new kinds of skill may be needed overall. Therefore the QCC studies to acquire the new skill. The company on-the-job training scheme provides skills needed on the spot. In QCCs, when the team presents its findings the learning of new skills is often discussed. If a new skill is identified the team leaders report to the appropriate section to deliver this new skill or ideas.

Horizontal expansion of projects.

Lots of companies fail to take advantage of the output from suggestion schemes and quality circles because they don't apply them across the company. Motorola, in its problem-solving methodology, talks of institutionalising the solution, by which it means communicating the idea to anyone else who could benefit. Their competitive improvement groups are assessed on the extent to which this has been achieved. At SGB, the UK-based contract scaffolding company, in the early 1990s we established a programme of Friday afternoon team-briefings as a mechanism to achieve this cross-fertilisation. Toyota too formally recognises this step.

When a defect in a machine is found it is conveyed to the workshop which can lead to not only improvement but also to design review of the machinery. The improvement is done for the whole company. There is a section that accepts recommendations of QCCs on behalf of the company, and an evaluation is done for any new idea or improvement suggestion. Suggestions and improvements used to be done individually and so the benefit from these improvements was very small. But QCC as team-work, when it is presented, improvement increased a great deal. In 1993 Toyota accepted 154,000 improvement plans or suggestions. Per employee that is 26. Toyota is not only proud of this number, but its rate of adoption is 99%. Of these suggestions about 50-80% are from QCCs.

When project themes are sought about ten different suggestions are made. The suggestion could be small, but by horizontal expansion can be spread to the whole company.

Measuring the benefits

As Russ Robinson from Motorola explains later, it is often difficult to assess the return on investment in teams. Organisations have to demonstrate faith that there will be one. Toyota too has experienced this and chooses to side-step the issues.

One of the largest returns is the growth of the individuals involved.

> One of the difficult questions is how much merit is produced by a QCC? It is immeasurable. The company's policy is not to expect a measurable merit to be produced, because improvement is not the primary goal. The integrational ability is recognised – this is most important.
>
> For individuals joining QCCs there is an individual merit – what is needed, what is lacking, this opinion is also presented by the QCC and the company has an ear to these opinions. The manager helps them to address these. Manager's participation makes a human relationship – in this atmosphere the able workers in a particular field can consult with the managers, who listen to these employees' choice of work and can help to assign a new job.

Employee development

Increasingly companies are having to invest in the development of basic skills for their employees. Toyota dominates the economy of its area, the city and the company taking their name from the family. Little surprise than that the local community college was provided by, and continues to be supported by Toyota.

> Toyota company has a professional school equivalent to a junior college; when the recommendation is made to send a worker to the junior college, a place is made available. At Junior College level, about 10% of the students are from Toyota – 3,000 is the capacity – it depends on the year; this is a regular college and competition is keen. It is a four-year course. There is also a General College in Toyota City, which advanced workers have the chance to attend. The capacity of the Engineering Department is eighty and Toyota sends two or three people every year.
>
> In Japan, the worker who leaves a company is not welcome to return to the same company. Companies provide benefits, health, schools, and so on, and takes care of all the workers. The company does not expect to recruit from outside: they want to train their own people.

To many employees the presentation of problem-solving activities to their managers is a high point and can be a tremendous opportunity. Many organisations run competitions for these presentations. Katayama witnessed one extraordinary event at one of these presentations.

> Employees have to speak in QCCs. Each Toyota Company selects ten QCCs and give rewards. It once happened that one employee wasn't able to talk [i.e. he was mute]. The QC members learnt sign-language to communicate with him. When his team received their award he started to talk!
>
> In Toyota factories in the US there have been problems with literacy, and when they are trying to form QCCs the company suggested forming them into ethnic groups – but one of the managers suggested forming them by language – this was very successful. Then we found that employees who could not speak English tried to join the English group to learn the language!

Involvement outside the company

Toyota is an active participant in wider exchanges between their teams and other companies.

> QCC is a national movement and in each district there is a chapter which is cross-industry. They have their own training courses and lecture programmes and their own QCC improvements. They are nationally divided into eleven districts. In ours, there are sub-chapters too. This makes them available to smaller businesses to take advantage of the education. Each local government has a system to recognise the QCCs. Local chapter conventions are held and small and medium businesses have their own. Big businesses have many QCCs but they have also dormant circles. The employers' interests in QCCs often develop through the local chapters.

7.3 GROUP DISCUSSION: EMPOWERMENT THROUGH SMWTs
Cellular Infrastructure, Motorola (Kevin Banks, Rick Chandler, Jaime Martinez, Tim Bell, Will High, Greg Holtz).

Rick Chandler, the local manager for Cellular Infrastructure at Motorola, has evolved SMWTs. His approach is both dynamic and empowering. To brief on the SMWTs within his area, he assembled a group of individuals from across the organisation. The discussion was free-ranging and open. The individuals included two shop-floor team-members, two team-leaders, one manager and a course-tutor in Organisational Development, who had been a team-leader a few months before.

Chandler began by describing why and how he began the movement towards self-managed team-work, and some of the preparation that was necessary. He makes it clear that he sees the transformation of the organisation as a cultural issue involving people's behaviour and not a three to six month process mapping exercise.

We thought we would tell you about our process here, because it is a little different for some people. We do not stage anything. We do not try to plan, we do not have any visitations, and so on. We are who we are. No more, no less!

It started about eight years ago. I wanted to go and do something fundamentally different. I spent time looking at what we needed to do to compete in the US on a world-wide basis. To do that, I spent a lot of time looking at what competitive advantages we have in America.

To be honest with you, I came up with only two. One is the diversity we have in this country; the other is that a lot of us have the attitude of what I call 'cowboy experience' – we are willing to go out and do things on our own. The raw materials, the technology, the automation, all of that's given. You cannot compete without that. So that is not an advantage. You need quality or you will be out of business. The market-place will let you charge whatever the market-place will determine. Because of the global nature of what we are in, you really cannot compete on a regional basis any more.

I looked at the group I was in and said, 'How do we take those potential advantages, develop them and make them useful?' The first step was to get a common language, because I felt we needed one verbal and written language – and for us it was English. The other common language was maths. You need a base in which you can communicate. We spent a couple of years just getting everybody up to seventh grade level for those two things. That does not get you anywhere; it just allows you to start.

We said we had a couple of missions. One was to serve the customer. The other was to get our people to work together to solve problems in their business; so that people gain a sense of ownership and pride in their business; so that we begin to deal with people as human beings and adults. We had to work on a process where they could all begin to reach their potential. It turns out that those few statements are big statements, because we ain't even close!

First of all, I made a commitment to treat all of us as human beings and as adults. That means that I am not going to check on you; I will not check on you if you don't do well; I will hire you if you do well; I will pay you money. It is a very simple deal, but it becomes very difficult because in our culture, we have a hierarchy system and people on the bottom 'aren't supposed to think'. People on the top are supposed to do all the thinking. Therefore, if you are on the bottom and you are not supposed to think, you don't have to do anything. You don't have to have any ownership, you don't have to worry about it, you just sit there until somebody tells you to do something. If you can get away with it, you don't have to do anything. That's a great system.

What we really did was to go to people and say, 'We are no longer going to do that. It is up to you to go and do that.' We are working to get the majority of our people running the business.

Somebody has got to manage the business. Somebody has got to plan, control and direct. That has got to happen. We run a very complex business. We have got to have some people here who are managing the business. The question is: 'Who?'

In our current system, it is the management who plan, control and direct, and they usually command. Ninety per cent of the people don't do anything but react. Somebody says, 'You sit down here and you do this'. They sit down and they do that. There is no thought. You are not buying into any of the person or any of their potential. What we are working on, essentially, is getting people to manage the business and getting management to provide the leadership.

That means that they have to know what the business is, they have got to know what they are supposed to do, and they have to have all of the information. We have to provide education, and it continues to surprise me how much education we must supply. It intrigues me that each time we turn around and get better at giving the business to people who are in charge of it, the better they do. It is amazing how much better the business will and can run if we do that.

But that is a cultural change, not a process change. It is not mapping. What we are working on is changing our culture so that it allows us to behave in a different way. We are talking about behaviour. People in management do not want to talk about that. They want to talk about 'What we can do in the next three months?' I find that fascinating, but it is of no use to me. Most people I meet in business talk about a three-month or six-month process. Whether you are going to assign Sam to be the champion of empowerment or horizontal organisation, or whatever it is.

We are working on changing our environment so that the people doing the job can run their business and have a sense of ownership, a sense of worth that makes them important, which says they have a say in what goes on. That gives them some degree of control over what their business is and what their life is. We work on providing educational opportunities so that they can begin to work on reaching their potential. We aren't there. That is what we are working on.

Introducing the teams

The benefits of teams depend on your perspective. To many employees the immediate ones are in terms of improving the environment in which they work.

We started this process eight years ago. The team was pretty much left up top. Here are the goals, let's get them done. What 'done' meant was that if you did a specific job and another team member depended upon you, then somebody had to be at the beginning and somebody had to be at the end, like an assembly line. If you do thirty, then he has to do thirty. Let us all work together, then if it doesn't get done, it's not just one individual's fault – it's the team's.

If you can do it on a weekly basis, then what you do on one day can help you out the next day, and so on until the end of the week. Everybody is not going to make the same every day. If you know what you need on a weekly basis, on a good day you can try to do more than you need to do. It just came to be that you were dependent upon your team. You knew that, if you needed a day off you would ask your team-members, 'Hey, I need a day off on Wednesday. Is that all right with everybody? Will we still be able to make the weekly goal?'

If there were any problems, I would not have to go to the supervisor to say, 'Hey, I'm not getting along with this guy as a team-member, – maybe my work will do better with someone else.' I'd rather go to a team-member and say 'I'm having a problem. Can you help me out?' It works out within your team. You are allowed to do that.

Flexibility

Self-Managed Team Working not only improves the environment we work in, it also develops our skills so that we have more flexibility. We can help other people out and, in turn, they help us out.

> What I like most about Motorola is the opportunity. You don't have to wait for somebody to say, 'OK, you've spent enough time here. It's time for you to move on.' When you feel you have done enough here, then you can go to other areas and say, 'Hey, you guys, have you got any openings?' or 'Can I help you guys out, we're a little slow?' That gives you the chance to gain flexibility without moving or without being ready to leave a job when you don't know it all. That is what I really like – the opportunity to go here and there without the supervisor coming to you and saying 'OK. Now it's time for you to move on. You have worked here enough.' If you wait for a supervisor, then you have got a long wait. I have to take the initiative to show that I can do something else. Flexibility is what it's all about, because there will be some slow times in one area where there may not be in other areas. If you apply yourself, then you can help other areas out.

It seems incredible that time-management has traditionally been seen as a management skill and not one for every employee. It comes down to juggling priorities. With teams, control is based on satisfying your peers – if you're skiving they'll know! Everybody is in the same boat – they are all developing their skills and resolving problems. Informal contact between people in different teams becomes an important channel to share ideas – and it's much more effective than formal procedures.

> The other jobs that I have had involved going through a chain of command to do anything other than your regular job. Here, you are allowed to approach another team-member on another team to talk about what they are doing in their area. As long as you are accountable, then you will not really have to explain, for example, why you were gone for four hours. 'Well, I was over here doing this and that.' When people know the type of person you are, then they know you are doing something constructive and not just hanging around. You aren't showing off by finding out what is going in other departments, because if you don't know, then you will never know.

They don't put any bulletins out saying what happens in this department compared to the next department. It is up to you to show initiative, to find out what is going on. If you work here in Motorola you should be able to say what goes on in other departments. I have been able to give tours because I know what other departments do, and how they function. I like that, it gives me an insight that there are better things to do than close-wave a circuit board. It has helped me out a lot, and I appreciate all the opportunity that I have had.

Talking and communicating is the big thing around here. You should be able to communicate with everybody around. You shouldn't be shy or feel that you can't go and talk because you're a regular employee.

Hiring

When we describe SMWTs to senior managers we mention the old adage about workers hanging up their brains before they start work – of course it's silly but often those senior managers will nod sagely and do nothing. When you suggest that front-line workers should interview new recruits, they throw up their arms and accuse you of being a crank or a unionist! The insights shared in the interview group demonstrate just how unfounded is the fear that managers have.

I was on an interviewing team where we really had an insight into what happens when someone new joins. You are going to have to work with these guys, so you might as well ask them some of the questions that actually happen in your department. It is a different thing from being on the other end of the interview and trying to figure out how to answer the question. I got to see how people respond to questions.

We were hiring a bunch of people, and our success-rate was pretty low. First of all, we started with about ten people in order to get one person in the door, and then about 10-15% of those left after about six months. This got very expensive. You have got to employ twelve or thirteen people to get one person who's going to stay for very long. This was not really profitable.

So we started talking about how to get a better success rate. A number of us sat and brainstormed, and the usual things came up. 'We'll do a buddy system. We'll do an introduction', and those kind of things. Those are fine, but they have all been tried before and the success-rate is marginal, from minimal to about zero. A couple of us said, 'You know, if you hire somebody and they are going to work with you, you don't have to have anybody trying to convince you to help them because you have already got a stake in this thing. If you hire the person and they fail, it's partly because you didn't do it right.'

It gets back to this whole concept of 'Let's give the people who are doing the job some of the tools they need to do it.' So we said, 'Why don't you let them go and hire the people?' The organisational bureaucracy around us said, 'Well, you can't do that'. Fortunately, we just ignored that, and we went and did it. It's not just changing some mapping! It's changing the environment in which we live!

> We had a group of people come in and sit down, and we interviewed them as a team – three or four of us with one person. We did not have a set of questions. We just had questions which we are not supposed to ask because of policy. We had that in mind. Usually the questions would be made up that morning, or we just went with some old questions. I think Personnel gave us that list. They were questions like, 'We can't ask if you are married or how many kids you have, because that is not relevant to hiring you.' We shouldn't have to ask irrelevant questions. When I saw the list of questions I put myself in the same situation, because I have been in an interview before where they wanted to know how old I was, was I married, how many kids I had. It was almost like going on a date. What has that got to do with whether or not I can handle a job, how I can handle it, how I get to work? How many girl-friends I have, how many kids – those aren't appropriate questions. My favourite question is, 'Why do you want to work for Motorola?' That was a good question because I found that most people knew more about Motorola's products than they actually knew about Motorola. They had no idea. After we told them that we were just regular employees, this made them feel more at ease than if they were talking to a supervisor or something like that. It put them at ease.
>
> After that I saw some of the people who I'd recommended to be hired on the floor, and they would come up to me and ask me questions.

No-one is suggesting that we suddenly go and get a team from the shop-floor and turn them loose on all potential recruits. As with every element of the change towards high-performance we have to prepare people, both with knowledge and confidence, to tackle new tasks. The difference is in the assumption that they are capable of learning it.

> This is a good example of what we had to do with education. We had to stop and spend three months teaching a bunch of people how to interview, and then we could move on. Because you can't just say, 'Go interview'. I see other companies doing that, which is really crazy. So we had to stop and say, 'OK, let's spend three months, not an infinite period of time, and teach you how to do it.' It is not impossible.

The relationship with supervisors

Every account of SMWTs explains the problem experienced by, and with, supervisors. Frequently, a supervisor is appointed because they are an able worker, but their role is to catch out people who deliver poorly. This can make the transition to self-management tricky. The purpose remains the same – it's the change in process that causes concern.

> Obviously this place is different from others. I came from the US Air Force which, like any military branch, is a dictatorship. This is totally opposite from that. All levels of supervision have given us the business, and it is up to us to

run it. If they see that we are having problems, then they get involved. As long as we are running the show and not having any problems, they let us continue. That gives us a sense of confidence, too.

There is no 'You will do this'. It is just, 'This is your job. You have the opportunity to succeed or fail here. You make the most of it. If you can prove that you can handle different situations, you are going to excel.' They give you what needs to be accomplished and you take the ball from there.

When something or somebody goes wrong, then your supervisor might get involved. If problems can be handled at a local level, we try to handle them there. If it is something serious, where there is going to be a problem in the future, we need to get the supervisors involved. If it's a product problem, then we get the appropriate engineers, so that it doesn't happen and the customer doesn't get disappointed.

It is a different kind of structure. We have say five or six people, who we call team representatives (we don't call them team leaders) who run the building. They represent our team to our manager. The team reps track everybody's performance. The manager always did that, and some people will say that the manager is just brushing off the work on you so that he hasn't got to do it. Sometimes it feels like that! There's quite a bit of work to do for monthly meetings, on top of your own job, so it takes time. We have just got a new manager whom we had to interview. That was different because we were also trying to make a good impression! It's a different outlook having to interview somebody who is higher, but he's a good guy!

How does the manager cope with being interviewed by the people they are going to manage? He didn't like it any better than you would! I'm sure he probably thought he was real good to do it that way. I think he was uncomfortable with it. He had been at Motorola a number of years and he was kind of looking down – we're still down here and he's up there, and he's looking down and thinks, 'What do these people know, and yet they can ask me these questions?'

The job of a manager is very different here. We have got people here doing all the work; all they are actually asking for is the goals to be set and a little bit of support, if they realise that things are going wrong.

I have about fifteen people, give or take a few, depending on whether I'm doing education assignment work. It's risky. I put the decisions in their hands. It's unsettling because I have had to force myself, many times, to stay out of situations and just let them go. Let them go and stub their toes, and learn from their mistakes. I try to come into the process in a way that provides some managerial coaching and leadership, rather than looking over their shoulder and making sure that they have dotted every *i* and crossed every *t*. It is sometimes hard not to do that.

The transformation is tough for the managers too. Not only are they learning to let go, to have confidence in others, but they need new skills to motivate and develop. Then, as their people grow, so the manager's job changes as they start to look at strategic rather than tactical problems.

I'll give you another perspective. It's easier to be a manager. Much easier. When I started, I could do my job in probably 35 hours. It was pretty easy. All I had to do was tell people what to do, when to do it and how to do it. It is much more difficult to get people to do that themselves. I ended up working 80 hours a week rather than 35 hours. It is much easier to play dictator. The work changes. My job changes. The questions I am asked change. I have to deal with things that are out six months to a year, as opposed to what is happening this week or next week. I deal with exporters and then I deal with 'What are we going to do to change our environment, to change our behaviour?' That is a harder job.

All this does not mean that the 'manager' loses touch with, or does not need to know, what is going on within their business. They still need to know what's going on, but it is managing versus doing. Letting the folks who really should manage the business. Saying 'go and do', and providing for them what they need to run a business.

We use the words 'coaching' and 'mentoring'. In any other business, they are supposedly there, but a lot of managers haven't got a clue what they even mean, let alone being able to do them. But there isn't a great deal of preparation. They can take advantage of things like Dale Carnegie, for example. That type of education provides opportunities for managers to be teachers. There is no formal approach to prepare someone to do this. We try to experiment and provide opportunities for managers to take initiatives while our cultural background sets the expectation.

Peer reviews

A lot of companies have experimented with alternative appraisal systems, regardless of the corporate strategy. Implementing SMWTs has implications for the way in which people are appraised. In most cases they end up with a system based on peer reviews.

I work in the Stock Room and I have been there for nine years. When I started here they were just starting on peer reviews. It was a nerve-wracking situation for me at first. I have got used to it and it's got easier for me to rate my peers and to be honest with myself and them.

Peer reviews should help as well with the feedback. The peer reviews are sometimes inconsistent because people are afraid of hurting other people's feelings. For a peer review really to work you have to be totally honest, and most people can't be totally honest because you're muscling in on someone else's life and money, in some respect.

At one time, we were reviewing people and we had to say what they were worth, from 0 to 4, four being the best. If you were given a 0 and you were currently a 3.9, you were going to lose money. Now they have changed – the structure to the point where you can't lose money for six months. So people are starting to be more honest and letting each other know that they have screwed up and should improve their performance or productivity. Motorola tries to encourage them. We don't rate people like they used to on a 1-to-4 basis. Now we just give feedback to the manager, so it has gone back to the manager actually having the final say.

There are a lot of things that come out of it. I deal with a lot of different people and I travelled a lot over the summer for Motorola. People would ask how peer reviews worked. They were tough for me as a team-leader. If I had to go to my manager and complain about somebody, then it's hard for me honestly to rate that person as being a good employee. If, for six months he has kicked me in the teeth every time I have tried to do something for him, then I am going to slam him.

You have got to be honest to make it at Motorola. I would like to get into management at some time. To do that, I have to either put my pride and my ego aside and let myself rise up and keep my friends, or sometimes I have to lose my friends.

The peer feedback processes, that we have engaged in for about four or five years, can be very painful. It started out as being called a peer review process, and we have since changed it to a peer feedback process. There is a lot of detail about the mechanics. We are still learning from it, and still going through a process to make it better. But the bottom line is that people really benefit more from feedback when it is given peer-to-peer. That is the most accurate, most constructive form of performance feedback a person can get. It is very difficult to go through, though. To sit eye-to-eye with somebody and give them information on how they are doing. We could have done a lot better job in preparing people for that.

I am one of the people who has been here a long time, and know operators who have been here fifteen or twenty years. They are not too interested in changing! They like the old ways; they find out on their peer reviews. In theory, every six months their salary would go down, but there was only one bad period and I don't think anyone in the building lost money.

It's alright as long as the feedback is constructive, and you realise the amount of damage you can do. Some people are good at giving feedback and some people aren't. We teach people how to handle feedback, how to give constructive feedback, how to take constructive feedback, how to deal with the issue instead of the personality. We teach them this by means of in-house courses. Sometimes it might take an individual more than that; it depends on the individual.

Training and development

A risk that doesn't feature very highly in the list raised by senior managers, but becomes a real one later is what to do if implementing SMWTs is a success! What will we do if people really do take to this?

Quite a few of us have mentioned things like, 'It's up to you to plan your life'; 'It's up to you to decide where you would like to go and try it out'; and things like that. Taking responsibility for your own life is important here. Motorola gives you a bit of help of course.

There are classes available to you. It is required that you take so many hours a year, but it is up to you. You can determine which classes you take. The opportunity is there. I was told, the first week I was here, that nobody is going to walk you through here. You're grown up now. I took that to heart. I never wait for anybody to say 'OK, you have been here long enough, time to move on.'

In a lot of other places, if somebody starts saying 'I'm bored here, I want to move on and do something else; I think I've done my bit here, I want to try something new, I want to be a manager', then the culture turns round and says, 'Hey, watch this person. He's grown too big for his boots'. That is almost the opposite of what happens here.

The managers today want you to progress because it makes them feel good, too. As managers, they are looking at it differently. When the people around you are shining and things are happening around your area, it makes you look good. It makes it look as though he is doing his job – which he is.

Now we have got the IWAS system. It is a system where they post jobs on a board. Different positions in different locations in Motorola all over the country. It is up to you: if you have the qualifications, if you have taken the initiative to go to school on the outside during your off-time, and you are gaining knowledge here, you have the opportunity to go as far and as high as you want.

Every day is opportunity. As soon as you walk through the door it is offered to you. So I have taken that and just kind of run with it. I plan to take advantage, to learn as far as I want, to go into education and help out the business.

Motorola will support you 100%, and they will pick up the tab for your education. Even doing outside courses as well as company ones. We also have our own internal courses.

I took a leadership course about a year-and-a-half ago. I said to my supervisor, 'I want to take this course. Here is how I am going to apply it to the business.' At that point he could have agreed or disagreed. He said, 'Yes. I would like to see an improvement, and if you can apply it, good for you. It will help out our business.' It helped out our business, it helped out our customers and even our department's understanding of the next department, which is an internal customer. Now people in our department sign up for that course.

I also find that among our peers. I will come to Greg and say, 'Greg, I want to see if I can get into the technical field or engineering. Who do I contact?' I have no doubt in my mind that Greg will back me up, give me the information I want and help get me started.

Reward and recognition

Reward systems are a common stumbling block. Managers must realise that they are not effective in the traditional organisation or they wouldn't be so ready to discuss changing them. However, changes of this kind are often put off for as long as possible. Most organisations have their own idiosyncrasies and no two systems are identical. The change is a motivating one though, as these comments reflect.

The pay system here is different in the amount of money, and the ways that people impact what they get.

There is pay for performance and also for merit. Merit is via the performance reviews which we were talking about, which are every six months, and pay can go up, down, or remain the same, depending upon how the performance review goes. There is also pay for job-knowledge which is a certification process. Different jobs have different certification points associated with them. We give those points for doing the job and so you will increase up a ladder and across a grid for the number of points you have. That was put in place to increase job flexibility.

So when somebody identifies a new job which they might move into, they have to go through a period when they learn how to do that task. Primarily it is all OJTE – on-job training and education. They have to perform that job for a specified amount of time, meeting the goals and quality objectives. Then they are deemed certified for that job.

There is a set time, usually two weeks; the goals are the goals for the department; and quality is perfect quality for two weeks. Then the supervisor makes the decision as to whether the person is certified or not.

Hierarchies

Even today, many years after Taylorism and scientific management were set aside, the concept of spans of managerial control are taught in courses to Personnel Managers. The idea that no manager can handle more than a few direct reports is so appealing! Ask people to draw their organisation structure and they'll apologise if more than half-a-dozen people drop out below the Chief Executive.

From the factory worker, say somebody who is on the floor from our level, there would be just us, a supervisor, and then their supervisor. That's about it.

In traditional organisations, the reporting process – the span of control – says managers can only handle five people at once, or something like that, so this is the justification for having a pyramid.

We have really got past that. If my job was to plan, control and direct you, I could handle about five to eight or even ten people, depending upon the activity. If it is a very repetitive activity, then I can handle a lot more. In a non-repetitive activity I have got to show your time-card, I have to tell you what to do, when to do it, how to do it, why to do it.

If I say 'Your job is to coach people and make sure that they are taking the right education and help them understand the business they are in', and if all those other things are done by the individuals. Then you get a different shift on how many managers you need.

I started out in a different direction because I did not think I would ever get through anybody's mind how to do all of this. I just said, 'We should have about forty or fifty people, or seventy people per manager'. I started off by saying seventy was the right number, but it led to a lot of interesting conversations! Part of that said, 'You are going to have to have peer reviews'. Why? Because the manager doesn't know everything you are doing. That means you have got to have a different mechanism.

Most companies have a ratio of managers to employees of about 4 to 4.5. We have a manager-to-employee ratio of 20 or 23, because the manager's activities are different.

Somebody has got to plan, control and direct. All we have done is say, 'Why don't you do that, we're going to make you smart enough to go about your business and do it...'

Customer contact

Again the obstacle to employee involvement with customers and suppliers is usually fear. In practice it improves communication and builds skills.

> We get lots of contact with customers. As a matter of fact, one of my supervisors, Mary, had some problems out in the field. Some of the engineers out in China had some questions as they did not understand the product. She gave the questions to me and I got back to those people. I called them up and sent them all the information that I could, and helped with the problem. Just recently some of our own workers went out to China to help set up and assemble sets. I was not involved in that, but a number of people from my area were. There is a lot of customer interaction in different ways.

> We focus on things like satisfying the customer. If there's anything you could ask people out there and get a consistent answer to – it is definitely on being customer-focused.

Lessons for others

It's clear that Motorolans are committed to this process. They haven't had anyone to learn from – but what are the lessons that they'd have liked to have?

> Probably the first thing I would do is teach feedback classes. Team-building is another. Eventually everyone will take that. Learning how to work in a team, because most people in this society want to be Number One and have everybody notice us, but that's not the way it really is. This place will still be running if I am not here tomorrow. A lot of people think that, because they are not here, the place is going to shut down, but I have never seen that happen. People do not realise that we have to be able to roll with the change and grow.

> You have got to have somebody who is for it, who is going to support it, who has to be a champion. That's our key ingredient. There are other things that we are talking about from a behavioural or an educational stand-point, but there also needs to be a person who is responsible for assuming leadership of the business. A champion.

You need to give people their own way of knowing how they're doing. You put a measurement up on the board and beat up on them often enough, and they get very good at modifying, not only getting better, but modifying that measure.

I had a group of people who said: 'If you're really serious about measuring quality – we think we should measure these things.' They were more severe than the corporation required for Six Sigma. The group came in and said 'We think we should measure all of these things too, because we don't think they're right!' I said: 'Fine, you measure what you want to – you do it your way. As long as you are measuring all that you should and it makes sense to you to help you run your business.'

My quality got ten times worse overnight – I was not real popular! I got a lot of phone calls. But we still measure different things from everyone else. The flack lasted for about two-and-a-half years! But I didn't pass it on – I just didn't tell anyone. The answer is, don't tell anybody about it. Just say: 'OK we're working on it!'

You get into a culture where, if one department does it, everybody does it. So part of this whole process was to allow different groups to do different things. It gets very confusing if you are trying to manage, control, plan and direct because I haven't a clue what is going on. If people within the group are doing it fine, because they know what time they started – no problem – but for a management system?!

People say 'empowerment' – it's the word I hate the most! Are they 'empowered'? – If I were truly empowered I would not work! I don't think that there's anybody here who, if they got paid and got all their benefits but didn't have to work – *they wouldn't be here*! So empowerment is an incorrect word. What we are trying to do is to get us so that, within limits – some kind of white lines – these are your boundaries. It might not be what you want to do. I don't get to vote on things – I was in here on Saturday – I didn't vote on that, I didn't want to be here Saturday. But I have some boundaries – all of us have some boundaries.

We learned very early on to stay away from buzz-words and jargon. We really look at it as a way in which we do business. We used to use the words Self-Directed Work Teams. That sent a message, 'I can do anything I want'. People got the idea that they could circumvent their supervisor and do *anything* they wanted! But there are boundaries – it isn't as if we don't have policies and procedures. They are there. So we try to stay away from jargon and buzz-words, and just say this is the way that we go about business.

Time and timekeeping

A very commonly expressed concern is that once you establish SMWTs the employees will start to go absent and timekeeping will seriously deteriorate. In practice (and it's been known for a very long time), the complete reverse is true.

The number of hours people work depends on the workload, maybe fifty-five to sixty per week. That's a good estimate. It's an honour system – we don't have time-clocks. Most areas have people sign in and out – but here it's an honour system – nobody is watching.

There's no rule here about the hours – everything is pretty flexible here in my eyes. If you know that the workload is going to be a sixty-hour week, and say something out of the blue happens – your baby-sitter is going to be on vacation – so you can't come in two extra hours. Communication! Just say to your team: 'Hey guys, I'm going to need to work only eight-hour days instead of ten-hour days this week.' The majority would say 'It's OK, we can get by with you doing that for a week'. It's not as if one guy is going to shut down the factory! You communicate with your team and you should be able to be pretty flexible with the things that you do.

In the four years that I have been here it has only twice been mandatory to work Saturday. That was just because the workload was so incredibly large. Other times it is strictly voluntary. The time that people spend here is good-quality time, and if the workload is there they'll spend that extra time to get the job done.

7.4 GROUP DISCUSSION: TEAM-WORK IN ACTION
Cellular Infrastructure Group, discussions with associates (workers) 'on the job'

Walking around the facility it strikes you how much movement there is. In any other setting this could be described as chaos or poor management. The difference is that the associates all have a purpose behind their activity. Because they know what they are doing, they do it. They don't wait for a foreman to come round and then ask permission!

Some team reps began by explaining what their role is and what it is not.

All the team rep is meant to do is to keep time – we monitor everybody's times, we monitor their attendance and we act as a manager when he isn't here. It is that easy.

From here you can see three teams – it is hard to explain, but everybody who works in that area eventually will be able to work in this area and in that one. They work together. So right now, these two can work together anytime – they have all been cross-trained. Everything falls into the line here, and so we all have to be able to get together and communicate with each other for that to happen.

There are times when we don't communicate, and you can see a big difference. For example, only last week, I got pulled into something and it almost turned into a racial thing – it was a bad situation and I backed off. These things get in the way – we are trying to get people to see that if there is something wrong with someone here you don't go to management, go to that person or to that person's team rep. That's the chain of command – if I have a problem with you, and your team rep is over here – you should try to go off with that person by yourself and work it out. If you can't work it out, then you go to the team rep, and the three of you work it out. If it's still a problem – then it goes to the management.

It's all to stop upward and downward stuff. If it goes to management, I can guarantee action will be taken – because the manager doesn't like to deal with this stuff. He shouldn't have to – he's not our baby-sitter. We are adults and we should be able to get on with each other.

Unions

Motorola is not organised by unions. At most levels people were of the view that a union would be of no benefit to them.

> Every place I've ever worked within Motorola has been very versatile. That's one of the advantages of not having a union. Most employees realise that bringing in the union would mess things up – we get paid well, we have all the benefits we need, we are paid to be flexible.
>
> That's why they pay so well. The pay is more than competitive – I make about $7 more per hour here than in other jobs, and I've done this work for five years. The building next door is unionised – they make $8 an hour and have to pay union dues: the average person here is making $10 per hour. Some make more – we've got profit-sharing and stocks – you can do anything with your money here. You can go into a purchase plan, and there are other schemes, like PRP, bonuses, flex checks. They are based on your gross salary for six months – it's based on what's been gated over the target. If you were working a lot of overtime, you'd get a big bonus!

Problems between teams

People often wonder how teams can communicate between one another in the same way that traditional organisations communicate between functions. One interviewee commented, in an aside, that the problem other places had was their egos. The teams iron out problems within themselves, but how do they resolve difficulties with other teams – without needing a manager to do so?

> We hold an hour-long meeting every Tuesday – everybody is welcome to go to it. It is a consistent problem-solving meeting – to deal with any problems in this building. If you have a beef about something, there's always a representative present from one of those areas. If you want to speak about something, or if you think a process or procedure is wrong and you want to improve it, a representative from each team is always there. Then they go back to their team and the following week you get your feedback as to what's going to happen. They give out minutes of the meeting to everybody. That's our only problem-solving team down here – it's not so much a problem-solving team as a process-solving team – that's what I

like to call it. We don't really have problems down here. Mostly it's our processes that need to be changed.

Certification of associates

People's pay depends on their skill-sets. As we heard earlier, after basic training an individual must demonstrate that they can do the job with no defects for a fixed period. Then they will be certified and paid an increment. What sort of problems does this present?

> Packing has to go for eighty hours without a defect; I watch people for a number of weeks, and if I find that they haven't made any mistakes and nobody has complained about them in that time, then after three weeks they can become a certified person. The volume isn't high enough in certain areas for people to experience the job enough. In my receiving area it's different – I'm always receiving something. In picking – I'm not always picking so I can't very well give somebody a week there. They may only get ten picks – that's not fair on the person who had thirty picks – so I have to base it more on a visual impression. We agreed that with my manager. It's the easiest way.
>
> If we take our packing department, they have a high turnover ratio because we're always taking people from packing to other departments. So they're always training people. They weed out the people.
>
> As Rick [Chandler] said, they let us interview people – if they don't make it, it means we were wrong too, that's one of the reasons they let us interview: we can't really complain about people if we hired them!
>
> Everyone wants to get to Materials. Someone can get all sixty points in the one location there, because we have more areas in which they can learn where they will be effective to this business. The job is just less varied in packing – that's why a lot of people start there.

The team-leader

Team leaders may be appointed by management, elected by the team, selected by other team-leaders, or rotated monthly, daily, by the shift or whatever. The role isn't permanent.

> If my group feels that it's time for me not to be team-leader any more, they can vote me out. When you get too big for your britches..! I had to go to Texas for Motorola, and I left my team in charge of one of the guys – he's a team-trainer. He's got his points because he can do any job around here. But I can go away for a couple of hours and he's real hard on them, and they'll be ready to do away with him! Something that happens a bit is that people will take things from their team-leader when they want to, but if they don't like it, they'll go back to wanting it from a supervisor or manager.

The caring culture

The associates themselves describe each other as Motorolans – it isn't PR hype. The organisation boasts many families as employees. There is clearly a commitment and an interest in work which exceeds that of many workplaces. What is it that makes it so different?

A Motorolan is someone who wants this business to succeed. There's a degree of ownership and people want to move on; there's a greater degree of that in Motorola than in any other place I've seen. My first manager was an older woman. She took me under her wing and said that she would help me if I wanted to be helped. I never got that offer at any other company. She cared, and she took the time to find somebody else who helped me kick some of my bad habits. That makes me have good feelings towards the company – it makes me more loyal.

We have a very good employee assistance programme – we extend the hand to anyone who wants help – even with really serious problems like drink or drugs, marital or financial problems. People may not think of going to outside help. My daughter wasn't well a while back – they gave me some parental sick leave – they didn't have to pay me, but they said: 'How much time do you want?' That's a big difference here – if you have a family or personal crisis, your job will still be here. They won't fill it.

If you wanted to take a year off, to do a tour or something, they would look after you when you got back. We had a guy who wanted to go to a Buddhist organisation for six months, so they gave him a six-month leave of absence to study his religion more deeply. He came back. In certain cases they actually guarantee you a job.

Fathers and mothers can take parental leave. I know some people who have taken their full thirteen weeks: one guy's wife took the first thirteen weeks and he took the next thirteen, so their baby got really good care for its first six months; and he came back, not to the same job, but to a similar one. They guaranteed him a job, but he was away for so long that things had changed – the business says what you'll do. This is a government thing – they are trying to encourage good family structures, and Motorola talks about good parenting, so it's pretty natural to allow this kind of thing. It's fair. It's not been that way for long – guys would often use their vacation time for family matters.

Just to stress the point about drugs: they have a random drugs screening – it goes to an outside agency. If they catch you, you are allowed two review processes, so it's the third time when you're fired. But then what you're telling them is: 'I don't want to work for you. I'd rather do drugs.' But they offer you help kick the habit. You go through analysis and they will screen you every ninety days – you don't know when, but it's once for every ninety days. If you've been clean for a year, then you're back on the random process. That applies to everybody – from the President of the company right through all of Motorola. In fact, it first started in the offices: there was a controversy at the time about whether it was an infringement of personal rights – actually Motorola got sued – it might still be in court. It is a very touchy situation –

where it's your personal life, you should be able to do what you want, but not when it affects others.

We operate an equal opportunity policy, and the balance is probably very fair. Women make up about half the workforce, and we have a good mixture of black and white, different religions, and so on. If an individual can prove themselves capable of doing something, then they can do it. We don't really think of things like this much.

When we are recruiting, Personnel do the initial screening and they then suggest the people for the jobs; we do the interviews and we try to pick the person for the job. On the job, a lot of times people don't even realise what is likely to upset others. Usually it only takes a word and they'll stop it. The Motorola policy states that if something is offensive to somebody, then it is a problem. It's possible to go to an extreme, but we have to look beyond that.

The company encourages us to help each other. You just work with people – it's much better than any other place I've worked. You don't have to jump into the problem with them.

As we walked the production area, a young electronics technician working on the line turned to a course tutor escorting us. The company had offered to send him to college to study for a degree in electronics. But he wasn't happy. A little while before, he'd attended a number of Motorola units on behaviour in teams and at work. After some thought, he wondered if they would support him to take a degree in Psychology instead. The tutor's response was immediate: 'Of course, come over and I'll give you the details of some places to check out'.

> Like Kevin this morning – no-one else around him knows which courses he could do, so it was right that he asked me for some help. This place depends on people saying, 'I'll help'. Not that you have to stop everything, but you judge their need and say: 'I've got a couple of things on now; let me finish them and I'll get to you later this morning'.

Activity 7.1 Your life-plan

As we have seen a vital characteristic of self-direction in any organisation is that people take charge of their own lives. SMWTs can only operate if each individual has a clear picture of where they are going, and what they are looking for from their work. So this activity is intended to help you to look at what you have done in the past, what you have enjoyed and what you have not enjoyed, and to begin to develop a plan for the rest of your life. We are going to use a technique which has been developed and applied by literally hundreds of thousands of people over the last fifty years. Although there are many variations on the theme, and despite the fact that it is a very simple approach, effort you spend on it now will be amply rewarded in the future.

Begin by taking a piece of paper and drawing a diagonal line across it. Ideally you should use a piece of paper of a size that is easy for you to handle. In the past this was easy. All we had to suggest was a piece of A4 or foolscap, but nowadays many people are carrying filofaxes or 'personal organisers' in various sizes, and it may be that you prefer to use a piece of paper that would fit into one of these. Whatever you choose, draw the line from the top left-hand corner to the bottom right, keeping the paper as if it were a landscape photograph. Mark the top left-hand corner with a zero and the bottom right with an 80 (we are not going to be too ambitious here). Divide the line in half and mark this point 40; then divide each of the sections in half again and again, until you end up with sections of your life marked off in ten-year intervals.

It does not matter how old you are, but mark with an x on the line your age at the moment. You will probably carry this paper with you for a decade or more (no kidding). So pop your name and the date in the top right-hand corner, well away from the line. You are going to write quite a lot of detail on this plan, so it is worth drawing and writing with a fine pencil, at least until you have got the hang of things. Now with a little mark, tick on the line your age at any memorable point or major event in your life so far. The scale isn't important and it is likely that there will be some crowded together. Be sure to show:

- the times that you have sat exams, and passed them;
- the times that you moved;
- changes of school and work;
- changes of job/career;
- promotions within the same company;
- particularly memorable holidays;
- major family events, such as meeting your partner(s);
- engagements;
- marriage;
- divorce;
- the birth of your children;
- and if anyone close to you has died.

It may be a squeeze to fit this all in. Avoid cutting off the early years, but you may find that is worth stretching the line or extending to two pieces of paper.

Most years will have something significant, though on average there will probably be between five and eight major events in every decade of your life. The more detailed you can be now, the easier things will be in the future. So far, you will have marked little ticks along the line. When writing the event, put positive ones above the line and negative ones below it to show how you felt *at the time*. Keep this piece of paper with you for some time, and mark on new events as you think of them. Try to include some items you recognise as being very emotional points in your life. Think of times when you were in a particular house or at a particular school. What was the highlight of your time there? Was it positive or negative? And mark it on your paper. Using a coloured pen or crayon, mark a green line under those events that you felt you had control over, and mark with a red line those that you felt that you didn't have control over. Most people find that they had little or no control over the positive events in their lives, while they can see that they had at least a part share in the cause of the problem in the negative ones. Whether or not this is the case, does not really matter.

You'll find that some events come close together, and that there were quiet phases too. Finally alongside, but slightly removed from it, try to record changes in your career direction, points where you felt that your direction was changing. Don't worry if some of these are slightly cloudy. It is useful to see what you have aspired to do over the course of your life so far.

You will probably find that most of your career choices so far have been made for you. There is nothing unusual in this, but we are moving into a new era in which you have to take charge of your own life, both at work and outside it. Whether you have ten, twenty or more years ahead of you at work, now is the time to start preparing for them.

Look back over the years at your hobbies and activities. Were there any that you said at the time you wished could be full-time? Perhaps when you were a helper at your children's clubs, you wished you could work full-time in a sport or social activity. Maybe on holiday you met someone whose way of life appealed. List these wishes on the line.

There are many excellent books available to help you in this initial stage of exploring alternatives. Don't let yourself be driven by what you think are poor qualifications or inappropriate experience. One thing you can be sure of today is that, if you have a mind to achieve something, you will be able to do so – even if it takes a while to get there. As somebody once said, nine-tenths of achievement is having the confidence to get there. For this reason, the kind of help that you need to look for is not just technical, but also looks at what drives you, making you happy and relaxed.

There are many books available to help you to look at your strengths and personal motivations before planning a new career, or developing the one which you are already following.

If you have decided to make a break, and pursue a new direction, then *What Color is your Parachute?* has become a classic and is annually edited and reproduced[1].

Activity 7.2 Preparing for the future

Armed with the emerging picture of your life so far, and the career moves that you have experienced, now is the time to look at the skills and qualifications needed to take you on to the next step. Whether you are interested in a complete change of direction or would like to step several rungs up the ladder of responsibility, you are likely to need new skills and qualifications. Although the world has become much more focused on paper certificates and formal qualifications, it has also become much easier for people to achieve them by routes other than the traditional schoolroom approach. Nowadays, any qualification can be achieved by a mature learner without previous experience or prior qualifications. In the last two years, we have seen a scaffolder working on an oil-rig, who left school at 15, graduate with a degree in Engineering, and an electronics technician embark on a degree in Psychology, never having been to university before.

Today, universities and colleges of higher education increasingly recognise the value of work-experience and the range of skills which you can acquire in that environment. The University of Portsmouth, for example, now offers formal degree qualifications, based part-time at the University and part-time at work, with a substantial number of marks based on your record of experience at work. Even if you have not decided on the direction in which you want to go, you can begin to prepare the ground. Nothing is easy, but this is a starting point.

There are two things that you can start doing now. First, begin to gather information about the training and qualifications you will need to get ahead. Local authorities, TECs, libraries and voluntary bodies like the Citizens Advice Bureau often have lots of general information available. If there is a professional body involved, such as the Institute of Swimming Teachers and Coaches, they not only have general material, but are probably able to put you in touch with both a regional co-ordinator and local members.

There are several ways of qualifying for most careers, so if one seems closed to you, look for others. If one career seems impossible, it is likely that another will be almost as good and might act as stepping-stone. Don't dismiss union headquarters – most have advisers who can help members looking for a change.

The second activity, which takes a lot longer than, you would expect, is to build up a record of your 'prior learning'. The chances are that, since you were last in formal education, you have done courses at work or in the evenings. Many of these have produced no formal qualification, but you probably learnt something useful. Use your time-line to jog your memory. List every bit of training that you have had, including half-day safety courses, and so on. At this stage, complete a simple record-card for each. Mark it with the course at the top right, and the date on the top left. In a couple of lines summarise the *content* of the course.

In the space below this, add three or four bullet points that spell out what you got from the course – you will be surprised, once you have started: it is very easy to do this.

References

1 Bolles R N (1990) *What Color Is Your Parachute?*, Ten Speed Press, Berkeley, California.

Learning Experience Record	Name: *Steve Jones* Date: *9 May 1995*

Event (length)	*Introduction to counselling (6 hours)*
Organisers	*Tactics*
What were the key learning points from the event?	• *Basic listening skills* • *Environment - confidential + open* • *Recognise your limits* • *Various theories: similar skills* • *Unconditional positive regard*
What did you find particularly good about this event and your involvement in it?	• *Amazing variety of people* • *Found out much more than I expected to* • *Really encouraging tutor - always said positive things* • *Made me realise how little I know about myself.*
What do you think you could do differently to get more from a similar event?	• *Re-read the course intro more carefully* • *Talk through my goals with someone beforehand* • *I need to practise the skills much more*
How have you applied the learning points to your life/work?	NB Complete this section 90 days later *I talked through the course with DT when I got back to work. She suggested using them in team meetings. It took a while but they are much better now. Also listened to Lynn much harder - I need to work on this now.*

Fig 7.2: A simple record of prior learning

8

THE UNIONS AND SELF-MANAGING WORK TEAMS

'I'm not going to tell you that you are not going to find models out there with non-union workplaces. What I am saying is you can find some excellent union-based models, and I think the union helps both the high-wage, high-skill strategy which we think is important for this nation. We have a consuming middle-class, and we are opposed to the ones that are going down the low road – it's not in their interest any longer in this country.'   (Bob Baugh, AFL/CIO)

- Where unions are operating it would be odd for the implementation of Self-Managing Work Teams to go ahead without their involvement.

- The relationship between unions and management is changing – old-style managers and old-style union representatives are finding the environment tough.

- There are many excellent examples of Self-Managing Work Teams being implemented with full union support – in a growing number of cases at their suggestion.

- The unions themselves are driving for enhanced investment in workers' skills – particularly on generic skills such as analytical and problem-solving skills.

- In the USA, the AFL-CIO is pressing for the output from business process re-engineering to be based on Self-Managing Work Teams. They argue that this is the best means of allowing individuals and teams to experience a wider share of the responsibility for their organisation's well-being.

INTRODUCTION

There can be little doubt that, where the front-line employees have already been organised into unions, it would be odd for the implementation of Self-Managing Work Teams (SMWTs) not to involve them. The degree of trust which a management team needs to feel towards the workforce means that they will have already dealt with the traditionally-expected adversarial role of the union before they countenanced (or even dreamed of) the concept of Self-Management.

There are many examples of organisations where unions do not exist and where SMWTs have been introduced – at Motorola, for instance, where unions have never been established. Similarly, many of the successful Japanese manufacturing operations have involved green-field sites, and their union system is based around employers anyway. Under these circumstances, as we have described elsewhere, the workforce has usually had a strong relationship with the management team, and there has never been a need for collective power as a negotiating tool.

Examples of unionised workplaces adopting SMWTs appear to be fewer – but this doesn't mean that the unions are not in favour of them – far from it, as we shall see. Perhaps the relationship between management and the union has not matured to the extent that the necessary level of trust exists; if this is the case, then there is a role for every manager and every union member in redressing the balance.

Unions do have some unique perspectives on their role, and this does have an impact. Whatever your own view, it is fair to say that the relationship between governments and unions has been changing throughout the 1970s and 1980s. Equally, the management-union relationship has changed. Whether SMWTs are fortunate in arriving at a time when all three parties are receptive, or whether they have emerged as a consequence of this shift in relationship, is difficult to say and probably will never be established.

WHY SHOULD THE UNIONS BE RESPONSIVE?

It is useful to remind ourselves of the difference in roles and organisation of a union locally and nationally. At a local level, union representatives are often called upon to react rapidly to a problem. They do not often have the opportunity to work strategically with management. Both parties may have a common desire to resolve those 'problems', but priorities may differ. As a result, even when both agree on the need for a solution, there may be conflicts. The only tools which the local representative has in order to force an issue on to the agenda are often confrontational. To many managers, the union's only 'face' is the local representative. In many ways this representative has shaped managers' perceptions of unions.

Nationally, on the other hand, there has been the opportunity to act strategically for a long time. Unions have had a tremendous impact on legislation in the past. This legislation has often focused on the protection of basic rights, such as safety, work hours, and protection from unfair dismissal. Again, this has reinforced a picture among managers of the unions as having little or no capacity for decision-making. Indeed, many managers believe that it is their prerogative to decide what work is done, by whom and when, how and where – after all what is 'management' otherwise?

In the past, the unions evolved as a form of collective power to address problems where they perceived that workers' basic rights were being infringed or could potentially be infringed. Wages and working conditions were given greatest emphasis, but unions have long held the view that their role was wider than this. Throughout the world, their objectives have included enhancing the quality of work-life, improving the skills and participation of employees, and creating industrial democracy. Self-Management, then, offers an opportunity for unions to move forward in their relationship and the image that they portray.

The new labour-management relationship

Where unions are already established, the relationship with management needs to move towards one of partnership – where both groups see each other as equals. This calls for a shift in attitudes, mainly at the individual level. Managers who have thrived in an environment of assumed responsibility, and who have become accustomed to issuing orders, need to change. Equally, union representatives who have depended on a confrontational and 'rallying' approach need to transform their style.

The nature of this new relationship is important because it highlights the failings of many companies in their adoption of 'empowerment'. Self-Managing Work Teams are not concerned with making employees feel good so that they work harder; nor are they about helping employees to achieve the ends that management has decided on. What they are about is a transition in the basis of decision-making, and it is here that the potential clash of ideologies can arise. From the managers' perspective, control – in the form of the power to make decisions – is being passed to the shop-floor team. Just as managers do not often talk in terms of individuals being empowered, nor do they mention a reciprocal transfer of influence into head office. To the union, however, this is exactly what is happening – the new work-structure is, they say, providing greater individual worker – participation in the workplace *and* enhanced collective representation on the corporate stage.

The importance of collective responsibility to the union movement is understandable. Since the movement's earliest days, collective action has been seen as a fundamental way of achieving fairness of opportunity. For workers in non-craft environments, the threat of lowest-common-denominator wages and conditions, and a constant undermining of self-achievement, could only be addressed by collective action, both in individual organisations and across whole industries. In many cases, the unions have been more effective at achieving this pan-industry collaboration than have management, for fear of divulging important information to competitors.

In a unionised environment, managers wanting to evolve SMWTs need to consider the increasing role of a collective workforce representation at the most senior levels. As Henry Bangser, Superintendent of New Trier High School summed up, the relationship is changing, but it has tended to focus on employment issues rather than operational ones: 'We work beautifully with the unions – if you're going to make a change in working conditions then they become strong – otherwise they let us get on. If you want people to work longer, then they'll expect them to be paid. We collectively bargain; if there weren't a union, a similar arrangement would work with a committee. But I do think that the prevailing view in the United States is that the unions are losing power – they are not as powerful as they were fifteen years ago.'

Equally, union leaders need to appreciate the limited consideration that this has received in management circles. Cases should be formulated, examples prepared, and methods of introducing them into the management forum need to be evolved.

DO THE UNIONS SUPPORT SELF-DIRECTION?

In the 1970s and only in the USA, a number of organisations implemented 'Quality of Work-Life' programmes. The movement was popular and attracted central government support, but it was never as successful as its protagonists had hoped. All the usual reasons could be given for its failure – though the commonest was, as ever, lack of senior management commitment. As with SMWTs, unless the most senior members of the established structure demonstrate their involvement in the process of change, little will happen.

A number of unions in the USA tried to negotiate the introduction of 'Quality of Work-Life' schemes of this kind. Out of the successes and failures came a number of lessons for anyone wishing to introduce SMWTs. In the USA, the AFL–CIO (the American Federation of Labor – Congress of Industrial Organisations) recently convened a study into these and other aspects of the evolution of work. They drew five principles which they felt were important to the success of future initiatives. In looking at them it is difficult to see anything other than an exceptionally well-considered endorsement of Self-Managing Work Teams.

1 The traditional view – that thinking and doing have to be achieved by different groups of people – needs to be rejected. The AFL–CIO point out that the workers who are actually doing a job are in the best position to make decisions about it. They don't expect to have the only say – simply a genuinely fair say. In order for this to be respected, and for it to be effective, the AFL–CIO add that a priority should be placed on developing workers' analytical and problem-solving skills.

2 Business processes need to be redesigned to allow individual workers, and the teams in which they work, to experience a much wider variety of tasks and therefore greater responsibility for the organisation's overall output. To achieve this the AFL–CIO committee specifically recommended the use of work groups.

3 They saw one of the consequences of the changes which are occurring as being a flatter hierarchy, and recognised that the traditional, autocratic, manager would have difficulty controlling such an environment. They saw few limits to the potential for these teams – including decisions of employment and financial responsibility as well as day-to-day operational issues. Given the nature of labour law in the USA, many managers find it difficult to believe that the union movement could be endorsing such a level of responsibility, as it would place many workers outside the protection of the current legislation.

4 Their fourth observation was that such decision-making mustn't be restricted to the daily operating environment, since this would restrict their input only to tactical concerns. Instead, employees should be involved as partners in strategic decisions too. The route by which the AFL–CIO thought this could probably be achieved was through the unions emphasising their collective representation role.

5 Finally, if the role of the worker is to shift so dramatically, there is a need for the whole process of recognition and reward to be changed. While basic employment conditions needn't be threatened, the unions are adamant that one of the reasons why 'Quality of Work-Life' programmes failed was because they didn't fairly distribute the benefits of the programme to those involved. The AFL–CIO takes a very positive stance when it points out that such distribution isn't expected to be equal – but it should be equitable. Again, they propose a collective negotiation of this arrangement. While, no doubt, some managers will react to this, it is perhaps difficult to see how it can be changed without creating a bureaucratic nightmare.

Labour representation in Japan is very different from that in the UK and the US, being concentrated on the company-union which is prohibited by

American law. Motori Hirose of the Keidanren sums up the impact of this style of representation: 'Remember, too, that the organisation of labour representation in Japan is different from elsewhere – our unions are company-unions and not national – this works very much in the employer's favour.'

As you would expect then, the support for Self-Management is equally strong among the unions in Japan, but this does not prevent them from taking action if they believe that their members' rights are being compromised. As Yasuhiko Inoue of the Japan Productivity Center explains: 'The unions are very positive – as they are enterprise unions – one company, one union – everyone joins the same union (managers and other employees). This means that everyone is in the same boat. The union performs its function but doesn't go outside this – the first thing is for the company to obtain what it needs, then, when resources are sufficient, the union can negotiate – collective bargaining or strike.'

Do the unions have a more significant role to play in Self-Managing Work Teams?

The US union movement is founded on the principle of collective representation, so it is hardly surprising this is reflected in their expectations of the new relationship in organisations. The AFL-CIO outlines four likely 'qualities' of the environment that will support SMWTs:

- mutual recognition and respect;
- collective bargaining; equality of responsibility:
- directed towards mutually agreed goals.

In each case, the union is seen as the representative of the workers. The emerging role is little different from that which the unions have had for decades, and although the words which are used appear to reflect a conciliatory stance, it is difficult to decide how this will be achieved in practice. In the USA, roughly one fifth of full-time employees (14,000,000 people) are believed to earn the poverty level. At the same time, deaths from industrial accidents continue to contribute an awesome proportion of the annual toll for people of working age. While statistics of this kind exist, it will be difficult to argue in favour of individual negotiation – especially when adult illiteracy continues to grow at a phenomenal pace.

So what can the unions do to achieve the new high-performance workplace? Firstly, they have to endorse the process of change – in the 1970s and 1980s a number of TQ processes floundered because of the insistence of unions locally to introduce participation as a negotiable commodity in the annual remuneration cycle. Often, their national representatives supported the initiative – and yet the message failed to reach local bodies until it was too late.

There is a growing tendency in the US, especially among medium-sized enterprises, for unions to be far more proactive in encouraging management to move towards Self-Management. Many national bodies have developed briefing documents for both management and union representatives. Some have gone so far as to provide training for local negotiators, to help them persuade the employers. Others have established training programmes to equip their members both to understand and implement these initiatives, and also to develop the necessary skills to enable them to participate.

At a national level, the AFL-CIO has adopted the role of resource co-ordinator, creating forums for the dissemination of materials and experiences of organisations involved in Self-Managing Work Teams.

A pioneering example – Ford and the Union of Auto-Workers

We describe the Ford experience at Romeo elsewhere in this book, but the partnership relationship between the UAW and the Ford management goes back much further. Together the two organisations have developed a wide range of worker involvement and co-operative initiatives. Ford attributes many of their commercial successes to these relationships.

Throughout the US there are about seventy joint facilities. In each, there are broad agreements for job security, information transfer and profit-sharing. Going well beyond US labour law, they address issues such as quality, personnel development, team working, business process re-engineering, safety, apprenticeship programmes, and academic research into management and social issues. In almost every case, the two partners discovered that a slow, evolutionary approach was far better than full-scale implementation, and that 'local' issues were just that – national intervention was largely counterproductive.

It was in 1979 that Ford and UAW formally adopted Employee Involvement as a voluntary process for local management-union partners to engage in. Between 1979 and 1982, the automotive industry suffered enormous losses – and Ford was no exception. In that period, Ford reduced its workforce by almost 50% – as well as introducting radically more efficient operating practices. In 1982, the partners signed a collective bargaining agreement. Among its terms were the provision of job-security measures and profit-sharing. At the same time, wages were frozen at current levels. Perhaps, though, one of the most innovative steps was the introduction of the 'nickel fund' by which 5 cents per hour worked were diverted into a joint training fund.

From 1982 onwards, workers who were to be displaced were offered help through Re-employment Assistance Centers. One of these centres, at Lima in Ohio, received the Presidential Award in 1988 for the innovative and highly effective support which they provided.

The mid-1980s saw the programme expanding, through the introduction of a number of ancillary support facilities such as child-care, health and safety, and employee assistance. The thrust of the training activities was largely to do with leadership skills.

By the end of the decade, quality had become a major focus: the two organisations planned together to implement improvement programmes. Profitability grew, and most employees received a substantial profit-related bonus. To achieve these returns, jointly supported teams initiated work in planned preventative maintenance (PPM), partnership sourcing, project management, team working on the shop-floor and, most significantly, in entirely new business structures.

CURRENT TRENDS IN THE WORKPLACE – AND THEIR IMPLICATIONS

Continuous learning

We have already alluded to some horrifying facts elsewhere in this book. Throughout the world, functional illiteracy is growing. Stop for a moment to understand those words. Functional illiteracy means that you can't understand a train timetable, can't interpret the instructions in a recipe or, worse, on the packet – and of course, the safety warnings on a drug bottle could well be meaningless. Functional illiteracy extends to numeracy: you can't check your change, can't balance your bank statement, can't understand the terms of the loan which you've just undertaken. And what happens when you need to complain about something – do you put it in writing? In the US, more than one in five new workers were functionally illiterate in 1990 – and the figure is growing!

But educational reform won't help. While it will redress the balance in the very long-term (it has taken us more than fifty years to get this bad) it does nothing in the short-term. More than 75% of the working population of the year 2000 have already started work. We need to help them overcome the disadvantage which has been created for them.

Of course, inadequate education is not the only problem. Again in the US, which is admittedly a culturally diverse nation, 60% of new employees are female and 25% are 'minorities' – yet the methods of teaching and training which have evolved over the years were driven by the needs of stereotypical white males. Whatever solutions we adopt have to allow for the special requirements of these new groups. At the simplest level, this means providing suitable child-care and travel arrangements. Far more significantly, we need to rewrite almost every text book with more relevant examples, and convey them in a culturally acceptable manner.

But this is a chapter about unions – so what is their role in this? Successful past initiatives highlight the role of local unions in the future. It is only at a local level that the psychological support, in the form of counselling and mentoring needed by existing employees, can be provided. Often the unions represent an impartial, or positively supporting, source of help to the very people who most need it. These people didn't succeed in an environment where such support wasn't available – perhaps this is one of the wider failings of our existing system anyway? This has many implications: one of the differences in the delivery of such programmes, for instance, has been the teaching style. The common approach is to identify the individual's lack of knowledge and then try to fill in the gaps; whereas the approach adopted by the successful programmes has been to use people's existing knowledge, constantly reinforcing the connections with this and emphasising the people's present ability.

Take the traditionally poorly-skilled and low-wage environment of the health-care sector. Hospital staff, outside the medical area, are often the most disadvantaged. In the mid-1980s the local branch in Seattle, Washington of the Service Employees' International Union, initiated a series of activities within two health-care establishments[1]. The union already had a strong presence in the two establishments, the Group Health Co-operative in Puget Sound and the Swedish Hospital Medical Centre. Both programmes were concerned with employee-focused, on-the-job skills development. In each case, success criteria were established in terms of the usefulness and effectiveness of the training, the success of participants in moving up to higher-graded jobs, and the extent to which employees themselves were involved in the programmes.

At the Swedish Hospital, the medical transcriptionists were the first to embark on the programme. Their skills have traditionally been acquired through many years of experience with very little formal training. Through their programme, general rules for establishing training needs and converting these into formal programmes have been established. So too has the importance of the mentoring approach to on-the-job skills acquisition.

The Group Health Co-operative took another area, that of medical assistants. This job is very diverse, providing support in countless practical aspects of care to the medical and nursing staff. It is important for assistants to have a much wider range of scientific training, as well as practical on-the-job skills, so the programme which was developed for them involved classroom work on two nights a week, half-a-day each weekend, and a further day a week on supervised on-the-job training. A schedule of this kind would tax most students, but the commitment of the medical assistants meant that they did all of this in addition to a full working week. Some traditional managers might be amazed to hear that the initiative for these exceptionally long hours was not taken by the hospital management team but by the local branch of the Service Employees' International Union.

The success of these examples has been ascribed to the ability of the union's negotiators. One of the tenets of the union movement, especially within the US, is that of collective bargaining. Until employers begin to pay more than lip-service to the development of their employees, and until we move towards a culture of personal responsibility for learning, it seems likely that it will only be through such a bargaining arrangement that sufficient resources will be made available. In Chapter 6, on the role of the government and legislators, we have looked at some of the ways in which this shift can be achieved.

New technology

The implementation of new technology goes hand-in-hand with changes in the structure of organisations – this is one reason why some companies mistakenly turn to IT professionals for assistance with business process re-engineering.

The introduction of new technology has had different impacts within different economies around the world. In the small proportion of Japanese companies with a large workforce, many new employees begin with a spell on the shop-floor, regardless of their entrance qualifications. In technical matters this ensures that they have a better ability to communicate outside their discipline. There are several other consequences of this. One is the way in which young people become involved in the education of their colleagues.

In Britain, non-academic routes to qualification, including the craft-work/apprenticeship ones, have been progressively diminishing – aided dramatically by the recession and the downward trend in first-job aspirations of graduates.

The French have experienced a similar trend, though theirs appears to have been progressing for longer. In many functions, as new technology has been introduced, a three-tier hierarchy has been established: those responsible for the introduction itself have taken a specialist role, between existing engineer/technicians and their professionally-qualified managers. The effect of this has not only been to extend the hierarchy, at a time when other companies around the world have been delayering, but it has also reduced the skills needed by existing engineers. They therefore become general dogsbodies, rather than pursuing a career path of their own.

A contrast has emerged in Germany, where the proportion of highly-skilled workers is greater. There, the distinctions between shop-floor, technician, engineer, supervisor and manager have been blurred for some time. New technology in this environment is often implemented by technically highly-skilled shop-floor employees. In a growing number of industries the competition for places on the professional-qualification ladder is getting stiffer and so, not only are the non-managerial staff seeking a place on this ladder, but they are also entering the system with higher qualifications. Thus it is more common in Germany than elsewhere for a secretary to begin work at the age of nineteen (two or even three years older than in the UK) having completed their university entrance examinations. Apart from the ability to use more complex technology, more comprehensively, their 'apprenticeships' prepare them for many activities on which they may only rarely call. Nowhere has this been more marked in recent years than in the area of languages. Many more German secretaries are bilingual than their British and American counterparts. But the distinction doesn't rest there – German secretarial staff are in a position to take on many of the tasks which have been performed by junior managers, including specialist research roles.

A combination of the strong union movement in Germany, coupled with their traditional involvement in a much wider arena than purely collective bargaining, and the legislation protecting employment, have led many organisations to adopt a highly participative approach to introducing new technology. Whereas in many countries (including the UK), the decision to implement new technology is taken by senior managers, often on the advice of their middle-management colleagues, in Germany there is a far greater involvement of shop-floor employees in decisions of this kind. In the US, one study has shown that less than 15% of employees are informed of a decision, let alone consulted before it is made, when new technology is implemented [2]. While the consultative approach can appear to slow down investment, it is said that the time taken to install, train and operate the facility is significantly shorter. The phrase used by many unionists to describe this approach is 'co-determination'.

Business process redesign

Of the tools and techniques which received attention in the 1980s as part of the Total Quality revolution, the 1990s have seen a resurgence of interest in one – business process re-engineering (BPR). As Carol Haddad of Wayne State University has reported: 'Instead of moving towards the high performance model ... many firms take a piecemeal approach to work restructuring – sprinkling in the ingredients that suit their particular recipes.' [3] The problem with this approach is that it rarely goes far enough for the organisation to reap the benefits of the re-engineering process. If a traditional organisation goes through this process, it will retain few, if any, of the functions that existed before. Most individuals will have a transformed role, being responsible for far more wide-ranging tasks and accountable for far more significant decisions. To achieve this calls for a flexible workforce, with a broad portfolio of modern and transferable skills, and a culture in which learning new skills is expected.

As with the introduction of new technology, the involvement of employees in the redesign process is rare. Instead, manufacturers in particular have often taken a redundancy-and-recruitment strategy to improve the relevance of their employees skills[4]. Not surprisingly, they anticipate a reaction from unions to this approach!

In the US, union intervention in business process re-engineering has largely been concerned with the preparatory steps, particularly in educating and reskilling employees for a more flexible role.

The decline in training expenditure, even before the recession, in the UK has been very thoroughly documented; and similar trends have been spotted in the US. Among the organisations to respond to this were the American unions, several of whom introduced training programmes, as we have already seen, into the collective bargaining process. The growth in this approach prompted the ASTD (American Society for Training and Development) to report in 1990: 'Unions are fast becoming leaders in providing career-related training to individual employees. Training programmes jointly administered by unions and management now spend more than $300 million per year and represent the fastest growing segment in the nation's learning system.'[5]

The argument for employee participation leading to empowerment has been advanced throughout this book. In describing ways of approaching and achieving this, we tend to take a corporate management view; interestingly this isn't the one that unions have taken, especially in North America. While it is obviously vital for individuals to have a repertoire of useful skills in order to participate in this new environment, there are many other aspects of BPR which have not been fully explored, and in North America many of the unions have taken a lead in practical research. The purpose of this research may initially be to improve the understanding of such issues as concurrent engineering, information-sharing processes and communication models, the integration of process design and manufacturing operations, and many more. But performing research of this kind has a second, very significant benefit: it demonstrates that front-line workers have a capacity to understand their own plants and businesses equal to that of their managers. It achieves this in a far more powerful way than many training courses could manage.

In Canada, some time before the left-wing New Democratic Party was elected, unions in Ontario lobbied central government successfully for a multi-million dollar grant to study the impact of new technology.

Apprenticeship

Just as the tenet of collective representation (and therefore bargaining) is central to the union movement, so to a greater or lesser extent is that of apprenticeships, tied as it is to the principle of seniority. Critics of the apprenticeship system point to its power as a regulator of industrial employment and as a mechanism to tie workers to the union for life. There is little to distinguish between apprenticeships and the training in many of the professions – e.g. housemen in hospitals and pupils in chambers. No doubt there have been instances where this fear has been justified, but if the crisis which we have described is to be addressed, we need every bit of training that we can get. Do apprenticeships hold part of the answer?

In the US there are many excellent examples of apprenticeship programmes, created and managed by the major unions, which have become virtually the sole source of affordable training for new entrants to a profession. Take the construction industry. When a need emerges for training in a particular area, a local joint apprenticeship committee (JAC) is established, consisting of equal numbers of employers and union representatives. The JAC appoint instructors – those who have not previously done this attend a formal instructors' skills course at a university. Unlike 'train-the-trainers' courses, these are comprehensive training development, management and skills courses – for example: the University of San Diego programme for the Ironworkers National Trust offers thirty-four such courses. The trainers have their technical skills updated, and are often introduced to new equipment and working practices by the manufacturers and employers. At a basic level, instructors themselves complete eighty hours of coursework before they are appointed. In some cases the courses are accredited for university engineering degree status, and the more dedicated instructors may well qualify in this way.

New entrants to the industry have their existing skills assessed by JAC panels, and are allowed credits for previous work, training and experience. With these, the apprentice begins a three-, four- or five-year training programme. Once qualified, they become what is known in the US as a 'journeyman' – a fully-qualified employee.

But their training does not stop there. We have discussed the need for flexibility and lifetime training. The JACs administer a wide range of post-experience courses. For example, in some states where hazardous waste is reprocessed, the construction skills needed to build waste-conversion facilities are far more specialised. Here, every journeyman has to complete a further forty-hour training course before entering the sites, and their instructors have had to take part in over a hundred hours of extra preparatory training.

By working closely with each other, the management and unions prevent the barrier of fear from developing. Such schemes not only serve the employers, the union and the workers equally well, but they also help remove the long-standing adversarial relationship which exists elsewhere between unions and employers.

THE FUTURE OF LABOUR ORGANISATION

Throughout this chapter, we have seen how the role of the unions can change. We have seen that they can take a far more proactive role in developing the labour resource of the future – perhaps by taking over (or at least supplementing) the provisions of State and employer.

The unions themselves speak of the need to address their relationship with employers – wanting to be seen as partners rather than adversaries. Where trust has been shown by employers, the new relationship has been profoundly successful – in some instances driven by the employer, in others by the union.

As have so many management consultants before, the unions point out how important it is for management teams to treat their initiatives seriously. Whatever the acronym – BPR, TQM, JIT, and so on – all call for a much greater level of commitment and involvement than have been demonstrated in many companies. No matter what the initiative, you shouldn't expect to recognise the organisation after it has been achieved. From the workers' perspective, the unions point out that this calls for radically more flexible employees. Traditional functions are disappearing and will continue to do so. Unlike many professional bodies, the unions are mostly organised by industry. This puts them in a better position to predict trends and to respond by equipping workers to meet new demands.

We have described the changing demographics of employment, but how will these affect the unions? These are four key areas:

- their members are increasingly from minorities;
- they have different expectations of the ways in which they will be consulted and represented to traditional members;
- they have different ways of learning and working;
- they have different models of reporting relationships.

All of these have an impact on a body that claims to represent workers. The union members of the future will increasingly be part-timers, some may even be portfolio workers. How will the unions cope with people who may traditionally have been excluded from membership for not being full-time? How will membership privileges and voting rights be affected when someone works in two different (often dramatically different) environments? Among the combinations that we have recently encountered are school patrols who also work as warehouse operators, warehouse operators employed as drugs counsellors, and drugs counsellors working as secretarial supervisors! Four occupations, four careers, four unions. What are the unique needs of these groups? At first, some unionists suggested that this was a transient population moving towards full-time, sole-occupation employment.[6] This is a dangerous assumption, and the problems which the situation poses are real – for example, how do the pension rights of a port-folio worker affect a collective bargaining arrangement when some employees are full-time?

Increasingly, unions are being joined by professional or white-collar workers. These groups were growing throughout the mid-1980s boom-time – now they are among the first to go from many service-sector companies. But do traditional union values of organisation, collective negotiation, state involvement, and seniority reflect the values of a group of the workforce who grew up in an environment of individually negotiated recognition and reward, where pay was entirely, or significantly, linked to performance?

INTERVIEW 8.1 TEAM WORKING AND THE UNIONS
Bob Baugh, Special Assistant to the Executive Director, American Federation of Labor & Congress of Industrial Organisations (AFL–CIO)

Employment is shifting towards the smaller businesses, especially in the service sector. This is an issue that the unions are having to address too, as their membership base also shifts. So how can we begin to influence the management of SMEs to go down the road of high performance and self-direction to the same extent as their manufacturing big brothers?

There are a couple of things:

- The manufacturing sector has been hammered heavily, but not as much as you'd think. There are several reasons why you see the focus there. Many of the practices we're talking about – that's where they're appearing for the first time: the advent of new technologies, not just computers, but technological change to the business all round.
- There's also been an actual growth in small and medium-sized firms in the manufacturing sector at the same time as the larger ones have declined, so over the last decade ironically you have seen 2.5 million jobs disappear in the large-firms sector and a growth of over 1.5 million jobs in the small-firms sector. A new study talks about that, because of the turbulence it's created.

If you look at employment in relation to the overall growth of jobs, the percentage of manufacturing has continued to decline but for its relationship to the gross national product, it's still a major player in terms of the economic generators.

Some of the reasons you continue to see people looking at that is that a lot of what is being done in manufacturing is spilling over into the 'service' sector. Service anyway is a complete misnomer. It's health care, it's janitors, it's lawyers; it's so big that it's very difficult to get your arms around it, and you see these initiatives cross the boundaries.

Much of the focus of change – indeed, one of the greater vehicles for change in the US – has been the quality movement. There was a fascinating, as yet unpublished, paper that appeared only recently which is all to do with the history of the quality movement, and what was the break-off point where change really began to set in to our industrial sector. It was in the early 1980s that the Japanese and the issue of quality came to the forefront, their ability to view quality as a profitability measure and as a productivity measure. It's a real change of the mind-set, because of the globalisation of our auto industry in particular, but we've seen it in other sectors too.

The tool in this country has been the Baldrige Award, but I see a much more subtle layer than that. That is an award, it's a prize, though it provided a template for states and governments and other businesses. They may not go for the Baldrige, but you see quality initiatives springing up all over.

Unions such as the Service Employees Union and ASME which is the Federation of State, County and Municipal Employees, representing both public-sector and private-sector service workers, are looking at quality-of-service issues. Governments are confronting these too – there are forty-two states which now have state-sponsored quality initiatives for the public sector. States which have set up these quality awards focused on manufacturing, but many are beginning to say we've got to include the schools, government, and the service sector. Manufacturing was also the biggest sector that was out there, with the most sophisticated ability to benchmark and measure itself. They have the most experience and they're also the ones that I would argue have had to be the most globally competitive. Our service economy isn't threatened in Wall Street to the extent that the Big Three automobile manufacturers are, so for a lot of reasons it's not surprising that this is where you see most emphasis.

The AFL-CIO and federal government

Just as the relationship between unions and employers is changing, so is that between central government and the unions. The AFL–CIO has had its differences with government, especially during the Reagan administration but nevertheless it is funded in part by government support.

In terms of our own base that's where a lot of our members are.

The AFL–CIO is the Confederation of Trade Unions – that's equivalent to the Trades Union Congress in the UK. In Washington DC we're the national organisation. Each state has an AFL–CIO which is a coalition of the local unions in that state. Then, in addition to that, you may have local labour councils at city level. We have currently eighty-four different international unions which comprise the AFL–CIO, and each of them has their own structure which may include a regional structure and then a local union structure below that.

In many ways that's where the power lies, within the individual organisations, not within the AFL–CIO itself. They're the ones which are involved in negotiations with contractors, and they are also politically active. We are partly the body that represents the united political voice as well as the individual unions. Then we also provide other service functions. The Human Resources Development Institute is part of the AFL–CIO, but we're actually a not-for-profit organisation, so I'm not officially on the AFL–CIO payroll. We're sponsored by government funds from the Department of Labor.

Nevertheless there's been a good deal of anger and frustration with the Department of Labor over the last decade or so. Previous administrations, which a lot of folks, including myself, feel were very insensitive to workers, did everything they could to dismantle the Department of Labor and its relationships with trades unions. You could liken it to some of the things that went on in Britain under Thatcher – there was a degree of symmetry between our President and your Prime Minister for a while there!

Some of that is changing now, because there has been a change in administration. This one is not at war with the labour movement and has a very different perspective on the role of government: there have to be partnerships of labour as well as business, and as a nation we've got to figure out how to do business differently.

The changing role of the unions

Changing the structure of the workplace inevitably affects the way in which people are organised and so the unions must adapt too. Nevertheless, before they can do so they need to make sure their members' employers are serious and that they are not simply paying lip-service to empowerment.

The role of the unions is changing. There's a very serious examination of our labour relations system in the United States, and the Dunlop Commission has taken a long, hard look at that and at the impediments both to change and organisational change.

This has very much to do with the labour laws; I would argue that we have the most restrictive set of labour laws of any industrialised nation in the world. People do not have the right to organise in this country, we've got it so tangled up in the legal system. There's a real serious look at what's going on here at least.

The AFL–CIO has recognised that in a empowered labour organisation, 'empowered workers' really implies that they have power. Yet it's often phoney change that they have a stake in. We feel that is wrong, that it's important that they have a legally recognised stake, and we feel that the labour unions have a place in the democratic process in this country. They play a very important role. For ten or fifteen years nobody wanted to have that dialogue; this administration certainly does, and they're raising the fundamental issue of fairness in our country. If workers want the right to organise and negotiate the conditions of their employment, isn't that right and just? I think that's an important move.

The unions themselves are in a tremendous state of change. Many unions had to participate in change in the workplace, and now the national organisation has reached the consensus that this stuff is safe, and it isn't the same as the quality circles of a decade ago. We've got to lead, follow or get out of the way, and it really is time we led. We have not paid attention to those who have been engaged in this reform, we have not assisted our members in the firing line – and it's time that we did.

Labour-management relations

Like any umbrella organisation the AFL–CIO has to monitor the interests of its subscribers and respond. With such a complex issue as the high performance workplace it is difficult to assess the interest and participation already underway.

Individual organisations have got involved to one degree or another. There was a meeting recently attended by hundreds of members of the machinist union, which had taken a position of not getting involved in labour-management co-operation efforts. In the middle of the speeches, somebody got up and asked a question; the speaker said: 'Well how many of you *are* engaged in labour-management co-operative efforts?' Nearly 70% of hands in the room went up – yet the International itself had told them not to (and thought they weren't)! In the State of Oregon, we looked at 1,800 workplaces and the amount of activity on Self-Directed Work Teams, and TQM, all the things that will be components of a high performance work organisation. There are huge amounts of experimentation, and you can see that a lot of it has gone wrong.

You begin to see that the unions are engaged. Two recent studies have looked at the places where unions are, and they found that they tend to be the ones where you find more of this kind of activity, or organisational-type efforts generally, and that they are more productive than other workplaces.

We want politically to get over the hump of how to deal with this. We've got to be more responsible for the management of an organisation, and it's a very uncomfortable and different role, and that's part of the change. But it's also coming with the recognition that we can't let these folks continue to manage by themselves. What has been a sacred contractual right for management in this country, called the Management's Right Clause, has strangled both of us, interfered with both sides and changed the way we do business – it says basically that the management make all the decisions.

Three years ago we did a high school conference. When I was trying to commit my friends in the labour-education sector to do this they said they'd be lucky to get fifty people in. We got 200, and we had to close the doors because the fire marshal said there were too many people – over 200 rank-and-file officers. We had different workshops, each with a set of common questions to address, then come back and report on as you went through the day. One was: 'What do you think of this? What is the technological change, work change and organisational change and labour management co-operation? What do you think of this – yes, no, good, not good? Shall we do anything about it?'

It was fascinating that every group came back with the same answers: that this isn't a question of 'if', it's already happening to us, and it's not that we don't want to deal with it, we want to know how to deal with it intelligently; help us build local union technology and education committees, help us acquire the skills so that we can do our best to represent our members and our organisation, and engage in this change and not be used and abused.

Preparation for change

Implementing the high performance work place in a unionised environment can mean that the union representatives need to change their attitudes and behaviours and that responsibilities of managers (even of the company) can be transferred to the union. As we've seen elsewhere, this has happened at Ford – and Baugh recognises, or at least expects, it to do so generally.

> The high performance workplace requires re-skilling of the workforce, which means talking about who really has a say in the agenda for training and education of the workforce. We need to defend that, and work for it so that it really does move to a high performance organisation; that's a change! AFL – CIO is getting a lot of industrial-based unions, or service-based unions, to zero back in on the training and education agenda that has been available to management and technical staff and which hasn't trained the workers of this country. There need to be changes from the traditional operation of grievance procedures, and union leadership roles which have always been adversarial to management. Now the union leaders are also going to have other roles – as communicators and coaches, which is just unfamiliar terrain to a traditional union leader; it calls for other sets of skills, and walking this very strange line between being a representative of the workers and the adversary of management, but at the same time being responsible for the management and decision-making within the organisation.

The structure of unions

Will multi-skilling and the increasing flexibility of people's jobs in a Self-Directing Work Group have an impact on the way in which the unions are structured?

> There are those who say that this organisation should move itself from being dysfunctional to being cross-functional. Do you practise what you preach? I think it will. It is already forcing people to think about strategic planning in a way that they have never had to do before. For example, we've put together a questionnaire about technology and training in the work organisation – we're starting to use it with the unions around the country. It gets used partly as a diagnostic tool, and partly as a discussion lever for training sessions. We're also trying to use it as the start of a national database, on just what is going on out there. We debated it at a conference last month. The last question was more of a customer survey: 'What do you think of us?' We had three categories – research, training, and development – and there were a bunch of sub-categories under those. We wanted to know what people's needs were; we were saying, 'As you've experienced this stuff, as it's happened in there as you're going through, what have you learnt? What is it you think you need?' 83% of the people who responded to this question said 'Train us in strategic planning'; another 60% said 'Provide technical assistance to strategic planning' – which shocked us! It was interesting that all these researchers think that's what needs to be done, but they

don't think the membership understands it. It just blew me away this; I walked in and I said: 'Do you know what the commonest response to all the questions was?' They said: 'Well, that's because we focused on strategic planning on the second day', and I said: 'We had all the surveys back before the end of the first day!' So people are recognising that there's a problem, and they don't quite know how to go about getting their arms around it, and they're telling us, 'Show us how to think about this'.

In a way, the challenge for the local union is to engage in strategic planning around workplace change, and it raises some fundamental questions about the union's role generally, because it's not just how the workplace changes but how the union engages in that change process, making it serve as a tool with which to strengthen and organise itself.

Co-management – the steelmakers

The trend in a number of organised plants has been towards co-management with the union. This has been more or less formalised according to the parties involved. It's easy to see this as a process which calls for a major shift in management thinking, but what about the unions? How do we begin to help them to adapt?

I've been facilitating the steel-workers' union in this country. It has negotiated a most startling line in a contract which really calls for the co-management of five major steel companies. I've facilitated a lot of these, including Bethlehem Steel Corporation and their Spares Point division which employs about 6,000 people. This is one of the oldest steel mills in the US with a history of a hundred years of class struggle, very much more on the traditional British lines than what you've seen in lots of cases in this country. They are engaged in this change, and I'm watching as facilitator for both – but they're using me as a consultant and mediator too. It's not crystal clear that I'm a neutral in what's going on here. I'm watching them try to change or think about the change.

They now have the words on paper. It's progress, but the euphoria of the first four months of having that paper has now worn off. You have both sides: a union which has a strategy that knows we need to engage in co-management, and some principles around that. They've got to share the information with the whole firm, it's the whole company, non-union employees as well. But if you ask them: 'Now what?', after that we're in deep trouble.

The company is no different, the company is just as liable to fall into its old patterns. I'm working with a CEO who does not have a steel-making background, but was a customer-service sales guy, who is very much into people, you know: 'Well, people, we can make this work!'

He's certainly got the right instincts; we've got to think differently. It's just that the behaviour is not there at all, in the sense that we're talking about. We want these area committees to examine a whole department. That means all non-union personnel and professional and technical people, as well as the bargaining union. We've just got to think. All of a sudden all the old industrial relations people are hammering on: 'Why did you do that?' and 'These guys are going to do this over here...', 'I remember in 1972 when they did it...!' There's a lot of history, and it's extremely difficult. I hope this works, but it's certainly challenged the union about who and what they are. Right now, they're still locked into thinking 'We know what management is doing wrong not to be a partner'; but they really need to think through, 'What do we have to do to become a modern organisation?' They've started meeting and, if it's going to work, they've got to come to the point, where they're going to do more critical self-examination about the changes they need to make. They even know some of them, they're talking about them, but they just aren't capable of making them happen yet.

Super unions

As jobs become multi-skilled, especially at trade level, the question arises as to which union is the relevant one for the individuals in teams. The natural impact of this will be for the smaller unions to progressively merge. The prospect of a super-union is not out of the question.

Is there a move towards a super union in terms of much more diverse representation? In this country, yes. Very quietly. If you had been here six or seven years ago you would have seen 100 or 100+ internationals, and now there's only 84. That's exactly what Australia did: they had 360 and they're now down to 20. And they did it in a decade. This all goes back to the change of the workplace and in getting management to modernise it; they took a look at themselves and said, 'This ain't going to work!'

People recognise that this needs to happen, but the impetus to make it happen is driven by the wrong 'energy' – it tends to happen out of weakness as opposed to strategic process; people aren't ready yet to let go of some things.

One of the big mergers which didn't happen, which I think would have been very interesting if it had, is the auto-makers and machinists. They came very close to merging a few years ago. It would have been a huge merger; it could have actually set a trend.

The benefit of union involvement

There's a lot of evidence beginning to come out now, in Xerox and Corning and places which are setting exemplary models of high-performance, that this offers great gains.

The evidence is not that those who aren't organised don't tend to produce the results. The tendency is that those who aren't organised are the last to go that way, to deal with it, that they continue to pursue a low-wage path. There's another argument that says because you negotiate better wages and working conditions, that helps drive the introduction of technology and productivity in the workplace. If you start looking now at the organisations which people talk about where they're really starting to make this transition, you tend to find a lot of fairly high-profile organised workplaces. That's not to say all. I'd love to see Motorola organised, but it's not! So I'm not going to tell you that you're not going to find models out there with non-union workplaces. What I am saying is you can find some excellent union-based models, and I think the union helps both the high-wage, high-skill strategy which we think is important for this nation. We have a consuming middle-class, and we are opposed to the ones that are going the low road. It's not in their interest any longer in this country.

The Labor Act and management unions

A lot of managers have said that the Labor Act gets in their way, because they perceive that there is a dispute about whether Self-Directed Work Groups are perceived as a management union.

In Japan by contrast, the main union organisation is the 'management union,' or the 'company union' as they prefer to call it. They don't have the national bodies to the extent that in Britain or America does. To what extent do these structures suffer from legislative barriers?

> I bet you 90% of the people to whom you've talked don't know what it's really about. A lot of assumptions have appeared in the literature. A Self-Directed Work Team can do all kinds of things, the issue is, when does it step over the boundary into what would be a traditional collective-bargaining relationship, like setting wages or, hours of work? Some of these things you could argue cross the line, but there are all kinds of things that don't. The Labor Act doesn't say anything about how you organise a Just-In-Time inventory system, how you organise your work around that or whether you have an assembly line or Self-Directed Work Teams and multi-skilling.
>
> I recently spent some time with one of the top officials from Ranco; he's out of the Toyota union and had been a white-collar worker, a technical worker, at Toyota before he became a union official. Their strategies are totally different. There are cultural reasons for all this, and I was asking questions about the union's role in issues of the skilling of the workforce. A lot of what you got is: 'Well, that's the company.' But the management is all union. It is difficult; I can understand what they're doing, but the cultural context just doesn't fit or work here – it's not the same.
>
> It's the same situation in Germany, you've got to learn where you can from that, and work out what have you learned and how you can then apply it in your own situation, your own culture. You're dealing in national culture here.

Activity 8.1 Our perceptions of union and management

This is not a trivial exercise. The more time that you spend on it, the more useful it will be. It could be worth carrying it with you for a few days – or longer, until you feel that you have done it justice. It is about understanding yourself, and why you hold certain opinions; it is also about other people and why they hold different ones.

Different people react differently to the same situation, or sequence of events. They do so not because the facts have changed, but because their experience has preconditioned them to do so. When we *observe* something happening, at first we *react* to it. Then we may think about it and make some more-or-less conscious *judgements* before we do or say something – or, in behavioural-science terms, make an *intervention.* This sequence is called the ORJI cycle, because what we say or do is another event for ourselves and other people to observe, and so on. In the book *Making Change Happen* (Pitman Publishing, 1993) we describe the impact of this process on teams of people

> '*Most management are comfortable, complacent, uncaring, members of the fortunate middle class. They are interested in doing things for themselves and out to screw the workers – though they would never see it that way!*'

> '*Most unionists are like sheep, following a few bolshie troublemakers. They are out of touch with the real world, putting their own interests above those of the company that employs them.*'

Either one or the other (or both) of the statements above will have made you think something: you may agree, disagree, or think that we're deliberately being naive to provoke you.

Let's pause a moment to look back over *your* experience to see what has influenced you and the way in which you interpret union-management relationships.

Step 1

On a piece of paper (a sheet from a flip chart would be perfect for this), mark off four boxes by drawing a vertical and a horizontal line. Above the vertical line write 'UNION' and below it 'MANAGEMENT'. On the far left put '-ve' and on the far right put '+ve'. Now spend a while doing a mini-brainstorm by yourself. Write down positive things that you associate with unions, unionists, shop-stewards and organised labour generally in the top left-hand box. Fill the other four boxes with equally appropriate lists of words.

Step 2

What was your earliest experiences of politics? Think back to your early school-days: what were your parents' views, those of your grandparents, and the community in which you grew up?

When was the first time you were aware of a clash between political views?

How old were you at the first elections that you remember? Can you recall which party you supported? Why? How have your views changed over time?

On a large sheet of paper (again a flip-chart sheet is ideal), draw a diagonal line from one corner to another. Mark it off in five-year blocks, since you were born to the present-day. (If you are 45, you'll have 0 in one corner and 45 in the diagonally opposite one – with nine equal chunks between them.)

On one side of the line (in one colour), mark major personal incidents in your life – changes of school and job, when you took up particular hobbies, when you married, your children's birthdays and so on. On the other side (in a different colour) try to fill in your political views, awareness and experiences. Now (in a third colour) mark your exposure to unions – important strikes, joining a union, leaving it, and so on. Finally (and in a fourth colour) add key elements of exposure to management – your head teacher at school perhaps, the appointment of a chairman or woman to your favourite professional sports team maybe, your first boss – perhaps from a Saturday job – and so on.

We did this exercise with a team of senior managers recently. Several were emphatic that they had never been union members. In fact, they had all been members of the National Union of Students. They learnt a lot about themselves and their views when they discussed what they thought of the students involved in the NUS at the time.

A small group of union members had a similar problem with 'management' One of them pointed out that, out of six, four were elected officers of clubs and societies outside work. In one case the individual had responsibility for the management of a larger budget than the turnover of his employer!

Step 3

Look over the first chart. Highlight the five most significant themes in each of the four boxes. Now turn to the second sheet. Try to pinpoint which events led to you holding those images of unions and management.

Activity 8.2: Labour-management relations

What is the recent history of labour-management relations within your organisation? It might be tempting to look at the last five years or so historically, but it is perhaps more useful to look at the degree of consultation and involvement that has gone on.

Take a document that represents all of the work that goes on. This could be a process flow-chart, an organisational chart, a site-map or even an internal telephone directory.

Now use a spreadsheet to document the extent of involvement. Firstly, list all the discrete parts of the organisation along the top row. Then against each, complete rows for the following (the symbol in capitals is a convenient shorthand). In doing this, remember that we are asking what *actually* happens and not what might, in theory, happen. For example, one major petroleum company has rules which say that managers can travel first-class on the train, while front-line staff must travel second-class. When they travel together, managers in some areas will put in a claim for both tickets at first class, others will travel together second-class, others will travel independently – often making some excuse that they have to go on an earlier or later train to avoid their embarrassment. We are not being judgmental here, we are simply asking you to make a thorough assessment of what happens.

- Front-line staff work individually (I) or in teams (T).
- Teams are temporary and only for problem solving (T) or permanent (P).
- Meetings of the group are held hourly (H), daily (D), weekly (W), monthly (M) or less often (0).
- Front-line staff are organised by a union (U) or non-unionised (N).
- Front-line staff elect their leader (F) or have one imposed by management (M).
- To what extent were front-line staff consulted in the last internal re-organisation? Not at all (0), some discussion (1), much discussion (2); they designed it (3).
- To what extent were front-line staff involved in preparing the last annual budget? Not at all (0); some discussion (1), much discussion (2); they prepared it (3).
- Front-line staff schedule their own work (S) or follow instructions (I).
- Front-line staff monitor timekeeping, absenteeism, sickness, holiday usage, etc. (F) or managers do (M).
- Front-line staff negotiate their salary (F), there is collective bargaining (C) or it is management determined (M).
- Front-line staff conduct training (F) or it is a specialist role (S).
- Front-line staff interview for jobs (F), it is done by managers (M) or it is a specialist role (S).
- How many new-product ideas or major quality/productivity suggestions did front-line staff contribute on average last year?
- What sort of social facilities do front-line staff have? Front-line staff-only club (F), staff association club open to both direct labour and management (S) or no facilities (0).
- To what extent do managers and front-line staff mix socially? Never (0); occasionally (e.g. Xmas Party) (X); regularly on formal occasions (F); routinely informally (I).
- Do front-line staff go to specialist conferences? (Y/N)
- If front-line staff and their managers go to specialist conferences, do they do so together (T), independently (I) or never to the same ones (0)?
- Do managers and front-line staff share wash-rooms? (Y/N)
- Do managers and front-line staff share catering facilities? (Y/N)
- Do managers have their workspace in the same area as front-line staff (F), close to the front-line staff (C) or on a different floor, building or site (D)?

Now review the spreadsheet. Are there any areas which you would say stand out from the others for greater or lesser involvement? Are there any issues that are universally non-involving? Are there any areas which you can correlate with what you know of morale, discipline, performance, productivity or quality with the answers that you gave? Spend some time poring over this chart.

References

1 Marschall, Daniel (ed) (1991) *High-Performance Work and Learning Systems – crafting a worker-centred approach.* AFL–CIO Human Resource Development Institute, Washington DC.
2 Haddad, Dr Carol J *A participatory perspective on technology and work redesign*, High Performance Work and Learning Systems, AFL–CIO Human Resources Development Institute, Washington DC, September 1991.
3 Op. cit.
4 Commission on the Skills of the American Workforce, *America's Choice: High Skills or Low Wages!* (Rochester NY: National Center on Education and the Economy, 1990).
5 American Society for Training and Development, *Put quality to work: train America's workforce.* (Alexandria VA: ASTD, 1990).
6 Sarmiento, Anthony *Cultivating a suitable workplace environment for workplace restructuring.* High Performance Work and Learning Systems, AFL–CIO Human Resources Development Institute, Washington DC, September 1991.

9

THE EDUCATIONAL PERSPECTIVE

'Factory workers today are very different, and so are the job-requirements. They have to be able and willing to learn, they need to be able to compute, to do math, to be able to work in a team, to be able to communicate, to make a presentation. They need to be able to take on a problem-solving role of their own.'

(Mary-Jo McCarthy, Motorola University)

- **Jobs are universally becoming more complex. Not only are the tasks themselves concerned with more technology, but they call for new dimensions, such as team-working, accountability, and minimal supervision.**

- **Literacy and numeracy are dropping – fast. In a national survey of 21–25 year-olds in the US, only one in four white adults could interpret a bus timetable!**

- **Industrialists feel that schools have lost touch with their needs.**

- **Teachers feel that they are appallingly under-resourced.**

- **Industry and schools need to work together – the competencies which are needed are defined, businesses need to help manage the schools, and become involved in resourcing them.**

- **The effectiveness of work-based training needs to be improved and its systematic delivery needs to be made an integral part of an employee's career.**

INTRODUCTION

This chapter is not for the faint-hearted: it covers issues which are complex and political. The issues involved are also at the heart of the high performance workplace. Everyone who has been involved in Self-Managed environments agrees that the pressing need is for a skilled and flexible group of employees. Most see this as a pre-requisite – you can't implement such teams if you don't *already* have the skills and flexibility. The issues highlight the imperative need for action. We don't wish to seem to be harbingers of doom, and there is something that we can *all* do to arrest the decay; but if we don't.... Read on!

World economies are crumbling. Even emergent ones that had been seen as bucking the trend, such as that of Korea, have now begun to totter. This is not something which the person in the street can address – it is an international crisis. If it isn't dealt with, wages will fall, social conditions will deteriorate, illiteracy, famine and disease will rise. The statistics are simple – we have allowed ourselves to create an environment which cannot support the current population, and is doomed in the future – unless we act now. This is not a third-world issue. In Britain at the moment homelessness has increased thirteen-fold in less than a decade (yes, that is 1,300%) – not in inner cities, but in the heart of the comfortable stockbroker belt!

The solution lies in education and employment. But the needs of jobs, in terms of skills and knowledge, are pulling away from the delivery capability of our educators. Confronted with underskilled employees, the employers are less likely to adopt a new organisational structure – after all, it is a risk. Yet if they do not do so, we cannot compete effectively on a quality or productivity basis, and there will continue to be a pressure to do so on price. Of course, competition by price favours the consumer in the short term, but it means that the long-term survival of businesses depends on their reducing costs – if they are not doing so by improving productivity and quality, they can only do so through subsidies or by reducing labour costs. We have already seen a dramatic migration of business (even from the UK) to the lower labour-rate economies of southern USA, Mexico and South America. In Japan, there has been an enormous influx of Korean labour. In the Gulf, Pakistani and Indian labour has been imported. Even across Europe, we see a migration of manufacturing to lower-cost economies in southern Europe and north Africa.

In the previous chapter, we saw how governments can intervene to encourage the adoption of Self-Management by employers. In this chapter we look at the prerequisites for Self-Management. We see the skills which today's employees must develop, and we see how some communities are trying to respond through education reform.

THE CHANGING NATURE OF WORK

It doesn't matter what the job, the expectations of the person doing it today are far more complex than they were just ten years ago. Entry requirements are higher; technical demands are greater; people are handling more diverse tasks, tackling problems, moving jobs, and relocating. They are increasingly working as a key member of a team, with minimal supervision and increased accountability. If you don't believe this, take any job and draw up a list of these items as they stand now and as they were in 1984.

The crisis in education

The crisis facing educationalists around the world is whether they can prepare people for this new workplace, and the new ways in which they'll have to work. Since the Second World War, most children have been educated in a system which concentrated on individuals passing exams, to show that they knew certain facts and could string them together in a reasonable argument, within a limited time.

In the 1970s and 1980s in Britain, at least, we experimented with alternative styles of teaching, concentrating less on *what* was being taught and more on how it was being learned. Now, in the 1990s, we are being asked to

Upward Shift in US Job Skills
source: Hudson Inst ('87)

Typical job skill ratings:

1 Unskilled labour   4 Teachers/technicians
2 Truck driver   5 Engineers/lawers
3 Administrative/construction   6 Nature scientists

Fig 9.1 The upward shift in US job skills

'go back to basics', as adult literacy is declining, and mathematical ability is poor. In both Japan and the USA there are problems – though the symptoms are not the same. In both cases, teaching methods are blamed. As Yasuhiko Inoue, of the Japan Productivity Center, explained:

'Educational changes are important – literacy is fine – but education needs to be much more creative. The average school-kid will have no problem with tables and so on. Two times four equals eight – they know, but not why. The creativity of education really needs to change. This hurts us in so many ways – but above all, we are less prepared to admit or even perceive new things.'

Essentially we have let down the present generation – we have prepared them for a world which no longer exists. Worse – as Yasuhiko Inoue points out – it is the new generation which determines the standards of society in the future. And those standards don't just mean behaviour in its commonest sense, but how money will be spent and how efficient our production will be:

'Our young people are absorbing a greater amount of information and becoming more sophisticated in their demands as consumers – they are reading newer books, watching new programmes, taking part in new leisure activities and so on, all of these are encouraging them to look for more detail in what they buy – they are becoming much more sophisticated.'

The competencies approach

For the new environment, a set of 'competencies' can be identified with which every school-child, every college or university graduate, should be equipped as they enter the world of work. Independently, industry in Japan and the US is identifying similar skills. While their expectations are unusual, teachers are eager to respond – it appears to be the government and further or higher education that are reluctant to support such a drive.

The new competencies

1 The skill of scheduling resources
2 Interpersonal skills
  – working with others to achieve results
3 Handling information
  – identifying, collecting, analysing, communicating
4 Thinking systematically
5 Coping with technology
  – selecting, using, troubleshooting, maintaining

Fig 9.2

1994	1984
'A' level or graduate	'CSE' or typing school
Handling computer software, fax machines, cellular comms, telephone or video conferencing and multi-channel telephones	Using a manual typewriter, perhaps an answer-phone, a telex machine, and a kettle?
Commuting 50 miles daily, travelling on company business, holidaying in the Med, and relocating to Swindon to continue their career.	Catching the bus, rarely leaving the office, holidays in Devon, and changing jobs rather than move.
They work with a team of others, on a project-by-project basis. They have no supervisor, reporting to the same 'boss' as other team members.	They are one of a pool, with a supervisor, reporting to the office manager, who allocates their work daily.
If they make a mistake, they share the blame and help work it out.	If they make a mistake, they are sacked.

Fig 9.3 The role of the secretary, 1984 and 1994

The response from industry

With its growing need for higher-skilled employees and more informed users of its products, a business has to ask whether it can rely upon the traditional providers of education to deliver all that it needs. Although state or community control of education has, in the past, been one of the social norms, many now feel that it is no longer tenable. In the UK, we have seen a growth in the number of schools 'opting out' of local government systems or seeking grant-maintained status. In the US, it has already been suggested that some employers would be interested in providing schooling for their employees' children.

The question becomes bound up with political dogma. Should schools be controlled by their customers – the pupils, their parents and the employers? If so who pays? If it is the employers, can they be fair and unbiased? And what if a child has an aptitude for a discipline which is of no use to employers but is potentially of value to society?

Managing the schools of the future

There has to be increased **dialogue** between the employers and the educators to define the requirements of those employers, and the standards which must be achieved. This applies in all parts of the educational spectrum, but it is vital at the secondary (11–16) stage, from which the majority of future employees (and consumers) emerge.

There appears to be agreement that the more permanent this dialogue can be, the better the potential exchange. On the odd occasions where this is achieved, it is usually through the employer's participation in the governing body of the school or college. There is less agreement as to whether this should happen on the basis of company-to-institution, or through individuals mainly representing their own views. An individual can't generally offer the desirable levels of resource and support and must rely on a central source of information within their employer which doesn't usually exist. If we are to achieve this transfer of ideas, employers need to invest in the collation of relevant data, co-ordinate its dissemination among the employees involved in schools, and provide suitable support for those employees to fulfil their role.

Resourcing the schools of the future

The second opportunity for employers to support education lies in the provision of **resources.** In the past, this has generally been restricted to employers donating specific, often unwanted, equipment. The opportunities, however, are much greater. Employers should be providing material for courses, such as case-studies and worked examples. They can co-develop complete teaching materials in virtually all disciplines. They can provide experiences for groups of students through site visits and 'guest' contributions to classes. To those of us who were educated in the 1960s and 1970s, such events were not unheard of – but today they are a rarity.

Similarly, organisations can provide opportunities for teachers to develop their own experience of the working environment, the challenges it presents and the skills it demands. They can also provide those teachers with the opportunities to broaden their own understanding of the industrial applications of their subject-specialisations.

The transfer of management methods

The other chance that exists is for **methods** developed in the management of businesses to be offered to schools, to help them become more effective and efficient. Many companies offer their employees structured development in techniques such as statistical process control, quality management, and interpersonal skills. These are not the exclusive preserve of commerce: many schools and colleges would benefit from applying them. For example, very few schools routinely assess the effectiveness of their classes or quantify the impact on learning of using different methods in a controlled manner. If the existing educational system doesn't provide these skills and encourage their application, then employers have two choices: do nothing and watch the quality of their new recruits progressively decline; or step in and provide the methods that are needed.

The smaller business constraint

Clearly there are financial and practical difficulties preventing smaller firms from becoming involved in educational management and reform to the same extent as larger ones. There is therefore a role for local employers' organisations, such as the Institute of Directors and the Chambers of Commerce, to facilitate pooled efforts. In the past this has been attempted on a piecemeal basis. It needs to be more widely recognised if it is to address the very real problems.

I'm ashamed to repeat this story – but it contains an important message. I used to work for a small consultancy practice, based in Oxfordshire and with a team of about a dozen consultants. We employed a dozen more 'support' staff, one of whom was an administrative manager. We specialised in an aspect of management development. When you looked at the consultants' out-of-work activities, very few of us did anything for the community with our skills. Only one person did. The administrative manager was also a lecturer at a College of Further Education, helping future generations develop the basic skills of business. It doesn't matter what your business is, or how large or small – there is something that you can do to help turn the tide of educational reform.

THE INTERVIEWEES

Three people, in particular, demonstrate how important these issues are and how we all need to become involved in addressing them. **Dr Henry Bangser** is the Superintendent of New Trier Township High School in the US. The High School has developed an outstanding reputation for the qualities of its graduates. This is not a new phenomenon, and as Bangser says it would be easy for them to become complacent. But they are not. Under Bangser's guidance they are initiating a massive programme of change. The way in which this is being achieved illustrates the degree of professionalism which is necessary, and the far-reaching scope of such programmes.

The growth of illiteracy poses an enormous potential threat to large organisations. To a global electronics manufacturer and communications service provider, like Motorola, it could mean losses of markets and revenues measurable in millions of dollars. But worse – as the proportion of skilled workers drops, so it becomes harder for major employers, like Motorola, to provide sufficient resources for their own production lines. **Mary-Jo McCarthy**, of the Motorola University Education Initiatives area, points out that the time has come for organisations to become involved. They certainly need to look at initiatives for incumbent-worker training. In theory this is easy – it just calls for a much greater investment than we have been used to making! But they also need to intervene in the education scene on a local, national and international level. She describes some of the imaginative and awesome projects on which they have embarked.

Picking up on the theme of incumbent worker training, which is an area that most organisations have some plans for, **Dave Basarab**, also of Motorola University, very neatly demonstrates why 'training' has such a dubious reputation in many boardrooms. As part of their drive towards Six Sigma, Motorola carries out a sophisticated assessment of most of its training activities. They do still carry out the basic 'smile' test for delegates to courses, but they also go a lot further. Their pioneering work is attracting attention throughout the USA and further afield.

INTERVIEW 9.1 CHANGE IN THE EDUCATION SYSTEM

Dr Henry Bangser, Superintendent, New Trier Township High School

Creating the stimulus for change

It's usually said that there are many stimuli to change, yet only one trigger. Henry Bangser gives three good examples of changes occurring. In the first, no-one really wanted to though there were many stimuli – so his role was to provide that trigger. In the second, everything about the area and the school was in flux, the issue there was managing the process. Now at New Trier, there are very few external stimuli – quite the opposite, as the community is stable and the school is phenomenally successful. Bangser has to create the stimuli, provide the trigger and manage the process.

> Probably my first involvement in strategic change, was in a one-town kindergarten-through-twelfth grade district with about 2,200 students. It is one of the oldest towns outside New York City, loath to change, a very conservative

community – yet there were a few things that needed change. At that time, no school district in the entire county of Westchester had ever done any strategic planning; we were the first to talk about it, but it was sort of rudimentary! So that was the mid-1980s.

The next place I went to was a western suburb of Chicago, in 1987, and between 1987 and 1990 we introduced a lot of change. It's said that organisations can have many stimuli to change and it takes only one trigger – well, I didn't have any trouble introducing change there – they had been ready for it for about four years. They wanted change. The demography was changing, up until the early 1980s it had been a predominantly middle-class river-town, about 15 miles west of Schaumburg, with a relatively small percentage of professionals; then from about 1983 on, because they had some open-land, the region became much more up-scale. So I arrived there at a time when there was a high readiness for change; we almost couldn't change fast enough – it was like the more the better.

New Trier is at the other end of the continuum. It is not experiencing significant demographic change. We're not growing very quickly – only about 2% a year. There's a significant amount of self-confidence, stemming from about fifty years of being told that they were doing it better than anybody else.

I believe that the way to change is to create a need or readiness for change. We tried to do that by using a combination of an intense introspection about ourselves, and then we brought in a team of 117 people for a period of three days to look at our programme. Out of the 117, probably between fifty and seventy were public high-school people, fifteen to twenty were educators but from private situations, and then there were about fifteen to twenty university types. This group of 117, in most other settings, would have had a maximum of forty people. We determined that we would do better if we had a larger group, so that we would have conversations as opposed to inspections. I think it worked well from the stand-point of the report being less of a document which told us how well we were doing, and how well we have always done compared to others, and more a document which said: 'Yes, we acknowledge the fact that you're very good – here are the things that we think you should consider for the future'. So the theory was that the process itself would establish a greater readiness for change on the part of the long-term staff than if I, the Principal, the board, or any other people with titles, said: 'We've got to change'. I think that in general it worked pretty well – it was better than anything else I could think of. I'm not sure in retrospect what else could have created such a readiness, though I have to be honest with you – I'm not sure we have that readiness quite now. It's higher that it would have been if we hadn't tried anything – that's to be expected.

A lot of times you get the external stimuli – it may be dissatisfaction with your organisation, or your products going down the tubes. What I've found interesting about Motorola is that they began the change when their product was pretty good. It wasn't all that it could have been, but it was still pretty good; yet people had the vision to say, if we don't change it won't be good. In our case, if we didn't change much we'd still be one of the best, however you measure that, or viewed as one of the best because reputations go on a long time – but we would know that we weren't, because other people would be better than us in part.

One of the frustrating things about the role of the Superintendent working with a board, being private-sector biased, is that of measurement. I've never really come across any satisfactory way of establishing whether your human resources are working effectively – in the public sector. Obviously there are test scores – people jump on those because they are real figures, empirical data – but if you set those aside (and people are willing to do that pretty quickly), how do you go about measuring those kinds of things?

One of the measures is 'cocktail' party talk. And I think it's pretty accurate! In the places I have been, if the cpt (child per teacher ratio) is high, you hear 'my child didn't get a fair deal', or 'I'm not happy with my child's teacher', or 'the school system is poorly managed', 'the teachers don't care', 'the quality of adults in the organisation is mediocre' – then generally there's not satisfaction either on the part of the people who are served directly or the 70% who are not served directly. That's a measure, and you tend to know that if you're a superintendent or board member.

For a community like ours one measure might be: 'How are our graduates being viewed by the colleges and universities to which they are going?' Is there any significant trend either up or down, for the broad band of universities and colleges to which they are applying, for percentage applied versus percentage accepted? We have been remarkably stable – it is not as good as I'd like, because I know that there is probably an equal number of students who were not accepted as were, and that next group will be as good or better than students outside our school.

Another area is how well our students do in jobs – only such a small percentage go out into jobs straight after school. Test scores are annually the highest in the state. They're not the highest in the country but they certainly are among the best. That's all sort of 'old products'.

The emerging role of the school

So we have heard that industry is not satisfied with the 'quality' of the young adults emerging from the school system. We have seen that achieving this is going to call for substantial change in the schools themselves and that one step along that road is for them to be able to 'measure' their own output.

The 'new products' were defined in the strategic plan which was produced in September 1993. In this we said that 18 year-olds in the next decade will be far more aware of, and engaged in, issues involving global diversity, technology and decision-making which will not be initiated by adults, but by them. We said that they would have the ability to interact among themselves effectively – so communication is very important, problem-solving, creativity, and risk-taking.

There is a trend to demand all of these – on paper though! It's coming from the American private sector. We hear that the American private sector doesn't much care whether a student can add or not: they want to know that people can work effectively together in groups, that they can problem-solve, and can communicate both in writing and orally. My impression is that, nowadays, 25 year-olds do a much better job communicating in writing than in speaking. Speaking skills are atrocious; writing is getting better.

From a school like ours, the basic skills are automatically there, but I think that the private sector feels that they can be produced by something other than the education system anyway. My impression of the sort of tests which people like Motorola are using, is that they are not so concerned with basic arithmetic or reading skills.

Our biggest challenge, though, is that we know that about nine out of ten of our graduates are going to go on to some kind of higher education. So the question is: for what are we preparing them?

So what we're about is providing the most diverse, exciting, intellectually challenging, academic and full-curricula programme over four years, which will give students access to things they wouldn't otherwise know about, both in the classroom and outside. We need to provoke their interest so that they might go on to study something that they wouldn't otherwise know about – to awaken them both to areas of study and outside study which they can then go on to study further. The Performing Arts programme is an example – at New Trier ours is better than that of most colleges and universities.

I don't think we are about developing an end-point academic experience in any subject which they will go out and implement – on an assembly line or anywhere else. We are creating an intellectual curiosity and love of learning, doing things academically and outside the academic life which will then cause them to be better judges of how they want to spend their next period of time, and create a sense of excitement about learning. That will cause them, at the age of 22, to be better, and different, from what they would have been if they hadn't been through this process as 14–18 year-olds.

You learn more when you work hard at something: high-school students do most of their hard work when they go home and they labour over the things which the teacher was talking about all day. I think they'd learn more if they used the time at school to work harder on it then.

Whether they are employed or not, the adult members of the local community can be expected to take an increasing role in the schools. Not only are they encouraged to do so for the children's benefit, but also for their own. Schools are learning to recognise that adult learners are an increasingly important element of their target 'market'. As lifetime learning develops, so the community will become far more proactive within schools. With the adults come a host of other social support provisions that might not before have been considered.

In general, for kindergarten through twelfth grade, roughly 20% of the community is directly concerned with a school. In our situation this is smaller still because we only represent ninth to twelfth grades. There are other agencies which share social responsibility with us, but more and more of these – such as adult education, family support, and child behavioural issues – have come our way because we are better funded than those agencies. That's hard when people say: 'Back in 1976 you spent this much, and now you spend this much; you've exceeded inflation'. If you list all the things that you have taken on since then, you sound defensive.

We do get involved in a wider social framework than many schools. You will hear debates at the business level of the school (the Board Meetings) about social issues such as substance abuse, sex education, family welfare, and involving the wider community in the school, rather than the relatively small proportion with children in our age-range. But all of this is only a relatively small part of our effort.

The changing nature of teaching

Rather like the middle managers in industry, the people who often have the toughest time in education are the teachers – they are blamed for poor standards while no-one gives them credit for their professionalism! So how do we introduce change without demotivating an essential part of the solution?

The measurement of teachers is neither well-received nor well done. If you've been a teacher for twenty-five years, in your first two years you were probably visited twice – once by your department chair and once by a Principal or Assistant Principal. For the next twenty-three years you were probably visited every two to four years – unless you're a problem – then you get a lot of attention.

The person at the top of a organisation can have an enormous impact – our Principal has, especially when her impact is through others and not directly attributed to her. My role is to support her. Change will inevitably come, but it has to be subtle and sophisticated rather than in the form of bomb-shells, because of the nature of the place, because New Trier is rich in history and reputation, the best of the best. Forget about the students – the community has to be convinced of the benefit of the change: they are paying substantially for it.

How do you define the 'product'? To be honest, I'm not sure how we define the product. In most places which are not focused on improving student-performance you will get a multi-tiered answer. The single biggest change in New Trier next year will be in staff training. In a commercial environment, the people whom you're training are there anyway; if they are being trained they are not working, so they are a cost. But in our case, it's more complex: when the 'adults' are there, they are theoretically with the children – if we are going to train them then we've got to do so when they're not with the children. So we either have to take time away from students, or have the teachers there more time – in which case we have to pay them more to be there – it becomes a financial issue. We know that if we want to bring in our faculty, and we pay them a per diem rate which is equal to what we pay them for summer-school, it would cost about $55,000 a day to bring everybody in; so ten days costs half a million dollars – that is about 1% of our budget.

We work beautifully with the professional staff associations: if you're going to make a change in working conditions, then they become strong – otherwise they let us get on with it. If you want people to work longer, then they'll expect them to be paid. We collectively bargain, and if there weren't a union then a similar arrangement would work with a committee. I think that the prevailing view in the United States is that the unions are losing power – they are not as powerful as they were fifteen years ago.

Developing the school plan

New Trier is following a common pattern – development of an overall mission followed by a cascaded involvement process through self-assessment. The concerns expressed by Bangser could be spoken by the CEO of almost any commercial organisation.

In early November we had a meeting of a hundred superintendents, at which I was in charge of the programme. One of the Motorola people pointed out that they can describe their product in just a few words, yet when you get education people to describe their product, they come out with the biggest set of platitudes – 'to create world-class global thinkers in the twenty-first century'.

Hopefully, after our planning process we shall be able to come out with something much more specific. We have two hundred people – creating eight Task Forces with an average of twenty-five people in each. There are eighty teachers, sixty members of the community, eight board members, thirteen administrators, twenty-five students, and about twenty support staff, and each of those communities is represented in each of the Task Forces.

We met for five months with thirty-six people, with each of those constituencies represented, and we held fifteen meetings – probably totalling 40–60 hours – to see what we thought the charges [terms of reference] ought to be. Then we created titles for each of those areas, which then became the Task-Force titles, and each Task Force has a series of questions which need to be asked. So those became the initial responsibilities of the Task Forces, then they'll branch out under their own means – and eventually we'll have to bring it all back together again.

After the next meeting I shall have the first meeting with the representative of each of those groups. We've had some meetings already, but just to converse; now we're going to try to bring it all together and figure out linkages to answer all those questions. We're not going to go too fast – people are very impatient – they get in these groups and go for the first answer, but these are not questions that you can answer in a month or two. It's important that the biggest constituency is the teachers, and the next is the community.

In a public setting, particularly where you are dealing with peoples' children, it can take longer than in a commercial one. There, if the CEO and the employees can agree on what the customers want, then you have less to worry about. If the planning process in schools involved only the professionals and not the community, then it would be a lot quicker. But you're dealing with their children – their most precious possession: if you try to make changes which affect their future, independent of their involvement, there's murder. A democratic system elongates the process. We don't have a particularly clear vision at the outset, so we have to take a risk.

There is a 'mission', and it's much more detailed than some of those which I'm not very happy with. We have a history of knowing what we believe in – it hasn't changed that much over the years. It is still not as focused as you would find in the private setting – a two- or three-sentence statement that tells me what you do.

Our motto is twenty-eight years-old: 'To commit minds to enquiry, hearts to compassion, and lives to the service of mankind'. If you look, it's believable, it can be understood – though some of the kids might have difficulty interpreting it – and you'll hear people talking about it; but it isn't particularly useful. I don't though know what we're doing to create an environment where we are focusing lives or hearts.

We have been challenged for not saying exactly what the vision is. It's there on paper quite specifically. We have the motto, and the philosophy too, which has been around for twelve years, and now we have the vision statement which is new but only known to the committee and Task Forces. I think that our challenge now is to define that better: what does it mean to have a school that is more 'student-centred', or 'values risk-taking, creativity and learning' more than what it does? It will mean something when the social studies class does not involve someone standing up and talking about the Civil War, but is where the students handle the key issues of the Civil War.

Predominantly, the teachers are not coming through with the skills to operate in this way, because the colleges and universities don't know anything about it. We're going to find what the private sector has already found, namely that people need training when they arrive. If we want to do those kinds of things in the classroom, we're going to have to train the teachers to do them. In our case, we are fortunate that we can hire a higher percentage of teachers who can already do it. We are a major drawer, and our money and reputation help.

INTERVIEW 9.2 EMPLOYERS' RESPONSIBILITIES FOR EDUCATION
Mary-Jo McCarthy, Motorola University

The startling difference between Motorola's initiatives and those of most other companies is the degree to which they take them. They research thoroughly, they implement thoroughly, they monitor thoroughly and then they do all that they can to disseminate the experience throughout the organisation. This is as true of their education initiatives as it is any other.

In the recent past at Motorola, it became very clear that, as the technology was advancing, the people who were operating with these technologies were lacking basic skills – reading, writing, language, computation skills – so there was a predominant place for retraining. In terms of self-development, the corporation has now taken a fairly new tack by empowering people to operate in teams, which requires people to have forty hours of job-related training, whether it is for the job today or the job tomorrow. A lot of work has been done in that area. It sounds very simple, but because so many of our jobs are decentralised and there are new technologies, it is a huge effort to track it. So there are some significant questions: what is the right training? What is training? It is up to the manager in that particular business to determine what is the right training for that particular person. What will the job require in terms of the needs of the technology? What will the organisation at the site look like five years from now, and what does that imply? This has set new questions and challenges.

Our company requirement is that everyone has an individual training plan. You work with your manager and decide what is going to be the right training for you, as an individual, in the next few years. Do you go back to college? Do you need to take a series of courses? What do you want to be when you grow up? So it's very much an individual activity. It is done differently in the different businesses. They each have their own training planning process-cycle, which is measured, tracked and reported on.

Managers are measured on their ability to develop a plan too. In our semiconductor business, they do things quite differently from our Land Mobile business. Our responsibilities are changing; our jobs are changing, what skills do we need in order to get it together and in order to contribute? For instance, if we are going to be developing new and glossier publications, maybe we need to go to school and take a photography course. We formalise what is expected of them, with their plan. In a performance appraisal, we will be assessed on our effectiveness.

To make sure that the education has been applied effectively, we can measure its impact on the bottom-line. If your business is not performing to its goals and objectives, and still you are doing all this training, maybe you are not doing the right training. The overall effectiveness of a policy is measured and judged by the business performance.

We have a couple of ways of helping people take what they have learned and apply it in their work. We have a group of people in Motorola University called the Applications Consultants. They were developed four or five years ago as the next logical development step for our organisation. We know how to develop training; the next logical step was how to apply this training back on the job. The Applications Consultants are, in most cases, long-term veterans of Motorola. They look at how the training is being applied to the business needs. They develop processes, solve problems and help managers to interpret the business requirements into better training.

Throughout Motorola there is the benchmark training model. We are trying to acquire the right training, at the right time, in the right place, and then apply it exactly to the right environment.

Front-line employees will be helped by the management. If they are not applying it, yet the manager is being measured on it, there's a strong incentive for them to help the employee.

The basic-skills issues are still being addressed. They can pull you back in a different way. They are now making it much more the responsibility of the individual. My manager will help me find a suitable course, a particular place or whatever. Adult illiteracy is serious. With the growth of Motorola, we have to interview and talk with almost 2,000 people before we can recruit 500 employees. This becomes very expensive and time-consuming.

Factory workers today are very different and so are the job requirements. They have to be able and willing to learn, they need to be able to compute, to do math, to be able to work in a team, to be able to communicate, to make a presentation. They need to be able to take on a problem-solving role of their own.

For the basic-skills area, Motorola has a basic-skills assessment which is given to all potential employees. Then there is an interview assessment.

The team-work issue is one that we are starting to work with. Motorola's message to schools for some time now has been that employees have to be able to work in teams. In the old days, everybody did their own work; now, we all have to work together and come up with problem-solving in all kinds of areas.

The company is undertaking a number of educational initiatives to help transform the skills of school-leavers. Several years ago Motorola realised that what we were getting from our suppliers in the public-school system was grossly inadequate. We were getting potential employees who couldn't read, couldn't write, couldn't do math, couldn't do computation.

Then we began to look at the root of the problem. The root of the problem is that the education system in this country is based on a hundred-year-old model. It was fine for the Henry Ford factory early in the century – and that is basically how our public schools are set up. One of our very valued employees, Ed Bales, put together a proposal about what Motorola should do because of our supplier-base and the people we were getting. He developed an initiative, the 'K through 12' education requirement, and began work to reform and improve the school system on a systemic level.

It would be easy to dismiss the investment that Motorola is making in education. They are a very large organisation and so can afford to be benevolent. They are also in high technology markets so their need may be more acute. Motorola have sent a great deal of time and effort investigating and interpreting the issues – it would be a waste for smaller, less challenged organisations to duplicate this.

Motorola's education initiatives

Vision: Motorola will be the global leader in establishing alliances that transform the pre-K through 16 education system, so all children develop to their maximum potential to function in the new world society.

Mission: To establish global alliances with school systems, private sector and not-for-profit organisations committed to implementing systemic restructuring which transforms teaching and learning so the exit-level competencies of graduates are equal to, or higher than, the entry level skill, behaviour and attitude requirements of Motorola and our suppliers and customers.

Core elements:
- Advocacy through partnerships
- Learning leadership teams
- Executive leadership Institute
- Effective parenting (child advocacy)
- Learning apprenticeships
- Motorola's Advocacy through Partnerships Process

Level 1: Policy

Collaborative efforts which shape the public and political debate, bring about substantive changes in state or federal legislation or local school governance, and affect the overall direction of the educational system.

Level 2: Systemic improvement

Partnerships in which business, education and community leaders identify the need for reform or improvement in the educational system, and then work over the long-term to make those major changes happen in the system.

Level 3: Partners in management

Partnerships which provide school officials with management support and business expertise in a broad range of areas.

Level 4: Partner in teacher training and development

Partnerships which provide opportunities for school personnel to update, upgrade or maintain their skills, or learn more about the labour market, industries, and businesses in the community, workplace needs, and career opportunities.

Level 5: Partners in classroom

Partnerships which provide business volunteers who improve the learning environment by bringing their business or occupational expertise directly into the classroom for students and teachers, or bringing the classroom to the business.

Level 6: Partners in special services

Partnerships which provide short-term, project- or student-specific activities or resources to help with a specific problem or need, such as awards, scholarships, donating or sharing equipment, educational material, sponsoring student teams, etc.

Looking at just one stream of their planned approach to educational reform demonstrates the thoroughness with which Motorola have planned.

Motorola's district learning leadership teams

An example of a Level 2 partnership

Mission: To achieve improved student performance through a collaborative-systems approach to transforming teaching and learning by building and supporting networks among school systems, business organisations, professional associations and state education agencies.

Focus: Improvement in the areas of:

- Curriculum – what is taught;
- Instruction – how it is taught;
- Assessment – are students learning?

Outcome: District Learning Leadership Teams (DLLTs) will develop, implement and evaluate comprehensive action plans which are designed to result in improved student performance.

Results and quality standards

1 A systematic framework for identifying and addressing critical issues established.
  Comprehensive action-plan developed aligned with systems thinking resulting in improved student performance.
2 Team-members have learned and practised team competencies.
  Individual team-members exhibit behaviours which contribute to effective team-behaviour.
3 District (system) teaching and assessment practices are aligned with state and national standards.
  Transformed practices will be documented and linked to standards.
4 Systemic change-initiatives that result in improved student performance are implemented.
  Initiatives and results documented.
5 State-wide network of DLLTs for support and information-sharing are established.
  Each team contributes data on successes and failures to network.

Membership:

Member of the Board of Education
Superintendent
Central Office Administrator
Principal from each level
Teachers from each level
Parent
School alumni
Business person or community leader
Human service providers
Internal facilitators (2)
External facilitator (1)

Development process:

1 Information meeting
2 Application process
3 Selection of DLLTs (and internal facilitators)

4 Selection of external facilitators and matching to DLLT
5 Facilitator orientation
6 Process training of facilitators
7 Team-process training
8 Facilitator debriefing
9 DLLT debriefing
10 Continuous training and development
11 Facilitator networking
12 DLLT networking
13 Programme evaluation
14 Longitudinal study

End result:

Transformed schools (the focus of change), as demonstrated by improved student performance.

It is, of course, too easy to pretend that poor educational attainment is due to schools. In many cases it is the child's experience with its parent(s) that determines how well it will adjust to education and what its attitudes and behaviours will be. So Motorola, along with many other employers, is encouraging its associates to develop an interest in, and commitment to, good parenting.

Motorola's effective parenting process

An example of a Level 5 partnership

Mission: To increase the awareness within Motorola of the role of parents and the extended family as agents of change in the pre-kindergarten through 12th grade education system, and to provide tools which result in the continuous improvement of the education system through advocacy, partnerships and improved parenting skills.

Goals:

1 To create awareness through the development and distribution to all Motorolans of:
• A brochure on the role of parents and extended family as first and most important teachers of children (must be validated, legal and unbiased);
• A bibliography of parenting resources with resource guides;

- A video on Motorolans as role-models of effective parents (to be made available through personnel offices or training centres).

2 To provide tools to assist in the restructuring of the education system, which include:
- Training and development programs;
- School assessment tools;
- School-board candidacy;
- Motorola PTA chapter;
- District Learning Leadership Team participation.

One of the significant problems faced by schools is a lack of resources. Again this is an area that Motorola readily responds to. The Motorola Museum is just one example of the firm providing access to its technology and research. Motorola is opening up its training courses to teachers and running summer camps for children.

We are working with the school-boards and the state governments. We have taken management training to school principals and superintendents, on the same themes as our middle-management courses in terms of creativity, risk-taking, communication and team-work. It has been very much an eye-opening experience for a lot of these people, because the confines of the school system are so rigid, so isolated, and so unaccountable. If a child fails, who is really failing – the child or the teacher? We have to help them look outside their system. Otherwise, we could face a future where people would not be able to man our factories or use our products and services!

We did something unique last summer with the development of a summer technology camp. The children came here, and to our sites in Austin, and in Phoenix. They were presented with a real, business case-problem, and they were told to go and find the answer. They weren't used to that. They were used to the teacher telling them: 'Study this chapter, this chapter and this chapter and that's where you'll find the answer'. They were assigned to work on teams, they had computers and research materials, and then they were challenged to make a presentation at the end of the week to a team of Motorola employees. It was not a classroom atmosphere at all. They were treated with respect. It was a very new experience for some of them. It was a bit strange when they first came in with their parents, but by the end of the week it was a very different group. They were challenged, and that was unusual for them too. This was made available for all Motorola families, so the kids came from that community. In this location, I would say that 80% of them were the children of executives who had themselves become intrigued by the idea and so put their children forward. In Austin, it was quite different – most of the kids there were from line employees. That experience last summer was the tip of the iceberg. It stimulated a tremendous demand.

Now we are being asked to do the same in Spain, in England, and in the Arlington Heights facilities. An organisation called the Young President's Organisation – high-level business people – have asked us to do a customised version for them. This isn't for their children – it is for them! Leadership Teams are also being offered for school principals and superintendents.

There will also be learning apprenticeships in the future. They may range enormously. My daughter may go to Belgium and I may have a French child on exchange, for example. Then we would need to address the cultural differences.

This work is being done in the United States, in those states where Motorola has a major presence – Illinois, Florida, Arizona, and Massachusetts.

This is not just for parents and teachers, mums and dads. Everybody is affected – everybody who pays taxes is affected by what is going on at school. If you don't have a good school in your neighbourhood, then your property value could decline.

There are other projects going on. For example, an electronics kit was developed. It is very simple but very well-presented, with the aim of teaching children the basics of electronics – like preparing a circuit-board and building a radio.

The parenting initiative is really a wake-up call. A brochure was sent to every Motorolan – it presents a series of very alarming statistics, comparing what is happening in the US with other countries. A video was also produced. But it isn't all bad news. It also outlined pockets of excellence among people who were trying new avenues to education.

INTERVIEW 9.3 CREATIVE EVALUATION OF TRAINING

David Basarab, Motorola University

Some companies, and some employees, treat training as a perk. As a result, it is often the first thing to be dropped either from the diary or the budget when conflicting demands have to be met. In the past some training companies have even pandered to the 'perk' idea by creating indulgent events and peddling them as 'rewards' as well as training. No-one is suggesting that training shouldn't be fun and enjoyable, but we are saying that it must be effective.

So how do you measure the effectiveness of training? Press a group of people and they'll usually dream up two ways – a course evaluation form and an examination of the course delegates. But one simply measures 'feel-good' factors, and the other places delegates under pressure when the area that should be under study is the training; the trainer, and the material itself.

Motorola, as you might expect within their Six Sigma process, have studied this problem thoroughly.

The evaluation of training and development

The university was built eleven years ago, and about eight years into that they decided to create an evaluation department. The evaluation department is chartered with establishing the processes and the collection of data to allow people to make decisions on two things:

1 On new products, the new courses ready for release, for instance when a cellular phone is introduced. Setting quality goals and working with people, building a new product and making sure that it meets its quality goals;
2 On continually tracking the implementation and delivery of training to make sure it achieves those goals. If it doesn't continue to achieve its quality goals from evaluation data, then to put some form of action in place to find the root-cause, and correct the problem. It is more than a monitoring activity, as the system actually tries to make corrections.

In each of our delivery-sites we have what we call continuous improvement teams, people who are responsible for reviewing the evaluation data, and finding the root-cause of any problems. These people have been trained by my operation on how to read the reports, how to Pareto the analyses. If you think about it, that's what we do for the training operation. The measures enable us to run the training to become the best possible, world-class training function, by setting proper goals ahead of time and then tracking those quality measures for the life of the course.

The training operation's span of control, in terms of the quality of the training, covers the design content, the instructor and the facility, until the student goes back into the workplace. Then, the span of control switches from training back to operations, to ensure that the people who have learned the skills apply them successfully back on the job. Our evaluation system is not based on the training community, but on the businesses tracking the quality of the application of skills. Let us assume that I train a hundred people over in Cellular to do something differently, and they learn to do it differently, and it becomes part of their behaviour. We then have a process for judging what kind of impact this new performance in skills has on the organisation – in other words, did we reduce cycle-time? Did we increase quality? Did we have higher productivity, more revenue, lower costs? What was the critical business issue?

Level 1

In the evaluation department we use four levels, numbered from 1 to 4. Level 1 is Customer Satisfaction for one group of our students as participants. We understand in the university that we have a variety of customers. The managers who send people for training are our customers, but we also have a variety of regional boards, corporate engineering councils, technology councils and manufacturing councils who are our customers and whom we have to satisfy. Level 1, then, is an interclass form. It is filled up anonymously by everyone to determine whether or not they are satisfied with the training programme.

258 Self-Managed Teamworking

Level 2

Level 2 is where we give people tests, and we look at mastering objectives. The techniques which we use for this level include an end-of-class form. In America, when you're in public school or college, you sit tests to pass or fail, to get a grade, and you are tested to see if you have mastered the course content. We turn it sideways, and we give the test anonymously. We don't look for passes or failures – we look at the class results as a group and, if we don't reach a certain level of scoring and of people achieving mastery of the subject, then we have a problem with the course or the test – not the individuals.

All classes that come out of Motorola University must have testing in place. Our goal is that everybody masters everything all the time. We give tests, but our people can use their notes and they can look at the study materials, unless the objectives say the student must be able to do this from memory, such as run the emergency shut-down routine on a machine. Then you would test whether they could do it from memory, following the five steps that they have to follow to kill the machine, or whatever. In those circumstances, it would not be appropriate to say, 'Wait, let me go and pick up my student manual so that I can shut down this machine which is on fire before it burns the place down!'

We also do a lot of team-testing, meaning that if the objective says 'the team will...' – you teach them the content as a team; then we'll put them in a group of three, four or five people and the team does the test. They each get a score, but if they get 90% on the test, they all get 90%. We don't determine whether one did all the work and the others sat round and drank coffee. So it is not individual testing. It's team-testing.

If the course objective says 'Describe lists to find', it's typically a paper- and-pencil test, but if it says 'Execute or role-play, collect, write, develop, analyse', then we do performance-based testing. We do simulations in a room and so on. So we do a combination of types of testing, depending upon the objective.

In teaching listening skills, for instance, we define the things someone would do when they are listening – such as, they won't cut an individual off in the middle of a question; they test for understanding: 'Let me give you back what I think I just heard'; they use probing questions when they need to get information, and then they close. Let's assume that those are the five or six things. We would then put one or two of the students in a role-play, and then we have trained observers who come in and observe the students using the skills. In that five or ten minute role-play, the observers look to see that the students either consistently, or at least once, demonstrate the five or six principles of listening.

We have done an incredible Level 2 study on a course called 'The Creative Manager', in which Motorola got the processes for measurement to define and create a process which a manager would use on their employees. We simulated the creative process within the classroom, and used an observation technique which had performance-notches. You had to understand and perform the creative process. We had two testings, which was interesting.

We have also added an element of play to testing, which has been very successful. In a Creative Manager course, for example, we created a crossword puzzle with the definitions over here and then you had to fill in the words. The students loved that. They also scored by it. We did one course called 'Gathering Software Requirements', where a software engineer goes out and gathers requirements from their customers before going off and designing a software system. To us, this game-concept meant gathering like on an archaeological dig, so we created 'Illinois Smith', cousin to Indiana Jones, put him in a cave of software requirements, and so on. It's good testing and can also be good fun.

So all of our courses have testing in which the key is programme evaluation and not personnel evaluation. It is anonymous.

The way we do it is really interesting. We give a module of instruction, then we administer a test, typically short, small tests. The students take the test, then we have what is known as a debrief. During that debrief session, the instructor gives out the answers. The students self-score, and then have an option of asking questions. But everything is anonymous. We train our instructors not to say, 'Graham, what did you get out of Question 3?' or 'Mary, what did you get on Question 5?' 'How many people got point A right?' We are not allowed to do that, because that would mean giving up the anonymity. But the student can say, 'I don't understand why the answers to Question 2 is 3.5'. When they have finished the students take their scores and put the percentage into a scannable form, before we go on to the next project. The students have told us that this is now the most important and reflective portion of the course. Before, we just gave a mean score and said 'Perhaps we might talk a little bit about it?' Now we really test them, and then go on to the next module.

Level 3

Level 3 concerns application of skills. There are a variety of post-course techniques which you can use to test application skills: surveys, self-reports, peer reports, and employee reports. We also use observations – we go in and observe people performing. For example, at our semiconductor sector in Austin, Texas, where they manufacture computer chips (a very capital-intensive operation), they handle wafer-boats which are about twice the size of a piece of paper and silicone. If you mishandle them, you could damage the wafers, and just one boat has between $10–20,000-worth of equipment in it. There are specific skills in handling the boats properly, and they found that people were not using them. So they created a training programme, and to make sure that the training was applied, they went into the plant with a bunny-suit on and watched the participants. They found that some of them were skipping a few steps or whatever.

Under other circumstances, we have surveys, observations, interviews, focus groups, and what is known as work output: let us say that I have just taken a group through a course on writing effective memos – so they send me their memos!

We also use action-planning. We go through a process: 'Here's the new behaviour that I want to learn. I am going to look at what I would normally do, the situations in which I would normally do this, what I am going to do differently, how I am going to measure my performance, what potential obstacles I can see that are going to stop me, and how I am going to deal with those.' We find that this takes about fifteen or twenty minutes per behaviour. Then the student goes through it. They fill out a form to plan generally what they are going to do when they get back to the job. The instructor and the student then sit down and agree what they are going to use, how they are going to do it, and so on. We find that a lot of times we have to rewrite the action-plan because the student has missed the target. So there are a variety of techniques: the first two evaluation levels are automated, and this one is not by design.

Level 3's application of skills are called STARs (Skills Training Application Review) – 'Level 3' is evaluation language, we call it STAR in business language. This is not automated because when we designed this process, our customers told us, 'We don't want a survey that goes out every thirty days. We also don't want a process that is done through corporate, and not in our operation. What we want is for you to define a process which we can execute – a process which is flexible and allows me to use a variety of techniques that my business needs'. So we do just that.

Level 4

The fourth level is what we call 'Organisational Impact' – better cycle-time or whatever. We use design of experiments to set up two groups – a control group and an experimental group. The experimental group are the people who have had the treatment, which is the training. You then track their business results to see if there is any significant difference since the intervention of training. You then do a longitudinal study on the same group of people, before and after training, but looking at the critical business issue, which has to be measurable, and the business cycle such as quality, productivity, defects. This is very sophisticated and becomes a hierarchy. You can't do this until you know that they have learnt what they need to learn to transfer the skill. What makes it a world-class evaluation is that you can hire a lot of people, consultants from the universities, who can do a course on levels 1,2 or 3. To me, that is not world-class. World-class is when you are using the same system. Every part of Motorola throughout the world uses these systems.

The training community does the initial levels because that is their job. Level Four is the businesses or, as we call them, the operations. At most companies they are lucky if they make it to the first level. To them, the definition of a good course is that they made it to Friday and nobody died. They liked it: they talked; they laughed; nobody complained too much. Well, we don't do that any more. Systemically, this is how we attack every process, and then we go after it.

Automation

Our Level 1 system is completely automated. You will see our end-of-class form translated into multiple languages – Chinese, Japanese, Korean, Malaysian, Spanish and French. It is a two-sided form which is scannable. Last year we did 104,000 of these assessments. This year there will probably be 250,000 assessments world-wide. The volume is huge. We count what we call opportunities for error: when we produce reports for our clients, how many pieces of information did we put out? Last year we did over 12,000,000 pieces of evaluation data just in this area alone. In turn we count defects, which would be when a customer comes back to us and says, 'The information on this report is incorrect'. We were zero defective in 1993. The way we do that is we make it a scannable form, we run it through an optical scan-reader, which turns each assessment into rows and columns: each assessment is one row in a file, and each response is a column. If you get twenty assessments, you will get twenty rows. We then take the data and electronically put it into an Oracle database running on a Macintosh computer. We distribute reports to our clients on a weekly, monthly and quarterly basis. Everybody in the training community has Macintoshes, and we have chosen Microsoft Excel for Macintosh for the output. When we query the database, the information is calculated in memory and then it goes out to an Excel template that sits on the disc and the report is created. We then electronically mail the report around the world, from here to your desktop.

When I first came here three years ago, this was not automated. It was a manual system in a different form, with seventeen questions. It took seventeen business days to get a piece of paper into a final report, laden with errors. We were only doing about 20,000 then. Now, when we get a piece of paper in-house, we can have a report back on your desktop, using the E-Mail system, in five minutes. We've gone from seventeen business days to five minutes, from laden with defects to defect-free. It flies, to say the least!

Wherever we have classes – China, Korea, Phoenix or Singapore – we have placed optical scanners in those locations. We scan locally; they send us the scanned results through electronic mail; we put them into the database; generate the reports in Excel; and E-Mail them back. That time is minimal too, instead of the days it would take a courier to get the stuff to us, or weeks if you put it through your normal mail; this system is used all around the world consistently. We now have non-Motorola customers – Texaco, Caterpillar, Dale Carnegie Associates, Goodyear Tire, the Internal Revenue Service of the US government, and we have seven community colleges which use us.

The benefit of being so speedy in our response-time is that, if our customers ran a series of classes last week, we get the data in here, and we will run the reports, and give them a weekly report on Thursday afternoon. They all have quality improvement teams which meet on Friday morning, because they are charted and constantly looking at the quality. If I couldn't get that data to them 100% accurately and in the time that they want it, I would never survive. So my value-added is 100% accuracy at all times, and, at the same time, that we must give the information to them in a timely fashion. About a year ago, we wanted to go from the single-user mode, where we produce reports, to a user dialling into a server and getting the report themselves. All our customers said: 'No. Why should we? All I do is drop an E-Mail to you and you give me the reports in a couple of minutes!' It makes sense. It is a service that they want, but they want it perfect, and they want it in a format that they like.

There are a few nuances in our assessments. For example, this course is for software engineers who work on certain types of project. It says: My job matches the description located in the last page of the Participant Guide, and the student says, 'Yes', 'No', or 'Expect to be within one year'. This is the first quality goal that our regional sites have. They report monthly to their bosses and, eventually up the line, the percentage of 'Yes' and 'Will be within a year'. Right now, we average about 2 or 3% 'No', but we don't want anybody in there who doesn't belong in there. There are some courses where there are a high percentage of 'Nos'.

We report percentages of customer satisfaction, so if someone marks their 'No', we count the number of Nos, but then we throw the rest of the results away electronically, because we don't want to react to people who don't belong there. We take each dot and turn it into a satisfied or dissatisfied response. So the 'course-content expectation' exceeded and met are the satisfied responses, and ideally none would be dissatisfied – we want 100% of these. Some cases were 98%, some cases were 85%, so what we then do is we Pareto the worst responses and examine those by course, and by instructor. I can go back three years and look at trend-data. I can look at a course which is being run in Austin, and the reactions to it in Beijing (China) and Korea. That is the beauty of having the same scannable form.

At the second level, students complete another form, which allows us to record each individual's test-score as a percentage. If they do a test and debrief, and let's say they got 18 out of 20 right, which is 90%, then the student would come in here, write 90, or fill in the bubble 90%: we allow up to 18 tests, we can also have a pre-test and a post-test. There is no way to capture any of the students' names or anything like that; we can only ask the course identifier so that we put the raw data in, we produce preliminary weekly reports, say, 'You have just run a course called X; did you meet your quality goal?' Now what is quality? 80% of the students must score greater than, or equal to, 80% on all the objectives. Then, if it didn't meet quality, give them a learning history report, which talks of learning to like the course. You may get a six-page report, and you're looking for patterns: Is it in any region? Is it by instructor? Is it just Test 1 vs Test 3? What is causing the quality to go down? Then they go away and do a root-cause analysis and fix those issues.

Interestingly, we found that we have to make sure, when creating tests just as when creating courses, that they are culturally and country sensitive. You wouldn't want to put a test in Korea that uses American baseball averages, or the football scores, or the Kentucky Derby. In Korea that means nothing.

You have to make sure that everything is appropriate – especially when we go and teach people whose second language is English. You may have a course which you would like not to translate; but if you are going to deliver it in English, with English materials, you must be very aware of using words that are not at too high a level, and are not American slang. That is difficult, because most designers and course-developers are Americans, so we have to be very aware of that. We have a parallel translation process, so that if we know we are going offer the course in Korea, besides translating from English to Korean, we also make the changes that are necessary to make it country-specific too. Their big thing may be speed-skating or water polo, or whatever. So we use this instead of baseball scores!

Some examples of Level 3 evaluations

One of our courses, called 'Managing Account-focused Sales People', taught managers how to manage their sales people who dealt with major accounts. Using the survey technique, supplemented with an interview, we found that 91% of the participants had successfully transferred the skills all the time in their job. The cost of the design, development and delivery of that training programme was $195,000. So that was $195,000 spent effectively in the training and the organisation; no problem.

Our Codex operation, which makes modems, were also doing a sales course, but they wanted their salesmen to start thinking strategically about long-range sales. So the Senior Vice-President of Sales went to the training operation, which hired an outside company to build this course. The first part of our evaluation process was to put these stake-holders together to talk about the performance issues. We got the Vice-President of Sales, the training director and the vendor in the room with the Human Resources and compensation people. Salesmen are driven by dollars. We found a complete disconnection. Fortunately, the operation decided not to purchase that course. If they had not done this study, they would have rolled the class out, and that could have cost them $360,000.

A performance management course for our semiconductor sector, taught managers how to conduct good performance reviews. This was a sixteen-hour, two-day mandated course from Phoenix. Our Austin, Texas, facility looked at it and said: "We don't think it needs sixteen hours. We think we can do it in six.' So they brought thirty people in and trained them on the sixteen-hour course. Then they redesigned the course for six hours, and trained a different group of thirty people. Then, using this process, they followed the application of the skills and found that there was absolutely no difference: they were both performing as desired. So they implemented the six-hour course and had 500 people trained. That meant they showed a course saving of over $250,000 and a cycle-time reduction of sixteen to six, in other words 62%.

Institutionalising the evaluation process

As we've noted before, Motorola is exceptional in the emphasis it places on institutionalising good ideas – that is, making sure that anyone who could benefit, learns about the idea and tries it out. The evaluation team's approach is an excellent example of how non-operational groups can nonetheless influence their mainstream colleagues.

Our customers wanted a process that works in any subject: the team created a three-day training course to teach people who to do this, and on the last day they do a test. It is a case study from beginning to end; the first two days are content – they are practising, and debriefing, and working just to get the knowledge and some practices. Then we put them into teams and they actually do a Level 3 evaluation or a Star from beginning to end. We now have 62 people trained around the world doing Level 3 evaluation.

The question is, how to institutionalise this around Motorola? So we came up with this concept of a world-wide Star network. We went to the businesses and said: 'You can voluntarily have someone come and join the network. To join the network you must agree the following things:

1 you must come to the three-day training class;
2 you will share with the process owner and the network owner; you will share with my operation formally what you do at Level 3, and any output that you create, like a plan; and we are concerned that this has momentum and it is maintained; so the final thing is
3 we hold an annual two-day conference in which all the training evaluators share information.

We may have some additional information. If we see you need some retraining, we will go back and fix it. So you get trained, but you have to share your results.'

We are not deliberately doing any Level 4 evaluations right now. We have a very, very enlightened CEO and general managers for all the businesses. They recognised that we need to institutionalise Levels 2 and 3 first, to get them working, and then – in three-to-five years – to do Level 4, because Level 4 requires Level 3, and so on and so forth. A lot of companies come up and say, 'Give me Level 4'. That's all they ask. They do not have the knowledge to get to this level. So we are putting all of our energy and resources in doing Levels 2 and 3. We do lots of things around the Level 3 Star network. We put out quarterly communiqués, mementoes to hang in your office, and all kinds of activities. We try to make these people special. This is the only cost they have – we charge nothing for training, consultation or the conference.

Ours is a professional way of running training programmes, and the added value which we are offering is the assessment. We have been benchmarked by AT&T, the American Society for Training and Development and Texaco. They are looking at all of our systems and methodologies for this. Some companies do some evaluation, but they do it not systemically. We let the businesses choose which courses get Level 3, not us. In some companies, the training community picks which courses to do Level 3 with, and also the ones that they think they have problems with.

Motorola is obviously very big, but this can be done in small shops, too. You don't have to have hundreds of thousands of people going through classes. It's just that people say, 'We can't do it.' 'Yes, you can!' It is a matter of culture and enlightenment. Most training communities are measured by the number of students they put through, and how many courses they have got on this month. That's good, but you need to balance that with the qualitative side, and that's what we're here for.

Finally, many of the training interventions which happen in organisations are not formal class-situations. We have a system for evaluating those too. In Asia, OJT (On the Job Training) is common, in which a junior person works near a senior person and is trained. We have actually created a Level 1 form for that. You are not allowed on the line until you demonstrate competence, so Level 2 is not an issue. We do a Level 3 on this though. If we have got twenty senior people mentoring 300 junior people over a period of a year, when they are on the line by themselves following the process, we can actually go and evaluate that.

Activity 9.1 The changing nature of jobs

You might like to think of doing this exercise in a group or with someone from personnel or human resources. You'd perhaps be surprised at the impact that a CEO, asking the HR Director if they can spare a member of their staff for a morning, has on the HR group!

What is the commonest type of job in your organisation? Pick three; there'll probably be a manager among them; there'll certainly be a front-line employee (perhaps two); maybe people from manufacturing, retail premises or offices.

Analyse carefully the three that you have chosen. For each question, draw up the answers as they were ten years ago and now.

- What tasks does the individual routinely do?
- What technology does the job require?
- What qualifications do new recruits have?
- What experience does a new recruit have?
- How do you assess their qualifications and experience?
- How much training is required for a new joiner?
- How are new joiners inducted?
- Do you link pay to a probationary period in a job?
- What is the remuneration package?
- How much of the pay is related to performance of the company, the individual, and the part of the organisation (e.g. team or works) in which they are based?
- To what extent does the pay-package contain non-monetary elements (e.g. car allowance, housing, pension, shares, private health insurance)?
- Who says that someone is 'capable' of doing a particular task?
- How have the job-procedures changed?
- What sort of activities do people get involved in outside work?
- Where do people spend their holidays?
- How do people travel to and from work?
- What sort of reporting-line do people have?
- How are people given information about the day's work?
- How many levels of management does the person interface with in the course of a typical week? And how close are these to the person at the 'hub' of the organisation?
- What would happen if this individual made a mistake in their work? What would happen if they made a series of mistakes?
- What would happen if this person did things that irritated their fellow workers?

Activity 9.2: Your involvement with the education system

In our experience, smaller businesses fall into two camps with regard to social policy: there are some who are so concerned with social issues that they lose sight of their commercial *raison d'être*, while at the opposite extreme there are many who to try to ignore the problems of the world around them. There are probably a number who do tread that difficult tightrope between the two extremes. In 1994 we witnessed the press clamouring at the doors of one of the few smaller organisations which does try to deal sympathetically with world issues, namely The Body Shop. This is hardly the kind of encouragement that we all need.

Larger organisations can take a stance – though few do, because shareholders' interests are not often seen in this light. Recently, one national bank has clearly positioned itself in support of global issues, but then the heritage (and shareholders) of the Co-operative Bank are probably atypical anyway.

So where does your organisation sit? Concentrate on the educational problems we have described. Again, enlist the help of a suitable colleague and set about answering these questions. Don't skimp on rough estimates. The absolute answer is less important than the small elements which you will unearth.

- How much contact do your staff have with local educational institutions? Include governorships, school visits, lecturing at evening schools and colleges of further education. If there isn't much, why not? Seriously. Ask what the reasons for inactivity are – it's only by asking that you'll get to the root of any misconceptions.
- How much of your staff's time is taken up with professional and trade bodies? To what extent are they involved in shaping the future generation of their profession or trade (as opposed to a purely social involvement)? How many professions and trades are represented? For each, get a feel for the one or two key issues of the day. What do your staff feel about them? Often, employees in a larger organisation are isolated from developments in their trade or profession. If this down-sizing phenomenon is anything other than a statistical quirk (and all the evidence indicates that it is), you'll be doing them a favour by spurring them into action.
- On what issues has the organisation and its staff taken a strong lobbying stance? Is there nothing that will affect your organisation's ability to perform in the future? Look back over the last couple of issues: who was involved in the lobby? What was the outcome? Are there any patterns here, and should they be broken? Is the Chairman the only person involved in lobbying of any kind? When representations are made, are they a management-only affair or do other people get involved? I recently sat through three representations from NHS trusts: two fielded management-only teams, while the third had a truly cross-sectional balance. You were left with the impression that the first two saw the problems they were facing as a management issue, while the other had taken the trouble to communicate them throughout and had seen the

much wider impact. So what if a couple of the people weren't used to making presentations? In fact, there were a few of the managers who could have done with some help too!

- Now that you know a lot more about people's activities, sit down with a team and draw up a social policy plan. Outline the amount of effort which you expect everyone to be expending on educational issues: most of us work 240 days a year – most committees (as just one example) meet between six and twelve times a year for half-a-day. So a simple equation might be that everyone in the organisation should be spending six days a year (just 2.5% of their working year) on educational issues. Decide how the organisation is going to co-ordinate its efforts: for example, who will be responsible? You need to make sure that their time (and therefore your money) is well spent, so someone needs to ensure that people are given appropriate resources and, if necessary, training. This doesn't mean controlling what they do or where they do it – it means co-ordinating efforts so that people who highlight similar needs get together. Not everyone will become a school governor (in fact, you might be lucky if 1% do), but remember that there are countless other ways to become involved.

10

THE PROCESS OF CHANGE

'In a one-year time-frame ... the contribution from the Direct Labor workforce, and the team solutions to problems, was roughly 42%. That opened my eyes up in a hurry, and the staff said: "Hey, if we give these people more things to do and delegate some of the decision-making responsibility once we've trained them, we can get a lot more out of them." That's how we stumbled into empowerment!'

(Russ Robinson, Motorola)

- **There are many consistent steps in most organisations' implementation of Self-Managing Work Teams. The first, and probably the most important, is to take time discussing the concept with the senior managers. Without this forum, ownership will be minimal and the likelihood of long-term success negligible.**

- **Measurement is vital – don't measure and you don't progress.**

- **A commitment to skills-development doesn't just mean training people. They have to be helped to put their new knowledge to work, and so to develop skills. This is the vital role of the new manager.**

- **People have to be motivated. If you are carry a burden of worries then you can't be motivated. Successful organisations provide confidential counselling support at any time, and employees are encouraged to make use of it.**

- **Implementation is an iterative process – move a little, train, practise, counsel – move a little more, train, practise and counsel – move a little more...**

INTRODUCTION

As you work with a growing number of organisations, introducing the concept of Self-Management, so you begin to recognise tactics which are consistently successful and those which are less successful. While there is a degree of truth in people's assertion that every business is different, the ways in which people behave do show many consistencies. People are not the same the world over, but they do have a lot in common! Over the last few years, we have also collected extensive case studies of successful change. From this accumulation of experience it is possible to recognise a model of the essential steps in any process of Organisational Development (OD). We do not pretend that this is our invention: the consistency of different situations is due to the underlying principles of OD which in turn reflect the consistency of people and their behaviour.

So important is each element that, we now find that, when an organisation reports that the process of change has been unsuccessful (and there are many like that), we can usually spot the elements of this model to which they gave insufficient emphasis. To help understand this model we have prepared a simple diagram (Fig. 10.1). Before we hear of our interviewee's experiences, let's go through the steps by seeing what happened at two real organisations – Motorola and Zytec.

The organisations

Zytec: Magnetic Peripherals Inc was a joint venture formed by four electronics firms and based in Eden Prairie, Minnesota. It was the subject of a leveraged buy-out in 1984. The HQ staff number around ninety and the rest of the 750 workforce are based in a factory just under a hundred miles away. The company, which took the name Zytec, has two principal markets. Its core business is a light engineering operation producing power supplies (PSUs) for the original equipment manufacturers (OEMs) of computers, medical and test equipment. Their second line, representing about 10% of turnover, is in the repair of power supplies and high tension devices, such as cathode ray tubes. The repair business even services the company's own competitor's products!

After the buy-out, the senior management team spent some time reviewing alternative strategies to develop their business. Their experience of the industry told them that service, quality and price were becoming increasingly important as competitive edges. For a while they looked at different approaches to achieve the kind of dramatic standards which they felt their industry would need. Eventually they decided that they could identify well with the fourteen points of quality guru, W. Edwards Deming. They

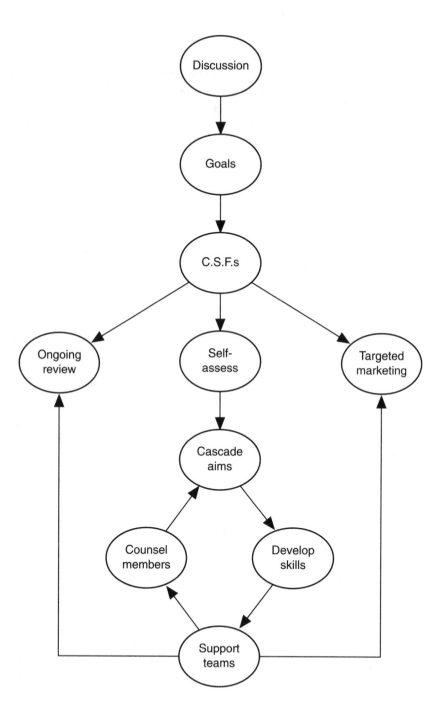

Fig 10.1 Implementing change successfully

decided to apply these throughout Zytec. The senior managers set themselves ambitious targets for productivity and quality improvement, with a vision of becoming the driving force in their two market sectors.

In 1984 the business depended almost entirely on orders from the former owners. By 1991 they represented only 1.5% of turnover, while their market position had risen to fifth in the USA in the AC-DC power-supply sector. But they haven't adopted a purely 'new business' sales strategy. The senior management team decided to develop customer-partnerships. Since 1990, they have supplied only twenty customers, but eighteen of those have single-source agreements – together they represent a turnover in excess of $50 m. In their repairs and maintenance area, often regarded as a low volume and poor margin business, Zytec are now the largest US provider, turning over nearly $6 m.

Their initial goal was to fulfil the requirements of the US national quality award, the Baldrige Award. They have begun a new process of change since they won that award in 1991.

Motorola: We have already heard from many of the people involved in the Motorola process of change. In this brief account, by describing the early stages in their pursuit of quality (starting back in 1981), we are just going to highlight how the elements of their voyage fit into the model shown in Fig. 10.1.

i Ongoing discussions

One of the first steps, for most organisations which are about to embark on a change process, is for their senior managers to spend time reviewing strategies and exploring alternatives. This process may involve away-days, seminars and conferences, and circulating interesting literature. These events may be driven by the parent company, by a local director or general manager, or by the industry's representative body: they can be organised by almost anybody. The content of the events is usually of much less importance than the fact that the individuals attending are surrounded by like-minded peers. They reinforce the fact that it is perfectly acceptable to challenge things in this way. The top team may never discuss the events together, or they may have extensive briefings and debriefings. A lot can be done to encourage people in this process, and to help them get the most out of their explorations. Although it may seem fatuous, this step is a very important one. Without it individuals can feel steam-rollered and may react negatively.

Zytec: As we have already commented, discussion at the senior management-team level has been a significant element of Zytec's development over the last few years. From their exposure to an eight-year process of quality improvement, which resulted in them receiving the Baldrige Award, the team obviously has had a substantial degree of broad agreement. A similar process then led to their adoption of a Six Sigma goal for high performance.

Motorola: The philosophical approach of Motorola emanates from its founder, Paul Galvin, and his son Bob. Since the organisation was founded in 1928, their approach has dominated decision-making and flavoured the business in many different ways. For example, few organisations publish their own library of corporate and personal philosophical texts for distribution to their employees. It might be argued that this is a vestige of the late 1920s, when the Dale Carnegie organisation was also founded; indeed, there are some striking similarities between the publications of Cargnegie and Motorola. Whether this is the case or not, the culture within Motorola is one of discussion and debate. Ideas are never *stupid* – they are always worthy of exploration.

It is hardly surprising, then, that their obsession with quality has almost universally been ascribed to one person and his intervention in one management meeting. But that intervention itself said nothing particularly new. Motorola had, for years, been a pioneer, and always boasted of its quality and customer-responsiveness. It was competing in a very fluid range of markets where new entrants with new technologies could effect a clean sweep in just a few months, and where reverse engineering was rife. They always had to respond to outside stimuli, of which there were many. So why this particular comment should have provided the trigger for a massive re-commitment to quality is difficult to understand.

Bob Galvin was bound to have lived in his father's shadow at Motorola. Paul's personality was that of the entrepreneur – loud, impulsive, and perhaps dogmatic. His son's was more analytical, cooler. Some observers have suggested that Bob was simply lying in wait. Motorolans are more likely to describe it as a succession. Paul Galvin's declining health meant that, over a number of months, Bob had taken a growing share of the overall responsibility for running the company. Nevertheless, without pretension, Bob Galvin introduced himself at functions with the down-to-earth reflection: 'One of the reasons for my rapid rise ... is the fact that my dad owns the joint!'

When Bob Galvin took over as president in 1956, it was obvious that he was a businessman of his father's calibre. Unlike so many heirs, he thrived on new technologies – Motorola is now the world's largest manufacturer of two-way and cellular telephones, and the fourth largest of semiconductors – but this technology is antiquated by comparison with the developments that they conjure with daily. Bob Galvin built up his father's business from a $227 million turnover in 1956 to one of $13 billion in 1992.

The event which triggered the latest generation of changes came during a company-wide officers' meeting. A senior sales officer, Art Sundry, made a comment that, in almost any other organisation, would have heralded his exit from the company. He announced: 'This is fine. These are good subjects, and we're making some progress. But we're missing the point ... our quality stinks!' George Fisher recalls even today that the group went through a denial process – trying to pretend that Art was wrong. The event proved to be a turning point for Motorola.

After Sundry's initial remonstration, Galvin and Bill Weiss (then CEO), in 1981, launched the business on a programme of change to enhance quality. Motorola was in a better state than many. Their whole business was founded on emerging technology and, as they had always tried to re-train rather than replace people with redundant skills, their staff were more aware of the opportunity than most.

ii Clarifying the goals

The next stage in the process is to reach a common understanding of what the new culture means, and how it relates to your organisation. You need to reach consensus on your vision for the business, and probably to identify some of the costs of *not* implementing it. You must agree where you are now and where you want to be. Most importantly you become aware that new behaviour has to be adopted if the culture is to change, and that interpersonal skills will be required to support this behaviour. Depending on the circumstances, and on the extent of previous discussions between the senior managers, this can take between two and six days. This part of the process usually starts with a two-day workshop, which is followed by a few half-day sessions.

Zytec: The Six Sigma standard cannot be achieved with traditional approaches to management. The Zytec team recognised this and began to formulate their vision of the future by building in many radical transformations. The lynch-pin is a programme known as 'Managing Through Planning' (MTP). This replaces the traditional management responsibility of goal-setting and planning with an employee-based one.

Motorola: The initial goal, set by Galvin and his top team in 1981, was for a ten-fold improvement in quality within five years. At that time such a target seemed impossibly high – but it turned out to be too low!

The biography of Paul Galvin, published by Motorola, begins with the story of a twenty-year-old operator in Malaysia who, when asked what she liked about the company, responded, 'The open door policy that was started by Paul Galvin'.[1] The woman was born after Paul Galvin had died, and yet the message of 'how we do things around here' was firmly established – not just in Illinois, but half-way around the world.

Taking the organisation towards their quality vision, Bob Galvin and his team had not only to understand the issue of quality, but they also had to be convinced of its benefits. The quality movement was well established in the US, with many gurus achieving popularity. Yet while the Motorolans learned all they could from them, the senior management team did not follow any one of them in particular.

There is a tendency for business people to be 'task-driven', often seen in an impatience to be *doing* something rather than thinking or planning. Of all the industries, the software and high technology ones are the most affected. Yet Motorola's top team largely resisted this temptation. They took care to support senior and middle management who would have to make the most significant changes. They recognised the value of education and training, and put into place some of the long-term initiatives of which we have heard elsewhere in this book. At the same time, they committed significant amounts of time in all their management meetings to reviewing progress and discussing the implications – turning the meetings into a learning experience for themselves.

iii Critical success factors

Having clarified the goals, the senior management team needs to take more time to develop the clear measures of success to monitor the improvement process. These measures require several strategic decisions, and they usually cover four main areas:

1 **The Customer**: How do your customers see you?
2 **Financial**: How do you look to your shareholders?
3 **Internal Business Perspective**: What must you excel at?
4 **Improvement**: How do you continue to get better?

There is little point in introducing change into a business if it does not produce tangible, measurable benefits. Too many organisations end up, three years down the road, doing all the right things but achieving little. This is generally because appropriate measurements of critical success-factors and short-term goals were not agreed at the outset.

This step is important. One benefit of doing it thoroughly is that it gives a further opportunity to discuss and clarify the idea of the new culture. Another is that everyone understands and has ownership of the measurements which are eventually agreed. This activity is a natural continuation of the initial clarification of goals.

Zytec: The senior managers have not lost sight of the criteria for the success of their business. Furthermore, they make them clear for all employees to see, and they update people on performance against them. Among the factors identified at Zytec were:

- sales per employee: they currently average $100,000, against an industry benchmark of $80,000;
- manufacturing yield: since 1988 they have achieved a 50% improvement;

- manufacturing cycle-time: in the same period they reduced this by 26%;
- design cycle-time: reduced by 50%;
- product costs: reduced by between 30 and 40%;
- product quality: (based on customer-supplied data) has risen to around Four Sigma. Specific measurements are used for different products and services, therefore:
  (a) mean-time-between-failures (MTBF) of PSUs is over a million hours!
  (b) on-time delivery now occurs on 96% of orders.

Motorola: Their initial experience confirmed in the minds of the top team the importance of quality as a competitive asset. The first wave of improvement had forced people to look afresh at their work, reassess the needs of their customers and put into place measures of these needs.

By 1984, on the basis of these measures, people were questioning whether the pace of change was quick enough. A presentation made by Bill Smith in 1985 confirmed these fears, and sowed the seeds of the Six Sigma process. An examination of the early-life field reliability of products showed very clearly that, if problems and defects needed fixing in manufacture, there was a good chance that the product would go wrong during its early period of use. If defects could be designed out before manufacture, then there was a much better chance of products not breaking down when the customer used them. The top team were discovering the importance of design.

In 1986, Galvin visited customers and began to grow impatient at the consistency of people's concerns: orders weren't completed, transactions were inaccurate, and deliveries were going wrong. It was obvious that that design emphasis had to apply to everything that Motorola did – not just to manufacturing.

iv Self-assessment

Most organisations which successfully adapt begin to look carefully at their existing business with the Critical Success Factors as a back-drop. They have already identified any major changes which are necessary to allow the new culture to flourish. These tend to focus on:

1 Customer orientation;
2 Organisation structure;
3 People systems (reward, recognition, appraisal etc.);
4 Internal communication.

The changes that many businesses need to make, even the best ones, are often substantial. If external consultants make the recommendations there is very little chance of them being carried out. Successful businesses may use outsiders, but they will do so only to support their own efforts. It is this stage which forms the basis of the book *Making Change Happen* (Financial Times/Pitman Publishing, 1993). Involving a team of people from within the business, to make the assessments and present recommendations, means that:

- the activities can be owned internally;
- the new culture of greater involvement can be practised (and any problems ironed out);
- the level of understanding can be raised around the company;
- senior managers can get some experience of practising the new culture.

Zytec: It became clear to the senior management team that highly-motivated employees were crucial to the success of their plans. The team carried out a survey of employee-attitudes. The success of this process and the benefits from its results have led to its adoption as a regular, annual process.

Motorola: There are many examples of this approach within Motorola: Galvin's own visits to customers were one and there was another which was to be as influential. When a company launches a quality improvement process, we often find that the most senior person with responsibility for co-ordinating the initiative becomes a focus for gathering performance statistics. Motorola was no exception: Richard Buetow, Senior VP responsible for quality, had carefully monitored defects in the Far East. The company was one of the best in the US, with defect rates of around 6,000 parts per million opportunities – but Buetow had commissioned a number of benchmarking activities which showed that Japanese competitors using the same equipment were achieving rates of less than four parts per million!

The internal assessments were supported by the use of the Baldrige Award criteria. That Motorola won this in 1988 was not a surprise perhaps – given their investment, commitment and *results* they deserved it. What is perhaps more remarkable is that, by 1987, Galvin and his team had realised that they were merely scratching the surface of the possibilities – major earthworks for other companies perhaps, but a scratch to them! Ironically, in the year when they were awarded the Baldrige, their RISC chip was months late to market because of design problems – highlighting the opportunity for further improvement.

v Cascade the aims

Organisations generally consist of senior management, middle or supervisory management, and non-managerial employees.

Often senior management has spent much time, quite rightly, getting to grips with the fundamentals of the new culture, and deciding how to fire up the organisation. The mistake is then made of cascading the message down to middle management and then to the non-managerial layers without sufficient thought for the consequences.

Non-managerial employees are usually quickly excited by the vision, because they are going to be listened to more, trusted more, and given more ownership. All good stuff. They then look to their supervisor for help and support, in the way in which they have been led to expect – and nothing happens. End of excitement. Beginning of disillusionment.

This is usually because the supervisor, who has perhaps the greatest behavioural change to make, has not had sufficient input into the process to have ownership of it. Neither has he been given the technical or managerial skills to support the change.

So following on and developing from your own induction, middle management must be brought into the picture. Ideally, they need as much, if not more, training than you have had yourselves. If this is conducted by outsiders alone, employees can see this as an indication of lack of senior management commitment. In some organisations, outside consultants begin this 'cascaded' process, but with the aim of getting the staff to identify how *they* want the communication process to continue.

The result must be that middle management is as fired up about the change as is senior management, which will result in their behaviour changing. As people are much more aware of what their managers *do* than what they *say*, this will have an impact on the other employees.

The cascade process can, then, in a properly supported way involving middle management, be carried down to the front-line employees.

Zytec: The introduction of new ways of working has built on earlier activities, and so an initial cascade process was not really necessary. However, Zytec's CEO, Ronald D. Schmidt, routinely holds face-to-face meetings with teams throughout the business as part of their MTP programme.

Motorola: Over the last few years the Senior Management Team at Motorola has reinforced its vision in a number of statements, although that vision was already well-established. In its latest form, it has been encapsulated in a plastic card carried by every employee, which spells out the fundamental objective of TCS (Total Customer Satisfaction) – while on the reverse are the key beliefs, goals and the current set of key initiatives. Armed with this information, no Motorolan should have difficulty weighing up a decision.

In 1987, the goal-posts were brought closer together. The target remained the same, but the new objective was to achieve a further ten-fold quality improvement in two years, and a hundred-fold improvement in four years, i.e. by 1992. This last goal was one of Six Sigma.

vi Develop skills

The Steering Group must establish some priorities for developing people's skills. They will focus on:

1. Skills of Management (known as Process Skills), which include:
   - Individual Behaviour;
   - Coaching and Counselling;
   - Team Behaviour.
2. Technical Skills for Employees, such as;
   - Problem Solving;
   - Quality Function Deployment.
3. Interpersonal Skills for Employees, including;
   - Team Working;
   - Customer Care.

We recommend strongly that the initial emphasis should be on the Skills of Management, and that the first managers to experience this should be the Steering Group.

Our own approach is an intensive four-day course, known as 'Empowering People For Change'. This course is presented in different ways to suit different companies. We find that this makes the senior managers much more aware of the real mechanism by which the new culture is put into place. The course is often the turning point for people in their understanding, and is very motivational. This being the case, the earlier the course can be held, the better. Suitably modified to specific needs, the course provides the basic training for all managers, facilitators, and team leaders – with variations in the programme to suit the specific needs of each group.

We usually help the Steering Group to select a suitable individual from within the organisation to be prepared as a trainer for this course (not necessarily from the training department).

Depending on the numbers of individuals involved we either run this course ourselves, or prepare your own staff to act as trainers. While this investment may seem large, it allows your own staff to conduct most of the subsequent activities themselves. The in-house leaders will probably act as facilitators for the initial improvement teams.

Zytec: Many organisations mistake the cascade process, in which basic corporate goals are communicated to all employees, for training, in which there is a transfer of genuine skills. Zytec did not fall into this trap. Instead they have a basic requirement for employees to attend 72 hours (ten days) of quality-related training each year.

This links to a revised employee-reward scheme. In the past, some authorities have argued about the effectiveness of these schemes, but Zytec has adopted a reward system which increases an individual's pay-rate according to the number of job-skills that they can use. The reward system, known as MFE (Multi-Function-Employee), encourages multi-skilling for each person.

Motorola: Despite the false start in the 1970s, Galvin and his team were now more convinced than ever of the importance of a highly-skilled work-force. Previously, training had been provided but was effectively voluntary, now, every employee had to undergo at least five days of training each year. Much of this was provided in-house by the Motorola Training Centre, which had been founded in 1981.

In 1989, the purpose of the Centre was reframed and Motorola University was founded. As Galvin himself pointed out, Training Centre sounds a lot less impressive than University. As yet, the University cannot award degrees, though that will probably change in the next few years. In the US, training facilities are superb and courses are provided by individuals, carefully screened, selected and coached. The company insists on providing its own syllabus, materials and even terminology to ensure that the message is totally consistent, not only within a given course, but also with others in their programme. It applies not only for internal training, but also for training contracted with outside suppliers. In Illinois they use staff from the North-Western Universities and the Kellogg School of Management. In France they work with professors of the Université de Technologie de Compiègne, and in Macao, with the Asia Pacific International University. In Britain, Motorola has forged links with the University of Edinburgh. The relationship with these universities is a fascinating one which other universities would do well to heed. Motorola sees itself very clearly as a customer. It deals with the universities just as it would with any supplier, precisely spelling out its requirement, not only in terms of the quality of the product but also of the process that leads to it. In the spring of 1992, they invited other institutions to attend Motorola University. The stipulation was that they had to adopt their TQ process for their own administrative systems. In an interview in *Fortune Magazine*, Michael Cummins of the University of Miami observed that Motorola was saying that if universities don't use these techniques to improve, then their graduates will become too expensive to employ. In 1992, Motorola's education programme cost some $100 million, but independent auditors showed that the return on the bottom line had been in the order of 33:1.

One of the concerns of Galvin's team before launching the Six Sigma initiative was that many of the line-workers lacked even the basic skills of reading, writing, arithmetic and taking responsibility. Their realisation was a decade ahead of that of the US government. A study by the National Centre on Education and the Economy warned of the dilemma facing US administrations. Many American workers continue to lack these basic skills, but they are not required in their day-to-day lives so there is no incentive to learn them. As long as American companies continue to use traditional management control to organise work, this will continue to be the case. Motorola is showing that this approach only works while labour rates are falling and technology is standing still. When you need to empower your workforce, they must have the basic skills.

Throughout this book, we have described a phenomenal investment of Motorola in the education of its employees. A prospectus from Motorola University reads like a menu of top engineering subjects from the best colleges, including short-cycle production, pool-production methods, advanced manufacturing technology and total productive maintenance. There are even courses that many universities have not yet been able to develop and run. There is a full range of management skills courses, and training in simple problem-solving tools and techniques. Essentially, the programme comprises interpersonal skills, technical skills and business skills. Again, ahead of its fellow countrymen, in 1992 Motorola committed $5 million to providing remedial education for its line staff.

vii Supporting teams

One cornerstone of the high performance culture is that people naturally work in teams. The Steering Group has to decide the extent and speed with which you want to introduce teams. These could be Task Forces, looking at a specific problem, or Quality Improvement Groups leading on to Self-Managing Teams (the modern equivalent of Quality Circles). It should be noted that Quality Circles often fail if they are operating outside the framework of a company plan. It is often best to start with Task Forces to look at a specific problem which management feels is important to the business. Quality Circles, by definition, look at areas of the business which are important to the employees concerned. These are not necessarily of the highest priority to the business. Quality Improvement Teams have a significant part to play, but need to be properly supported and the participants given the necessary skills.

You must be prepared for the fact that it takes a minimum of five years to develop an organisation into a true, self-sustaining culture. This steady improvement process needs to be accompanied by lots of short, sharp initiatives which bring quick results. Every success reinforces the programme and gives it momentum. It also boosts the confidence of the teams involved.

If facilitators have been trained, as part of the process described in the previous section, they should be able to support these teams.

Zytec: As they develop their skills, so teams of people are encouraged to run their own departments. These Self-Managing Work Teams are not the only teams at Zytec: for example, a cross-functional team manages product design and development. This work passes on to other teams for implementation. These teams are all empowered to resolve customer and supplier issues, and anything that affects quality performance.

Motorola: Motorola's development of teams may superficially appear to be less extensive than that of other organisations. In fact, they have taken the approach that there is no point forcing team working into a facility or plant which is currently performing acceptably, and where the management team has not yet fully bought into the need. As we have seen elsewhere in this book, there are many examples where the management team has perceived the need and has probably got further in the implementation of Self-Directed Work Groups than many other organisations. Self-Managing Teams are seen by most OD specialists as a natural consequence of the TQ culture. When establishing them, the majority of companies begin with teams made up of individuals from different areas working on topics identified by the management group, so-called Task Forces. Before becoming institutionalised as SMWTs, they either evolve into cross-functional (but choosing their own problems), or departmental improvement groups, still working on management-led problems but within a particular area.

There are two initiatives which are moving Motorola in this direction – a participative management programme and the TCS teams. As one form of sport for these teams, Motorola has implemented an international competition for its employees. The TCS teams may be cross-functional, but are more likely to be functional. They choose a problem, usually directly related to their work, and then set about using a simple six-step problem-solving process to resolve it:

1. Identify the product;
2. Identify customer requirement;
3. Diagnose the errors to be eliminated;
4. Define a process for doing the task;
5. Ensure the process is mistake-proof;
6. Put permanent controls in place and institutionalise the change.

If applied by individuals, this problem-solving process lacks the power of group-process to improve its effectiveness. It is a normal divergent/convergent thinking model of the type which has been widely described since the late 1950s. Variants of these models are taught on management and problem-solving courses around the world. Nevertheless, the dramatic results achieved by teams which use them are a good indication of how poorly they have actually been applied!

The Motorola teams, known internally as TCS teams, can, if they wish, present their findings to panels of managers – and from 1993, to customers too. They are judged on criteria including project selection, team working, analytical tools used, the evaluation of alternative solutions, quantifiable results, the extent to which they have been communicated and adopted elsewhere and the team's presentation itself. Winners at various levels progress to national, regional, and international finals, the results finally being included in the company's annual report. In 1992, there were about 4,000 TCS teams, representing nearly 24,000 employees – or 25% of the workforce. Roughly half of the teams join the competition. Some experts suggest that creating internal competition is likely to undermine a quality process in the long-term. Whether the TCS teams become institutionalised, and whether they evolve into SMWTs, remains to be seen. As you will have seen from several of the interviews, some of the areas that have most progressed in the development of SMWTs have in fact been the least involved in TCS teams.

viii Counselling members

Once the front-line employees have been empowered, real improvements start to take place, often with stunning rapidity. This often catches out some middle managers, who are caught in their traditional role of monitoring and disciplining and have yet to feel comfortable in the coaching and supporting culture.

In any traditional business, counselling is usually seen as a soft activity. Yet those businesses who succeed invariably provide some form of confidential counselling for their managers. A good example is British Telecom, who have committed an entire department to Management Counselling. Obviously this is not a major element, and we usually find that our consultant takes on the role until a suitable individual is identified. This support is provided at any time – though most on-site meetings are timed to coincide with the Steering Group sessions.

Zytec: The role of the manager at Zytec has changed. Unlike their peers in many other businesses, the Zytec managers rarely get involved in day-to-day fire-fighting. Their job throughout is to provide the support and coaching that individuals or teams need to develop their own skills.

Motorola: In the early 1980s, Motorola began a programme of participative management. Exactly how successful this has been is difficult to establish, though several of our interviewees referred to it as a significant turning-point. Again, participative management is a transitional state. Nobody responds to being told that they are to take part in a participative management programme. It usually means that they will be asked their opinions and then given no credit when the managers implement their ideas. Worse still, it means that the line-workers' ideas will be sought and then ignored, in favour of pre-determined solutions. At Motorola the participative management programme appears to have been another name for departmental improvement groups. These teams received incentives for the improvements that they achieved. The key to the transition to greater involvement, which is what the Motorola programme sought, is taking full responsibility and authority at the front-line and this revolves around the attitude and behaviour of the managers. Anyone asked to change from being responsible for something, to handing over that responsibility to somebody else, finds it difficult to accept. It is particularly hard to swallow when that person was previously regarded as several steps lower down in the hierarchy. Managers need to adjust, not only to cope with this loss of personal power but also to change their management style from that of controller to developer of people. To help them do so, most successful change-processes include off-line counselling for the management team. At Motorola this support has not been provided directly, but through a combination of the management skills development work, and the introduction of team coaches and course tutors – together with a major investment in interpersonal skills. The support is being provided by an alternative structure to the traditional hierarchy.

ix Ongoing review

Organisations commonly, at this stage, set up a Steering Group. The purpose of the group, its composition, how often it meets and how it communicates with the rest of the company, need to be agreed.

Most companies use the Steering Group as a means of trying out different ways of meeting and working, and for learning new skills.

Most organisations settle for a monthly meeting lasting about half a day. For many of our clients, this is the main input they have from our consultant, in which case this meeting usually extends to one day.

Zytec: Besides the annual survey of employee attitudes, teams routinely review the performance of the various parts of the improvement process. The MTP programme, for example, calls together 150 employees for a two-day planning event. At this session the proposed five-year plans of six cross-functional teams are reviewed and revised, in line with, and leading to, corporate goals. Drawn together to form a coherent package, these plans are then reviewed with selected customers and suppliers in an almost unprecedented partnership arrangement. In several areas the organisation has contacted other businesses to provide a benchmark for their own process. Again, the results of this are regularly reviewed by the senior managers.

Motorola: With quality remaining on the agenda of every Motorola Management Meeting, the process is subject to constant review. We have already seen one complete cycle of revised goals, recascaded aims and an improved change process. Stories of success at Motorola are rapidly assimilated into the culture, and are reported widely. They are justly proud of their achievements; when talking to employees, you hear little of the failures. Nevertheless, the infrastructure of TCS teams and close communication between managers around the world exist to address these problems, and the overpowering drive to Six Sigma means that few will be allowed to slip. George Fisher reported that, overall, Motorola had achieved 5.3 Sigma by the third quarter of 1991. One good example of a non-production improvement was the month-end financial procedure. In a typical month, they would handle over 2,000,000 transactions in their general ledger. Each of these was a chance to make a mistake. By February 1991, they had reduced their error rate to 0.08%, a sixteen-fold improvement in two-and-a-half years. In terms of the time saved, the company was able to close its books in four days rather than eight, which represented 576,000 man-hours – or $20 million saved each year.

x Targeted marketing

Throughout the change process, you need to develop plans for a targeted approach to marketing the new culture. This begins internally, but eventually includes external marketing. Initially it is intended to create a demand for the new culture, and later to explain the detail of the process.

The external phase, which would probably begin between six months and eighteen months into the process, involves suppliers and then customers. You have only to look at the recent campaigns by Xerox, Federal Express, and Texaco to see the importance of this step.

The role of the Steering Group is to establish a marketing strategy for the new culture, identify the resources necessary and allocate appropriate budgets. This is monitored for effectiveness, and they need regularly to review the approaches. Our organisational development consultants have worked alongside our marketing consultants to develop considerable expertise in devising and carrying out such strategies. We have recently, for example, supported cultural changes in the Department of Transport by facilitating their senior managers through a targeted communication process.

Clearly, the professionalism of this process is critical. We usually expect the planning of this activity to begin at the Steering Group after the first three or four months.

Zytec: Most organisations can benefit internally from the systematic use of their marketing activities. Zytec clearly gained a tremendous boost in its profile when it was presented with the Baldrige Award. This coverage, and subsequent interest in the company, provides a great incentive internally too. Using such impromptu material, the management team constantly reinforces the key messages to its employees.

Motorola: At the management level, articles, videos, booklets and courses all reinforce the message of Six Sigma. While some companies expend a great deal of energy on this process, at Motorola it is part of the culture and probably has been so for a long time. We have already described the card-in-the-pocket reinforcing the goals of the business; the TCS teams are also exposed to corporate messages in other ways, and a variety of materials is provided to plant managers for general distribution, including a library of corporate philosophy. For many office employees, the corporate culture is again the key to the internal marketing process. Informal and formal networks exist throughout, and while some companies are afraid to use the grape-vine, Motorolans do so to great advantage. While a formal organisational structure does exist, it is widely superimposed by a matrix of responsibilities and mutual interests.

INTERVIEW 10.1 TEAM WORK IN ACTION
Russ Robinson, Operations Manager, Land Mobile Products Manufacturing, Motorola

We stressed the importance of a common vocabulary among the members of the senior management team. This is one of the reasons why SMWTs are easier to establish on green-field sites. The next best thing to this approach seems to be a clean sweep of the management team. Russ Robinson explains how they used this to kickstart the change process at Land Mobile (LMPM).

> In 1987 we had a traditional manufacturing operation with 900 employees. Today we have 500 direct labour (DL) people. We had fifteen 'On Q' or quality teams. We were management-driven and had about five layers of management. There was no flexibility and a manual quality system – which had a delayed feedback. If there was a defect at the end of the process, we were already working on something different at the beginning, so we couldn't do a repair. There were finite job responsibilities for layers five to six.
>
> I came into the operation with a whole new staff and the first thing we did was to put in a pull-system on our printed circuit-board operation. This really is where it all started – that improved our defect-rate down to 185, and now we're down to 140 hours. We put in the pull-system in three days – it was phenomenal – we just got everybody to co-operate! I think the employees were really sceptical about this being another management programme – they would go along with it... but we stuck to it. Today it exists everywhere.

Introducing problem-solving

LMPM are perhaps typical of many organisations. Their first experiments in team-based problem-solving were the result of a corporate quality improvement initiative. Management identification of the areas for investigation ensures that the themes are significant to them and create a sense of worth for the team members. As the teams produce satisfactory results, so they reinforce the management team's decision.

> So this is how we ran from 1988 to 1990, when we introduced PPS or Pro-duction Problem-Solving teams. Our Training Department had come up with a 'six steps to problem-solving' course. We put that training out on the factory floor and walked them through that process very simply. We also gave them some training on basic SPC diagrams, histograms, etc. At that time we formed about twenty-six teams, ranging in size from five to twelve people, and we iden-tified a project for them to work at. We gave them an hour off the floor every week, and a meeting session. Seventy per cent of our factory participated, although we twisted a lot of arms to get them on those teams. But we started to become more team-driven, championed by an engineer. So we'd have an engi-neer or two to eleven DL (direct labour) people. We had an 'I recommend...' employee suggestion scheme – but it was too management-driven.

People are sometimes afraid that Self-Management is about losing con-trol. Throughout this account Robinson demonstrates that he is still 'in control', with a consistent set of measures. One of these, at least, is less a measure of control but one of its relaxation!

> We were around three jobs per associate, and had a vision of what our facto-ries were going to look like down the road. We were just starting to put that vision together – we had gone down to four layers, were starting to conduct more designs of experiment in the factory, and our ppm and our cycle-time had started to drop.

High Performance Work Teams

In 1991 the TCS (Total Customer Satisfaction) process began. We started more SPC training, and more appropriate training in the factory relative to the busi-ness. Forty-two teams represented 80% participation. We also formed some Zapp! teams, with their concept of empowerment, and started-up ten High Per-formance Work Teams as pilots, although I don't think we had a very good vision of what they were then. Our employee suggestion programme was now called the 'Impact' programme, and was managed by the people in the factory. Today we are really proud of that because we average twenty suggestions per employee, which is our best domestically at Motorola, and I think that includes international as well. With some cross-training, each operator was capable of four or five jobs, and number of layers was reduced to three.

As managers became more confident of the results from the teams, so they were prepared to 'risk' more. OD consultants often talk of the need for many small gains along the way to a major breakthrough. Such results demonstrate to employees that they are capable and also act as a confidence-builder to doubtful managers.

> We stumbled into empowerment. Through these problem-solving teams we started to recognise the contribution that people on the factory floor could have. At the time I had engineering and manufacturing responsibility, and not enough engineers to go down on the factory floor and work on these problems. In a one-year time-frame, the contribution from the DL workforce, and the team solutions to problems, was roughly 42%. That opened my eyes up in a hurry, and the staff said: 'Hey, if we give these people more things to do and delegate some of the decision-making responsibility once we've trained them, we can get a lot more out of them.' That's how we stumbled into empowerment!

The self-assessment step is an important one in the transition. It is very common for a small team to study alternatives to the organisation structure, where necessary polling customers and staff on their opinions. This can lead to functional reforms. In LMPM the self-assessment team has become two permanent steering groups reviewing progress in an ongoing manner.

> We put a design team together in the latter part of 1991; it has been meeting weekly since. It is a cross-functional team of manufacturing people, some support people like Human Resources, Compensation, and a couple of people from Personnel who were part of the sector corporate group, and we spent two to three months laying out what empowerment was. We did some surveys on the line – things like that.

The transformation of an organisation to the high performance workplace is unlike many other changes of culture, in that it depends upon a substantial increase in basic skills. As people progress at different paces, some will be ready much sooner than others. This transition needs to be carefully managed.

Many people considering this strategy baulk at the extent of the training necessary. Yet, as Robinson points out, it really is necessary.

> We really have three factories – the traditional people run some semi-automatic equipment and the job task is very repetitive, whereas the new factory – the high performance areas – has automated equipment, a higher skill-set, and everybody has passed testing so we know they have the basic skills to take part in the team meetings which go on in that workplace. The transitional areas have a mix of people, some with the basic skills, some not. They will be high performance areas in 18 months or so. We are moving the people who aren't capable of passing the test – with the investment in training that we have given them – to the traditional areas, who those in the transitional areas who have that basic skill set into high performance areas.

To address the lack of basic skills, we started a programme in 1988 called 'New Directions'. At that time, we recognised that a lot of our workforce had trouble with English. Communication was a problem, and people didn't have good reading or math skills. We hooked up with a local junior college, and sent the people there for two hours a week. That didn't have much success! So the following year we changed that to four hours, and then a couple of years ago we hooked up with a commercial company from California who use a phonetic process which looks at visualising and verbalising to concept imagery. They came in with a different approach, which has been more successful. Between 1988 and June 1994, will have put everybody through the programmes – currently we invest in 240 hours for reading and 240 for math – although math seems to be a little easier than the reading. We are pushing people to get through that, which is six times the company minimum.

If you go through 240 hours and you still don't pass the basic skills test, we encourage you to go outside Motorola to seek continuing education – and if you have proof that you are doing that, you can come back in four months and resit the test. If you don't go outside and get help, then you can come back in six months and resit the test. We also meet with our employees four times a year, and we give them hand-outs of the places where they can get outside help. I talk to them about how the future in these traditional, old-technology, products is diminishing, and the number of jobs is dropping. We are not saying that the people will go. We believe in the integrity of the individual and if you have been with us for over ten years, then we have a big investment in you and we will find you a job – but it may be something else.

No person in the new factory wants to go back to the old workplace – sitting in a work-station placing components all day long, when you could be doing a little bit of that, running a piece of automated equipment, assuming the role of a team-leader for a day – it's much more challenging and rewarding. We put team-based pay in last year, which supplemented what we were doing with the empowered teams.

Big changes have gone on, and the results in some of the teams are tremendous. Rather than compare traditional, which didn't necessarily have automated equipment, with the new factories, we looked at manual processes that we have in both these areas. You can still see improvements in productivity, but they're not improving at the same rate – there was 16.6% improvement in the old as compared to 28.3%, service level was at 78.6% versus 91.5%. There were eleven basic tasks in each of these factories. We found that if you cross-trained somebody in a traditional area, as they don't have that basic skill-set, they weren't able to retain that cross-training. So you train them, put them on their old job, then put them on the job you trained them on, and they couldn't do it at the same quality-level as they did when we were training them. It is phenomenal. Employees' suggestions (our Impact programme) were 11.8% here, as opposed to 28.9% in the new areas where people have the skill-set to be creative and can visualise some solutions to problems on the factory floor. The transitional area is a mix of people, so their levels fall right between them.

It's worth reflecting on the record that Ross Robinson gives. Most organisations do not measure aspects of their organisation like this. Even fewer can track how they have changed. Virtually none set targets or objectives based on these measures.

The changing nature of middle management

There is often a debate among members of the senior management team about the future of middle managers. Many companies have 'down-sized' by stripping out layers of managers. BT, for instance, is reputed to have removed 17,000. Most people have difficulty imagining what effect introducing teams will actually have on the structure. Yet, at Motorola with its Job for Life after 10 years' service, what do you do with those managers who are no longer needed?

> We have gone though quite a transition in the middle-management level, and eliminated a lot of layers. I don't know that we have any production supervisors. The new factories operate with a team-leader – and some teams are ready to take the step of incorporating that team-leader as a functioning team-member. They will then report directly to a pretty high level of management. The supervisors who had good interpersonal and facilitating skills and were able to train and coach, we've retained – but changed their role to team coach. Those team coaches are deployed in the traditional areas. Our vision is that we can still have empowered high performance work teams in the traditional factories, but they need someone to facilitate that process and the rate of improvement, or change is going to be much slower. So we are deploying some of the middle management in those kinds of roles – some have gladly accepted that others have moved into individual contributor-roles in other places in the organisation.

Rewarding the teams

The issue of compensation is a difficult one for many people. In the past renumeration systems have either been very simple or extremely complex. The prospect of changing the pay system terrifies many organisations and is regarded as totally immutable in some! While there are bound to be exceptions virtually all the successful SMWTs that we have encountered here used a skills-related incremental system.

> In the past we would rate on a zero-to-four basis. A hundred per cent of their score was subjective, on the part of the management reviewing the employee. We have been in team-based pay now for two years, beginning with a pilot area. Eighty per cent is based on individual performance and then 20% is based on

the team's performance. We measure eight criteria throughout the factory, for each work-cell, and you therefore get a score that can be higher or lower, depending on both: 80/20 isn't going to have much of an impact, but we are moving towards 70/30 next year and maybe 50/50 after that. In the past, we also gave out standard cost-of-living increases which were basically the same amount to everybody in the factory. Today, Compensation can provide us with the percentage pool that we have to distribute, but now we look at the teams and their scores – let's say we have a merit pool of about 6%. We would take that and reward the top team with the 6% or more, and put in a formula so that the lowest team might end up with 2. The manager of that operation would have to look at the 80/20 split and distribute that 2% among his performers, while the best team would have 6% or more among that pool split. This makes it a lot better when you have more money to distribute.

The first year it was in place, not everybody understood – I had a stream of people in here after we went through the first merit package where we had good performers on a low-performing team. Were they doing a lot of complaining! So there was a lot of peer-pressure right after that. A lot of team scores have been improving significantly over the last year. As it gets to a 50/50 split, you are going to see a lot more peer pressure.

The eight factors in the team scoring were set by our factory team, who came up with quality, service level, cost, cycle-time, impacts, training, factory audits and scrap. We took a look at the percentage that is the typical corporate standard for percentage continuous improvement. Quality is at 68%, service level is at 50%, cost 20%, cycle-time 50%, etc. So these are the criteria. We have a grid which shows a baseline of the fourth quarter of the previous year, and that would be 'doing the job', and then we construct improvement percentages if you move to different percentages. Each week you score from 1 to 4, and the scores are averaged and plotted. So the team can see how well they are doing. We also had some weighting. Four years ago, quality would have been 30-40%, but today we feel that we have got our act together pretty well on quality. Service level is important as well as cost, so we have identified a higher percentage weighting there.

The team does all the collection of the data, and they have teams which set up the objectives. These teams study eight criteria that correspond to the objectives matrix. We set up the objective matrix teams so that if a work-cell has, say, twenty-five members we would ask for volunteers to go on each one of these teams and we would rotate. They stay on each team for thirteen weeks, and during that time they collect data, by going through the six steps of problem-solving. They document it and hold a review on a monthly basis. After thirteen weeks, the idea was to have the people move to another team so that over a two-year period, each team-member would be associated with every important business factor and understand it. The documentation would start to build from each of the teams upon each other. This is all with the idea of moving to high performance teams, and is very effective in the new and transitional areas. People were given a little colour-coded card based on the criteria. We call them challenge teams, so the card has a memory aid based on the word CHAL-LENGE. The member who was responsible for cost would wear their card under their badge. Cost-cards are green. Anyone with a question on something to do with cost would turn to that person.

Performance in teams does fluctuate – you can see that in the team-based pay. The teams can see why they lost it in a quarter, and can zero in and improve so that their salary will increase. It even happens in traditional cells – with a bit more facilitating. We have a job description for each work-cell, and there are more than enough tasks to get through, that training would probably take a year or a year-and-a-half. We also have a member/ partner arrangement. Once you know 80% of the tasks in a work-cell, you become a partner and your pay-range is expanded. We consolidated the grades so most people are either A, B, or C – typically A's would be working on a very manual process, but if a person didn't pass the basic skills tests and was content to stay there, they could increase their pay over time by learning 80% of the tasks. Through our manufacturing opportunities system, if you pass the tests you can 'escape' the traditional by moving to the high performance factory.

To be successful, you have to have a workforce that has the basic skill-sets to work on – reading, English and math – and then start giving them the other training to form good teams. Business performance here is the key link and that's what we're all here for – we've seen it, we can make a correlation between basic skills and business improvement.

I think that managing change has to go along with the rewards. One of the good things that we did from the start was to involve Compensation. In years past we would do something in manufacturing – which is often the more aggressive because it is closer to customers – but we wouldn't have involved Compensation. We decided to be cross-functional when we saw what some of the teams were doing before the design team. They were on board in a lot of the brainstorming, and I think that this step was excellent – it helped make the process much quicker. I might still be figuring out how to keep these people motivated if I didn't have a pay-plan. I would not recommend with hindsight not to have something at the same time going through.

You can always get people motivated for a period of time, but then they lose it because they start to ask: 'What is it getting me?' It varies in different cultures, I assume. We all know that some of our facilities in Malaysia have different values from those in the US. Tying-in a reward system to the US one, to which they can readily contribute, I think helped us escalate performance here. Sure you can get people motivated with a nifty communication plan, but I think you'd lose it after a period of time.

Continuous improvement and flexibility

Team-based pay has allowed people to look at A, B and C and move from member to partner, so for the next year-and-a-half we have settled. You always have to continue to motivate people, though. You can't put a programme in place and not build upon it. In three to five years, team-based pay may prove to be gain-sharing. If the teams are really doing well and we get to this 50/50 split on team-based pay, then the team is probably going to want to start sharing in the dollars that we are saving. We are brainstorming those things, and trying to stay on top of people's needs and expectations. If you don't do some forward planning and try to be visionary about this, then you'll just get trapped.

Right now we have the DL operators on team-based pay. There's a proposal that the technicians are put on it as well, and we are looking at all the support groups, to see if we can tie a person to a team. There's some thought of looking at some of the middle managers, coaches and so on. Maybe that will expand down the road to some of the engineering ranks. Certainly, if we can do a good job of associating our people with the performance of a team, you'll see a lot more of what we have done in the factory start to take place in other areas. Managers are heading in the same direction. If I am tied to a team out there, and they are taking the ups and the downs, I guess it's a reflection on my coaching and leadership that I'm not doing a good enough job to get them out of that, so maybe I should not get rewarded as much as I did in the past. But if my team is out performing, then it must mean that the team and its resources are doing a pretty good job, and we should share those rewards as well.

Recognition

Some organisations revel in recognition schemes; others revolt! Some people admit that they enjoy occasional recognition; others spurn it. Most people, though, enjoy a pat on the back or a quiet gesture. Russ Robinson and his team have gone several steps further by proactively encouraging good performance through recognition.

People are very visionary – they come up with clever little things like the challenge cards. During meetings we have brainstorming sessions to see what we can do to improve motivation, continuous improvement and so on. We had Zapp! teams present solutions to different problems, and I would give out lightning-bolts badges each month. Anyone who made a presentation for twelve minutes had a lightning bolt!

I used to sit in meetings and present business performance charts. Everyone would sit and listen but didn't ask questions, so you figure they know what you're talking about. Yet you go out later and talk to them and they didn't understand a thing. So in 1989 we had this idea of putting out thirteen weeks of little cards containing key business words, which we use in our day-to-day operation, with a quick definition. We passed them out on a Monday. The words were things like TDU, process control, kanban and so on. On Friday we would go around at random and test an operator on the line. It was fun, and it was also really good at getting management out on the line talking to their people! It also got people on the shop-floor more comfortable talking to management. So I'd pick someone and say, 'Can you tell me the definition of kanban?' If they came up with the definition I'd give them a calculator which was marked Total Customer Satisfaction, and so they'd have a tool that would help them with some of the things they were doing. Then I took them over to a board in the hall-way that said, 'you've passed'. We had a contest later, ran a raffle, and gave away some good prizes. If they didn't get the definition right, we would sit down with them and go over the definition and walk them around it and so on. Thirteen weeks of that and I couldn't believe how much more attention people paid to the charts and graphs in the presentations!

Measuring empowerment

Will it work? Implementing SMWTs calls for an act of faith. The returns are rarely immediate and depend on considerable investment and commitment. Sales courses describe the measurement fanatic as typical of one form of resistance. In the senior management team too, when someone demands that measures should be made of the empowerment process, it can usually indicate someone who hasn't fully bought in.

> A lot of companies want to measure empowerment. How can you say that quality improvement is tied to your high-performance enterprise or your empowerment activities? We struggled with that. The biggest problem lies with the fact that when you go into the high performance concept, it is a long-drawn-out process – it's probably three to five years before some teams are capable of handling it. Early on, there is such a heavy investment in training, on-the-job cross training, additional training to understand the business. I don't think you see the pay-backs like you will later on. I don't know that we have yet really realised the results of what we have done in the last two years. Management's focus is always on short-term results:- 'You can't take those people off the floor because your productivity is going to suffer!' I think you've got to make a stand – if you think their productivity is going to improve somewhere down the road, and it's going to get to a higher point than you can ever achieve by doing the things that you are doing today, then you've got to try to convince other people into doing that – that's the struggle.
>
> Most management structures are so dynamic that you might have a manager starting to put high performance into place and be gone a year from now, and you're back to someone who doesn't believe in it. This is one area where we have to improve, because we are very dynamic. Some teams tend to be moving along and then they'll fall down until the next guy picks them up, and they move a little faster. Day-to-day you don't see the results; you build it slowly, and hopefully when you are all done you have a lean, mean fighting-machine.

While measurement isn't usually easy, recording key events can be very effective too. We often suggest a round-the-table review at the end of management team meetings as a means of eliciting examples. Anecdotes of significant events are also excellent material for targeted marketing, both internally and externally. In recent years the Marriott hotel chain has used exactly this kind of information as the basis of its very successful advertising campaign.

The guys on the shop floor – you can see the growth in them. We are always going places. In years past I would have been giving the entire hour-and-a-half. The other day and I gave a talk for ten minutes and the team spoke for fifty. And they're so polished. Years ago they would have said: 'You're not getting me up in front of a group of people. I don't know how to use a computer. I don't know how to make a slide. I can't speak to this'. Now you get lots of volunteers to take part in these presentations. They do the slides, they get up. It's a trust level – there were a lot of questions asked the other day, and I was thinking to myself: 'Years ago I would have jumped in and tried to answer every question – I didn't answer any.' At the end of the session the chair-person got up and said: 'You know what amazes me? There is such a level of trust that we are asking questions and you are allowing your team-members to answer.' I could have left that session as far as I was concerned. That is one area in the growth of people which I readily see. This happens when you go to town-hall meetings, departmental meetings, and so on. They understand the business and what we are telling them.

Creating a momentum

It's surprising how often managers decide to implement team-based structures, tell a few people and then wonder why nothing has happened. This process depends on visible commitment from senior managers. Robinson and his team introduced a 'Flash' meeting – a three minutes every two hours review by all the team. This provided a consistent boost to any sceptical manager, or employee, as well as resolving many practical problems on the site.

One of the supervisors came in early on and said: 'What do we do to motivate these people to want to cross-train? To make decisions on their own?' We brainstormed for an hour and came up with the idea of putting up a board to show the output levels and quality levels over a twenty-four-hour period, for the three shifts, in two-hour increments so that we knew where we had to be in output and quality. Every two hours we went out, called a 'Flash' meeting and had the team talk about whether they were going to make their targets in the next two hours. We facilitated – we were running all over the factory as management resources. The first few times, I remember going out there and saying: 'Well, you're at this point and you need to be here in two hours – what do you need to do?' They'd sit and look at each other, talk about something else and then the timer would go off and so we'd send them back to work. We just kept that up for a couple of months. Today you go out there, the Flash meetings are three minutes, we don't go. They gather around their board and talk about what they have got to do. You hear them volunteer. 'Where's the bottleneck? Well, three of us, let's go there'. I can't tell you what that means to a manufacturing operation!

They elect for themselves a quality leader and a linearity leader – the linearity leader's job is to go to the customer during the day and find out what is really needed, to make sure that we're working on it. So in those two-hourly meetings they are reporting too. The quality leader goes over the defects in that three minutes too – it's phenomenal!

We don't measure individual productivity any more. There are no rates on the jobs – it would be mind-boggling to do that. There's a trust factor – you know how much you've got to produce, so you just go out and do the best you can to get the job done. They know when they fall behind.

You might think that implementing SMWTs is fairly straightforward. But rather like measuring, Robinson stresses that teams will continue to develop and evolve. His next target might seem as though it's the end of the road, but in practice he is already looking at the future.

We aren't perfect – we have a long way to go on the empowerment continuum, but we're making a lot of progress. In three to five years, most of these teams will be reporting to a director of manufacturing, and there won't be anything in between – they'll be making all the decisions, and handling budgets.

We are trying to link the eight criteria into the business – we have created a business school and are talking about finance and so on. We have some people who are able to do that really well, and others who are still struggling with it. We also still have this mix of people who don't have the skill-sets that we're looking for, so we're still working on that issue too. The end-result, after another two years, is that people will migrate across these different categories – they'll be able to do that.

We are piloting an interpersonal skills course. We realised that after going through the basic, technical on-the-job training – if they are going to take on board leadership responsibilities, the one big need is interpersonal skills.

The teams interview prospective applicants, whether they are internal or external, and they make recommendations to the coach or the leader as to whom to hire. We have got to do more training in this area too. They interview as a team, and we have gone over the questions that you can and can't ask, but they have to understand this better.

We want them to do peer reviews next year – we started last year, and it worked in some cases but not in others. There has to be an understanding of how you say things in different cultures – and how you can say something to a person from another culture, and it may mean something different to them. That's what we're working on. Today, we're going through listening and feedback. Down the road are coaching classes for the people who want to move into that role.

There is a lot of training. We talk of forty hours, but our teams last year probably averaged 120 hours, what with cross-training. We try to give them maybe eight or sixteen hours of what they think they want to take, and if it accords with what we want them to know, then we let them go ahead and do it. A few years ago, a lot of manufacturing managers would have sent people on that forty hours and not have thought what they were going to get out of it; today, we are trying to be more specific – we are doing a much better job in conjunction with the

296 Self-Managed Teamworking

Training Department identifying our needs. At the end of the year, they come down and do surveys of the different population of leadership to find out what the guys need. Then they do the same for the factory floor. They go back and do some out-sourcing and say: 'Based on the needs that we have, and what we have seen, this is what we think.'

I am responsible for the training budget. I have so many dollars, and I have to look at the training I am going to do, at the cost of the classes. I may be given a total dollar budget, but I have to make sure that I have enough room in there to take care of all the classes. Training is getting costly so what we are doing today is taking many of our team-leaders off the floor – those who have the ability to teach – and we're sending them off to 'train-the-trainers' courses. So we'll get training from somebody like Motorola University, and we'll deliver it ourselves. We've got some really good people who are doing that. Right now, the team-leaders actually teach – they take them off to a classroom.

The role of managers is crucial, but this is more demanding than you might expect, as it affects not just skills, but behaviour too. With these individual qualities come changes to many basic processes, such as succession planning.

I think management is its own worst enemy in terms of trying to get high performance teams to be successful. We have got to do a better job of communicating success stories. You need good coaching – managers who know the business in different areas and who have coaching ability. We don't take a good look at areas which are doing well. We'll move managers, but not take a hard look at whether we should replace that manager with one who has the same philosophy.

Hierarchies at work are not based on any rational criteria. The people 'at the top' do not have any particular skills or talents that others couldn't possess. Nor do they necessarily have any more experience. It can be a sobering experience as a manager to spend some time asking why you reached your position, removing the generic ('I work harder than others') and looking specifically at each promotion.

As we dismantle the existing work hierarchy to allow teams the flexibility and scope that they need, so others crumble too. Social hierarchies and social iteration change. Union hierarchies too will be affected. Russ Robinson illustrates the opening-up of the workplace.

The question of unions is interesting – companies which have them are interested in finding out how to achieve this. We get questions about what do you do with people who can't function in this environment, or managers who can't adapt. Above all else, it's a question of motivating people, and keeping them motivated; helping to break down traditional ideas of who does what.

We have put together a talent show for the last two consecutive years – lasting three hours each. We had one operation with 300 people – 100 of whom volunteered. You could only have people within your work. We've got it recorded on tape; I went with one of the other managers as the Blues Brothers – we did live singing with a back-up band behind us. People talked about that for weeks and weeks. Instead of calling me and referring to me as something – I was Jake! 'Hey Jake..!'

I think walking the talk is important – that works in a social way too. This place lit up when people realised we're as human as them, and we can have a good time together, not only after work but during work. Before we started this, there was an us-and-them attitude.

There are often many hidden fears on the part of senior managers as teams are established. One of these revolves around the contact between team members and customers and suppliers. It is very difficult sometimes to get individual managers to say what they are afraid of, such is the power of these taboos. Usually they feel that shop-floor workers are socially inept and commercially naïve. They are afraid that they will create a bad impression of the company and blather uncontrollably about all the company's commercial information!

One of our TCS teams had a supplier in it. He would come in and be with the team every week, and we gave him a trip to Hawaii because that team was selected to go. We also had a Schaumburg police lieutenant on one of our teams – he came in each week – a great guy, but his force wouldn't let him go to Hawaii! We have lots of external participants on our teams – one of our suppliers came in and looked at what we're doing from a team standpoint – and he formed a team. Now we have a 'partnership for growth' concept with our suppliers; we're starting to look at the team activities. Motorola now has a team competition for its suppliers too, so we're trying to get everybody involved.

If we look back to the early work on excellent companies there were four characteristics that were identified as setting them apart: customer obsession, employee involvement, transformed leadership and masses of innovation. As Russ Robinson neatly summarises, this source of new ideas is not just conceptual – it's about practical ideas. But the fount will dry up if you don't put those ideas into practice.

We believe in giving things a try – if it doesn't work and you gave it your best shot, then find out why – but you've got to try in the first place. What's important is to recognise as managers that you aren't losing face by doing that.

Activity 10.1

a The nature of change

Ask the Personnel Department to tell you who is your oldest employee and who is the longest-serving. Take them out to lunch – use the canteen or a pub.

Get them to describe the business as they remember it when they joined the company. Really encourage them to reminisce. Take notes. Get specifics. When was new technology introduced? Were pay and employment conditions always the same? Which changes do they remember? What were they doing when Kennedy was assassinated, when the *Queen Elizabeth II* was launched, or when man walked on the moon?

b The pace of change

Take your organisation's annual reports and identify the major events in its history. Plot them on a time-scale to see if any patterns of change emerge in the industry, in technology, in markets, etc. Show mergers, acquisitions and so on.

Histories presented graphically can be far more revealing than prose. ARCO, the Atlantic Richfield Oil Company, displays its history as an evolving chart in the reception halls of its head offices around the world.

c The *status quo*

Load up your camera with a roll of film. Walk the job taking snapshots. The technical merit of the photographs is totally irrelevant, so don't get the company photographer to do the job. Just make sure that you capture every aspect of the work your organisation does. As a minimum, the snaps need to include:

- The salespeople;
- Goods inwards;
- Any raw materials holding-yards;
- Pre-production processing;
- The production line itself;
- Scrap heaps and rework piles;
- Goods outwards storage;
- The loading bay;
- Distribution;
- A delivery being made;
- The accounts department;
- The head offices.

For some reason CEOs and senior managers are sometimes uncomfortable doing this. If you are, it's worth asking yourself why. A common reason is embarrassment at being seen doing something that is considered inappropriate for someone in authority. To help overcome this, one favourite trick is to take a young son or daughter around at a weekend. This doesn't get quite the same results, because there are usually fewer people around, but it is better than nothing.

d The inventory of change

Now that you have begun gathering information, think back to ten years ago. Use the inventory of change (below) to summarise these events.

An inventory of change

- How have your main facilities changed?
- How has the product-range changed?
- How have the numbers, types, mixture of employees changed?
- How have working conditions changed?
- How has the production process changed?
- How has the company funding changed?
- How have production statistics changed?
- How have the customers changed? Are they the same or different?
- What sorts of product do these customer buy and in what volumes? How have these changed in the last ten years?
- How has the remuneration package changed across the range of employees?
- Have there been any significant disputes? What were they about, how long did they last, and how were they resolved?

How do you *feel* about these changes? Have they been positive or have there been setbacks? Were they avoidable, inevitable or deliberately engineered? Are there any that you would rather forget? Some things will have remained the same. Should they have – or would you rather some had changed? Make a note of some of these. Finally, jot down any of the things that you already expect to happen in the next decade. Do you see these as positive or negative? Do you think that they are inevitable, or do you have some degree of control over them?

Activity 10.2

Fig. 10.2 represents the generic model of change which we have described above. Using the research which you did for Activity 10.1, identify the various steps that you have gone through in recent months or years. Remember that you can expect to have to go through this sequence for almost any change. If you have introduced any strategic process recently you should spot them. Alternatively, you may feel that your organisation has already begun its current change-process, and you might want to record events so far.

References

[1] Petrakis H.M. (1991) *The Founder's Touch: The Life of Paul Galvin of Motorola.* Motorola University Press, Chicago.

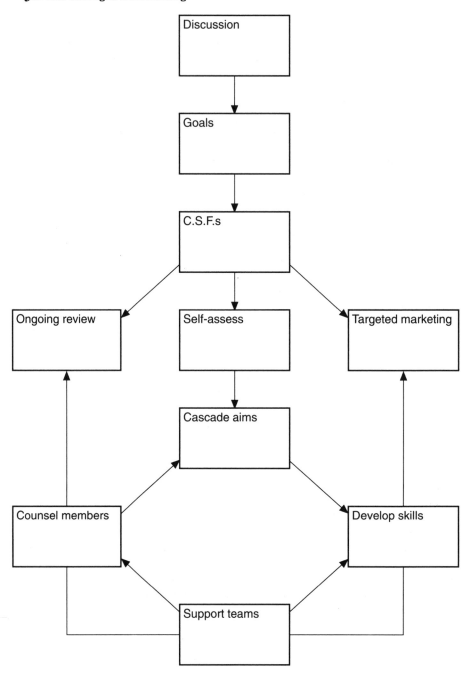

Fig 10.2 Successful change model

11

THE HIGH PERFORMANCE STRATEGY

'One key ingredient gets at the notion that none of this happens differently. You have got to have someone who is for it, who is going to support it, who has to be a champion. That's our key ingredient.'

(Cellular Infrastructure, Motorola)

- You need to have a clear vision – not a summary of what you are already doing, but a picture of where you want to be.

- Set yourself outrageous goals.

- Look at your present investment in people – now put more and more effort into it.

- Pilot a team-based workplace. Try it somewhere. If necessary, admit that it is an experiment. But do try it!

- Involve your employee-representatives. They don't have to be a one-way communication channel. Just because you didn't select them doesn't mean that they can't do their job.

- Broadcast your initiative – involve schools, government and other businesses.

This look at the organisation of the future has been wide-ranging and controversial. It seems appropriate to summarise the territory that we have covered, and look at some of the practical steps which you could be considering in the next few months and years. The questions in this chapter are addressed not to our interviewees, but to you, the reader, to help you evaluate your own organisation in the light of these changes.

THE HIGH PERFORMANCE STRATEGY

One of the 1980s management gurus once described a mission statement as a stake in the ground. It was, he said, a way of measuring how far an organisation was progressing. Today, many OD specialists would probably take him to task. Few of us dispute the importance of clear vision – but many of the 1980s and 1990s 'Missions' were little more than summaries of what the organisation was apparently doing already.

What is your organisation's mission statement? When was it developed? What is currently being done to instil its meaning and values at the shop-floor level?

For most organisations, the journey beyond has usually been one of slow but steady improvement. We have provided ourselves with a plethora of milestones: ISO 9000 first, then Investors in People (IIP), followed by EFQM – and for the most adventurous the European Quality Award or in the US, the Baldrige Award. Achieving any one of these is a tremendous accolade to the employees – and the directors should be congratulated for their foresight and commitment, for without this nothing would have been achieved.

As we have seen throughout this book, while most of us have been struggling with the procedures of our quality system, a quiet revolution has been taking place.

What has happened in your organisation since the development of the mission statement? Had you already achieved ISO 9000 or have you done so since? How many people are in the workforce now who were also in it then? What sorts of improvement initiatives have you undertaken, and what awards have you won? What has been their net worth to the company?

Outrageous organisations

A handful of outrageous organisations – among them Baldrige winners – have set themselves extraordinary goals. One example we have referred to a lot is Motorola, whose process of continuous improvement still raises aggressive cries of disbelief from the managing directors of other companies. In the early 1980s, Motorola began its process of improvement with a simple target – one that most people could relate to, though barely conceive achieving – a ten-fold improvement in 5 years. They made it. They did it again and again, and in the process they won the Baldrige Award. But they haven't stopped there.

We have seen that Motorola are quite exceptional for their strategic planning. If we are honest with ourselves, most organisations with a strategic plan pay it lip service at best, and flaunt it at worst! To an extent, strategic planning has become a nonentity in many organisations. By way of contrast, Motorolans, particularly those near the centre, frequently and very seriously look at their fifty-year strategic plan!

What is your organisation's strategic planning process? Is it a joint development or is it the brain-child of just one person? Is the plan regularly reviewed, and if so, when, and how often? If it isn't, how is it disseminated and agreed upon? What successes has it produced?

Extraordinary improvements

It is only with this far-sightedness that Motorola, IBM and others have been able to sustain their *Kaizen*-like process and remain on track to achieving the goal of Six Sigma. Six Sigma is a simple concept based on statistical process control principles. The idea is that every process you operate should have a target performance: for the manufacturer of plastic bottles, this might mean that there is a target proportion of defective bottles due to contamination; to the railway operator, it could mean the number of trains arriving on time; or to the manufacturer of radio-pagers it could mean the number of demands for payment which cross in the post with the payment cheque!

Either side of the target there are tolerances outside which the company would prefer not to stray. Natural variation means that there is always 'wobble' around the target. The more variable the process, the greater the wobble. It is by comparing the wobble with the tolerances that we know whether our processes are capable of delivering. Wobble (or more accurately 'statistical deviation') is measured in units of variance known as Sigma. Typical applications of SPC talk of levels of 95% of variability falling within the tolerances – that is, two standard deviations either side of the target (a condition known as Two Sigma).

Very few companies get this far, because this isn't the sort of thing that makes you shout from mountains! Which is why the success of organisations like Motorola stand out: not only have they created a fascination for variation among virtually all their employees world-wide – those employees have also begun to achieve Six Sigma levels of performance regularly – representing no more than three items beyond the tolerances in a million opportunities.

Be honest with yourself. Obtain some figures from your production area. How near are they? Are they measured? What about figures from non-production areas? Are they measured? Is the measurement part of the management support system, or is it accessed by anyone?

Incredible transformation

You don't achieve this standard easily. It is beyond the capabilities of most of us to comprehend it, let alone achieve it. The level of transformation which is necessary has led to the shop-floors that are responsible being dubbed *high performance workplaces*. Increasingly, organisations as diverse as carpet-makers, bakeries, auto-parts manufacturers and car rental firms are realising that, unless they set their own sights at this level, someone else will.

The high performance workplace involves a combination of tough targets, investment in automation and a highly committed workforce. Achieving such a level of commitment goes beyond most normal organisational structures.

How well are your competitors doing? Have they disappeared in the recession or are they thriving? What changes do you know about which are going on in the industry? How do you get this information? How well is it distributed throughout your organisation?

Industrial anarchy?

It is important for the people on the front-line to be so strongly motivated that they won't let performance drop, and to be continuously on the look-out for better ways of doing things. Most of the organisations which have made this transformation have stumbled on the same approach. Organisations should not motivate people by pandering to their basic needs, but by stimulating their desire for self-achievement. They are doing this by creating Self-Managing Work Teams – or more accurately, Self-Directing Work Groups, since they direct themselves rather than 'simply' managing, and because their members often work in comparative isolation, despite quite large sizes of group.

A SMWT is a group of employees who collectively manage the processes on which they work. They do so without management intervention – except as trainers or coaches. A typical SMWT will have 20–25 employees handling all aspects of their work. SMWTs often give workers the incentive to contribute that they have been denied for years. They work through a combination of individual motivation, peer-pressure and self-constraint. The control which is exerted in these ways is far more effective than anything which can be imposed by a manager – except in one respect. Teams are universally more creative than individuals working in isolation.

What have you done to promote the use of teams in your organisation? How well have they worked? What proportion of employees are currently members of teams? What have you done to equip them? Are they concerned with day-to-day operations or with special projects?

Creativity without limit

Whether they are the true, Japanese-style Quality Control Circles, Western Quality Circles, task forces, improvement teams, or SMWTs, a group working together will, after just a little preparation, outperform the sum of the individuals any day. That's why team sports work, and it's why we use juries in our judicial system.

THE DOWN-SIDE

Sadly, there is a down-side. Even in industries which seem to have stayed the same for decades, jobs (and life in general) is becoming more complex.

Look at your own home. There are many anecdotes about most people who own a video-cassette recorder not knowing how to programme it. Lower your sights a little. Think of the equipment you have, and for how much of it you have needed to turn to the instructions. Now think back to 1980.

How much of that equipment did you have in 1980? Did you have alternatives? Did you read the instructions for those?

Whether it's new technology, sophisticated replacements for old (such as digital telephones for the old dial ones), or just more complex engineering than old (have a look under the bonnet of your car), the things on which we depend are getting more complicated. To handle that technology we rely on having more skills – basic skills as well as technological ones. Sadly many of us don't have those basic skills...

This might seem a little tough for you to swallow. You are reading this book. But what about your colleagues? Statistics of illiteracy and innumeracy are not easy reading. They can cloud the issue. The National Assessment of Educational Progress (NAEP), conducted by the US Department of Education on 21–25 year-olds, put the figures in more graphic form:

'Only three-fifths of whites, two-fifths of Hispanics, and a quarter of blacks could find information in a news article;

Only a quarter of whites, 7% of Hispanics, and 3% of blacks could decipher a bus schedule;

Only 44% of whites, 20% of Hispanics and 8% of blacks could correctly determine the change that they were due from a two-item restaurant meal.'

There is a crisis in education, and it isn't restricted to the US. School-leavers are emerging with fewer skills than their brothers and sisters just a couple of years ahead of them, whether they were educated in Britain, Japan, or the US.

Discuss this with your personnel officers. What experience do they have? Do you have job descriptions? (Many companies no longer bother – jobs change too fast and descriptions hamper creativity and risk-taking!) How long ago is it since they were updated? Pick one, and compare it with reality. What skills are people joining with? How are those skills changing?

The crisis in education is a crisis for both producers and services

A few products are so well-established that you don't need any instructions on how to use them. Anyone who has travelled in an undeveloped country will know how children flock around foreigners. The guidebooks tell you to take cheap objects such as pens, pencils and crayons to give these children, rather than encouraging them to beg for money. If you take their advice – what do the children do with the pens, etc.? The popular, romantic image is that they rush off to their classrooms with an indispensable tool for their future! Of course they don't.

It is likely that pen-and-pencil manufacturers will never have to worry unduly about providing instructions for their use – though many do. But anything more sophisticated, from a breakfast cereal, baby milk, telephone, radio, cable TV, and so on – all of these need instructions. The instructions need to be provided in such a way that people can understand. You can rely on the written word if you wish, or you can experiment with cartoons, free training, free cable TV channels, even videos! Whatever the medium, you are expecting a level of educational achievement which simply can't be assumed. What's more, that level is decreasing.

As a manufacturer, you need to decide how much action you will take to remedy this. If your products are safety-critical, perhaps you will feel more responsible than others. If your products could injure large numbers of people, perhaps you will take a community-wide stance. One highly responsive pen manufacturer has been providing free pens and teaching-aids to school-teachers and pupils for decades.

As a service provider, don't think that you have escaped! If people can't read and understand the forms that you produce, can they be held responsible for the consequences? Perhaps they can now, but for how much longer? If you had a reading difficulty and you were presented with two versions of a loan application – one in the usual cumbersome pseudo-legal jargon and the other in simple words and graphics – which would you sign up against? If you find this tough to answer, pretend that you are a well-educated graduate with many years' management experience – now say which one you'd prefer to sign!

What about your organisation's products and services? List a few – how do the buyers know how to use them? Do they make assumptions about the educational level (let alone the basic language capability) of the users? Are any of them particularly critical – for safety or PR reasons, for example? Take a worst-case scenario – if an illiterate user tried to operate your product, or took up your service, what is the worst thing that could happen and what could the actual or PR consequences be to your organisation?

The crisis in education is a crisis for employers   *Demography*

Not only are products and services becoming more complex and the educational standards of school-leavers dropping, but there is also an age-related bubble in the population. The average age of workers is increasing. So you can't rely on younger employees being recruited. The pool is diminishing in size. The people who work for you will mostly be with you for some time to come. If any of your products, services or working methods have become more sophisticated, then you've got to take action now.

What are the demographics of your organisation? Are the people older, younger, immigrants or not? What educational background do they have? What has been your organisation's experience when recruiting – is it easy or tough to get people of the right 'calibre'? Are your working methods getting harder or easier? Do you have a quality system? Is it written so that people can really understand it? Do you provide people with training? How do you assess its effectiveness and value for money?

THE WAY IN WHICH YOU ARE ORGANISED

The traditional approach used by employers to control the output of their workers was to provide a hierarchy of decision-making. This works on the basis that limits are set on the decision-making ability of employees at each level. When confronted with a decision which is beyond their imposed level, the employee turns to their boss.

There are problems with this in that it undermines people's confidence, prevents spontaneous decisions (although they are sometimes necessary for customer responses), removes decisions that affect productivity and quality from the workplace (often preventing all the facts from being known by the person making the decision), and can build in unnecessary numbers of managers to prop up the hierarchy.

There was a wonderful concept known as span of control, which was often interpreted as saying that individual managers could control up to nine people but no more. So for an organisation with eighty-one shop-floor workers you needed nine supervisors and one manager – three levels in the hierarchy – and so on. Even today, consultants are to be found using this 'principle' as part of business process re-engineering, to determine minimum numbers of employees to support the process. No-one seems to challenge the basis of it.

If you are trying to control those employees' behaviour, then perhaps it is true that you can't manage more than nine direct reports. On the other hand, if you leave those people to control each other, perhaps you don't need anywhere near that number of managers and levels of authority?

Organisations around the world have recognised the importance of managing customer-driven processes. They acknowledge that managing discrete activities leads to functionalisation, and that this has a knock-on effect on communication, product quality, ownership and customer satisfaction. By organising themselves along product- or service-related process lines, with appropriate degrees of multi-skilling, they find that flexibility, responsibility, quality and productivity soar.

How old is your organisational structure? Who was responsible for it? Are there hidden assumptions in its design? Does it follow lines of customer contact? How many contacts can your customers have with your organisation? How are they co-ordinated? Do you promote within functions or rotate among them? What do you do to give aspiring promotees a role-model for their future job, and the skills to achieve it?

RELATIONS WITH THE UNIONS

The relationship between employers and unions has dramatically changed in recent years. Much of this change has involved reducing the power of the unions. In high-performing organisations, the relationship has gone one step further. By demonstrating a trust between the management team and the union, and by calling on unions' national experience, opportunities exist which wouldn't otherwise have been created. The unions in these organisations still hold some collective bargaining responsibilities, but more importantly they share in the responsibility for the plant output.

In some instances, the union has helped with training and development. In others, it has taken the lead in strategic planning – even buying out existing facilities and operating them collectively. In the majority, they have simply been invited to share in the decision-making processes.

Universally, where a union exists, the relationship between managers and the union is described as one of partnership. This is not a case of lip-service, but reflects the transformed role of both managers and union representatives.

What is the extent of worker-representation in decision-making within your organisation? Is there a union, staff association or similar representative body? What is the nature of the relationship between the union and managers? What are the barriers to their involvement in routine decision-making? Are these impenetrable, or can you plan to overcome them? Will union representatives be involved in your strategic planning, or in the programme of discussions that precedes any major cultural change?

The union perspective

If you are a unionist reading this book...

What research has your union done to examine Self-Direction and the high performance workplace? Has it established any policies? What experiences do you know of in other countries (and in the same industry)? Which organisations are considered to show best practice, in your experience?

What is the nature of the relationship with management in your organisation? If necessary, could you change this? Are there union functions – locally or nationally – to which you could invite 'senior management' from your organisation? Does your union offer vocational training? If so, could it be offered to managers within the organisation as well?

What can you do to encourage a positive working relationship with the management team? Remember that if you are going to take the lead, you need to maintain good personal relations with them.

BARRIERS TO CHANGE

[handwritten: Govt Barriers to snow?]

How ambitious are your plans? In pursuit of high performance you may well identify obstacles to change which you can't readily work around or which you feel are unjust. For example, an employer might decide to take the logical step of giving employees their own budget for training, rather than controlling this centrally. But, in Britain, you would then become liable for employers' National Insurance contributions, and the employees would be taxed for their additional income. British tax legislation assumes that employers provide all, and that full-time employees rarely, if ever, contribute to the well-being of their company other than with their hands and

[handwritten: Tax]

minds! You might decide to lobby for changes in this or one of countless other barriers to change.

Perhaps you feel that the local provision of education is simply inadequate and that you would like to provide the opportunity of private, company-funded secondary education for all employees. The barrage of obstacles which you would face (legislative, financial, PR, and so on) could well prevent you from starting. You might decide to grab this by the horns rather than allowing the system to preserve the *status quo*.

Then there are issues of immigration – you have plants in different parts of the world and perhaps you would like to transfer employees from one to another (previously the sole preserve of managers, but increasingly common at the shop-floor level). You will soon find yourselves in the middle of an immigration nightmare. If this is close to your organisation's values, perhaps you'll decide to champion cross-border employee interchange.

Policies obviously differ from one country to another. For example, within Europe the requirements of different countries vary enormously on the structure of the boards of directors. In Germany the two-tier system (recommended, in concept at least, by Cadbury in the UK) encourages union participation in strategic planning, whereas in the UK the single-tier system does not. Perhaps this is your burning barrier.

Germany, too, has a unique structure to its Chambers of Commerce, with obligatory membership for most commercial organisations. This enables the Chambers to become very strong representatives in local government – especially with respect to education, transport and issues affecting commercial development. If you are involved in lobbying for local issues, perhaps you'd like to promote your cause through local trade bodies and at the same time promote the Chambers of Commerce, or some other organisation.

What experience does your organisation have with local, regional, or national lobbying? Have you been successful or not?

Activity 11.1: Reactions to change

The diagram, Fig. 11.1, is taken from *Making Change Happen*. It represents the variations in morale which most organisations will go through before reaching their new culture. Try identifying features which your own firm is going through, and firstly, record them on the table, and then summarise them on the diagram.

SYMPTOMS OF CHANGE

1. **Numbness**

   Situation:

   Circumstances:

   How long did it last?

2. **Denial/Disbelief**

   Situation:

   Circumstances:

   How long did it last?

3. **Self-doubt/Emotion**

   Situation:

   Circumstances:

   How long did it last?

4. **Acceptance/Letting Go**

   Situation;

   Circumstances:

   How long did it last?

5. **Adaptation/Testing**

   Situation:

   Circumstances:

   How long did it last?

6. **Searching for meaning**

   Situation:

   Circumstances:

   How long did it last?

7. **Internalisation**

   Situation:

   Circumstances:

   How long did it last?

Fig 11.1 Reactions to change

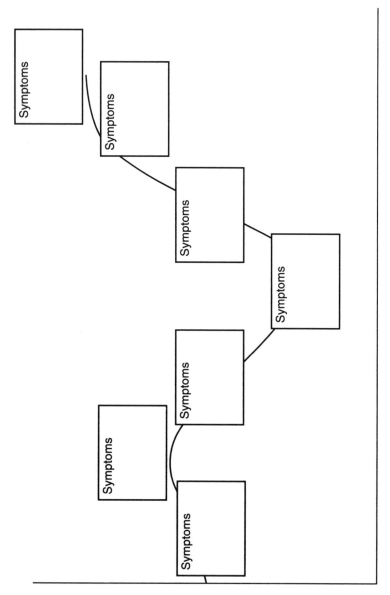

Fig 11.1 Reactions to change (continued)

INDEX